Reconstructing
RAGE

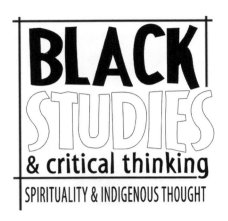

BLACK
STUDIES
& critical thinking
SPIRITUALITY & INDIGENOUS THOUGHT

Cynthia Dillard, *Series Editor*

Rochelle Brock and Richard Greggory Johnson III
Executive Editors

Vol. 25

The Black Studies and Critical Thinking series
is part of the Peter Lang Education list.
Every volume is peer reviewed and meets
the highest quality standards for content and production.

PETER LANG
New York • Washington, D.C./Baltimore • Bern
Frankfurt • Berlin • Brussels • Vienna • Oxford

Townsand Price-Spratlen & William Goldsby

Reconstructing
RAGE

Transformative Reentry in the Era of Mass Incarceration

PETER LANG
New York • Washington, D.C./Baltimore • Bern
Frankfurt • Berlin • Brussels • Vienna • Oxford

Library of Congress Cataloging-in-Publication Data

Price-Spratlen, Townsand.
Reconstructing rage: transformative reentry in the era of mass incarceration /
Townsand Price-Spratlen, William Goldsby.
p. cm. — (Black studies and critical thinking; v. 25)
Includes bibliographical references and index.
1. Criminals—Rehabilitation—United States. 2. Ex-convicts—United States—
Social conditions. 3. Ex-convicts—Services for—United States.
I. Goldsby, William. II. Title.
HV9304.P724 365'.6630973—dc23 2012034617
ISBN 978-1-4331-1473-1 (hardcover)
ISBN 978-1-4331-1472-4 (paperback)
ISBN 978-1-4539-0847-1 (e-book)
ISSN 1947-5985

Bibliographic information published by **Die Deutsche Nationalbibliothek**.
Die Deutsche Nationalbibliothek lists this publication in the "Deutsche
Nationalbibliografie"; detailed bibliographic data is available
on the Internet at http://dnb.d-nb.de/.

The paper in this book meets the guidelines for permanence and durability
of the Committee on Production Guidelines for Book Longevity
of the Council of Library Resources.

© 2012 Peter Lang Publishing, Inc., New York
29 Broadway, 18th floor, New York, NY 10006
www.peterlang.com

Printed in the United States of America

Townsand's Dedication

To my four grandparents. To Mr. and Mrs. Price, you created and raised well a caring, exceptional daughter. For doing so, I thank you both. To Pastor John the Baptist Spratlen and Mrs. Lela Dobbins Spratlen, you created and raised well an extraordinary son. By doing so you gave a gift to me and many others. Thank you. I am eternally grateful to all four of you. May this book grace your memories well.

William's Dedication

I dedicate the words of this book to those resting in the red soil of Alabama and in our souls. I dedicate this book to Townsand Price-Spratlen for his trust in me and internalizing the mission of Reconstruction. Finally, I dedicate this work to Elaine Selan for her technical professionalism towards the finish line of this manuscript

Table of Contents

Acknowledgments

Townsand Price-Spratlen

First and foremost, I give thanks to my known and unknown Ancestors. I am particularly grateful to the many forced to take the journeys across the Atlantic Ocean's waters, and those among them who survived and flourished beyond bondage. I am grateful to you in ways I will never be able to put into words. My faith leads me to believe that I was in your dreams then. And I hope and pray that I am a worthy expression of your hopes and prayers.

A book is a process. It is the product of many contributions including and beyond those of the authors. In these few words below, I will acknowledge what is most surely an incomplete list of those contributions which matter most. On the foundation of our Ancestors, I thank my co-author, William Goldsby. We first met in 1981, and across multiple moves and life changes, we stayed in touch. In the fall of 1990 I first visited him in Philadelphia when I was in graduate school. William had kept me aware of his (at that time) two years of progress in building the foundations for what would become Reconstruction, Inc. Shortly after my visit and return home to Seattle, I asked him if I could write my dissertation on the organization. Though William said no, the possibility was planted. Thank you William, for finally saying yes a few years ago, and then moving forward with the intensity, passion and craft that is your way.

Like the words above, my many other comments of gratitude are far too brief for the depth, quality and longevity of support, guidance and generosity I have received from those I have remembered to mention here. Cynthia B. Dillard, you are so much more than a friend and series editor. You are a special Blessing. Thank you for your timing and enthusiastic support throughout this process, and for your Spiritually-grounded feedback when this book was little more than a few formative words on paper. Ruth D. Peterson, perhaps the only thing greater than the quality of your scholarship and willingness to support the growth of others is your humanity. Thank you for the support of the Criminal Justice Research Center (CJRC) under your leadership, and for the seed grant that made the generation of these data possible. It was a project well-outside of the type the CJRC has typically funded. Thank you for taking that risk. I am honored to know you as colleague and friend. Lauren J. Krivo, your merge of friendship and vocational productivity with Ruth over many years has been amazing to observe. From the first family dinner I shared in at your home in 1995, you and Bob were willing to welcome me. Especially during my challenging pre-tenure years, thank you for all of your mentoring and support. Barbara Reskin, thank you for the vision and advocacy of your leadership as my first department chair. The mixture of your profound scholarship and intense desire for justice continues to inspire.

Avery M. (Pete) Guest, I am grateful to have been trained by you to be a "Husky social demographer." The quality of your scholarship and your guidance during and after graduate school is the strong foundation I could not have done without. Hubert M. (Tad) Blalock, I am so thankful to have been in your final methods sequence cohort. Sharing time with you during your office hours throughout those two quarters refined my ability to engage themes sociologically, and to model and refine conceptual relationships with greater care. Robert (Bob) Crutchfield, know that several of the thoughts we shared during your advising of my master's thesis project, inform these data and this book. Thank you for your advocacy and guidance at such a vital time in my life. Barrett A. Lee, you too being a legacy of Pete's guidance, you made my two years at Penn State a productive platform for my career. Your focused feedback and input when we worked together helped me to know better what productive research partnership can be. I also share thanks with Linda Burton for your patient kindness, and demonstrated excellence in making the most of a longitudinal, multimethod, qualitative project. I will forever value the caring and content of our "This way forward!" meetings those many years ago. And special thanks to William H. (Bill) George. Thank you, Bill, for providing me with my first research opportunity. You thoughtfully introduced me to the setting, sequence and uncertainties of academic research.

My thanks go to the many, many Reconstruction affiliates who opened your lives, memories and visions of a possible present and future for yourselves, your families, the neighborhood and the organization. I especially thank the following persons: Hakim Ali, for your profound dedication to the Reconstruction mission, and for sharing your many skills of craft and caring with so many; Khalifa Shabazz for your work with Gathering of Men, and for your timely help in organizing the archival materials that were so important to this book; Patrick Murray for so many things, but especially for your quality meeting minutes in the early years, and for providing primary leadership to the production of Reconstruction's documentary, and the building of the Club House, two vital moments of the organization's progress; Cameron for your patience during my first project interview. Your willingness to continue speaking with me beyond the point of fatigue, your help in refining the interview guide, and in sharing your story with such vulnerability and strength rests with me still; the Philadelphia Research Team members (William, Hakim, Dr. Kristi Brian, and Thomas Ford). Your help and support in generating these project data were essential.

My thanks go to Maren McDaniel for the responsiveness and caring detail in your interview transcriptions, and to Elaine Selan for the quality of your work in formatting and preparing the page proofs of this manuscript. And a special thanks to Muge Galin for your thoughtful, specific and extremely helpful editing as William and I built this manuscript, from formative proposal, to final text.

Finally, I share thanks with my family. Pamela, your profound career success and life mission of place and faith explorations on many foreign soils has been a joy to observe and share in from time to time. Pat, your Olympic excellence, sense of family (wow, what high-quality kids you and Rick have gifted to the world), and willingness to risk and re-create your vocational and personal selves continues to amaze me. Paula, your dedication to the craft of education in challenging settings, focus on family and church, use of sport as a space of faith and mission, and your loving enthusiasm and unyielding faith in the face of profound tragedy and loss, continues to inspire me and many, many others in so many immeasurable ways. Khalfani, your unique strengths, and life embrace of being a culturally-grounded agent of change has been wonderful to see and share in. I am grateful to have the four of you as the siblings I measure myself by. And last and most, my thanks to my parents, Professors Lois Price Spratlen and Thaddeus H. Spratlen. Well beyond my birth, rearing, and the many unspoken sacrifices I will never know that created our family, these are just a few of the reasons words cannot possibly describe how, and how much I am indebted to you. May this book be one small part of the many ways I can only begin to thank you. Dad, simply put, without you, this book would not exist.

William Goldsby

The ancestors and our God, who created me, are at the center of these acknowledgments. Since I did not understand nor appreciate how acknowledgments should be written, I asked a few people for some advice. What follows is the result of this exploration.

It seems that acknowledgments are that which we appreciate about people in our lives. And to some degree, they are prayers. To that end, I appreciate life itself for its many gifts, and my evolving relationship with life, humanity, the struggle of being human, and the influences of time, space, and love as phenomena we have yet to understand or figure out.

I acknowledge and give thanks for the natural energy and life force that continues to guide and protect me, and is at the center of this book and the work of Reconstruction. I acknowledge humanity and our collective force, in spite of individual trials, tribulations, and celebrations. I acknowledge my mom, sad, brothers, sister and all of our family for allowing me to exist. Within humanity I acknowledge and appreciate many personal and professional partners. This includes Patrick Murray for his presence and consistent spiritual search for the truth; Lucinda Hudson and her family for being the rock of life for me in Philadelphia; Hakim Ali for his spiritual presence and his ability to think with precision; I appreciate the powers in the universe for placing in my life Butch Cottman, the Morrisons, the Whitfields, Reconstruction's first and present Advisory Council, past, present and future Board of Directors of Reconstruction Incorporated, and all of our supporters. Without the members of each of Reconstruction's committees and programs I am not convinced *Reconstructing Rage* would exist. As a founder of Reconstruction, I humbly acknowledge the masses of people who have suffered from the oppressions of the many empires and who have yet to receive justice from an unjust society. Most importantly, I acknowledge children as our future and as a bridge to our history as a current event regardless of the time.

I acknowledge time and space because it is time and space wherein all of this exist. To that end, it is important and worth acknowledging the colonization of Africa throughout human history and the many colonized places on earth. The colonization of the Americas and, the ending of the Atlantic Slave trade, when the last slave ship anchored on the gulf, the time of the Reconstruction era in America, that later gave birth to the National Association for the Advancement of Color People (NAACP). I acknowledge the Jim Crow laws that were adopted and affected every human being in this country. I also recall when the Communist Party almost had a stronghold in Alabama in my birth year of 1949. And the MOVE bombing in 1985 was essential to when, how and why Reconstruction was founded in Philadelphia with the support of the American Friends Service Committee's National Community Relations Division (AFSC-NRD). Although, the overlapping of space and time is significant, space warrants being acknowledged for many reasons as well. I give thanks and much appreciation for the donation of 1808 Tioga St. by Ms. Emma Ward of North Philadelphia who deserves high praise for the timeliness of this gift and the space itself.

Finally, I continue to grow, seek truth and acknowledge the importance of understanding the presence of God, love and the collective force of humanity, and the vital roles that time, space, and silence have in our lives, and specifically the writing of *Reconstructing Rage*.

Prologue

He responded to a Calling more than three years in the making. Move. As a verb, an action word, demanding motion for a changed location; a changed state of being. MOVE. A predominantly African American organization in Philadelphia, Pennsylvania, that values "decision-making that is nonhierarchical, nonauthoritarian, and open to the entire membership." Also a humanist organization that "does not claim to be a substitute for revolution in an oppressive society"[1]. After completing his second period of Peace Corps service in Central America, William Goldsby moved to Philadelphia in February 1988. At the time of his arrival, the second MOVE confrontation had taken place three years earlier on May 13, 1985. Seven years before that, a 1978 series of armed hostilities between MOVE and the Philadelphia Police Department left one police officer dead, three other officers severely injured, and four firefighters shot. Despite ballistics evidence that the police officer's fatal bullet most likely came from *behind* him as "friendly fire," the unfriendly outcome was the convictions of nine MOVE members, all of whom are now serving century-long sentences for that officer's death. From these two incidents, many unhealed wounds remained, just three years after the 1985 tragedy.

> I want to speak on the word ostracize. Most of us are very shocked walking the streets when we see a young Black man. White people. They move over when they see a young Black man. A lot of people in here would do the same thing. We talk about hatred. And we say don't harbor hatred. I'm angry. And unfortunately or fortunately, I've learned how to deal with my hatred. I've learned how to deal with my anger. But, for the most part, young Black men have not. At this point, I want to offer us a *solution*. I challenge the organizations here to include in your program [a] mechanism for young, Black men to deal with the hatred that we have. Otherwise…it will continue to resurface. Be it MOVE. Be it me if I walk out of here, and say something that is not…appropriate. The bomb will be dropped again. Because we are not allowed to express that anger. So, if there are any organizations here, I will volunteer time to help implement those programs…and I'm willing to deal with *those* causes, and help people implement solutions on *those* issues. Around Black men and how we are ostracized from this society.[2]

Culture

Culture is all around us and is many things. It is the symbolic and material content, texture, and tempo of all persons, activities, events, and priorities that occur among and between groups within a society. A culture is often marked by, and understood through, critical events that define it and raise questions about how and why critical events occurred, and how they are to be historically understood and responded to—both immediately and long after the event(s) took place. The 1985 MOVE confrontation escalated from standoff to tragedy when

Wilson G. Goode, the first African American mayor in Philadelphia's history, secured a military-grade bomb and authorized it to be dropped on a house—inside the city he governed.

The house was defined by some as a MOVE "compound" or "stronghold." And, like all symbols, the chosen language mattered then, and matters now, shaping memory and perception. Framing justification and placing blame. All of which make up the content, the texture, and tempo of historical memory and meaning. Whether, or how, the events are to be returned to and what strategies of action define the "shoulds" associated with the moment, the memory, and its meaning. Compound, stronghold, or whatever the chosen adjective, the facts of the confrontation remain. A military-grade bomb was dropped on a row of homes with connected walls, on a densely built block in a West Philadelphia neighborhood. The subsequent fire it ignited was then allowed to burn freely. Sixty-one homes were destroyed. More than 250 persons were left homeless. All this took place on one block of Osage Avenue, named after an ethnic group of Native Americans. And that block of Osage Avenue has never been the same.

This curious, inhumane process of administrative mismanagement, excessive force, and violated human rights resulted in the deaths of eleven Philadelphia citizens, five of whom were children, 9 to 14 years old. What segment(s) of what kind of culture values a bomb being dropped on a row house in an inner city neighborhood? What kind of culture leads a group of (Quaker) Friends to act with empathy and compassion, to—three years after the event occurred—then memorialize a humanist, non-hierarchical, African American organization's moment of profound loss, while also seeking to nurture a possible progress? These and other questions occurred to William when he first heard about what happened in Philadelphia. Between his two periods of Peace Corps service in May 1985, he briefly returned to Seattle and worked at El Centro de la Rasa, a Latino community social service agency. "My reason for coming to Philadelphia," he said, "was because I was intrigued with that whole [MOVE] tragedy."

Community

> The Osages are so tall and robust as almost to warrant the application of the term gigantic: few of them appear to be under six feet [tall], and many are above it. Their shoulders and visages are broad, which tend to strengthen the idea of their being giants.[3]

Community is both place and process. A community is made up of members in a location, who feel and share bonds or a sense of attachment in some way, and who share in patterns of exchange that those members' value, and that reinforce the bonds of fellowship to one another and to place. Beyond the physicality of historian and adventurist John Bradbury's observations, the Osages were both a culture and a community. Nearly three years after the tragic events that occurred on Osage Avenue, and after having moved to make his home in Philadelphia, William's community development Peace Corps days were behind him. Now, other unfinished business remained. Via long-distance learning, and their acceptance of transfer credits for degree closure, William was taking the final course to complete his Western Washington University bachelor's degree at the Community College of Philadelphia (CCP). Walking around the CCP campus after class in April 1988, still very new to the city, he wanted to get a better feel for it and its possibilities. He knew doing so would require some intimate investments of time, faith, and focus. He looked over several CCP bulletin boards. Entertainment, political, leisure, and otherwise, notes and flyers were haphazardly posted, inviting those who might be interested to attend various events. William's eyes stopped on one flyer in particular, promoting a three-day weekend set of activities commemorating the 1985 MOVE tragedy. William returned to his feelings from three years earlier when he first read of the bombing and related events. Implicit in the activities of the weekend's commemoration was an invitation. A call to action for anyone who might be interested in moving from memorializing an injustice, to nurturing justice solutions as an agent of change.

> I saw the announcement of the Memorial Service and where it was going to take place, then went to 1501 Cherry Street [the national office of the American Friends Services Committee (AFSC), the event's primary sponsor]. I had not given much attention to Quakers, regardless of their history around slavery or anything like that... When I walked into the space, even though it was pretty lax there, being new in Philadelphia, there was still somewhat of a tension. "'Who are you? What do you want?"' The person at the desk called the next Black man she could find that worked there, [chuckles] since I looked lost to them. I told [Darryl Jordan] what I was looking for. He shared with me what was going on, introduced me to the locations, and that's what brought me to the event. (Personal Communication, n.d.)

Capacity-building

[Valuing the assets of others begins with the choice to act with courage to value one's own.] Once that occurs, the ongoing process of capacity-building can begin. Capacity-building, or maximizing the local area assets of individuals, families, organizations, and others, can then be brought together to share in and collectively nurture an improved quality of life within that local area. And the lessons this process teaches can benefit those individuals, families, organizations, and others, who live within and well beyond the borders of that local area. Fellowship with others both similar to and different from one's self, is a long-practiced and critically important cultural and capacity-building strategy, which often begins with a single, simple moment of being at the right place, at the right time, with the right willingness and availability to act with conviction and Calling. For William, the CCP flyer moved him to action.

Perhaps it was simply something to do to productively respond to an otherwise open weekend. Perhaps it was just a brief moment in passing, of hoping to fellowship with the assets of many others that organizing for social justice provides. Just another moment in a lifetime that began and was defined by many such moments in a 1950s childhood in small town Alabama. While it may have begun as any one of these—or any number of other possibilities—attending the AFSC MOVE commemoration activities became an event that changed the course of William's life and the lives of many others. It was the genesis of an organizational effort to proactively, productively implement solutions on the issues around how Black men are ostracized from this society. It was a moment that changed the process and practices of post-incarceration re-entry and reintegration for a growing number of former felons and their families in one North Philadelphia neighborhood, and in many other communities in the city as well.

> I don't think I remember anything that was said, no more than, "We want to prevent such a tragedy [from happening again]." And I had to subjectify the comments. Because, from what I was hearing, the MOVE [members] had been alienated from society, [and] were mad as hell about a lot of things. The oppression of Third World people. Poor people. And I felt moved to just stand up and *to challenge… them to meet me halfway* to design an organization to deal with the rage of Black men. In that challenge, I remember sharing that people are afraid of Black men. Young Black men. Black men in general. Even Black women clutch their purses when we walk behind them …or across the street from them. And any time a group of people is feared, it creates an element of rage…[and the need] to design an organization that would deal with the rage of Black men. (Personal Communication, n.d.)

Culture, community, and capacity-building each extend from a collaborative foundation. Proactive strategies of cooperation. Relationships that are informed and enriched by reciprocity and respectful negotiation. An ongoing process where consensus is the desired outcome, and hierarchies and other structures of status and difference are acted against so that mechanisms of control can be exchanged within and beyond ritual in a spirit of equity. With comfort and shared power. While such a foundation may be more ideal than real under many circumstances, the process of nurturing its realization is valued and practiced by many as both the means and the ends of social change. If, as we are often told, "charity begins at home," so too does collaborating across differences and creating sustainable alliances, shared resources, and improving the ability of all to challenge injustice successfully. Responding to the MOVE–Philadelphia police confrontations and tragic, life-taking outcomes, and connecting them to larger local and societal challenges, are risky long-term processes that continue today. This is the work of learning from and moving beyond the critical lessons of both recent and more distance history. This is the work of reconstructing rage toward realizing a possible justice.

On that May weekend in 1988, the MOVE commemoration events were informed by a collaborative spirit and included various speakers and workshops. The general theme of preventing future tragedies was coupled with an exploration of how the events of May 1985 could have occurred in the first place. Details were recited and chronicled through multiple media. Importance— however partial—was given to placing the tragic outcomes in a process or sequence informed by history 100 years and more in the making. How might the MOVE moment in 1985 have been connected to, and informed by, events that preceded it by more than a century? In part due to the depth and demands of this question, the ease and convenience of an ahistorical, liberal distance was an all too common tone of the commemoration's events.

In spite of the best intentions, lamenting injustices that may well be difficult to explain, with only a minimal commitment to deep explorations of more complicated relationships, was repeated again and again that day. A dialogue addressing these deeper explorations, and the process of structuring organizational and community collaborations to address them, was begun. Between individual and collective agency for actions our worldviews may well otherwise oppose. Between law "enforcement" for the sake of collective safety and abusive social control. Between the visible and less visible, structural and interpersonal ostracizing of one cultural group, and how to proactively use the rational rage resulting from it. All of these and other similar continuums and contradictions of injustice were reflected in the institutional decisions and individual actions of another day's urban tragedy more than 25 years ago. And the unjustifiable deaths of eleven African American citizens that resulted from a bomb authorized by the African American mayor of their city remains another one among them.

[The MOVE tragedy] just burnt me to the max…I have always been addicted to risk. Being in the Peace Corps, and every time I turned around I was being challenged. My soul. My spirit. Everything…coming to Philadelphia with nothing was [a necessary risk]. Arriving, I was an open vessel. Reading. Observing. Taking in everything…[After] I challenged the organizations during that Saturday morning [at the AFSC event]…this one women, Mary Norris, was a committee member on the Community Relations Division of AFSC. She came up and grabbed me as I was leaving. (Personal Communication, n.d.)

William and Mary briefly spoke that day and then set up a time for their next and much longer meeting. And with that one act of outreach, a formative collaboration began. So, too, did Reconstruction. Reconstruction, as the name of an organization dedicated to a process of productively responding to the rage of Black men. An organization that finds truth in the words of Professor John Henrik Clarke that "*history is a current event.*" A grassroots, culturally grounded, capacity-building organization whose origins rest in an intersection of risks and vision, and a willingness to move from commemoration to acting as an agent of change. Reconstruction. As an era in U.S. history, of many unrealized possibilities, when the meanings and protocols of African American citizenship were being formed and reformed, and the interracial processes of, and potential for, institutional and resource capacity-building beyond the Underground Railroad were initially given voice. An era where promissory notes of profound importance were informed by absent sincerity, written in invisible ink, and never fulfilled.

The bridge between, and building a possible future from, the historical era of Reconstruction and a contemporary organization of the same name is analyzed in the following pages. Its foundation rests on culture, community, and capacity-building. What began as a response to a flyer on a community college bulletin board has become an organization with a history of more than two decades, and a set of collaborations and healing outcomes informed by a reach and legacy far beyond its sizeable mission and small size.

This book is in part an institutional ethnography of Reconstruction's organizational development and community capacity-building. It is partially a participatory action research analysis and assessment of collaborative practice in grassroots organizing. It is partially a historically informed exploration of evidence-based principles and practices for post-incarceration reentry and reintegration. And it addresses the 21st century present and future crisis in prison funding and social policy. Through archival documents, focus groups, and extensive in-depth interviews of past and current short- and long-term members and affiliated others, ethnographic data from various organization activities and events, and many other data sources both large and small, this is the story of Reconstruction Inc. It is an exploration of an organization you'll come to know and value in the pages that follow. It analyzes a healing community that is giving greater meaning and method to dismantling mass incarceration. It chronicles the many challenges and contributions of a grassroots organization giving direction to successful reentry and reintegration into post-prison family and community life, and the principled transformations these successes demand.

Part I
Culture

Part I, Chapter One

Echoes of Rage:
AEA, Resilience, and Healing

The mood and temper of the public in regard to the treatment of crime and criminals is one of the most unfailing tests of the civilization of any country...an unfailing faith that there is a treasure if only you can find it, in the heart of every man—these are the symbols which in the treatment of crime and criminals mark and measure the stored-up strength of a nation, and are the sign and proof of the living virtue in it.
—Winston Churchill to the *British House of Commons*, July 1910

A true spirituality cannot be constructed or assembled. It has to be recognized in the daily life of people who seek together to make sense of their existence and find meaning in life for themselves as individuals and in their collective experiences.
—*Hidden Wholeness*

Winston Churchill's statement from 1910 regarding civilization and the treatment of criminals is perhaps even truer today, especially in the United States. The United States has an incarceration rate of 754 inmates per 100,000 U.S. residents.[1] This is by far the highest documented rate in the world and is comparable only to Russia (602 per 100,000). Explosive prison growth in the United States began in the early 1970s, in both the number of inmates and institutions. The post-industrial economy had begun, globalization had gained momentum, and the echoes of the Civil Rights Movement had been stifled, not five years after the murder of Rev. Dr. Martin Luther King Jr. This "new *Jim Crow*" led the late 20th and early 21st centuries to be viewed by many as the era of mass incarceration.[2] Still, more than 96% of incarcerated persons are eventually released. They typically return to communities that have been made worse by their removal and the many disruptions to individual, family, and community that incarceration imposes. What is the mood and temper of the public—and of former felons in it—as they return to their families and communities? Rage is warranted.

For these former felons, their families, and communities—and the general public to which they return—how can a "true spirituality" of hidden wholeness be more fully recognized, to bring the wholeness out of hiding?[3] One organization's mission uses rage as a resource for growth beyond resilience. This chapter analyzes one program of one organization to explore how rage and resilience are used to heal and build capacities beyond the many wounds of its members. Due to the uneven distribution of who is imprisoned, reentry, the return of persons from jails and prisons, will disproportionately impact African American families and communities for the foreseeable future. One unique organization, Reconstruction Inc., is among a growing number helping the United States to pass "the most unfailing test of the civilization by enriching treasure resting in the heart of every human who comes into contact with it.[4]

Currently, there is very little research that longitudinally analyzes organizations in the reentry and reintegration process. Even less research explores how sustained affiliation with a reentry organization informs individual, familial, and communal desistance (i.e., ending criminal participation). Still fewer of these studies analyze organizations that are neither state-funded nor faith-based, and that take a family-centered, spiritually grounded, and holistic approach to reentry and reintegration. And none have evaluated an organization that, despite these characteristics, has existed for more than two decades. This chapter and this book is a helpful next step in this research. Reconstruction Inc. is a grassroots, community capacity-building organization formed in 1988 to value, redefine, and respond to the rage of Black men. In its history, curricula, structure, and strategies of action, it is a learning organization, that is, one that is "skilled at creating, acquiring, and transferring knowledge, and at modifying its behavior to reflect new knowledge and insights."[5] It is also an intimate collective of resilience and healing. As William Goldsby, its founder and Chair states, "[The] collective conscience is what I consider to be love. [Our] community capacity-building curriculum goal is to teach members how to counter alienation by building connections with this collective conscience and divinity source. Personally, familially, and communally." The Alumni Ex-Offenders Association (AEA) is one Reconstruction program that builds and renews those connections. AEA is a collective response to the call to action in Winston Churchill's words.

This chapter explores how an organization influences emotional, spiritual, and cognitive factors that contribute to desistance from crime and successful reintegration, providing useful information for reentry interventions.[6–9] It begins the exploration of relational resilience and *un*hidden wholeness; that is, how the spiritual influences of Reconstruction Inc. are expressed in the history, meetings, and other current activities of one of its programs: the Alumni Ex-Offender's Association. Reconstruction revises the long-standing phrase that "charity begins at home." It recognizes that community capacity-building does as well. In AEA, ritual, reciprocity, and rage are intersecting resources that, together, enable resilience, and enrich capacity-building outcomes.

A Core of Faith and Fury[10]

But real anger accepts few substitutes
And sneers at sublimation
The anger-hurt I feel
Cannot be washed down with a Coke (old or new) or a Colt 45
Cannot be danced away

Cannot be mollified by a white lover
Nor lost in the mirror reflections of a Black lover
Cannot evaporate like sweat after a Nautilus workout
Nor drift away in a cloud of reefer smoke
I cannot leave it in Atlantic City, or Rio
Or even Berlin when I vacation
I cannot hope it will be gobbled up
By the alligators on my clothing
Nor can I lose it in therapeutic catharsis
I cannot offer it to Jesus/Allah/Jah
So . . .

I must mold and direct
That fiery cool mass of
Angry energy—use it before it uses me!
Anger unvented becomes
Pain unspoken becomes
Rage released becomes
VIOLENCE !!!
Cha, Cha, Cha

First of all, rage is an emotion, and, is a real strong emotion. And, there's a lot of passion behind it. I don't think anyone can actually control their emotions. But they can intelligently respond to their emotions. So, the notion to remove it, or the notion to tell people to not exercise their rage would not be very effective....So, the people that was on the Advisory Board, and myself, agreed with identifying all of the emotions that was a part of the participants in the program. The joys. The happiness. The pain. But more importantly, identify what are the actual experiences people had in their past that resulted in rage. To deny that is to deny those experiences. So, the idea was to unite with those experiences—to identify [them]. Whether you've been hungry in your life. Or you've been raped. Or you've been abused. Or you've been disrespected. Silenced. All of those...are experiences that bring one to act out violently.

The reason for not removing rage. One is that you can't remove it. [Instead], dissect it. And [then] put it in its historical place. Rationalizing the condition within the household, within the family, that created that emotion [to] move forward….To have rage is legitimate. To have rage is valid. To be able to understand the causes of that rage, and all of the elements that create that rage [and] why it exists….To understand how we have [been] arrested in our emotions. At what point we're arrested in our emotions. To understand it, and to begin to look at it both objectively and subjectively IS rationalizing it. It is the point by which you can then be a spectator of your emotions…[and] you move forward by not being a slave to your emotions. Your emotions don't dictate behavior. You recognize that, although the urge is there to rob someone with a gun. The need is there because your family is going without. Because you recognize that someone has disrespected you or your family very violently. *You don't commit a violent offense against people or the community. Because…you're able to be intelligent about what you feel.* Your feelings are very present. But you are not a slave to those feelings. (William Goldsby, Personal Communication, n.d.)

Rage is a given in the Alumni Ex-Offender's Association (AEA) of Reconstruction Inc. However frequent or rare, acute or long-standing, rage is a reality in a life lived with virtually any depth or substance. This, especially, when one has experienced the spectrum of oppressions intersecting marginalization within this society imposes on far too many, far too often. Over and over again. Exclusion alone is reason for anger. And with oppressive repetitions, anger can quickly become rage. And the intersecting oppressions of race, class, and gender within the criminal justice system, that is, the status of a Black male residing in a poor, urban neighborhood—especially here in the era of mass incarceration—lead rage to make a great deal of sense. From Grier and Cobbs[11] to bell hooks,[12] to Stanley Tookie Williams,[13] the role of rage in Black life manifests both as problem (i.e., a resource for self- and group destruction) and solution (e.g., a resource for passionate purpose, transformation, and social justice).

As Stanley Tookie Williams notes while explicitly telling his own story, and implicitly that of many other African American men, *"My rage was nourished by the hate I saw and felt from mainstream society and white people, a hate based on my black skin and my historical place at the nadir of America's social caste. I was filled with hate for injustice. Yet my reaction to the hate was violence directed only toward blacks"*[14] [emphasis added]. At once, rage is both problem and solution, both poison and antidote, the two sharp edges of rage are in line with the long-held saying from Black folk culture: "That which don't kill you, makes ya stronger." It does so *"within a society that systematically denies or neglects responsibility for its crippling oppression"*[15] while tailoring new and innovative marginalization strategies still strategically anchored in a system seemingly long past. So says the illusion of a "post-racial"

America. In contrast to that illusion, the many markers of a living, breathing racial reality remain. As Professor John Henrik Clarke observed many years ago (personal communication), *"History is a current event"* [emphasis added]. As a result, "We have not ended racial caste in America; we have merely redesigned it."[16] Reconstruction and AEA are designed to work within and counter these caste truths by first acknowledging and then nurturing the many assets of their members. This is the beginning of an often long and nonlinear process of individual, familial, and communal growth—of reconstructing rage.

As Wenning (2009) has stated, "Often rage is an appropriate response to injustice and serious wrongdoing…[and is] a major tool for creating justice and gaining power [by] the oppressed."[17] In AEA, as reflected in William Goldsby's words above, rage is a capacity-building resource, a means through which one heals, individually and spiritually. Within one's family, and within the program, organization, collaborations, and community, *"rage can be an emancipatory force that does not simply expose violations but at the same time brings about an engagement to correct them…. In the face of blatant injustice there is a need to offer a different vision"*[18] [emphasis added]. Through AEA, Reconstruction members nurture and share with others the emancipatory force within themselves. This force is then made stronger still through collective engagement to correct whatever exposed violations are shared in that particular meeting, event, or initiative. Be they violations of honor, of dignity, or of justice. AEA is a healing collective, with rage as part of the means through which the healing occurs. Linked with the stigma of soiled honor, rage emerges in a cultural milieu of (the myths of) American individualism and the consequent alienation from a fundamental yearning for significance felt by so many.[19] The reconstruction of rage rests in relational resilience[20], which we will document and explore in this and the coming chapters; it is a *"grassroots movement with a shared sense of indignation, a shared vision…[and] message of hope in a better world"*[21] [emphasis added]. AEA moves with, and builds from, the hearts, minds, families, and environments of its membership. Like intersections of the built environment, members' diverse characteristics and histories make up the internal, personal intersections of their lives.

Intersections and Sacred Space

Turning at the intersection of these two quiet streets is an invitation: to a shift in focus; to an exchange of second sight, sharing in a power to perceive things not present to the senses; to a place on a pathway of change that Reconstruction Inc. encourages, in fact, demands of all who affiliate with it. It is a simple street corner in North Philadelphia, not unlike many others in the neighbor-hood or in the city. On one corner is an open field with a mixture of concrete pieces and overgrown grass. A hollow reminder of where houses and apart-ments long ago torn down once stood. Across the street heading south is a newer multiuse building. It contains a daycare center, a treatment center where 12-step meetings are held daily, and a residential space for those in recovery from abusive substance use. Moving west across the street is a fenced yard adja-cent to the small apartment building a few feet further west. Across the street heading north to the final corner is a church, large enough to fill a corner but not a small city block. Gray bricks housing a chapel that was once full. Now the era of "commuter pews," neighborhood decline and the decline of the neighborhood church, for many, have left the congregation small and aging with parishioners who no longer live nearby. This is the corner's turn toward a possible transformation. A corner's invitation to an exchange of second sight.

An intimate pathway begins here. Now heading east, these steps, both in motion and location, are steps to a sometimes Sacred space. A building and a room that many know as welcoming and value with a feeling of home. These steps on this avenue called Tioga lead up to a set of row house buildings, with multiple units behind every front door. Near the street's end is 1808. Old. Brick. With a wrought iron, knee-high fence in front that meets the sidewalk, preventing the entry of no one. Reconstruction Inc. is in this building, with a small, green grass yard on the side to the left, with a smaller garden between the sidewalk and the raised front porch. The brief path to a five-step walk up of offset steps. The unassuming front porch is nearly empty most of the time. A folding chair here and there. The front window's upper half greets the viewer with a large decal on the window's inside surface that reads, *"Changing Ourselves to Change the World"* [emphasis added]. This is the political line of the organiza-tion and is its political, social, and spiritual mission. Focused. Clear. With enough unknown for curiosity, and the sound of being principled, with a spiri-tual possibility. Maybe even a spiritual demand. How members live these ideas together is critical to the organization's work.

The building has the look of many multiunit row houses built in this era, in this first capital of the United States. Especially in this part of the city. There are many large, beautiful, abandoned buildings nearby on blocks yet to be bitten by the tensions and false promise of gentrification. The building has a look of old brick and layers of unspoken history, holding all of the words to all of the memories of each person who has ever entered there. Once inside, the front door has a small foyer where the mailboxes are. Then the entry door to the hallway of the first floor units to the left. Or the staircase to the right and the multiple apartment units on the floor above. With only a hint of irony, entering the Reconstruction office demands a quick turn to the left. Upon entry, this is the place that centers the craft of reconstructing rage, one meeting at a time. This is the secular, yet Sacred space of a converted studio apartment. The office space is cramped with a table too large for the floor space at the center of the room. The mantle above the closed-up fireplace is the first visual greeting upon entry. A large monthly calendar is there and almost always full of various meetings, organizational events, and other social justice commitments documenting the collaborations of caring members of Reconstruction. Though cramped, the office is marked by the absence of wasted space. To the left of the fireplace front in the northeast corner are half-sized filing cabinets, with once-working computer parts stacked on top. A keyboard here, a monitor there. In the opposite northwest corner on the other side of the front window, rests a stack of five large framed images. Each one of the 4 feet x 5 feet frames contains 50 or more Polaroid images of persons serving life sentences. These "lifers" are among those who carry the membership and the message of Reconstruction inside prisons.

Not accidentally, the decision of Ms. Emma Ward to sell this building to Reconstruction for one dollar in 1993 initiated a firestorm of neighborhood concern. Concern about "those people, criminals and such" being on this quiet residential block. *Tioga*, or *Teaoga* as it has also been spelled in the past, is a Native American word meaning gateway, or the meeting of two rivers.[22] As a place, Tioga was an especially strategic location. It was "a natural watchtown where many important Indian [rivers and] trails converged"; a key pathway to new and unknown spaces, rich with danger, uncertainty, and opportunity.[23] Tioga is also the name of an ethnic group of the Seneca Nation who once inhabited diverse areas of North America. The Tioga were known as a people who gave special priority to "knocking the rust off of the chain of friendship" to enrich alliances within their group, and between their group and others, in hopes of enhancing a possible future.[24] Like the street name where it is located, all Reconstruction programs merge multiple life pathways as their mission. Their method is one of nurturing the resilience of intimate renewal beyond whatever rust may have formed on the faith, friendships, and families, extending from the tensions of a criminal past. Tioga. This is the street, the office space, the meeting place, where the organizational and spiritual praxis of "*changing ourselves to change the world*" happens as a daily Call to Action.

AEA: A Brief History

The Alumni Ex-Offenders Association is a group of people who have either been incarcerated or join with those who have. AEA members are united by the facts that all persons possess excellence, have been exposed to varying degrees of unhealthy socialization, and have a history of life stage outcomes informed by both truths. Members are people who have robbed banks, taken someone's life, raped another person, been raped, used and dealt drugs or guns or both, or had family members doing all this and more. AEA members are also persons with no criminal or substance use history of any kind, who just want to help. They are students, people from all races, economic backgrounds, sexual prefer- ences, and religions. They are affiliated with the criminal justice system as prison administrators or who serve in other criminal justice roles. This rich mix- ture shapes many moments in each meeting. There have been moments where members found out that they and their spouses or partners are expecting a child, or that a child has recently been born. Moments where a loved one lost their life only a few minutes earlier, due to a criminal act or a health challenge. Moments when a member relapsed and returned to active addiction. Or re- turned to prison. Or received a phone call from another member they had not seen or spoken with in many years. AEA members nurture principled transfor- mation by enriching the assets of its members. It sustains growth built on col- lective, culturally anchored accountability, a spiritually informed search within and beyond one's self, and a restorative, critical awareness and insight that val- ues ongoing relationships between the personal and the political. Participating in AEA is a means by which former felons and interested others change un- wanted behaviors in all their forms, including spiritual, emotional, political, psy- chosocial, and intellectual. AEA is an environment where personal and social struggles are embraced as fuel for further transformation. It is a culture of so- briety marked by all forms of recovery, and it celebrates people who are gradu- ating from penal and all other oppressive institutions. For many, AEA has been and remains a lifesaver.

AEA began at Hospitality House, a halfway-back facility that housed parole violators. Hospitality House kept them from returning to prison for minor in- fractions, and they were required to be there for six months. Although Hospi- tality House prevented men from returning to prison, it did not have an interactive program that addressed spirituality, politics, family issues, or even how to navigate the relationship between parolees and parole officers. During the early 1990s William Goldsby became a member of the Village of Kumbaya and participated in the village's monthly meetings. The village was named for the Gullah phrase for *"Come by here* [Lord]" [emphasis added], an African American spiritual from the Depression of the 1930s. Like the Gullah phrase itself, this Afrocentric collective was founded on the ideals of human and spiritual unity, closeness, and compassion, and the potential for collectively realizing Afrocentric awareness, the fifth and highest level of individual and collective transformation.[25] William was also involved in a political study group, the New African Voices Alliance. As a result of his membership in the two groups, he learned more about the necessity of people being open with their personal issues, and understanding the ways in which personal issues are indeed political.

By 1997, Brother Joseph Dudek, the CEO of Hospitality House, had served on the Reconstruction Board of Directors for more than two years. In that same year, Bro. Joe asked William to consider condensing the Reconstruction four-year curriculum into a six-month format. This four-year program had been successfully facilitated at the prison in Graterford, Pennsylvania. Bro. Joe understood that addressing rage was at the core of the original curriculum, and he also understood that the curriculum was designed to include the active collaboration of family members, city agencies, and local institutions. It was structured to engage diverse units in an exchange of resources, and, by doing so, to collectively build the capacity of each collaborator. More importantly, Bro. Joe knew that the curriculum was interactive and taught participants how to set and follow an agenda, and how to facilitate meetings as they facilitated their own growth. In February 1997, William completed the redesigned curriculum, and he began facilitating this condensed version in the Hospitality House Life Skills Program.

As the initial implementation of the revised curriculum progressed, it was agreed to change the title of this program from Life Skills to Leadership Development Program. Several discussions around life skills versus leadership took place. William suggested that in his view, many, in fact, most of these men already had life skills, though they may not have been using them appropriately. This was much more than a conceptual dialogue or exchange of semantics alone. Life skills emphasize the individual and self-development. Leadership implies group, community, and other systemic collectives. The Reconstruction leadership development curriculum was facilitated for nearly two years. During this time, the men began to see themselves as a community. They organized and hosted two graduations for current and former residents. They initiated a house committee that provided leadership to all residents, whether or not they were participating in the leadership groups. As they graduated from Hospitality

House, reentered their family households, and struggled to settle into their civilian lives, their challenges became more difficult to manage.

In 1998, after the first two Hospitality House groups graduated, a trio of graduates from the six-month program approached William and asked him to assist them in creating a support group for ex-offenders. It was clear that these three former residents had

met themselves to discuss their needs before they approached him. Hospitality House employed people who had been formerly incarcerated or who were in recovery and had long-term sobriety. Despite these elements of empathy, and consistent with the prevailing individualized life-skills model, the staff did not demonstrate a willingness to build collectively on a community level. These graduates were concerned with how to best navigate their own behaviors, family situations, and race and class issues between themselves and their parole officers. William then asked Hospitality House to sponsor another graduate group in addition to the in-house, morning leadership development group. When officials said yes, a weekly, Friday evening "After-Care" ex-offender group began. This small group of men met for nearly two years defining and refining what they needed to help them move from a space of initial reentry to one of sustained, successful reintegration into the lives of their families and communities. Less than a year later, women from Hannah House, a women's halfway-back house, began participating in the morning group. Soon thereafter, a group of young men who had been sentenced to penal boot camp also began attending. This group of young men would later form the genesis of Leadership, Education, Advocacy, and Development (LEAD), Reconstruction's youth program (see chapter 6). Whether focusing on the After-Care graduates meeting or the in-house leadership group with its new women and youth members, AEA community leadership emerged because every individual learned from each other how to run a meeting, set an agenda, and list issues within an agenda topic, to make the most of its capacity-building potential. Furthering a nearly constant dialogue between structure and principled action, this capacity-building potential was realized as these participants improved their leadership skills with each meeting.

During these meetings, one issue consistently provided an avenue for the men and women to exercise their collective power to gain knowledge and organize among themselves: community support of persons on long-term parole and the time they would have to be under penal supervision. Two years into its development, AEA furthered its momentum by hosting a meeting with one of Pennsylvania's former lieutenant governors. Organized through a collaboration of current and former residents, AEA members wrote the meeting request, set the agenda, invited neighbors and interested others, ran the meeting, and offered to pay the lieutenant governor's honorarium. The purpose of this meeting was to ask him what it would take for the community to support parolees who had five or more years on parole. They wanted to know if these sentence lengths could be reduced with a good record and community support. The growing group of current and soon-to-be former felons discussed these related issues of sentencing policy, reentry, and reintegration in fellowship with this high-ranking state government official. It was a critical turning point in the maturation of AEA. This was the first time these men and women had the opportunity to sit with someone of that caliber.

William began to include the worldview and strategies of action from his memberships in the Village of Kumbaya and New African Voices Alliance into the Leadership Development groups at Hospitality House. This encouraged participants to become more open and trusting, and to value the depth of strength required to be vulnerable in these new ways. The practice was to share deeply held secrets and begin to connect them to motives, decisions, and destructive behaviors. This awareness within the group created a culture where personal issues were openly shared. A process of getting feedback from the group regardless of the issue that was shared became ritual, and individuals began to view themselves as valuable members of their group and community. This practice also allowed participants to begin looking at their negative or hostile feelings. Without these and other healing initiatives, these feelings could have easily devolved and been expressed as violence. Or they could have led to relapse back into active addiction. If such negative situations occurred between meetings, those involved were expected to state their role in the situation and contract with the group what they would do to prevent it from happening again. This, too, remains a practice within AEA: redirecting rage as a capacity-building resource that strengthens the personal, family, and community dynamics of its members.

Most AEA members who graduated from Hospitality House and others who became members of AEA learned and understood the mechanics of running a meeting. They also learned that being disciplined, structured, and focused are imperative and are at the center of self-governance. And that priority is given to shifting participants' thinking to move them in thought and action from individualism to collectivism. Members have struggled to understand that building consensus is implicit in democracy. To that end, from the beginning to now, members continue to struggle with collective decision-making. And in this process, it is essential to record any minority perspectives so that they can be effectively considered during upcoming evaluations. This adherence to structure and related discipline was matched with a willingness to collectively respond, to practice these principles in the everyday experiences that arose in participants' lives.

Many years ago, a situation occurred in an AEA meeting that gave rise to the Emergency Response System (ERS). ERS is now Situation Management; the second pillar of the organization's curriculum (see chapter 2). Avoiding the language of "crisis," it was named for responding to an acute or chronic circumstance in an AEA member's life that demanded a timely, collective response. In 1999, an AEA member was keeping the group updated about his common law marriage. At that time his parole home plan was at the home of his common law wife, where two of his wife's adult children were living with her. When tension arose between the AEA member and his wife, her son and daughter both got involved. This led the disagreement to escalate, as the voices of the AEA member and the son got louder and more abusive. In an act of aggression that happens far too frequently, his wife's adult son then went outside the home and onto the sidewalk, challenging the AEA member to join him there.

At that moment, the AEA member had the presence of mind to call another AEA member *before* he stepped outside to respond to the son's challenge. Prioritizing a principled choice of relational resilience, the AEA member he called, in turn, called another member. As geographic proximity and caring response times allowed, less than ten minutes later, ten members were outside their home. AEA members separated the two men, and the situation was kept from getting worse when AEA members then assisted in the decision making of first dividing, and then hauling the members' furniture to a local church. No fighting. No police. No handcuffs. No arrests. Just collectively building capacity by engaging in shared respect and avoiding further escalation. This happened on a Saturday night after 1:00 a.m. This type of responsiveness, and the galvanizing of members that results from it, continues today.

This process of curriculum refinement, improved self-governance, and collective practice lasted from 1996 to 2002 (see chapter 7). In 2001, a new Board of Directors was organized. AEA continued evolving from being a leadership program at Hospitality House, into a separate ex-offenders' support group, and later to a program under the auspice of Reconstruction. AEA later gave rise to the youth work and program that became LEAD. Since AEA had become an accepted force in the community, with participating members at Hospitality

House and Hannah House, the members decided to accept only people who volunteered for AEA and to not accept people who were stipulated into AEA as a condition of their parole. This remains a policy today. AEA's original and continuing goal is to help formerly incarcerated persons, their families, and the community at large to better understand the plight of people returning home from prison and to use the meetings in the Reconstruction office as a learning environment to establish and refine capacity-building skills.

More recently, through AEA, Reconstruction's spiritual leadership enriches several collaborations discussed in detail in Part III. These resource exchanges are informed by the Reconstruction commitment to further capacity-building and collective leadership, both intra- and interorganizationally. And what this demands is the nurturing of shared expertise, so that skill-set dependencies occur seldom, if ever. When sharing with another organization, the goal is to nurture the skills within that collaborator such that in the future they can engage it with equal success toward whatever goals they solicited with the participation of Reconstruction. For example, the late Father Paul Washington was one of Reconstruction's first advisors. Father Washington presided over the Church of the Advocate, whose history included having been a safe haven for the Black Panthers to organize during the 1960s. When Father Washington passed, Father Isaac Miller presided over the church. Like other community leaders, Father Miller, then and now, called on Reconstruction and AEA to provide direction on how the church can best assist people returning to the community from prison. Along with this outreach, Reconstruction expects people to take ownership of a process. When Father Miller called Reconstruction many times in the years since, each time he would say, "I know you want to educate our congregation on how to do this work ourselves." The calls to Reconstruction and AEA continue. When other organizational collaborators continue affiliating with Reconstruction within a service-provider model, this model most often leads them to refuse to take ownership of the process because of a lack of capacity, or because they will not take the time to learn how.

Father Miller had in his church a family with two sons who were often in trouble. The older of the two had been referred to AEA in August 2009. He contacted Hakim Ali, but he was rearrested for a parole violation between the time he contacted Hakim and actually making it to an AEA meeting. Unfortunately, the morning of the AEA regular meeting, the youngest son of this family was found murdered with his face cut up by a knife or a razor blade. The oldest son was so full of hurt, pain, and rage, he walked to the AEA meeting the same day. The rage was worsened because he knew or had a good idea who killed his brother. Coming to AEA allowed him to function with that rage as he walked the streets in his neighborhood, all the while knowing that he was likely passing his brother's killer. The wounds that this situation created are profoundly present, with echoes that will always be heard and deeply felt. The surviving son is now an active and contributing member of AEA, reconstructing his rage with each moment of fellowship. He humbly offers and provides his time to the organization whenever it is needed or requested. He is also very sensitive to the struggles of others, caring for and with them as deeply as the feelings that remain from the loss of his brother. Even though he is available for AEA, he continues to have some major struggles. He is presently attending school, parenting his son, and strives to maintain a principled relationship with his son's mother. He is currently without a steady income and is (still) on both state and federal parole. Reconstruction members, both former felons and interested others alike, are sharply aware that there are hundreds and thousands of young men and families in similar struggles. *"Changing ourselves to change the world"* is a long walk of many lifetimes and many lifelines. Built on the foundation provided by the curriculum considered in chapter 2, through its meetings and mission AEA is one of them.

AEA Praxis in Motion

Meeting Segment 1

"They made me walk a chalk line earlier today," William comments to Tod, the only one of the four members in attendance not aware of the real circumstances William describes.

"Made you walk a chalk line? Who is they, and why did they do so?" Tod asks.

"These two made me do it," William says emphatically, referring to Hakim and Sonya. "And, I don't know why they did it to me. You'll have to ask them."

The exchange continues, ending with Sonya saying to William and all who would care to listen, "William, you know what they say. A little torture every once in a while is good every once in a while for the soul."

"Is that right?" William responds. "Uh, huh. Well, whose soul, exactly?"

All the while, Hakim simply signifies gently, "Uh, uh, uh."

Meeting Segment 2

Lendell opens the meeting, "Okay. Right now, um. Right now, I want everybody to be really sincere, um, about the meeting. Like, first of all, like I said I had a pretty good day. I had a very enjoyable day. So, I want everybody's focus to be very clear. Ask any questions, at any time. And so, right now we're gonna reflect on …Y'all gotta bear with me. This is [only] my second meeting. {Slight chuckle} I'm also asking for help. If anybody wanna fill in. So, I guess we should deal with, um…old business?"

"Check in," Tod suggests, to which Hakim signifies, "MY man!"

Lendell then begins the check-in with Sherece, his wife, who is a healthcare worker.

"Well, while I'm checkin' in, I have a client of mine, who, I can just say, could use this support group. Actually, I said something to William about him earlier. I need the information, when the next support group is so that I can invite him to it. 'Cause he says he will come, if he knows it ahead of time. He will come. I have a card for William that I brought with me…with his name and number on it. So that if y'all want to get in contact with him at some time so, I just handed it to Hakim. He was the one I was tellin' you 'bout, that when he finds out more information about Reconstruction.…He was talkin' 'bout gettin' the papers, and gettin' the apartments [to renovate], and settin' them up, so that when people come outta jail, they'll have a place to go. Also…trainin' the guys to [re]build the places, so that there'll be somebody [on site] to help with up-keep of the places, as well as havin' somewhere to stay. He has the son, who had gotten shot in the head, a few years back, that he's been taking care of by his self. So, he's been sayin' he could use this work. 'Cause, like I was sayin', he said his wife left him, in the midst of all this…and he's been doing er'ything tryin' to get his son back. [First] from a coma, to then being a vegetable, to walkin', [and, now] talkin', you know. So, he's sayin' that he could use all the support he can get. So, that's my check in for today."

"Are we goin' all the way around first?" William asks Lendell.

"Ya, we should go all the way around. Uh. No. Actually, can we ask questions [after each individual check in]. Since it's a small group?"

"It's up to you. I'm cool [with doing so]," Hakim responds.

"Question, William?" Lendell asks.

"Ya. Questions for Sherece. Two things. One is, I say this in support of you, Sherece, and the struggles that you goin' through right now. And I guess it's a question just to see where you at. Are you prepared to ask for support when you need it? That's a general question. And the second one is, the meet-ings that we have are the first and third Wednesday. These are Member Support meetings. So, this is similar to the question that was asked, when you raised this issue [recently]. You're a member of this organization. And I'm just wondering how much leadership can you give to the direction—What kind of information you can give to this guy?"

"Well, I can—" Sherece begins.

William breaks back in and briefly completes his questions.

"So that's the—How much support can we give you? And, do you know how to ask for support? And secondly, you being a member, I would hope that you give some leadership to bring this guy. Introduce him to us. And it's not my organization. It's just as much yours as it is mine."

"Yes, well, on that note. Yes, I know how to ask for support; know how to ask for help when I need help. But, I've given this man all the information that I can give him that I know about the group. So that's why I offered, told him, about comin' to the group. So that he could hear, could learn more about it himself. 'Cause, like I said, I've only come in here, sat in here. Learnin' a little bit about the groups, when I can [manage to] come here, you know, due to my job. So, to me, I don't really know about each myself, to where I can go 'head and explain everything to him. So that's why I asked him, invited him here to witness it, and hear about it for himself."

Then, Hakim and Sherece have a brief exchange which Hakim begins by first asking Sherece the son's age. "We can deal with this thing in more detail, once we start dealing with our issues. But, how old is his son? // His son is 34. // 34 now? // Yes. // Did he tell you how old his son was when he got shot? // 16 years old. // When he got *shot?* // Yes. // Wow. // And [as a result of the damage the bullet did to the young man's brain stem] at this time he's got the mind of an eight-, or ten-year-old. // Okay...Wow...Okay, thanks. That's it."

Reflecting on the first Meeting Segment, William is legally blind and would not be in a position to walk any line, chalk or otherwise. And the two members he is referring to, Hakim and Sonya, would not force William—or any other AEA member—to adhere to that, or any other sobriety checkpoint policing procedure. Yet the joke continued. The exchange is shared with a chuckle and sense of familiar among all members. A play of caring. The reference to, and play with, police procedure. The willingness to render one's blindness as a source of humorous play as abusively imposed policing. The use of humor to introduce two members to one another (Sonya and Tod) who, at that time, were strangers to each other, grounded in a caring mockery between intimates. And the process of all involved, being willing to be patient while waiting for other members to arrive so the meeting can then formally begin. To share in this exchange extending from a simple wordplay on an event that would never take place was a single meeting moment. Yet it was reflective of the many rich intimacies among members, renewing even before a single meeting begins, the Reconstruction mission.

Then, just a moment later, the meeting is brought to order when Lendell and Sherece arrive. William reminds Lendell that he has agreed to facilitate the meeting. Lendell then welcomes everyone and begins a moment of silence. Then, having attended many meetings across the years but having facilitated very few, Lendell searches within the meeting and within himself for the text and tone of principled leadership the facilitator role demands. He is allowed time and latitude. To struggle and be unsure. To request the support of others, while still reluctantly taking leadership. To build his own capacity for facilitation and the many skills associated with it, learning in the practice of a new role in a single meeting and within the organization, as well. "The role of leaders in organizations is to set the necessary conditions for the organization to develop an effective learning capability", including the struggle to find voice, follow through on a prior commitment, to develop new skills for guiding other, far more seasoned and familiar members to make the most of a new and challenging role.[26] It was "only" a new facilitator's struggle. Yet, within it was layered much, much more.

Once Sherece had checked in, William challenged her on two counts. First, to assess her understanding of the reciprocity between strength, vulnerability, and fellowship in the ability to request help when the need arises. Healthy leadership and healing are both enhanced when those places of strong vulnerability are shared with others to further fellowship, and they collectively grow stronger through the sharing of both with others. And second, William challenged Sherece's comfort with being, in effect, an ambassador for AEA and Reconstruction. Expertise is not something that rests outside of members, however new. Now, as members, expertise and organizational ownership are as collective as the organization's consensus decision making. Sherece emphasized that she has shared the extent of her organizational knowledge and that what was then needed was his meeting participation. William pushed her. He invited Sherece to a new self-understanding: to see herself as having all that is needed to provide this potential new member with that which could get him to the Reconstruction office to participate in a support group meeting. William's follow-up to Sherece further demonstrates the intimacy and compassion central to the capacity-building protocol of AEA and the Reconstruction mission.

How Healing Happens

AEA provides a shared space where more and less common aspects of navigating life as a former felon are discussed and explored in a challenging environment of compassion, empathy, and love. Given the complexities and opportunities of the reentry and reintegration process, this is done to enrich strategies of action for possible change so that an improved quality of life can be realized for individual members within their families and communities. AEA typically gives leadership to processes, procedures, and action items both large and small, with two different kinds of meetings: work plan and membership support meetings. Both are facilitated in the same way and consistent throughout Reconstruction. True to the organization's mission, membership in AEA and Reconstruction are open to anyone willing to *"change themselves to change the world."* Membership moves from the general mission to a more specific process when an individual interested in the organization attends an orientation.

By taking the time to orient new members to the opportunities and responsibilities of membership, Reconstruction creates a more educated membership and a more productive organization. The orientation introduces how the organization is governed, its history, what its programs and protocols are, prior long-standing discussions, and any current initiatives that are being prioritized. It motivates excitement through a dialogue between new and experienced members, and it emphasizes the practice of being membership-run. This is vital in an organization defined by collective ownership and decisions that are arrived at by consensus. After attending an orientation, it is vital that the interested person first clearly understands and then unites with the philosophy. Thus, a discussion in depth about the meanings of, and challenges within, the philosophy takes place as new roles and new ways of knowing oneself continue to unfold.

As the introduction and brief history above demonstrate, this happens in many diverse ways in the lives of AEA members—both formally and less formally. Perhaps the most formal expression of AEA fellowship is meetings where AEA models principled relationships. These meetings provide general support among members, their families and other loved ones, assists members with the proactive management of various situations, whether understood as "crisis" or not, educates itself and others about the connections between personal, familial, and communal issues, and enriches the structure, discipline, and focus of members as well as the community at large. AEA also facilitates the Reconstruction community capacity-building curriculum and serves as an ambassador to the community on behalf of Reconstruction.

All meetings begin with a moment of silence. Understood as a recognition of a shared spirituality between and beyond all the present members, and being affiliated with a rich diversity of faith paths, the shared absence of sound is a reciprocity within and beyond the Christian tradition of "the substance of things hoped for, the evidence of things not seen." During this time, some members may bow their heads and say a prayer in silent conversation between themselves and the God of their understanding. Some may reflect on a moment of anguish or triumph from earlier in the day. Some may return to a space of solitude they cherish as a Sacred memory from many years ago. Other members simply sit and share in the fellowship of caring silence. Perhaps paradoxically, the shared silence of attending members in the room is mixed with any number of sounds and activities engaged in by others just outside the meeting space. Tenants in one of the building's apartments come and go, opening and closing the front doors and head up and down the old, wooden staircase, as they need to. Adult conversations from the adjacent front porch punctuate with loud words and louder laughter. The occasional car passes on the street, with its stereo system being played loudly enough to be at a "see and be seen" volume. And the voices of children playing on Tioga remind members of the present and next generation of agents of change nearby. The silence at the very start of every meeting is a shared peace. Not as if one is in a place where noise, trouble, or hard work are absent. Rather, together, attending AEA members are in a place where those things are also present, yet they still share a space of calm in their heart and mind.

This moment is then followed by an introduction and/or an orientation, if either is needed. Here, need is determined by which members are in attendance, the level of familiarity they have with one another and with the organizational mission, and with the purpose for this particular AEA meeting. If there is limited familiarity with any one of these things, the facilitator asks each attendee to share in the ritual of a brief description of themselves, how long and in what ways they have been and are now affiliated with AEA and Reconstruction, and then contributing to the details of program and organizational introduction to a new attendee.

A facilitated check-in follows. During the check-in, those in attendance are giving the choice to share whatever they want to share. It may in part be an informed answer to the question and greeting, "How are you?" The details of a troubling day. A brief update of an ongoing family challenge. A new triumph or refinement of a skill that few knew that member had. It may manifest as little more than wordless emotion; near silent tears of joy or sadness and the safety for them to be shed in this space of shared respect and caring. As a result of past grief or present pain or for the recent arrival of very good news. During the check-in people say whether or not they need or want a subgroup to meet on their behalf in order to get deeper into one or more personal issues. The meeting proceeds with old business where minutes from the previous meeting are read. Action steps: considered, taken, and not taken. Outcomes or other points of change; of closure, and those still unfolding. Shared in enough detail for points of progress and ongoing challenges that remain to be recognized and understood. With enough caring and intimacy for privacy to not be abused, with success and vulnerabilities, movement and stagnation alike, recognized and valued for the contributions to capacity-building they all share.

New business is conducted next, where new items are considered and re-sponded to, followed by an assessment. All AEA members are clear that the moment of silence at the beginning of all meetings means that the Ancestors are very present during the meetings and in members' daily lives. That the check-in allows the issues or topics of most pressing concern to be given voice and support shared as a result. That the business, both old and new, and the assessments that end all meetings are also essential resources for the capacity of each member to be enriched and the process of refining and renewing the or-ganization mission to occur with each ritual, process, and organizational action step. And that innovation is borne of the creativity that necessity often de-mands. The work plan meeting involves dealing with the organization trainings, public relations, fundraisers, and other business planning. To exemplify por-tions of this AEA meeting process of reconstructing rage, what follows is a brief composite of segments from a recent AEA membership support meeting. Some names have been changed and the specific circumstances of situations have been altered to protect the anonymity of all involved.

Conclusion

A single meeting from a single program of an organization can only begin to present the layered dynamics that inform the comprehensive praxis of its mis-sion. The AEA support group meeting detailed above began with a simple question and dilemma: how should those in attendance best adapt, given that the person who agreed to facilitate that meeting had not yet arrived. A decision was made by consensus of the five members in attendance to begin the meeting just five minutes late. Consistent with AEA's desire to use structure as an ally for disciplined transformation, all meetings begin and end on time unless unexpected circumstances do not allow that to occur. Lendell had previously agreed to chair the meeting, leading to some uncertainty regarding how to best proceed. While the five attending members already there waited (sharing in patience and compassion), they shared intimacy—the "loudest" unspoken resource in Reconstruction. Rage was reconstructed with craft and caring, so that the capacity of all those involved could progress.

AEA Praxis: With Love as the Cultural Core
This introduction to AEA shows a very few among its many intense and unique moments of the Reconstruction mission. Through AEA, Reconstruction enriches an ever-present dialogue between rage and love, recognizing both as vital resources for capacity-building and furthering organizational progress. Reconstruction engages love by staying true to the forces from which it grows. It grows from a history of humankind struggling to make the world a better place to live and by resisting any forces that could oppress humankind. It grows from a history that recognizes that each human being and all life forms are all complete reflections of all elements from which life is created. This collective force is what many AEA and Reconstruction members consider to be love. A love that is an energy that fuels and fertilizes the practice of this work. Where no one is put out of the organization for their behavior, because regardless of their behavior, the members are still humans. And each human being is a reflection and creation of the Divine force. Thus, love is the essence of the feelings that create behaviors and move humanity toward a collective conscience and toward Divinity. AEA, like all Reconstruction programs, is driven by a community capacity-building curriculum goal to teach members how to counter alienation in all its forms by building caring connections with one another and with this collective conscience and Divinity source. Personally. Familially. Communally. The next chapter will explore how Reconstruction moves its members toward this Divinity, by structuring and facilitating its curriculum to bring together and engage in a dialogue of rage, resilience, discipline, and healing—with love as the cultural core.

Endnotes Toward Principled Transformation

Extending from the process of restorative healing in the culture of Reconstruction, three possibilities toward principled transformation emerge:

- Transformative Trainings—It would be helpful for affiliates of non-profit organizations to better understand how their work both enhances—and prevents—real social change; that is, how their decisions and actions can enrich or act against the shared mission. Similarly, it would be helpful for well-intentioned funders to understand better the (many) differences between charity and transformative change, in the interests of furthering the latter.

- Resolving Rage—The resolution of rage most often begins best when people are met where they are, are acknowledged for their brilliance, where members connect with one another in many different ways that are both more and less formal, and provide many structured, disciplined opportunities for both new and longtime members to take ownership of the organization.

- A New Justice—To nurture a new justice paradigm, the contributions of each member should be recognized and celebrated for being Sacred and valuable. By nurturing a culture within the organization of equity and trust, affiliates can understand better that a new justice—a true justice—is within them, within each of us. Right now.

Part I, Chapter Two

When Love Is the Cultural Core: A Curriculum on Race and Rage

...the Negro is a sort of seventh son, born with a veil, and gifted with second-sight in this American world...the end of his striving [is] to be a co-worker in the kingdom of culture...to husband and use his best powers and his latent genius.

—W. E. B. Du Bois

Reconstruction engages love by staying true to the forces from which it grows. It grows from a history of humankind struggling to make the world a better place to live, and by resisting any forces that could oppress human kind...love is the essence of the feelings that create behaviors that move humanity towards a collective conscience and toward Divinity....This love is an energy that fuels and fertilizes the practice of our work.

—William Goldsby, November 2010

At its core, Reconstruction Inc. is a capacity-building organization focused beyond reentry and reintegration with a membership of former felons, their family members, and interested others. It nurtures the assets of all who come into contact with it, as its founder William Goldsby states, "engage[ing] love by staying true to the forces from which it grows." Reconstruction grows from a history that recognizes each human being and all life forms as complete reflections of the collective force of all elements from which life itself is created. In the eyes of the founding leadership, this collective force is love—the organization's cultural core. Yes, some members may have robbed or assaulted others, may have used and/or sold drugs, and, in some cases, may have taken a life. Yet, within and beyond the AEA program, each member has chosen to come to an organization that prioritizes and gives meaning to principled transformation. In short, Reconstruction affiliates live a pedagogy of principled transformation. They come together to embrace their roots and be accountable for their past actions, to be "co-worker[s] in the kingdom of culture" in their life's explorations of trust, faith, vulnerability, and strength in the Divine. To proactively participate as cultural coworkers, they engage in a set of transformations guided by the curriculum analyzed in this chapter. These transformations occur in a learning organization "skilled at creating, acquiring, and transferring knowledge, and at modifying [individual, family, and organizational] behavior to reflect new knowledge and insights."[1]

By enacting its learning organization activities, and maximizing member, organization, and local area assets, Reconstruction builds community capacity, bringing together and nurturing the interaction of human capital, social capital,

and all other related resources "that can be leveraged to solve collective problems and improve or maintain the well-being of that community."[2] Because a
peer-based, former felon–founded and led "approach to mentoring ex-prisoners
is relatively new, there are as yet no 'best practices' that have been identified by
research."[3] Doing much more than individualized mentoring, Reconstruction
Inc. has effectively merged these organizational frameworks across its history.
From its origin to the present, it continues to innovate best practices for grassroots organizational participation in the reentry and reintegration process by
including, and moving well beyond a mentoring model. Perhaps above all, Reconstruction renews itself as a secular sanctuary—a loving and spiritual organization. It is one in which leaders and all members (as all members are leaders)
are guided by and vested in a vision and "sense of calling...that their life has
meaning and makes a difference [and they] have genuine care, concern, and appreciation for both self and others, thereby producing a sense of membership
and feeling of being understood and appreciated."[4] This grows from a curriculum that fuels the organization's work, striving for an egalitarian atmosphere in
all settings and believing strongly that excellence already exists in each person.
Whatever the nature, type, longevity, or severity of a former felon's past, the
curriculum exists to manifest that excellence within themselves and their families and in fellowship with interested others.

The success of learning community capacity-building and spiritual growth
often rests on the clarity of mission and quality of curricula as a plan of action
guiding the organization enacting them. One vital element of Reconstruction's
success is the organization's strong and flexible capacity-building curricula from
its origin to the present. These curricula are the designs and strategies of transformative action that guide the teaching and learning, or pedagogy, of the mission: *"Changing ourselves to change the world, uniting [with] the many to defeat the few."* By
exploring the original and most recent curricula, this chapter details the themes
and practices of Reconstruction's pedagogy of principled transformation. The
foundation these curricula have given the organization to further the spiritual
growth of its members extends from leadership and members creating—and
maintaining over time—an organizational culture of relational resilience; that is,
an exchange between individual and collective "strength forged through adver-
sity."[5] A spiritually grounded, egalitarian exchange of information enriches an
individual, familial, and organizational culture of resilience. Resilience within an
organization's culture nurtures success beyond survival. It fosters a return to
form and effectively function as the echoes of rage and prior trauma are explored and understood. Its impact can be channeled to fuel many constructive

ends. For Reconstruction, resilience occurs in reciprocity between pedagogy, principles, and transformation. This transformative resilience is a rhythm, a tempo of purpose and possibility. It is a process and program of action. Relational resilience is pedagogy, a means by which a critical awareness of one's life and current circumstances are facilitated. Relational resilience occurs as the curriculum is engaged. It includes a setting in which investments in—and commitments to—individual and social transformation are nurtured when doing the intimate, political work with former felons, their families, and interested others. And, from its origin to the present, it is in this intimate, political work that principled transformations take place, with the curriculum as the guide.

> Education either…facilitates the integration of [people] into the logic of the present system and brings about conformity to it, or it becomes the practice of freedom, the means by which men and women deal critically and creatively with reality and discover how to participate in the transformation of their world.[6]

First Steps

The genesis of the Reconstruction curriculum is in William's journaling from late 1982 and early 1983 before he entered the Peace Corps, and more than five years before he arrived in Philadelphia. While he was working with several employers in Seattle (e.g., the University of Washington School of Social Work, the Federation Production Group), he wrote, "…the plight of Black men is the same as the plight of Black women." On January 20, 1983 he wrote:

> How the Black Man can live longer when we are controlling our own lives: by utilizing a future plus goals.
>
> 1. Take responsibility
> 2. Recognize barriers (hypertension, food seasoning, smoking, drink ing, constructive use of time towards a healthier self)
> 3. Discover alternatives
>   a. Ask for help
>   b. Develop a willingness to receive help
>   c. Take risks
>   d. Affirm a healthier and successful future for ourselves
> 4. Cope with unemployment
>   a. Create support groups
>   b. Develop skills
>   c. Use time effectively
>   d. Get into a training program
>   e. Educate yourself
>   f. Plan for tomorrow

    g. Believe that the man has power

    h. Grow crops

    i. Treat looking for a job like work

5. Inter-racial relationships.

    a. Is that a threat to you individually?

    b. What does it do to the Black Man?

6. How to treat a woman: by loving and respecting ourselves.

Therefore, we can love and respect women. By developing a future for ourselves, we thereby are more able to accept a life partner to share a future together. By recognizing our fears and weaknesses we can better comfort and support each other as men and women. Where do we go from here? Do we continue, how and where, and what is our agenda?" (Personal Written Communication, n.d.)

In the development of any curriculum, the social context of the persons developing it is a vital point of origin in the specification of what themes are featured, why those chosen themes are featured, and how they will be explored. As William continued developing the formative steps for Reconstruction, many of the early advisors encouraged him to explore what was inside of him that led him to think that a particular concept or activity would work in fellowship with incarcerated men. This autobiographical reference point was beneficial since he was a former felon himself. The organization began from a one-page document written for Barbara Moffett and Bill Meek of AFSC. They suggested that William design the curriculum to help these men explore their spirituality. Spirituality can be understood as "finding the divine within [oneself, through] the expression of key values [in] a process of learning to love and trust again."[7] Thus, in the view of Ms. Moffett and Mr. Meek, any curriculum that was to successfully engage and nurture change among these men should build on a spiritual foundation. That guidance began the collective design of the original Reconstruction curriculum.

Journal Entry, May 1983—We will discuss our life goals, dreams, fears, hopes, successes, and beliefs. We will share growth, self-control, and we will synchronize the whole by looking at the stars in the universe, the earth and the nuclear family. (William Goldsby, Personal Communication)

As William began to develop the feasibility study exploring service delivery in Philadelphia that in any way provided services intended for African American men, he began to refine these global goals into a focused program. During this time, there was never a formal discussion about a curriculum or a syllabus. What was to become Reconstruction was always categorized as a "program." The idea for a formal curriculum was mentioned occasionally, yet there was no text offered outside of community resources that were available to fulfill the needs of the program. After securing the support of Dr. Molefi Asante and the prospective access to Temple University students with a graduate concentration in African American Studies, two meetings were planned on campus with them. Surprisingly, these meetings did not lead any students to express interest in this effort. But one student, Yumy Odom, saw William in the hallway and expressed his curiosity about the feasibility study. He was the only student to participate in any way as he agreed to assist William by editing the feasibility study and join the Advisory Board.

Consistent with the journal entries from years before, what remained was William's original goal: to establish an ongoing support collective for African American men struggling with seeking employment, having health issues, and securing resources to achieve other life goals. As the refinement of the goal became a specification of a target population, the idea became geared toward men who were incarcerated. William's inclusive process of taking every new idea to his advisors for their critique and input was imperative. This consensus-building approach had always been a part of his makeup. Its importance was further reinforced formally during his post-military college years in the Western Washington University College of Education "college without walls" construct. There, he learned how to research community-based social service organizations, facilitate personal growth groups, and listen with a critical ear. William thus combined the participatory pedagogy of the college without walls with the consensus emphasis. Both became intricate parts of the Reconstruction protocol. He gradually took the diverse advisors' different ideas and, through consensus, all agreed upon a curriculum.

Beginning With the End in Mind: Three Original Components

In April 1990, William shared the following in a memo to "Committee Members." The Board and the Internal Advisory Committee were introduced to each of the three parts of the curriculum first. This was done by engaging them in a workshop for each part. Then the curriculum was introduced to Graterford Prison administrators during an initial orientation with nearly 200 inmates. It was then more thoroughly introduced and covered during each part of the first year, within-prison curriculum, with each part lasting between three and four months. Though the topical focus and themes changed, for each curriculum component there was a thorough discussion held, where participants were given an opportunity to raise questions, complete necessary research, develop vi-

gnettes and other related role-plays, and present or facilitate their learning in
fellowship with other participants.

Education and Self-Reflection
Founded on the ideal of an "intentional community," the first component of
the original Reconstruction curriculum valued the acquisition and interaction of
information exchange (education), and introspection in fellowship with others
(self-reflection) as its two critical aspects. Thus began their pedagogy of principled transformation. An intentional community is:

> a group of people…sufficiently organized [and] acting with responsibility …in mutual
> love and respect…[and] in continuous active fellowship to work out effectively the to-
> tal way of life to which they are dedicated.[8]

Valuing its contradictions from the moment of its initial within-prison curricular engagement, Reconstruction turned the state imposition of incarceration
into an asset-affirming environment for shared resources, mutual love, and respect. The original orientation group of 200 inmates was pared down to an accessible intentional community of 24 persons. It was essential for participants to
research their family background for as much information as possible. "Education" was much more than the accumulation of external facts. It was also a
means to understand the historical legacies of their families and uncover any
family mental or other health issues that may have existed. Introspection was
engaged by placing themselves in the context of family; in other words, returning them to reference the first intentional community for most persons.

To enrich both the education and self-reflection aspects, each participant
maintained this family background information and all other reflections in a
journal they gradually added to during their within-prison year. These journals
were revisited as they prepared to leave the institution. In addition, within this
curriculum domain, focus was placed on life areas of arrested development and
emotional blockages that likely were at the core of their self- and other destructive behavior(s). Though clear in its design, the layers and interactions of this
dynamic were often quite complicated in their execution. It was quickly discovered that many of the men had never had connections with their families. Others had to stay away from their families because of parole stipulation—a built-in
alienation by legal mandate.

One serious example of this was when the release date for one participant,
Robert, was quickly approaching. Robert had done extraordinary work
throughout: in the group work, with homework, and with all assignments. As
the time for him to begin preparing to leave approached, several issues surfaced.

When members of Robert's Reconstruction release support team approached the Pennsylvania Adult Probation and Parole Board with his record and request for proposed release, they realized that Robert's family was blocking his parole. They found out that he was serving time for having killed his brother. The killing had happened during a Sunday dinner when Robert's brother had begun to share a family secret: that his mother had murdered one of their other siblings. Through his journal writing and after meeting with the Parole Board, Robert came to realize that he had killed his brother because of the rage that had festered inside him. Once it was determined Robert would not be released on the date that he had understood, he deliberately acted out, was written up, and placed in the Restricted Housing Unit (i.e., within prison punishment). While Robert's circumstances were unique, many, if not most, of the seeds of principled transformation rested in the detailed exploration of the past, present, and future elements of challenging moments of discovery. In addition to their journal writings, participants wrote, staged, directed, and performed skits and other role-plays. Assessments were shared, and the relationship of these moments to the "whole way of life" of their intentional community was returned to repeatedly. Some skits dealt with deeply held secrets within their individual and/or family histories. Some dealt with misunderstood feelings, and the decisions and actions of themselves and others associated with critical moments of that particular emotional misunderstanding. Some dealt with desired interactions that may or may not ever occur.

Through it all, each of the men was provided with many opportunities to explore how this or other related moments may have prevented their emotional or spiritual growth by imposing an emotional blockage. How these moments informed destructive behaviors the men exhibited in that moment or far later in life assisted them in going beyond that moment, initiating areas of new growth that may have been arrested. Relationships between criminal arrest and arrested development were frequently made directly and indirectly through the recognition of the participants and the information shared with them when various speakers came to the workshops. Strong relationships were also made between the three core themes of the original curriculum. Many of the issues uncovered during the Self-reflection component were closely tied to the Medical Care component, and affected the Employment Resource component, as well.

Robert, whose family blocked his release, explored why he really killed his brother and how painful that situation was for him. He had not previously dealt with that—even during counseling sessions in prison. This also showed how profound his alienation was from his family and how strongly his family wanted to keep it that way. This situation was one among many clearly demonstrating that Reconstruction's curriculum was holistic, yet incomplete. Though effective, all participants and their families would not be saved or necessarily even helped. This humility began to unfold with most of the men. With self-reflection they began understanding where and how they were arrested in their development. Assignments also demonstrated that many of the men needed assistance securing Supplemental Security Income (SSI) due to a disability and that, for some, seeking work would not be an option.

Medical Care Program

In his journal entry from January 1983, "How the Black Man can live longer when we are controlling our own lives," William identified the necessary act of recognizing barriers. And here, all of his example barriers addressed health and wellness: hypertension, food seasoning, smoking, drinking, and the constructive use of time toward a healthier life. Just as in the foundations and practices of Reconstruction that continue to shape the organization today, in this entry William also moved from problem awareness, to information sharing, to strategies of action for principled transformation. "Discovering alternatives: a. asking for help; b. developing a willingness to receive help; c. taking risks; and, d. affirming a healthier and successful future for ourselves." Six years later, this focus informed the second wellness component of the original curriculum. This component also extends from the interdependence of multiple trinities that inform William and the founding leadership of Reconstruction, one of which is mentioned here: I-We-Thee. I-We-Thee is the recognition that one's soul or Spirit—the I in me is spiritually interdependent. It is connected to the next person and, in fact, to all persons, thus forming the We. This nurtures a need to constructively interact, sustain relationships, and share resources in order to nurture individual and shared growth beyond survival. This fellowship exists in an environment well beyond the individuals themselves. A larger entity, or "God," is Thee. I-We-Thee is in a Sacred reciprocity with Body-Mind-Soul: three entities of an individual: the physical, the mental, and the spiritual. This trinity is increasingly recognized as central to a holistic approach to wellness.[9] In 1990, the Reconstruction leadership defined it as a vital second component of the original curriculum.

This decision also extended from work William had done years earlier. In the late 1970s he worked with Dr. Lois Price Spratlen, a member of the Nursing School faculty at the University of Washington. Dr. Price Spratlen was researching adolescent hypertension and the relationships between genetic predisposition, behavioral choices, and environmental elements informing hypertensive outcomes. William was a research assistant on this project. Given the racially informed disparities associated with it and its other related health challenges, that experience gave rise to the need to focus on hypertension as a critical wellness dimension in the first curriculum and in Reconstruction as an organization.

Like the Education and Self-Reflection component that preceded it, this second health component was introduced in the same way. Inquiry into the participants' family dynamics of health was then followed by self-reflections on the meanings and impact of that which was discovered. Its relationships to arrested development and self- and other destructive decisions, actions and outcomes soon followed. What differed? With this health dimension, Graterford Prison was more directly engaged institutionally. Participants were encouraged to seek and complete medical assessments with physicals, dental, and eye appointments. They were informed about the role and pledge of assistance the University of Pennsylvania Hypertension Clinic provided. Findings extending from these health service assessments then informed the skits, role-plays, and other related strategies of engagement to enrich the health practices of participants.

Employment and Resource Bank

In that same journal entry of January 1983, William specified what would become the third component of the original Reconstruction curriculum, specifying strategies of action to better navigate job loss and related economic hardships. "How to cope with unemployment: a. create support groups; b. develop skills; c. use time effectively; d. get into a training program; e. educate yourself; f. plan for tomorrow…and, treat looking for a job like work itself." Strategies of presentation and participatory engagement used were similar to those in the prior two components. And again, the process of family history related to job regularity, job loss, and economic well-being were an essential part of engaging with this final portion of the curriculum.

The value-added within it was in another of William's 1983 journal entries: "Employment Resources = Participants will bring job listings with them to every weekly meeting, work on resumes, writing skills, and job developing techniques." This is what was done over the course of these final months of the in-prison curriculum. Moving with and beyond the first two components and the often-subtle transformations associated with them, each team of support persons met with each participant. These meetings included everything from simply assisting them in documenting their work history, developing a resume, mock interviews for their post-release job search, and making participants aware of viable job contacts; in other words, others they knew and associated with. Each two-person support team had been orientated about Reconstruction and introduced to the curriculum to help make sure the participant they were working with did not forget or get overwhelmed by the newness of this final part of their reentry process. Information from the Self-reflection component improved their understanding of how and why the participant behaved as he did and had the health issues he had.

The support team met with the participant during their last three months of the in-prison phase in order to set up employment and health clinic appointments. To proactively address their substance use recovery, many participants were directed to treatment facilities rather than employment. And for others, the process uncovered more serious mental, physical, or other health issues that would likely prevent gainful employment. It was sometimes decided not to share these concerns with the larger group. Instead, these concerns were sometimes shared by breaking into small groups. Or, depending on the issue, they were shared with the support system by Graterford Prison counselors. This again demonstrates the interdependence between curriculum components and patterns of resource collaboration that were central to early success.

The process and strategies outlined in the curriculum were evaluative. As information was gathered, decisions were made to move forward and regarding the direction that movement would take. For example, Elton, the first participant released into the residential facility after completing his in-prison phase, had completed a little more than two years of college. He was also a barber and wanted to work in a barbershop. Elton also had a serious addiction to crack cocaine. He lived in New Jersey before he was arrested, and his daughters were currently living in New Jersey. These challenges, combined with his parole stipulations, influenced his likelihood for getting immediate employment, and where and whether he should seek employment at all. As a result of this type of case history contingency, for Elton and other participants, the assessment and transformation process strategies had to be flexibly engaged. The original curriculum provided the procedural and conceptual foundation for Reconstruction's pedagogy of principled transformation. While various curricular changes have occurred across the years, they have been guided by the original component trinity presented above. The second curriculum explored in this chapter is the organization's current one. While the history of its development warrants a more detailed consideration (see chapter 7), we present it here as a curricular "bookend" to the original within-prison curriculum discussed above.

Capacity Under Construction

In their seminal book, *Building Community Capacity* (2001), Robert Chaskin and his colleagues provide a "relational framework" of community capacity and the process of community capacity-building. They chronicle a diverse set of community organizations from across the United States. The book describes and evaluates their six framework components to demonstrate how local area organizational collaborations contribute to the quality of life among local residents by developing leaders and relationships among those leaders to further program development and to improve the quality and accessibility of available resources and the delivery of human services. In the book's final paragraph they suggest "building community capacity can help communities provide what can be provided locally, by crafting mechanisms for responding to local problems and opportunities. And it can help consolidate locally based constituencies."[10] Reconstruction's original curriculum was directed at their initial constituency: a group of currently incarcerated men soon to be released from Pennsylvania's Graterford Prison. Its current curriculum responded to Chaskin and colleagues by addressing a local problem—the reintegration of former felons—extending from a global system of institutional injustice. In order to do so, Reconstruction expanded its original service model constituency. It now brings together former felons, their family members, and a critical mass of interested others who collectively nurture a broader justice to dismantle the prison industrial complex. Since the Alumni Ex-Offenders Association (AEA), for the most part, gives leadership to the rest of the organization, their Internal Development Committee took the responsibility for developing the current Reconstruction Community Capacity-Building Curriculum (see appendix).

Collective Appeal and Trinitarian Foundation

Beyond its theme-specific content, perhaps the most critical aspect of the current curriculum is its brevity and focus. This one-page document is the outcome of many months of idea sharing and consensus building on the part of the Internal Development Committee of Reconstruction's AEA program. It is the product of many years of weekly political education that began with William's early participation in the Village of Kumbaya, under the leadership of Shafik Asante, and the New African Voices Alliance that was the political arm of the Village. After Mr. Asante passed, Butch Cottman was asked to mentor a group of Village participants who sought to maintain the momentum of cultural pedagogy and critical consciousness. That is why the current curriculum greets the reader with an inclusive invitation. All persons are either "in or outside of institutions." The collective appeal to institutional awareness, and placing any person within a proactive trinity of self, family, and community, is an essential introduction to the organization. This is then followed with a statement of belief in the sacred nature of each human being and a spiritually informed equity—recognition of already possessing an inherent value or set of assets that fellowship with the organization seeks to nurture and maximize. This is the *"Assets First"* focus of Reconstruction's spiritual pedagogy. Related necessities that begin with critical thinking and end with changing the world invite the reader to place themselves within a broader set of interdependent collectives. This is consistent with the Du Boisian view of seeing oneself as, "a co-worker in the kingdom of culture, to escape both death and isolation, to husband and use [one's] best powers and latent genius."[11] It is consistent with the historical recognition of interdependent civic engagement domains: self, family, community, nation, race, world. It is consistent with, and extends from, the organization's mission: *"Changing ourselves to change the world, uniting [with] the many to defeat the few."* The three pillars of the curriculum provide an overview and guide of how these transformations unfold as one collectively proceeds through the strategies of action associated with each pillar.

Three Pillars of Contemporary Capacity-Building

Pillar I: Leadership Development
Nurturing the organization's mission begins with leadership. In Reconstruction, leadership and its development is not a linear process of accumulation, status, and socialized dominion over others. Leadership development is recognized to be a dialogue of transformation, a set of reciprocities. Leadership development is the dialogue between giving and receiving that reciprocity demands. Between the objective and the subjective, rage and emotional intelligence. Between healthy and less healthy decisions and actions, the personal and the political. Between two persons sharing information, with both being in the equitable role relationship of servant-leader. Leadership development is a dialogue of dialects toward growth and new possibilities. As Fry and Cohen (2009) state, "Leaders play a major role in creating and sustaining an organization's culture…[as] the source of beliefs and values …organization members use to deal with problems relating to external adaptation and internal integration."[12] In Reconstruction's curriculum to enrich the organization's culture and foster growth, leadership is learning to engage critical consciousness. It begins with the critique of one's self by recognizing behaviors that foster stagnation or, worse yet, regression (i.e.,

that are self- and/or other destructive), then using these recognitions and behaviors as necessary fuel for transformation.

These four dialectics (from alienation to building community, etc.; see appendix 1) were designed by Butch Cottman to foster an exploration of self central to the New African Voices Alliance's commitment to the necessary intimacies of political education. The starting point of alienation immediately challenges the "culture of separation[13]," that is, the aloneness, commodification, and one-dimensional self-understanding that too often occur in contemporary post-industrial life and is often magnified among the marginalized. This introspection, and then relating this intimate process to economic, political, and other institutional realms outside of oneself, enriches a critical consciousness central to vision, clarity of Calling, and the nurturing of belief in a possible future. Without critical consciousness, learning as the practice of freedom, "the means by which men and women deal critically and creatively with reality and discover how to participate in the transformation of their world,[14]" cannot take place. Critical consciousness is "learning to perceive social, political, and economic contradictions, and to take action against the oppressive elements of reality" to further one's own growth, exchange with the growth of others, and, by doing so, contribute to the realization of social justice outcomes.[15] It is an essential process if leadership is to develop, as critical consciousness is both highly individual and profoundly communal since it is best practiced in fellowship with others. Leadership development and critical consciousness are two essential resources in the curricula for Reconstruction's capacity-building and spiritual pedagogy.

A Brief Example of Leadership Development

When Reconstruction's youth program, Leadership, Education Advocacy and Development (LEAD) was facilitating groups at a youth opportunity center, one of LEAD's participants, Shandra, was 16 years old. Her 7-year-old brother had been born with a hole in his heart. Shandra had been in and out of juvenile centers for violently acting out her rage, and she had never gotten along with her older sister. She had participated in LEAD for about four weeks when her brother passed away from his heart condition. This was a tragedy for all involved, with such a young person passing, and the additional pressures beyond the grief this brought onto her family. On the day of her brother's service the LEAD facilitators conducted the moment of silence with Shandra's brother and his family in their prayer.

All those in attendance were surprised when Shandra appeared in the group at that moment as they assumed she would attend her brother's service. In the midst of her moans, the tears shed by many, and Shandra's struggles to explain her emotions, she explained to them that, with the help of the groups, she had become sharply aware of her feelings. And she knew that if she had gone to the service, she and her sister likely would have fought at it, bringing still more stress and pain to the family. She also shared that the moment of silence and the spirit of the group helped her deal with her brother's passing more than she thought the service would have. This is leadership development on an intimate, personal level and is one example of Reconstruction's principle transformation. For Shandra, this moment sealed the reality that this was a necessary and vital component to LEAD's curriculum. She struggled very hard to stay involved. But the lack of resources and the lack of family support prevented Shandra from further involvement beyond her participation with the youth opportunity center.

Pillar II: Situation Management
Once the process of leadership development is underway, Reconstruction affiliates build onto this foundation by refining their critical consciousness and the transformative dialogue demanded by individual, familial, communal, and organizational progress. Pillar II continues nurturing the praxis of Reconstruction's mission in a dialogue between theory and action. To do so, they raise and answer the question, "How acute and potentially detrimental is a particular situation?" Answering this question and the many related questions it fosters, then defining one or more strategies of action to address current circumstances while exploring aspects of the situation from more than a single viewpoint, are among the many components of Situation Management. Perhaps the most critical resource for this process? Discernment; the steady, thoughtful assessment of the tasks, tensions and take aways related to a particular circumstance. Discernment comes from the combination of two Latin words, *dis* or "apart," and *cernere*, meaning "to sift." Discernment is the engagement of perception, understanding, and wisdom. It is "the act or process of exhibiting keen insight and good judgment...in action-directed thinking that relies on values-based...skills to increase the probability of the preferred outcome."[16]

A "crisis" may arise when shared meanings that previously served an individual, family, or community well significantly change. This "cultural collapse" or breakdown in shared meaning, investment, and appreciation of valued relationships has often been initiated by some triggering tension or event.[17,18] When these factors are mixed with short or long-term misunderstandings of some kind, a severe moment of discord is experienced as a crisis, "the aftermath of [which] includes the eventual collective adaptation and replacement of old practices and relationships."[19] And it likely takes some amount of work to arrive at that new, transformed moment and place.

Within Reconstruction, this second pillar can be more efficiently facilitated once the personal, familial, and communal connections in any situation are understood. And it is this collective assessment and situational understanding that enriches the intentional community foundation central to the Education and Self-Reflection theme of the original curriculum. More recently, in 2007 a group of young people in the Reconstruction network was meeting to refine a curriculum that would assist them in their community organizing with other young people around justice issues. They approached William and Hakim Ali and requested their help in addressing a set of issues both personal and political. As a part of this work, they insisted that William and Hakim help them explore conflict mediation and related problem solving. William and Hakim included a diverse set of situations that were directly applicable to young people's lives to exemplify these skills and their flexible application necessary to effectively mediate both short- or long-term challenges. Collectively, they changed the name of this theme from Conflict Mediation to Situation Management. What emerged from a rich set of diverse questions and dialogue was that:

1. There are many different types of situations: good ones, bad ones, and many types in between.
2. Crises within their families did not make them a dysfunctional family.
3. Tensions, be they political (e.g., cultural oppressions) or personal (e.g., sibling rivalry), does not mean that conflicts necessarily are constant; and,
4. In order for them to fully participate in this process to manage any type of situation, four basic skills were needed: emotional intelligence, active listening, looking at one's position objectively, and extracting available skills toward managing the situation at hand.

After repeated workshops guided by this pillar, William, Hakim, and the young members of the organization found it was easier to begin to develop these four skills within the Situation Management Pillar once a strong foundation had been laid from the first pillar. Founded on a quality understanding of Leadership Development, Situation Management then builds on it because participants can more clearly understand why they behave as they do. And it is this

understanding that lessens the scope of the situation being faced. As Jerry Hawthorne, the skilled therapist and organization leader of Continuing Opportunity
For Family Education Enrichment (COFFEE), has stated, "The more we know
about the problem, the smaller the problem becomes. We cease to judge others
and are not as hard on ourselves once we begin to know how we are conditioned by religious authority and the education system to behave as we often
do." This is not to ever excuse or to promote behaviors and decisions that are
not principled. However, with this kind of unfolding of historical and personal
conditions, it becomes more apparent that each person needs collective feedback and support in order to maintain this personal and collective growth in
challenge and struggle.

A Brief Example of Situation Management
The nephew of Joseph, a member of Reconstruction's AEA program, con-
fessed to a rape. Joseph asked Reconstruction to meet with his sister, his
nephew's mother. This process took a few meetings with Joseph to address
various concerns before members finally met with the family. Although Joseph
was the one who sought out the support, consistent with the organization prioritizing a person in the context of their family (and community), they insisted
on meeting with the family. To their surprise, this meeting was very impressive
because it was attended by more than ten family members: other siblings, aunts,
and uncles. All of the adults in the family were working- and middle-class people, and they were extremely interested and engaged in the process. Reconstruction's Situation Management approach is always to educate about the legal
process and to assist the family to separate what they think may have happened
in the alleged crime from the legal process. In this particular situation, their
primary goal was to help the family members understand the differences between the legal process and the moral aspects of the crime. Consistent with the
therapeutic element of intentional community, assessments were completed to
understand which family members would likely have the most difficulty listening to the harsh details of the crime and then hear from the nephew what actually happened.

Once the assessments had been completed, and the persons who needed to
remove themselves did not return to the subsequent meeting, the process of
managing this situation could proceed. Reconstruction's experience has proven
that without dealing with the legal and moral issues separately and without also
addressing readiness for being aware of and processing the details of the crime,
either or both of these often destroy the family, affecting every decision they

have to make. Most critically, these processes assist the family to better understand the victim's situation as well. Otherwise, as in the case of the rape Joseph's nephew committed, it becomes too easy for the family to blame the victim by saying she came on to him, or she asked for it, or in some other way removing responsibility for the actions of the nephew. And any kind of perception like this would be entirely inconsistent with Reconstruction's mission and simply must be challenged and productively, collectively changed.

Pillar III: Support System Development
Reconstruction Inc. is a membership learning organization; in other words, it has an equitable power structure, consensus building decision making, and a collective leadership of shared investment. It is guided by flexibly engaged protocols to reveal and enrich existing assets to build individual, family, and community capacity and thereby nurture a broader justice and dismantle the prison industrial complex. Because of its grassroots membership focus, it is imperative that members understand, internalize, and get others to unite with the curriculum. Its history and foundations, together with its current concepts and processes, shape the means by which its organizational mission is achieved in the everyday actions and interactions of its membership. Thus, Pillar III builds further on the two prior pillars and is a compilation of an intentional community model from the 12 to 16 months in-prison, four-year (total time) original curriculum.

Two types of meetings are held within each of Reconstruction's three programs: work plan progress meetings and member support progress meetings. The focus of Pillar III is the second of these two. Member support meetings are informed by the therapeutic expression of Reconstruction's intentional community model. According to De Leon, "Meaningful change cannot occur without individuals experiencing feelings, their own as well as the feelings of others ....Empathy and compassion are the emotional domains of social relatedness through which the individual gains deeper self-understanding and acceptance...[and] are essential mechanisms in the change process itself."[20] Because Reconstruction is a Philadelphia-based grassroots organization, with diverse, disparate members living all over the country, these caring dynamics are essential for the sustained engagement of principled transformation. Placing priority on sharing personal issues for collective support came from William's participation in the Village of Kumbaya. The structure of collectively managing a changing agenda to respond to emergencies came from the empathetic, procedural innovation of Alumni Ex-Offender Association meetings. And the strategic use of subgroups for more concentrated, collective interventions extend from their use of an adaptive agenda.

Subgroups are, in many ways, the clearest procedural demonstration in the organization of how the Black feminist sensibility is enacted; that is, "the expansion of the feminist principle that 'the personal is political'"[21](see chapter 4). Subgroups are proposed when a member, during their check-in, shares a serious life challenge, the details of which warrant a level of depth and duration perceived by consensus to be beyond the scope, current time availability, or topic of whatever meeting in which the member shared it. A smaller group of typically two to four members volunteers to gather in the near future with the member independent of any other organizational meetings, to secure a more complete understanding of the situation including assessing the level of potential harm that could come to that member. Immediate or longer-term precautions that may be warranted are discussed at that time, and a preliminary agenda for the subgroup is specified. Subgroup members then agree to report back to the larger program regarding their progress, strategies of action, or other decisions and the short- and potentially long-term outcomes resulting from them. Implicit in all of this is the need for patience, the expectation that each person take an informed position on any topic presented for discussion, and the understanding that being "liberal" with an observation about another member's negative behavior is the same as symbolically writing a blank check. This blank check might then be cashed in some literal way that bankrupts the organization of its available assets. The primary goal of the situation management pillar is to prevent harm upon oneself, one's family, and community. It is the learning organizational expression of the Hippocratic Oath. This is done by teaching members how to become more skilled and confident technicians in each of the four primary skill sets discussed above in Pillar II. However, this goal also heavily informs the Support System Development pillar. Moving beyond harm prevention is the means by which challenges become assets, which can then be maximized in fellowship with the assets of others to further the capacity-building process central to the organization's culture. And all of this extends from the original goal of the original curriculum to establish and sustain a spiritually informed, intentional community for individual, family, and community growth.

A Pedagogy of Principled Transformation

In May 1988, many more questions than answers were set in motion when Barbara Moffett, Bill Meek, and a (very) few interested others within the American Friends Service Committee (AFSC) were willing to respond to William's MOVE Memorial challenge and meet him halfway in addressing the rage of Black men. Soon after William affiliated with the Middle Atlantic Regional (MAR) office of the AFSC, the questions before the AFSC-MAR Executive Committee included:

1. What form and function would this Reconstruction initiative take within and possibly beyond the AFSC-MAR?
2. What process of engagement and information exchange would structure the form and function of the Reconstruction initiative?
3. What themes or components would be featured in the curriculum to effectively respond to the rage of Black men?
4. What outcomes would result in the lives of participants after having been a part of the Reconstruction initiative?

Informed by these and other questions, in fellowship with a few caring others, William developed the original three-component curriculum discussed above that has been reflected across its history, including the current curriculum.

Sustaining a Pedagogy of Principled Transformation

Reconstruction Inc. has established and maintained a pedagogy of the spirit. A pedagogy of critical consciousness. A critical pedagogy and emancipatory process of profound transformation.[22–28] A principled transformation. This chapter explored the meaning, methods, and mechanisms of these concepts and relationships by analyzing the past, present, and possible future of the curricula that have been its pedagogical foundations. These foundations, from the original themes to its current pillars, are the outline for the strategies of action that nurture principled transformation by building the capacity of its membership and all others who have ever come into contact with it. Individually, familially, and communally.

Richly reflected in the past and present curricula explored above, Reconstruction Inc. is a learning, community capacity-building organization that has developed and consistently practices a pedagogy of principled transformation. Within the organization, "personal transformation is seen as the key to social transformation" recognizing reciprocity between them.[29] Thus, it is essential that the reciprocity between these transformations be guided by a highly principled worldview and sense of self and others. At its core, Reconstruction is a safe space that extends from a strong, yet flexible curriculum. The collective engagement with the curriculum components informed by the four transformations central to the current capacity-building curriculum detailed above, nurtures a sense of community and a shared investment in the organization as an intentional community. Like the brief, libratory 19th-century era of Reconstruction, albeit on a far smaller and contemporary scale, Reconstruction Inc. offers a "homeplace," where former felons, their families, and interested others affirm their minds and hearts and, by doing so, heal many wounds. However fragile or tenuous, this homeplace has a radical, political dimension, where members nurture their spirits and restore themselves to a level of dignity often denied them on the outside in the public world.[30-37] Individuals arrive at this safe haven informed by a variety of motives and desires, and then, over time, contribute to and share in an environment of support and possibility in which their limitations and challenges fuel change, and their assets are enriched and made stronger. Reconstruction is a collective environment in which members are constantly changing themselves to change the world, living this as much more than just a slogan. In fact, living it as a way of life deeply embedded in and extending from the curricular foundations of the organization. In doing so, Reconstruction members do much more than "just" skill building for successful reentry and sustained desistance, though this remains central to the organization's work. Members use dialogue to engage in "conscientization," or "developing consciousness that is understood to have the power to transform [their own lives, as well as] reality [itself]."[38] From Freire, this means developing an understanding of reentry, reintegration, and desistance—whether or not those words are ever actually used—but also building an understanding of what needs to be changed within them and within the world, and how best to do so within and beyond organizational membership.[39-43] In brief, Reconstruction engages a critical pedagogy of, and for, principled transformation, grounded in three elements critical to how it engages its mission: spirituality (as a pedagogy), cultural priorities (as principles), and a relationally resilient therapeutic foundation (for transformation). In order to do so, the curricular foundations of the organization bring together and express these elements, symmetrically and simultaneously, nurturing community in the most intimate and political senses of the term. We discuss this process and praxis of community further in Part 2.

Endnotes Toward Principled Transformation

Extending from the culture of Reconstruction reflected in its curriculum, three possibilities toward principled transformation emerge:

- Transformative Trainings—Symbols of significance enrich the culture of an organization. Because organizations are given names with significant meanings, it would be helpful to train affiliates how to best internalize and manifest the names, their meanings, and the related organizational practices extending from both.

- Resolving Rage—The resolution of rage can be enriched by bringing to light and exploring the ways we are conditioned to alienate others, be arrested in our development, and establish and sustain codependent relationships. In turn, we can collectively act against the harms of individualism by developing curricula that move toward a global community, collective determination, and shared responsibility for our global future.

- A New Justice—To nurture a new justice paradigm, engaged citizens can help develop more inclusive curricula to expand the current trend of decriminalization of substances and groups of people, including those with mental illnesses and others. The funding of family reunification initiatives and assisting youth aging out of Department of Social and Health Services (DSHS) facilities are among the beneficial family-centered public policy initiatives of a new justice.

Part I, Chapter Three

A Fragile Justice: Reconstruction's Organizational Origins, 1988–1992

Hope for emancipation of the oppressed [is] in the oppressed themselves....In dialogical cultural action [when] the people who were hitherto objects now become subjects and in cooperation with each other they act to transform their social reality....According to [Paulo] Freire, *the first element of dialogical cultural action is cooperation.*

Samuel Zalanga

This increase in the movement from prison door to community doorstep comes at a time when traditional mechanisms for managing reentry have been significantly weakened.

Jeremy Travis

On a cool, rainy spring afternoon in 1983, 11 African American men stood on Broadway Avenue in front of Seattle Central Community College (SCCC). Their gathering had recently ended. There was some laughter among them, mixed with uncertainty and anticipation of a possible future. These were the "stragglers"; though their meeting had ended some time before, they did not want to leave one another. They had all responded to a call to action made by William Goldsby. The call invited "Black men, unemployed, ex-offenders, smokers and non-smokers" to the SCCC auditorium. William made the call, motivated to establish a safe space where Black men could share their personal struggles and collectively figure out where to secure resources to meet their needs. Those who came, stayed, and participated were a select group, as invitations had most successfully been spread by word-of-mouth among a few friendship circles. William's promotion of the meeting had also been presented much more broadly through an ad in *The Facts*, Seattle's longtime African American community newspaper.

These men shared a sense of hope that they might have just begun something valuable, in support of one another. Something of consequence, both for themselves and for others they knew. Rich with diversities, they were tall and short. Older and quite young. Gay and straight. College educated and not. Former felons and persons with no arrests or citations of any kind. Those who had been participating in "identity politics" and voicing a sense of social justice for many years and those who were just learning to value the voices and visions they did not know they had. These men were from a set of social class standings and connections to William that were as diverse as any other aspect present in their fragile, formative collective. Any move toward political engagement of, by, and for Black men at that time in that city was a profound accomplishment. The meeting was a success. Feelings were voiced. And a sense of shared spiritual and political possibility was established. But it initiated an uncertain pathway to an unclear destination and soon ended, crushed under the weight of unmet expectations. But for that rainy spring afternoon grounded in the greatest good of hope and the unknown, these many uncertainties were all the men needed, to know that they were right where they should be.

Five years later in early 1988, William moved to Philadelphia from Honduras. Having left Seattle to enter the Peace Corps, his multiple Central American assignments were now over. He was in search of a new challenge and a new set of risks for merging a penchant for social justice with his desire for collaboration and bringing together individuals who likely would otherwise not meet. Nurturing an abiding cultural anchor in a Divinity shared by all who came, William searched for an environment of support where he could further service a safe space for dialogue and social change. Then in May 1988, William needed three math credit hours to complete his Western Washington University bachelor's degree. The university's liberal transfer policy allowed him to complete them in almost any accredited college. While on break from his math class at the Community College of Philadelphia, he noticed a flyer announcing an upcoming event that seemed perfect. Risk. Human rights. Social change. The possibility for collaboration. Sponsored by and held in the event space of the American Friends Services Committee (AFSC), AFSC is a Quaker organization guided by the principles of the Religious Society of Friends. Having themselves escaped persecution, albeit for religious reasons, from the late 1600s on, the Society of Friends was the first recorded religious body to oppose chattel slavery in the United States. It also was the first such Caucasian collective to openly advocate for the abolishment of slavery and were central participants in the Underground Railroad. William attended AFSC's MOVE Memorial weekend-long event (see prologue).

The workshops and teach-ins sought to sustain necessary attention on the (second) major MOVE tragedy that had taken place in the city just three years before. William was then, and remains today, engaged by the questions. What kind of city and city leadership drops a military-grade bomb in a neighborhood within the urban core? How do the residents interact with and experience one another? What are the dialectical relationships between justice and injustice in such a place? While attending that MOVE Memorial, he began to get some answers.

I challenge the organizations here to revise...your program....Otherwise...the bomb will be dropped again. Because we are not allowed to express that anger. So, if there are any organizations here, I will volunteer time to help implement those programs...and *I'm willing to deal with those causes, and help people implement solutions on those issues* around Black men and how we are ostracized from this society.[1]

Soon after William shared his challenge at the MOVE Memorial, he gathered his things and his thoughts and prepared to leave. A few new persons met, acting on the opportunity to share time with like-minded others living possibilities of a different justice and to begin a new familiarity with AFSC. As he was about to leave, Mary Norris called out to William and shared a shoulder's touch to gain his attention. "I'm glad that you said what you said earlier today. Your words made an impression," William remembers Mary saying. "I'd like you to meet someone who shares your interest and values your words as I do." With her act of willingness, a fragile collaboration was sparked, and the multiyear process of Reconstruction's formative steps began.

Program Building Begins

In 1989, Reconstruction conducted a feasibility study, investigating local programs which provide services to the homeless and ex-offender populations in Philadelphia...it was determined that the area lacked culturally sensitive programming that is responsive to the varied and complex issues of ex-offenders, particularly African-American males.... Reconstruction was conceived by an ex-offender, and further refined by the Board of Directors and prison inmates from the State Correctional Institution at Graterford....Nearly one-third of the Board of Directors are ex-offenders, and many other members of both the Board and Advisory Council work directly with offender populations...this particular group is keenly aware of both the pitfalls and the needs of the constituents whom Reconstruction seeks to serve...the overarching aim of Reconstruction is the facilitation of a grounded re-entry into the community for repeat offenders.[2]

As the summer of 1988 began, William started volunteering at AFSC. After first meeting William (Bill) Meek, William was introduced to Barbara Moffett, and met with them both. Bill Meek, a longtime Friend, would sit and talk with William for many hours—probing and sharing with one another in a deep search into William's soul and his background. These explorations took place at the same time he was attending more and more MOVE events and Quaker meetings. All this was grounded in an uncertain pathway to an unclear destination. Despite the uncertainties—and because of them—William continued to trust where he was being directed.

At the time, Barbara Moffett was the executive director of AFSC's national Community Relations Initiative. Though she was not Quaker, she had worked for the AFSC for more than 30 years. She valued and knew well the Quaker way—their processes, their worldview, their motives for change—and their contradictions. And though she was not an advisor to William and his program building, she provided advice and many other resources to him. From the beginning William was interested in using rage as a resource for healthy transformation. He generated a one-page overview of his formative program idea. This was consistent with Barbara and Bill's request that he start off with an initial exploration of the spirituality of persons who were to participate in this program-under-construction. Once he completed it, this one-page document led Bill and Barbara to call and share William's document with Vernon Seybold who was then the director of the Middle Atlantic Region (MAR) office of the AFSC. After the four of them met about the many programmatic possibilities beyond the words on the page, Mr. Seybold introduced the concept paper to the Executive Committee of the MAR.

The summer of 1988 turned to fall then winter, and Barbara Moffett continued her support of William's efforts. She too was intrigued with the question of how to best frame the feasibility study's text and focus, as that would be critical to figuring out how to get more Quakers' support for Reconstruction. In her role and life, Barbara practiced an unyielding commitment to the idea that AFSC should be in the business of listening to the disenfranchised and the marginalized. She believed that members of those groups with an appreciation of the meaning and consequences of that marginalization should be primary contributors to the direction AFSC takes. In addition to these affiliations and consistent with Barbara's worldview and personal practice, William became affiliated with and a participant in the Executive Committee of the Middle Atlantic Region. In his first meeting after Barbara's nomination and his successful approval for membership, neither he nor this formative program were on the agenda. But as a result of Barbara's soft-spoken manner, appreciation of William's sense of mission, and principled leadership in AFSC meetings, she made it possible for him to speak and share the idea of Reconstruction. This moment was an essential point of progress, enriching the possibilities for a formative idea to begin moving from conception to formal program design.

William then devoted countless hours to developing this concept over the following year. This formative document became the outline for a much more extensive feasibility study of other organizations providing social services for Black men. The study was guided by the central questions of: How feasible was a program that could effectively work with the rage of Black men? What, if any, programs were currently available in the city that in some way addressed the emotional and spiritual well-being of African American men? What value-added could a more holistic program provide to do so better? This feasibility study was later accepted by the Mid-Atlantic Region office of AFSC. William met and talked with many persons throughout the city as part of the resource assessment of the feasibility study. Social service workers and social justice advocates. Teachers and artists. Politicians and faith leaders and many others in diverse roles, who each approached the questions of nurturing the possibilities of Black men differently, if at all. These persons moved from organization leaders, to key informants on city resources, to program advisors contributing to this formative program development.

While William's research proceeded, he was introduced to the Pennsylvania Prison Society (PPS). PPS had two foci: prison inmate services and prisoner advocacy. After meeting with Janet A. Leban, the PSS Executive Director at the time, William was introduced to a group of influential inmates serving their time at Holmesburg Prison. These inmates were creating a program on the inside to establish and sustain them in a post-release form in the community. They asked William to initiate a program. This post-release group was called People United Together (PUT). PUT had secured major funding support from both PPS and the Cookman United Methodist Church. The church had a building they offered to PUT for their residential program to begin. This was another set of rich yet fragile organizational relationships that helped to establish a formative foundation upon which William could build his AFSC program.

To suggest that these steps were a part of a constantly comfortable and clear process would be to misrepresent the many large and small challenges William encountered. It took at least six months simply to establish a meeting with Dr. Molefi Kete Asante. Dr. Asante founded and was then chair of the first PhD degree–granting department of African American Studies in the United States. Motivated by a desire to have as strong a leadership for his formative program as possible, William asked Dr. Asante to serve on this formative program's Advisory Council. Though Dr. Asante initially declined, he soon agreed to do so, furthering the momentum of this formative progress. During this time, William also met with Fallaka Fattah, Executive Director and co-founder (along with her husband, David Fattah) of the House of Umoja in West Philadelphia. Sister Fattah and the House had been recognized by former president Jimmy Carter, and the facility remains open today. Then, as now, House of Umoja (which means *unity* in Kiswahili) is the,

"...first inner-city Boystown" in the U.S. [where] up to 25 young men, mostly black, are in residence at any one time....Most are adjudicated offenders for any offenses except sex crimes....Umoja creates a sanctuary, a sheltered environment that...fosters a sense of togetherness and group unity by imparting the values inherent in African culture...[and] addresses the youth's well-being, including regular health checkups, clothing, food, and recreation.[3]

The House was originally established in an effort to reduce gang warfare, needless violence, and lost life. It resulted from a 1969 Temple University study that found that the primary motive for gang affiliation was the desire for belonging.[4] Though Sis. Fattah did not have any specific input for the in-prison curriculum William was developing; she freely offered suggestions for the post-prison, reentry residential component. These included painting the resident rooms with warm colors, having plants in the common areas, and a fish tank somewhere in the building. Sis. Fattah also emphasized the importance of family involvement as soon as possible so that program participants could rebuild a sense of their familial selves as they began to reestablish their post-prison lives in a space for them to flourish. She spoke with William about the importance of a holistic focus, including healthy food, good hygiene, and civic engagement as a necessary part of their return and resilience.

Consistent with Sister Fattah's recommendations, William spoke with health care professionals to enrich the wellness domains the program would address. This included a meeting with a psychologist, Dr. Thomas Gordon. Dr. Gordon was the first person to introduce William to the idea that the program's curriculum must address arrested development. In the eyes of Dr. Gordon, this far-too-common state was a central process in the lives of Black men and all persons who had experienced any form of institutionalization, including and especially incarceration. Dr. Gordon put William in touch with a specialist in unblocking areas where one may have had their development arrested in different stages of their growth.

Tensions of a Tempered Inclusion

RECONSTRUCTION does not intend to be easy or safe. The safe way would be to work with *non*-violent offenders, to *integrate* racially, to get it done *quickly* to process as *many* people as possible, and to concentrate on *physiological* causes instead of spiritual [ones]. In some ways, RECONSTRUCTION proposed the opposite of these expected approaches. Violent offenders will be allowed to be non-violent; a period of separation of races will allow them to integrate peacefully; and both physiological causes and spiritual causes will be examined and linked. The past year has uncovered a constituency waiting for a project like this to present itself.[5]

As the spring of 1989 arrived, William continued gaining more familiarity with Quakers as a faith community and their relationship with the American Friends Service Committee. Prior to the MOVE Memorial event, he had never intentionally had any direct contact with Quakers. Despite this, he experienced a sense of familiarity in their silent meetings. In these meetings, those attending were invited to speak if they were moved to do so. They spoke of seeing God in everyone, in a Western sense of *Namaste*, the Sanskrit term meaning, "I bow to your form," and "I see the God in you"; in other words, a shared presence of the Holy within us all. And they expressed a strong sense of patience and investment in a labor-intensive process of shared investment, making progress by building consensus. They repeatedly engaged in thoughtful self-criticism, as individuals and as members of meetings or other collective processes taking place.

All of these qualities were familiar to William from his days as a young person helping to raise his sister's five children as his own. It struck him as strange that Quakers and other AFSC affiliates interacted with one another and him, as if these practices were somehow uniquely "theirs." Meditation as an active part of quality listening in meetings was another part of a familiar newness characterizing much of his early AFSC volunteering time. As William's presence and investment grew, Barbara Moffett continued to be supportive of his program-building initiatives. She nominated him to the AFSC's Community Relations Division National Committee. Within weeks, William was nominated to also serve on the Third World Coalition Committee, both in the national office and in the Middle Atlantic Region office. As a result of Barbara's nominations, William began to attend and actively participate in these meetings.

On February 24, 1990, William wrote a memo of organizational progress to the MAR Executive Committee. In it, he described having brought together and consulted with supportive persons who guided his development of the organizational proposal. They included Professors Philip Harris, Peter Jones, and Kay Harris of Temple University's Department of Criminal Justice; Barbara Auerbach and George Sexton of Criminal Justice Associates, a nonprofit organization; and, Fred Braun, a wealthy entrepreneur who set up and maintained a private sector, for-profit business in a Kansas state penitentiary. During this same period of his increased presence and participation, a series of events demonstrated the challenges of race, justice, and a tempered inclusion of him as a new volunteer and program initiator at AFSC.

Near the time his nominations were being moved forward, the values and stated mission of AFSC were challenged, literally and symbolically, at their doorstep. One day, there was some commotion going on outside of their international headquarters in downtown Philadelphia. Jealous T. Street, a self-named homeless Black man, had set up a makeshift temporary dwelling in the small stone plaza just outside the front door of the AFSC building. Reminiscent of the "I am a MAN" placards used during the 1968 sanitation workers' strike in Memphis, Tennessee, Mr. Street wrote the words "I AM" on the cardboard box he knew as home, less than five feet from the AFSC Friends Center front door. This created a stir in the office. In its organizational mission statement, the AFSC defines itself as

> ...a practical expression of the faith of the Religious Society of Friends (Quakers). Committed to the principles of nonviolence and justice, it seeks in its work and witness to draw on the transforming power of love, human and divine....The AFSC draws into its work people of many faiths and backgrounds who share the values that bring to it a rich variety of experiences.[6]

As local echoes from Ronald Reagan's presidential policies of reduced public welfare intensified, larger and still larger holes in the safety net among the most marginalized emerged, leading the 1980s to close with substantial increases in the number and visibility of homeless persons.[7,8] What happened when, in 1989, into that "rich variety of experiences" of the AFSC came Mr. Street, an African American homeless man seeking shelter on its doorstep?

William remembers the newspaper articles read: "There was this huge black man living at the front door of AFSC." But he remembers on the contrary. He was little more than 5 feet tall and dark in complexion. "I was asked to join a small group in the national office to deal with this situation," William recalls. "This was my first formal invitation to deal with a conflict, [as] several meetings within AFSC tried to figure out what to do." During this time, at the national level, the Third World Coalition along with other AFSC staff were advocating for, and demanding affiliation with, a union. The AFSC position against its own workers unionizing was a blatant contradiction. This, because AFSC was supporting union organizing throughout the country. More specifically, AFSC stood with migrant workers organizing for fair labor laws, along with boycotting Coca-Cola, which was spearheaded by the Community Relations Division (CRD). All of these events occurred quite close together in his first year of AFSC affiliation and were powerfully eye opening for William. They gave him a greater understanding and appreciation for the mission, motive, and management challenges experienced by Quakers. Like First Nation people living on reservations and being exploited by gambling casinos. Like issues faced by Latinos and others on the borders, and the historical conflicts between Islamic and

Jewish nations. They broadened William's awareness and appreciation of the larger, globalized landscape in which his program development was taking place.

On one level, William felt he was welcome with open arms by many, if not most, within the organization. On another level, he was dealt with at a distance, manifested in many ways, both inter- and intraracially. This included many judgments and nonverbal demonstrations of disapproval by well-schooled African American AFSC employees directed at his college-educated yet deeply southern manner of speech and interaction with others. Welcomed with open arms and dealt with at a distance, creating a vocational and spiritual space of tempered inclusion, William struggled to bring these two things together. At AFSC, he was invited onto the CRD Committee in order to make it more diverse. Extending from this dynamic of tempered inclusivity, he remembers attending a few meetings and learning that Quakers call each other Friends with a capital F. They also made it clear that non-Quakers are friends with a lower case 'f.' This symbolic distinction had practical, interpersonal consequences. William did not like this difference and thought it reflected how he was accepted within the Society of Friends.

"The Most Dangerous Weapon Was the Food"

William continued nurturing his program, gradually generating more support as his first years of AFSC affiliation came to a close. His participation in their activities increased, and more Friends gradually learned to value the overlap between William's mission and their own. At the same time of William's programmatic efforts working toward its elimination, the process of mass incarceration was of course being magnified, both locally and beyond. On May 23, 1989, local events of mass incarceration had a meaningful impact on the program building of what was to become Reconstruction, as things were more tense than normal at Holmesburg Prison. Holmesburg, a maximum-security institution in Northeast Philadelphia, was then a nearly century-old facility. It had a troubled history of unrest and inmate exploitation dating back to the 1970s and before. The prison was then running at 56% *above* its court-mandated capacity. That day, severe overcrowding coupled with prison tensions and surpassed the tipping point.

A disturbance erupted during lunch. Lasting for nearly an hour, riot gear–equipped guards responded to the incident involving about one-fifth of the prison's inmate population, and an uneasy order was restored. Press M.

Grooms, the prison's warden, said that the incident "was almost like 'Animal House,'" a 1978 college fraternity movie in which a comical food fight occurs. "There was not much physical contact. The most dangerous weapon was the food."[9] Food was the closest resource to express opposition to these many problematic circumstances, and a work stoppage that same day preceded the disturbance. A group of inmates sat down and refused to prepare breakfast to bring to light other inhuman and unjust prison conditions. These included many broken toilets that had remained broken for some time, leaky ceilings, severe rat and roach infestations, and cutbacks in food and personal supplies. These systemic conditions likely had far more to do with the lunchtime act of resistance, beyond the overcrowding alone. When things changed little in the months that followed, tensions increased.

Just over five months later, in late October 1989, weapons far more dangerous than food were a part of a Holmesburg Prison rebellion that left more than 100 inmates and nearly 50 prison guards injured. When a large group of inmates from I-cell block were not fed dinner in an orderly fashion, this was the tipping point for unrest. Desks, chairs, metal bunks, mattresses, and homemade weapons, including clubs made of batteries taped end-to-end, all were parts of the October uprising. While all the reported rioting took place in (only) one of its ten cell blocks, in addition to the human injuries, a great deal of damage was done to the cell block itself. One month after the October uprising, 27 inmates filed a lawsuit contending that they had been beaten without cause. After the October incident was returned to an unprincipled peace, corrections officers created a *gauntlet*, that is, parallel lines of officers "swinging clubs, sticks, fists, feet and metal bars," as the inmates were forced to go through it. These parallel beatings slowly proceeded for longer than a football field. The inmates were exposed to this twice, given the gauntlet's pattern adjacent to their cells, its weapon-heavy construction, and the space through which they had to crawl to safety. According to their suit, after these beatings the men were confined to the prison gymnasium and "kept in inhumane, unsanitary conditions" for eight days.

In 1986 a Holmesburg inmate–initiated lawsuit had been filed without success. That suit alleged that the inmate had (also) been beaten without provocation by two guards while he was showering. Now three years later, with many inmates sharing in this legal truth claim, it was taken up by a Philadelphia law firm. And this time, the inmates won their suit. As a result, the state was ordered to contract an independent agent to create and facilitate a thorough investigation that would occur as a follow-up to any inmate allegation of assault by a guard. William Goldsby was asked, interviewed, and agreed to serve as the independent agent. He designed this exploration process and conducted the interviews for more than a year. During that year, he followed up on as many Holmesburg inmates as he could, who were at the time sentenced and were serving their time in state prisons. This led him to go to most of the state prisons throughout Pennsylvania and gave him a vast amount of knowledge and experience that later informed the development of Reconstruction.

Placing Oneself at the Center

Yes, Reconstruction is an Afrocentric organization because it is my belief that to be Afrocentric is to see ourselves. To see the African self. To see us as an African people. To see that as a centrality of [our] existence. It is the center by which that Sacredness begins. By which that origin, or that Source is. So, it's Afrocentric in that, on a spiritual level, that Sacredness is the glory. The Spirit of the Ancestors that guide us. And Afrocentric is those involved being able to come from that center and recognize all things that [are] *not* of that center…to strive to understand and make the connection between Afrocentric or Afrocentrality and other realities. It's an inclusive paradigm that embraces everything else, [without] alienating everything else. (William Goldsby, Personal Communication, August 2007)

From its organizational origins, Reconstruction extended from the belief that a lack of emotional intelligence hinders understanding, with rage being an explosion of that lack of understanding. Violent offenses are the historical manifestation of that hindered emotional intelligence. What had begun in Seattle as an effort to address the holistic well-being of "Black men, unemployed, ex-offenders, smokers and non-smokers" had been refined into a program bridging the divide between incarceration and successful reintegration. For these reasons, William, in collaboration with the group of advisors he was putting together, collectively decided that the primary focus during the first years of the organization would be to address the rage of Black men. To do so, men would be guided by a holistic curriculum and be for those with at least two violent offenses, such as simple or aggravated assault, armed robbery, and homicide. This was also motivated by the contributions of several parole officers familiar with recidivism rate variations. This "violent offenders only" decision increased the likelihood of success in the form of higher probability for reduced recidivism and successful desistance with and beyond their post-release reintegration.

But perhaps the most pivotal collective decision in its organizational infancy was the choice of Afrocentricity as a guiding foundation for this program-under-construction. Before any curriculum draft was designed and presented to

AFSC, or the first penal institution the organization would soon enter, the decision was made that the program that was to become Reconstruction should be guided by an Afrocentric paradigm. In his landmark book of the same name, *Afrocentricity*, Molefi Kete Asante (1980) defines this as

> ...an ideology for liberation [that] must find its existence in ourselves. It cannot be external to us, and it cannot be imposed by those other than ourselves. It must be derived from our particular historical and cultural experience...recognize[ing] all that has gone before us and all that is to come upon us...the Afrocentric perspective [is a] testament of NJIA, the ideology of victorious thought.[10]

Liberation. Victorious thought. Resisting the imposition of any ideology outside of the historical and cultural experiences of Black people. These were the critical elements that had long been discussed and presented in African and African American history and texts and were popularized by Prof. Asante's book, and his many related books that followed. The discussion of this and what it would mean for the program became the focal point of many, many meetings with various advisors, both formal and less formal, and with persons asked to join the Advisory Board. Yumi Odom guided a full day's exploration of the meanings and probable implications of the term for various domains of the formative program. Navigating a great deal of discomfort and lack of point-specific unity with all of what it was to mean, a consensus was reached among the leadership that it made sense for Reconstruction to be an Afrocentric reentry program.

This same dialogue was then held with representatives from the Hypertension Clinic at the University of Pennsylvania, the Pennsylvania state welfare office, the Pennsylvania Department of Corrections Adult Probation and Parole Board, and the Executive Committee of the Middle Atlantic Region of the American Friends Service Committee. Described by William as "a laborious and tedious conversation," after the MAR-AFSC deliberated, they left the final decision to William. At great risk to the fragile momentum of this new initiative, William remained steadfast in his position that this should be an Afrocentric program. Throughout, there was a lack of willingness to more thoroughly explore the (very few) tensions and rich worldview symmetries between Quaker consensus and sense of the shared divine and Afrocentricity.

In the end, Afrocentricity focuses on one's cultural center to nurture "victorious thought"; that is, a sense of self and the sacred that enriches the value one places in oneself and *all* others. Despite this, AFSC representatives present at the meeting made it very clear they could not recommend, affiliate with, nor in any way support a program that "discriminated on the basis of race." It was agreed that language be crafted allowing the program to proceed, maintaining its AFSC affiliation, and focusing on African American felons, while being open to all races, a position true to the Afrocentric paradigm. Once that language was agreed upon, several AFSC representatives supported the program. Yet despite these lengthy dialogues and collective decisions, a short time later the AFSC-MAR office faxed a communication—to Barbara Moffett, not to William or any other program volunteer—that explained that they could not support Reconstruction any further. This decision fueled three characteristics that continue to inform Reconstruction as an organization: financial uncertainty, a clarity of mission, and a very small, devoted critical mass of organizational leaders and committed supporters.

As noted previously, various tensions of presence and worldview informed the process of William's affiliation at the AFSC office. Perhaps no element demonstrates this sustained paradox of tempered inclusion better than the early effort to secure office space for this formative program. Some staff in the Middle Atlantic Region resented William's work in Philadelphia. This was because prior to his appeal, the MAR office already had ongoing prison work taking place in Baltimore, Maryland. Plus, this Baltimore initiative had not received the type of recognition and support some felt William was receiving. These internal tensions were intensified when access to office space came into question.

Continuing her sustained support, Barbara Moffett arranged for William to meet with three elderly Birthright Quaker couples (i.e., those born into the faith). In the meeting, William explained his program and its mission. Barbara and William then suggested that the support of the Birthright Quakers could include joining the Philadelphia Yearly Meeting Social Justice Committee, the committee that governed Quaker prison work. These Birthright Elders agreed to join the Social Justice Committee and support the Reconstruction initiative. Extending from their respect for Barbara's values and vocational practices, they suggested that Reconstruction be housed on the first floor of the Philadelphia Yearly Meeting space. Grounded in Birthright Quaker support, fundamentally important given their leadership role and power among Quakers,[11] a series of intense meetings was held at the Arch Street Friends Meeting House that neither Barbara nor William participated in. Many of the employees from AFSC and other Quaker organizations housed at their headquarters attended these meetings. They raised serious objections to Reconstruction being housed on the first floor of the Friends Center.

In their overt, recorded language, those who opposed a first floor Reconstruction presence spoke of concern for costs, rent, office supplies, and related administrative upkeep. But in the off-record, informal texts, (un)spoken concerns were quite different. Perhaps they were motivated by fear. Fear of difference. Fear of a program that addressed prison issues. Fear of a prison issue program that included former felons who were no longer behind bars. Fear of these felons having a violent past. Fear of a large number of these felons with a violent past being African American men. And a fear of these persons coming into and out of the Friends Center and having to be near them. All of those who voiced concerns were White women. And this series of meetings were taking place a very short time after George H. Bush had successfully further criminalized African American men, using the Willie Horton work release incident and tragic rape-murder case to full effect in his successful 1988 presidential campaign.

In spite of this opposition, it was finally decided that Reconstruction would be housed in the Friends Center. On the first floor. And this formative program that became Reconstruction remained there for more than two years and could have been there longer. Its move from the building was made by choice to the donated building that, from then to the present, houses the Reconstruction office. This decision of first-floor office access would have quite likely never been made without the organized support of Birthright Quakers before, during, and after the contentious meetings at the Arch Street Friends House. These same supporters later made it possible for Reconstruction to secure other Quaker funding.

Soon after the "withdrawal of support" fax was sent to her, Barbara Moffett and Bill Meek again demonstrated their unyielding support for the Reconstruction mission. They quickly secured an attorney who was paid to assist in the process of organizational incorporation. Their support merged their caring with their financial and other contributions. In November 1990, an interim Board of Directors was formed so that the incorporation process could begin. Five months later, the formal Domestic Nonprofit Articles were signed by Phyllis Jones-Carter, Frank Lang, and Ethel Napper-Johnson, and Reconstruction was incorporated on April 11, 1991. This first interim board was comprised of the three persons who signed the Articles of Incorporation and Anthony Jacobs. Not unlike many organizations at the very beginning of establishing their formal bureaucracy, the terms of these initial incorporators as an Executive Committee were extended indefinitely until a formal election of officers could take place. Less than two months after incorporation, five persons began their three-year terms as Reconstruction Board members: Jonathan Lewis, Patrick D. Murray, Lori Popa, Todd H. Tyson, and Tyrone Werts.

Considering the makeup of both the Executive Committee and the first organizational Board, these persons together reflected both genders and a rich mixture of education levels, racial sensibilities, class backgrounds and current class standings, sexual identities, worldviews, and other elements of individual and collective difference. True to the recommendations of Black feminist sensibilities, taken together they formed a

> ...fund of necessary polarities between which our creativity can spark like a dialectic. Only then does the necessity for interdependency become unthreatening...with different strengths, acknowledged and equal...to seek new ways of being in the world...[and to generate] true visions of our future, along with the concomitant power to effect those changes which can bring that future into being.[12]

This reflected, and was consistent with, the strong foundation William had built both inside and outside of the American Friends Service Committee in a very short period of time.

Getting to Graterford Prison

As the fall of 1991 began, Reconstruction Inc. experienced the growing pains of its recent incorporation in April, mixed with the primary tenets of its organizational history: financial uncertainty, a devoted critical mass of affiliates, and engaged strategies of action to further the organization's mission. The result was steady progress, albeit in an environment of limited funds and the difficulties of sustaining affiliates willing—on a purely voluntary basis—to search for, research, write, and submit grant proposals to funding outlets open to grassroots initiatives. During the October 1991 Board meeting a bank balance of $289.48 was reported. A proposal for $500 had recently been sent to Bread and Roses, while a proposal to a funding outlet for $5,000 was "to be sent" in the near future. William expressed the need for a long-term budget (i.e., four to five years), including consulting fees and the funding of special projects. During this same meeting, decisions to be tabled for future discussion included board meeting attendance, number of board members, organizational bylaws, and the tasks associated with the role of project coordinator. Toward the end of the meeting a seminar was to take place in just a few weeks (November 16) at the Graterford Prison.

Graterford is the state prison closest to the city of Philadelphia, 31 miles west of the city. Built in 1929, it is the state's largest maximum-security prison. In 1989, an $80 million construction program was completed that added a new administration building, a 28-bed infirmary, and 371 additional cells. Fewer than two years after the prison construction program had been completed, Reconstruction initiated a resource partnership with the penal institution. Understanding itself as a service organization providing access to a reentry program, William had begun writing the State Commissioner of Prisons shortly before incorporation had been finalized. When he received no responses after having written for nearly two months, William traveled to state capital Harrisburg, Pennsylvania, and entered the commissioner's office. Having been employed in administrative gatekeeper positions for much of his post-Army life, William appreciated process and protocol, and he knew the value of informal intimacies with first-line administrative staff members. After he shared his story with the receptionist, she introduced William to the commissioner's secretary, whom he met with for more than a half hour. Consistent with the secretary's suggestion, geographic access, and the suspicion and uncertainty of William's first contacts at local county facilities closer to, or in the city, made Graterford the best institution to begin the within-prison, reentry preparation phase of the program.

Pennsylvania's "largest and most violent" prison, Graterford was originally built to house Pennsylvania's most violent offenders. It has been called "The Farm, The Camp, The Fort, and Dodge City...is reminiscent of a dungeon; dark, dank, and dangerous...   [and] has never been called safe."[13] As one Graterford lifer states, "When I was in the county jail awaiting trial, I saw grown men cry because their counselors told them they were being transferred to Graterford."[14] William met with Donald Vaughn, the Graterford Superintendent. Mr. Vaughn let William know that he had already spoken with the Commissioner's secretary. After meeting with him, Mr. Vaughn invited Thomas Stahalic, Graterford's Deputy of Treatment, to join them during his second meeting at the prison. In this meeting William shared with them that his program was affiliated with both AFSC and PPS. These affiliations enhanced his credibility and administrative "buy-in" for this initiative.

Affirming Alliances by Placing One's Self and Others at the Center
Nurturing the prison's administrative investment was essential to the eventual success of the Graterford mission. Mr. Vaughn made clear to William that (1) his entire staff had to agree and accept him and Reconstruction; and (2) if Mr. Stahalic didn't accept the idea, William would not be going any further at Graterford. William quickly got the impression that neither of these men (and other DOC administrators) seemed particularly impressed, and Mr. Vaughn confirmed this with William. William suspected that this was a product of a dismissal of ego and self-protection; in other words, much of the reason was

that they perceived Reconstruction as doing something the prison should have already been doing. When William mentioned that he had served in the Army and had volunteered in the Peace Corps, Mr. Stahalic's reserved, soft-spoken demeanor became much lighter. He, too, had been in both. William was the first person Mr. Stahalic could recall meeting with that common history.

That symmetry led him to be much more affirming, going so far as to assign Bessie Williams, a member of his staff, to be the program liaison. The tone of Reconstruction's within-prison process had now been set. The program and process were inclusive and everyone's voice was important. To that end, it was the consensus among William and the leadership that they needed to create an Internal Advisory Committee (IAC), a leadership collective of respected, current inmates to establish an internal legitimacy and to reach out to others by framing Reconstruction's formative program in a proactive, inmate-centered light. Ms. Williams shared a few possible names with William for him to meet. One was Tyrone Werts, a lifer who had recently had his sentence commuted by Governor Rendell. William met with Mr. Werts, who was impressed with both the mission and the process of Reconstruction. He then called another meeting with other men there who all quickly agreed that the next need was to invite the president of the inmate organization to make recommendations to the IAC. Soon thereafter, an IAC of Graterford inmates had been formed, and the within-prison program had truly begun.

Endnotes Toward Principled Transformation

Extending from the cultural foundations of Reconstruction's first 5 years, three possibilities toward principled transformation emerge:

- Transformative Trainings—This involves training persons to develop critical listening skills, separating feelings from thinking regarding a given situation, and identifying and reciprocating with the expertise of each person regardless of their cultural caste.
- Resolving Rage—Justice-affirming risk taking, which challenges power and one's place of comfort, is an essential resource for resolving rage. Examples include William's call to action at the 1988 AFSC event (individual level); AFSC's willingness to be a "friend of the court" on behalf of MOVE (organization level); and prison decision making, be it prison uprisings against overcrowding, abuse, or other injustices, or prison administration and staff collectively not impeding or, better yet, supporting the efforts of a new, unknown, grassroots reentry organiza-

tion (institution level). As a cultural transformation, this risk taking can include examining what we are willing to sacrifice to redistribute economic and political power in the United States and the global community beyond our borders.

- A New Justice—To nurture a new justice paradigm invites people to celebrate themselves as agents of change and the equity-affirming meaning that can be given to that phrase. This might include exploring and challenging paradoxes associated with the worlds of wisdom, experience, and spiritual and other possibilities behind the rage of Black men and others. Understanding that there is something far deeper than violence alone in the ways they contribute to the "fund of necessary polarities" is essential for social change.

Part II
Community

Part II, Chapter Four

"There Is No Progress Without a Woman in It!" Women's Experiences in Reconstruction Inc.

> I find myself as a woman of insight ascending into my highest powers, my greatest psychic strengths and my fullest satisfactions....The women who sustained me through that [challenging] period were black and white, old and young, lesbian, bisexual, and heterosexual, and we all shared a war against the tyrannies of silence. They all gave me a strength without which I could not have survived intact...[now] I feel more deeply, value those feelings more, and can put [them] together with what I know to fashion a vision of and pathway toward true change.
>
> Audre Lorde, *Sister Outsider*, 1984; *The Cancer Journals*, 1980

> While engaging [with] others who have been involved with Reconstruction, I have developed a voice I never knew I had. And I took that voice and extended it to my family; some who were incarcerated. I didn't know how to do that in the past....Once I became a part of Reconstruction, it really shaped me, and developed me into a stronger woman. Definitely into an activist. And also, I'm not so quick to judge others. That's how Reconstruction has helped me.
>
> Jamilla Vorn, Reconstruction Member, Women's Focus Group, August 2009

Women have been and remain central to realizing the mission and vision of Reconstruction Inc. What happens when, building on the observation of W. E. B. Du Bois from more than a century ago, women are proactive "co-worker[s] in the kingdom of culture" in a capacity-building reentry organization?[1] The praxis and paradox of women's inclusion is defined and redefined in the reflections and lived experiences of women's diverse affiliations with Reconstruction Inc. across its history. Women have been called "the afterthought in [postprison] reentry planning."[2] But they have been integral to the success of Reconstruction Inc. across the years. They have served in the most long-standing leadership roles. They were the original initiators of the organization's first collaborative ties. They have been the primary drivers of the Fight for Lifers (FFL) program of the organization. They have been and continue to be the strongest family supports and the central guides in navigating the tensions of empathy, risk, and rage. From the moment of its 1988 Philadelphia point-of-origin, to its initial board leadership, to various women-centered initiatives across the years, to a current moment of rich contradictions and egalitarian engagement, women's footprints and fingerprints have refined and continue to nurture the mission of the organization. In this chapter, we analyze the ways of being and strategies of action of women within the organization, and investigate how those ways and strategies have shaped challenges within, and the achievement of, the organization's mission.

Reconstruction is an organization that nurtures social resilience, that is, "a community's capacity to respond to challenges."[3] Women's diverse affiliations have been, and continue to be, central to this process of resilience. Since its founding, Reconstruction's focus has been and remains engaging the organizational mission within one's everyday activities, consistent with the "personal is political" phrase framed and popularized in the Black feminist-Womanist paradigm. The phrase encompasses the ever-present relationships between global and institutional structures, and the structural forces associated with them, and the day-to-day realities in the lives of Black women. Theirs is a critical expression of the literal, lived reciprocity between these two macro and micro groups and processes. That is, Black women are in a unique space of intersection, living a Sacred exchange among and between Black and other women and men, and how those women-centered exchanges extend from and contribute directly (back) to those ever-present and ongoing relationships between global and institutional structures and the structural forces associated with them. This personal-is-political reality is a thread running throughout the experiences of women in Reconstruction Inc.

While the conception of Reconstruction Inc. dates back to the early 1980s, its organizational birth occurred when William attended the AFSC MOVE Memorial event and shared his call to action with those in attendance (see prologue). It became a collaborative possibility when Mary Norris responded to his call, shared her appreciation of his words with him before he left the event, and established a meeting between William and Ms. Barbara Moffett. This moved William's call from an individual statement of willingness to a formative programmatic idea of potential collective investment. That moment on that day in May 1988 marked the coming together of two individuals in an environment of support and dialogue about justice resting in, and nurtured by, the lessons of a shared tragedy from recent history to further social resilience. That moment was illustrative of women's willingness to partner with William and move from vision to action to social justice outcome. We are interested in tracing how women have nurtured, and been nurtured by, Reconstruction Inc. from that 1988 moment to today. In chapter 4 we answer this question by focusing on the theme of community.

Othermothers of Reconstruction Inc.

The capacity-building leadership of Reconstruction Inc. has been and continues to be nurtured by the contributions of many women. A comprehensive exploration of these organizational "Othermothers[4-6]" could be a book in itself. "Women's activism within Black families meshed smoothly with activism as community othermothers in the wider Black community as 'family'…[where women worked to create] female spheres of influence, authority, and power that produced a worldview markedly different from that advanced by the dominant group."[7] This chapter is an affirmation of gratitude and exploration of these many rich contributions.

To say that women have played a central and centering role both acknowledges yet understates their importance. A letter from William to an aunt in 1983 was a valuable catalyst for his search to further develop an organization to address the challenges of Black men. The decisions and actions of Mary Norris and Barbara Moffett noted above were central to the momentum of the organization's earliest years. Phyllis Jones-Carter was the first and longest-standing board president and was one of the three signers of the 1991 papers establishing Reconstruction's 501(c)3 nonprofit status (with two of these three signees being women). And in 1993, Ms. Emma Ward chose to sell a sturdily built, structurally sound brick six-unit apartment building in North Philadelphia to the organization for $1.00. It was this building that established Reconstruction's neighborhood home—the reentry space for former felons from the first Graterford prison cohort to establish their residential reentry roots for principled transformation. We consider a few of the Othermothers of Reconstruction Inc.

> Community Othermothers work [and express]…ethics of caring, personal accountability, transformative power and mutuality.[8] Such power is transformative in that Black women's relationships with…vulnerable community members is not intended to dominate or control. Rather its purpose is to bring people along…so that vulnerable members of the community will be able to attain the self-reliance and in[ter]dependence essential for resistance…even in the most troubled communities, remnants of the Othermother tradition endure.[9]

Reconstruction's othermothers embody and engage with the best of the organization's pedagogy of principled transformation. Their many forms of reciprocity (i.e., sacred exchange) of information, skill sets, vision, and other principled assets in a tempo of information exchange and purposeful growth have nurtured the best of what Reconstruction Inc. is and ever will be. These othermothers have embraced and, in many ways, defined the mission of Reconstruction. By doing so, they have transformed themselves individually and have made substantial contributions to the principled transformation of their and others' families, workplaces, neighborhoods, the organization, and the larger community.

Othermother Capacity-Building Domains

The presence and, far more critically, the participation of women in Reconstruction Inc. are reflected in every expression of its realized and unrealized capacity-building possibilities. As a result, all of the capacity-building domains and contributions of women within Reconstruction would be nearly impossible to list and explore. What follows is a beginning. This because without Mary Norris's decision to speak and express an interest in speaking with William Goldsby, after responding to his call to action, it is unclear when that idea and call would have manifested its organizational potential. This because, in the archival records of the organization across its first 15 years of monthly or bimonthly organizational board meeting and other meeting minutes, there is only one meeting on record that did not have at least one woman present. In most of those meetings six to ten members were present, and there were typically two or more women engaging organizational leadership and moving all in attendance well beyond a gendered tokenism and further in the development of organizational initiatives and other assets among women and men. In Reconstruction, to be present in a meeting IS to participate by definition, with all engaging in an equitable exchange of ideas and actions.

The process of women's participation in any capacity-building initiative is reflected in their engagement of vision through strategies of action beyond mere presence. The process of empowerment and movement toward emancipation within Reconstruction Inc.—as within any (other) learning organization— must have "a strong emphasis on feedback, creativity, teamwork and problem solving."[10] This process of empowerment is central to their affiliation and participation. Many data sources have informed this book (e.g., focus group data, paired parent-child interviews, organizational archive, in-depth interviews, participant observation of meetings from 1990 forward, and an ethnographic record extending from these and other related sources; see appendix). From these data, four domains most consistently emerged as the capacity-building praxis of Reconstruction's othermothers:

1. Voice and transformative action.

2. Critical awareness.
3. Balancing tensions as beneficial dialectics.
4. Calling and spiritual mission.

Each domain is explored.

Voice

Perhaps the most critical domain or capacity-building resource among women affiliates of Reconstruction Inc. is voice. In the simplest sense it is the willingness to risk and speak, the process of speaking truth to power and, by doing so, affirming the power in one's self in fellowship with the shared power of others.[11] Voice in the sense of bargaining and engaging in the consideration of valued options of visibility and self-affirmation.[12,13] Among women who have served in a wide range of roles and participated in numerous activities in the organization, the praxis of voice is far more than simply the articulation of sound. In her seminal essay, *The Transformation of Silence into Language and Action*, Audre Lorde (1984)[14] raised essential questions related to women's lives that are relevant to their organizational participation, "What are the words you do not yet have? What do you need to say? What are the tyrannies you swallow day by day and attempt to make your own, until you will sicken and die of them, still in silence?"[15] Women in Reconstruction nurtured this transformation, perhaps reflected most clearly in the comment of Jamilla Vorn above: "While engaging with Reconstruction, I have developed a voice I never knew I had. And I took that voice and extended it to my family; some who were incarcerated...[which] shaped me, and developed me into a stronger woman."

In addition, on many occasions women in the organization identified what, in their view, were contradictions warranting opposition. As one example, in 1997 the residential reentry phase of the original curriculum and program had begun for the initial Graterford cohort of former felons (see chapter 5). Controversy arose on the Board of Directors surrounding the overnight presence of loved ones, especially children. The challenge of a potential contradiction—a family-centered organization restricting access to the family of current members—was voiced in empathetic advocacy. Lucinda Hudson spoke at a board meeting on behalf of residential clients not represented on the board. Informed by the dangers of legal liability and a set of related concerns, meeting minutes reflect that William Goldsby "had no problem with telling the daughters that they cannot spend the night." In a principled challenge to William's position, Ms. Hudson felt "that we are essentially breaking up [a] relationship between father and child which is so badly needed, especially in the Black community."

A motion to not let anyone connected to residents of the Reconstruction reentry program spend the night passed unanimously, though all those in attendance did not share in that position. Lucinda abstained from voting and challenged the unanimity of the vote. She prioritized Reconstruction residential space as a "homespace"[16,17] supporting a means of family reconciliation as central to the reentry and reintegration process in "the nature of the intimacy achieved by the occupant...[within] the boundaries of communal space."[18] Hers was a voice of organizational procedure, empathetic advocacy, and strategic opposition.

A third aspect of the capacity-building resource of voice among women in Reconstruction is valuing what one hears taking place behind prison walls. This is reflected in the dialogue on both sides of the wall and the centrality of women as a mission bridge, nurturing that dialogue.[19–22] Inside the institutions, they share hope and possibility as prison personnel furthering principled prison practices. And outside the institutions where specific internal concerns among current inmates are given a broader audience, and where the dynamics of transformative actions beyond advocacy are furthered, virtually every affiliate regardless of gender nurtures this part of the resource of voice. As longtime member Prof. Kay Harris notes:

> Two years ago we had a meeting set up to bring in Reconstruction board members to meet with PSI [Public Safety Initiative, an inmate-led, community well-being effort] to talk about the reentry initiative and how we could connect the outside-inside pieces. And we finally got a date. And we had it all scheduled. The staff liaison who handles [a different inmate program], is not the same one who handles PSI. So [when] he heard about it at the last minute because it had gone up through PSI to get approval, he said, "I don't know anything about that. This is denied!" [After many months of organizing] we had a daylong meeting cancelled...and then the prison decided none of these people could come in because they have criminal records, which we told them all along. (Personal Communication, n.d.)

Without the willingness to enrich this dialogue on both sides of the wall— despite the setback of event organizing denial in the chain of command of prison staff approval—information exchange continued. Within Reconstruction, the praxis of voice in women's leadership demands it. "The message is to continue the connectedness of self with others, to persist through the responsibilities of hard times, because understanding and change will come."[23]

Critical Awareness

Another aspect of the social resilience of women-centered affiliation with Reconstruction is how women have nurtured a consistent refining of other's understanding of the world in terms of depth, power, and praxis. *Depth* is defined as one's level of familiarity and willingness to expose and explore one's self and other dynamics of interaction and information exchange. Power is appreciation for and engagement in different roles, relationships, and patterns of influence extending from both. And praxis in terms of an appreciation of the exchanges between concepts, conceptual relationships and actions extending from, and back to both. This underlying reciprocity is one among Reconstruction's most fundamental attributes. And depth, power, and praxis are among some of the rich characteristics of the organization's conscientization—in other words, the critical awareness or critical consciousness of social and political contradiction in both intimate and more public contexts.[24,25] This has informed much, if not all, of Reconstruction's organizational mission, and it has emerged repeatedly in more and less overt forms within observed interactions and in-depth interviews of women affiliates. Sometimes this critical awareness among the organization's women is of a more global and philosophical nature, demonstrated in one affiliate's reflections on freedom. Imara is the youngest of her siblings. She is a member of multiple women-centered groups, is a fierce agent of change, and a principled business woman. Here, Imara reflects on her earlier organizational development effort to establish and sustain a women-centered initiative. For example, when asked about what she was most proud of when considering what affiliates gained from Reconstruction's short-lived Women's Warriors fellowship, she responded:

> We all began to understand what freedom really is. [Too often] we think that freedom means being able to do whatever we want when we want. But sometimes freedom is freedom of expression. Freedom to be creative, and not being afraid of what somebody might think because we drew a picture…or wrote a poem that is not mainstream. Or, we took an action that's not mainstream. But it just seems right. So I would say the thing I'm most proud of is that we started to gain that feeling of understanding freedom. (Personal Communication, n.d.)

Redefining freedom by acting on the willingness to risk, challenge mainstream participation, and value that other women and men in the organization are there to support and refine these new understandings as a part of women's affiliation is one element of how women engage critical awareness in Reconstruction. And this process of risk-taking often extended from innovative participation. Laralynne is a teacher, married with two daughters, and resists sexism daily as she struggles with her class and race privileges at the same time. In the following, Laralynne was introduced to the Fight for Lifers program of the organization by another longtime (woman) volunteer and now values her membership in a learning organization of political engagements.

Getting involved in different prison related initiatives were really important for my political development. Reconstruction has definitely filled that void. I think I benefit most
because of the community that it provides. And a politicized community especially.
There's a sense of community in my neighborhood. But we can't talk about the critical
problems of the world with that community. I can try to. But it doesn't go as far as
talking about those things with the Reconstruction community. (Personal Communication, n.d.)

Laralynne compares her access to critical engagements within the Reconstruction community with her residential neighborhood to illustrate differences
she experiences as an asset to organizational membership. The boundaries of
awareness within her neighborhood are in many respects more consequential
than whatever geography markers she experiences within it. And through Reconstruction, that void is filled given the many links between the critical problems of the world and the organization's prison-related initiatives.

Sometimes the critical awareness of Reconstruction's women affiliates is far
less global, far more intimate, and far more rooted in the processes and protocols of the organization. This includes something similar to Buddhist mindful-
ness or caring attention to the process of listening and engaging in a particular
meeting or organizational event. Tamika is a mother whose husband was recently released from a long-term stay in prison. At the time of our interview,
she had recently lost her job and wanted information about starting an organization that would assist her husband. Tamika illustrated this caring attention:

[I] listened and I paid a lot of attention to different people's reactions to what other
people said [in the organization meeting]. And once I found out that it was supposed to
be a support group meeting, where we're supposed to extend our support to one another, I guess I started looking for, I started observing in which ways different people
were willing to support each other instead of just listening to what they were saying....The different people's backgrounds and levels of education—sometimes you
view other people's [stuff] in a different way and it makes you respond to it differently.
And that blocks some kind of support that you can give. (Personal Communication,
n.d.)

Here, Tamika engaged critical awareness by moving from focused listening,
to gaining knowledge of a meeting's purpose, to specification of distinct forms
of expressed support within the meeting, to background characteristics that
inform the willingness, style, and substance of that support, to her assessment
of how education and other background characteristics matter, to how those
ways of mattering inform her response(s), to a recognition of the supports that
she herself can and will give. She later focused on how these steps in her criti-
cal-awareness process informed a similar process in others attending and not

attending that meeting and how all of these dynamics shaped both her varying investments in the organization. This most intimate critical awareness is both distinct from and consistent with Laralynne's comparison of Reconstruction and her residential neighborhood, and her appreciation of the rich, political engagements of a learning organization, and Imara's effort to establish and sustain the Women's Warriors initiative. All are women-centered, "glocal" examples of critical awareness, or, conscientization, in other words, extending from and enriching a resource reciprocity between the global and more local expressions of the Reconstruction mission.

Balancing Tensions

Community capacity-building in virtually any form is consuming and competitive. It is consuming in that time, energy, and effort are demanded for the generation of beneficial outcomes that are, by definition, both multilayered and multidimensional. It is competitive in that any organization that operates with the thinnest of fiscal security, yet still also possesses an extraordinarily strong "labor of love" sense of affiliation among a small critical mass of members, must engage affiliates in multiple and varied competitions of the spirit. These competitions of the spirit, or tensions, are another asset that emerged as central to the praxis of capacity-building among women of Reconstruction: the relationships among tensions, risks, and balance. "Persistence is a fundamental requirement of this journey from silence to language to action."[26] Like voice, analyzed above, tensions between risks and balance are also a critical part of women affiliates of Reconstruction hearing and heeding "the message ... to continue the connectedness of self with others, to persist through the responsibilities of hard times, because understanding and change will come."[27-33] Doris is a mother of three sons, a professional child care provider, and a person with a strong, abiding faith. She originally came to Reconstruction to support someone else and has now been a member for nearly twenty years. When Doris shared what informed her affiliation with Reconstruction she reflected on the relationship between family and faith.

> My ex-husband's brother was a juvenile delinquent. At the age of fifteen, him and a few of his friends robbed someone's home and the individual was there. He just happened to have an ax by his bed and my brother-in-law picked it up and with the hammer side began to beat this man because I guess it startled him. So it wasn't really premeditated. [He] wound up getting a life sentence behind it and the other two individuals did very little time. So that, along with—I would always go with the family to visit him. Then the church I'm affiliated with [had an initiative that] didn't start out as prison ministry. But that's what it ended up as, because the son of the mother of the church got in

trouble. He was given a life sentence and we began to visit him. And he gathered other lifers whose family had pretty much wrote them off, or didn't have visits. He would put our names on their lists so we could bring them out. And when I looked around and saw all these young men, I thought about my sons because they were in middle school and high school at the time. And I was like, how do I keep them out of here? And that's how I started. (Personal Communication, n.d.)

Doris lived a critical tension very early in her new marriage. In her early 20s at the time, robbery turned to murder in the life of her then-15-year-old brother-in-law. When the balance of nurturing familial bonds included visits to the prison to share family time with this young man, reciprocity among risk, faith, and family balance began. This was later moved to another expression of continued connectedness of self and others when the son of a faith leader also was sentenced to life in prison. Engaging a tension of faith, Doris simultaneously shared with and nurtured in others a faith with persons who had taken lives, assaulted others, robbed, and otherwise imposed a negative will into the lives of other individuals and families. Then, as now, Doris's Christian faith is the essential resource that became the critical fulcrum for the maintenance of her balance and modeling a possible balance to others. Change can come, including the faith-informed changes of a woman informed by love, continuing her connectedness of self with imprisoned men as they did hard time. All of these persons, on both sides of the prison's walls, bear the responsibilities of diverse expressions of "hard times," all in the pursuit of what would come to inform Reconstruction's mission of "*changing ourselves to change the world by uniting [with] the many to defeat the few.*"

Related to the "how" of the organization's mission, another aspect of balancing tensions is the many members who appreciation and enrich a consistency between expressed values and organizational strategies of action, and how that consistency then nurtures a balance among reentering former felons affiliated with Reconstruction. Kay, a prison abolitionist and supporter of the oppressed, is a pillar for academics and activists alike, and he has a powerful intensity that is a joy and a challenge to fellowship with. Kay made a direct comparison of how Reconstruction differs from other inconsistent organizations and why, as a result, she values Reconstruction's influence on her leadership:

Reconstruction has been influential in my leadership by both modeling certain ways of operating that reflect values that have all been so clearly thought through and a commitment made to operate in that way—and then to indeed operate in that way. So it models that and it inspires me because it helps me have faith that it's indeed possible to operate in this way. There are all these organizations that say they do reentry. First thing, none of them really deal with that values piece. I mean one of the things that for me has kept me interested in supporting Reconstruction over the years is the clarity of the values and the nature of those values. [Other organizations] don't necessarily do a good job of dealing with the day-to-day realities that [former felons and their families] live. It's not about housing. I mean housing and jobs and all of that are, of course, real issues. But it's also what happens when you get in a fight with your mother or your child? How do you handle that? With supportive, tangible values. [Reconstruction nurtures] an environment where you trust the people who are there. (Personal Communication, n.d.)

The tensions here are layered and multidimensional. There is the tension between what an organization may speak of doing that is inconsistent with how they actually function. Kay values that, in Reconstruction, this frequent tension is almost entirely absent because of the clarity of thought given, and commitment consistently made, to live them among individuals, families, and collaborators in and of the organization. She also calls attention to the specificity with which Reconstruction organizationally models these values so that the inclusion of new former felons into the organization is made through the everyday praxis of these values. Any possible tension of having to struggle with whatever difference may exist between one's present decisions and actions and Reconstruction affiliation is embraced as a living contradiction and a resource for new understanding of leadership. Also, within Reconstruction, there is no tension between the material resource focus of many reentry programs and the relationship-centered interactions with family and others. This, because for Reconstruction members, the centerpiece of affiliation rests in the values that enrich the relationships between them both, and priority is given to the nonmaterial because it guides and informs so much else in their individual and familial lives. According to Kay, a longtime member who has affiliated personally and professionally with many prison and reentry organizations, Reconstruction is unique in making the most of material and nonmaterial contradictions for values clarification, elaboration, and engagement.

Some women in Reconstruction came to the organization after realizing they were in a career they came to see as inconsistent with the values they possess. Jackie, social worker and mother of three, came to the organization after waking up from a 25-year marriage. After several years in law enforcement, Jackie realized:

I definitely don't want to be one of those who are on the end where I'm the oppressor. To me as a deputy sheriff you're the oppressor. So, I got out of that....I don't have any immediate family members that I know who's in jail. [But] I still have that empathy, because I had the experience. I was in jail for four years, because working [in the sheriff's office] it's just like being in jail to me. (Personal Communication, n.d.)

For Jackie, law enforcement had no place in principled transformation. Years before she began affiliating with Reconstruction, she resolved this tension by leaving that career path and entering social work and social service. "I understand my leadership role and its purpose, which is, to undergird the mission by utilizing my skills, abilities and resources that are accessible to me." However, in contrast to Jackie's experience and choice, the beneficial organizational dialectic associated with this law enforcement role among Othermothers is that two of the most vital women in Reconstruction's history worked in prisons for much of their careers. These women saw their work within the prison as beneficial forces for justice change. They were essential resources through their prison staff positions in Reconstruction entering multiple prisons, establishing and sustaining long-term, within-prison initiatives instrumental in the principled transformation and successful reentry of many. Rather than any stress of inconsistency, these women nurtured symmetry of shared intent and remained highly supportive of, and active in, the organization throughout their careers. The beauty of this dialectic, or any other capacity-building resource, is that just as these Othermothers, any two members can experience the same reality in very different ways, with both being beneficial to achieving the organization's mission.

Yet another tension balanced by women in Reconstruction is the paradox that the very principled transformations the organization nurtures within its members are the very changes that might lead that same member to move away from the organization. Nurturing a desire to explore and understand new self-definitions likely also nurtures a desire to value the fit of other changes. Addressing both the motive for sustained affiliation and the motive for new experiences of self occurs at the same time members engage a communal ethic that is often in opposition to socialized, societal desires. As one member stated:

We're conditioned in this society to look out for ourselves and not necessarily [look out for] other people. And so for me the struggle is just to make sure that I am connected to a community that's willing to do the hard political work that needs to be done for social change—and still explore the world. For me, I want to leave Philadelphia, not because I want to leave [Reconstruction] at all. But because I feel like I need to throw myself out into the unknown a little bit and see what I can come up with. (Laralynne, Personal Communication, n.d.)

I went to a place I've never been before and started working in prisons trying to help on the other side of the [U.S.]. Just trying to take what I learned from here to Colorado to see what I could do to help those over there in that Republican state. (Doris, Personal Communication, n.d.)

As reflected in these members' eyes and experience, and in that of several Othermothers, the Reconstruction mission should be shared with others in many ways. For them, one means of doing so is bringing it to other places by moving away from Philadelphia, the very place of its origin and critical mass. True to many dialectics within an organization, this tension of transformation and place is consistent with the "exploratory" process of Reconstruction's genesis. William Goldsby was living in Seattle, Washington, when his formative ideas first germinated in his journaling, family letters, and in collective expression with bringing the men together for the 1983 meeting at Seattle Central Community College. He then refined its possibilities through more journaling and multiple Peace Corps service periods in Central America, assessing the benefits and severe limitations of the Peace Corps model of development. While in service, he periodically returned to Seattle to work in both social service and the private sector. Then, motivated by the 1985 MOVE tragedy and its aftermath, he came to Philadelphia and what would come to be known as Reconstruction took root as an American Friends Service Committee program, nurtured with the guidance and caring counsel of Barbara Moffett. A journey of growth, exploration, changes of place, and refinement of mission—just as current members engage in their own tensions of mission, exploration, and place.

Finally, in addition to the intimate tensions of (blood or church) family members' criminal consequences, the tension between the articulation and consistent practice of egalitarian and transformative values within the organization, role tensions of law enforcement vocation, and the tensions of place and exploration, women in Reconstruction also navigate diverse interdependent tensions of civic engagement mission. These collaborations are lived within their ethic of caring so consistent with Othermother praxis of community involvement. How should one best sustain long-term affiliation with what might appear to some to be an organization with dissonant mission? One part of this answer is simply by living the symmetries between them. June's daughter is serving a life sentence without the possibility of parole. She has raised her two grandsons to young adulthood, one of whom recently began acting out his place of rage regarding life's circumstances. June sustains her commitments as a steadfast woman of quiet strength. For more than 20 years, June has comfortably lived a paired affiliation as a den mother in the Boy Scouts of America and an active member in the Fight for Lifers program.

I've worked with the Boy Scouts ever since my [now, 45-year-old] son was old enough to be into Scouts. Up until last year I was a regular volunteer with a group of Cub Scouts and Boy Scouts.... I was really involved with the Scouts from about 1970. After my son, both of my grandsons was into Cub Scouts and Boy Scouts. My youngest grandson stayed until he was an Eagle Scout. I'm still a member of the Boy Scouts. (Personal Communication, n.d.)

Over its many years of challenge and change, the Boy Scouts of America Mission Statement remains: "[T]o prepare young people to make ethical and moral choices over their lifetimes by instilling in them the values of the Scout Oath and Law—On my honor I will do my best to do my duty to God and my country and to obey the Scout Law; To help other people at all times; To keep myself physically strong, mentally awake, and morally straight."[34] June has won awards and been recognized for her community service in both organizations. Some may view this as a tense partnership, at best, between a grassroots community organization that addresses prisoner advocacy for persons serving life sentences, youth prevention, and the reentry of former felons built upon an ethic of family first. However, June does not live these affiliations as an unsettled tension of some moral uncertainty. Instead, she lives them as a comfortable symmetry. Like so many women of Reconstruction, June nurtures distinct fellowships by balancing the two as concordant missions to improve her personal, familial, and communal well being.

Calling

Exploring a calling is the final, most salient capacity-building theme emerging from available data on the experiences of women in Reconstruction Inc. Repeatedly, both explicitly but most often implicitly in their decisions and actions, women affiliates would speak to, or otherwise place value on "calling," in the sense of building, having, or refining a spiritual mission and the role of the organization in doing so. Here, we treat calling, mission, reflexive spirituality, and engaged servant leadership as synonyms for one another, each of which describes "that internal mechanism that guides human beings to make meaning for their lives, to establish purpose for themselves, to enter into [spiritually-centered, value-driven] connections or relationships with others, and serves as the facility for people to create through inspired imagination." [35–41] In exploring the components of her calling, Doris stated:

I do things out of love for people.... I reach out to people, I embrace them and just like with Avril who's battling cancer that has two sons in prison. I'm not overly concerned. But I'm concerned about her because she's living alone and stuff like that. So I kind of go out of my way and things like that to help other people.... Because in any organization like this, it's a lifetime effort and you have to work at it every day. (Personal Communication, n.d.)

The genesis of Doris's calling is love for people. Though she herself has not had any children in prison, this love as empathy nurtures a concern for others, here for another mother of two sons in prison who is not a part of the organization yet not a great deal different than herself. And, like most if not all callings, according to Doris, when this love manifests collectively one is called to engage it on a daily basis during one's lifetime.

In addition to the organizational actions of empathetic love, experiencing a developmental turning point also emerged as a component of calling among Reconstruction's women members. Be it recognition of class, race, sexual identity, or other difference(s), some form of openness to the "fund of necessary polarities" was nurtured when that equity sense was "tested."[42] In a memorable moment of oppositional intimacy, Laralynne states that she

> ...grew up free from poverty, violence, and any real conflict. But I [had] some early confrontations with race and racism in my [small, Midwestern hometown]. Like much of the Midwest it was very segregated. I became aware of that without really having any kind of language to understand it at a pretty early age. I also had a really racist uncle. And I was the one to confront him. Which was troubling because I didn't really know how to and I didn't have any sophisticated language to do it. At some point I was able to say, "I don't like what you're saying, I don't agree with what you're saying." And then my mom sort of followed after that. Once I was able to make my own choices and have some freedom, I was the proverbial "tracks crosser." I recognized that the Latino kids and the African American kids were living in the south side of town and I lived on the north side of town. And I felt like life was more interesting in some way on the other side of town. And so I developed a lot of [African American and Latino] friendships, which I think is pretty standard for a lot of white Americans. That's how a lot of us come to confront race is through friendships and dating. I have this vivid memory of driving down Main Street with my Mexican-American boyfriend at the time, [and] taking some heat for that relationship. Not so much at home. But just sort of generally. And I [thought] that I want a life that in some way opposes these ideas. That opposes these backward ideas about race and difference. (Personal Communication, n.d.)

Laralynne's layered quote illustrates a developmental equity and othering component of calling. Here, the beginning was a sense of wanting to oppose backward ideas about race and difference. In her formative exploration of race and class privilege, she engaged in an openness for the observation of resource differences that was not rooted in a "blaming the victim" tautology (i.e., because of their personal unworthiness, those unworthy people in that unworthy setting deserve to be in that unworthy setting with unworthy others). Like many

Reconstruction members, Laralynne's outcome is a long-standing life tempo that those "backward" ideas of her uncle were then, and remain, different from the values she holds as she nurtures a justice sensibility in her vocational and volunteer work.

As Audre Lorde (1984) observed, "Difference must not merely be tolerated, but seen as a fund of necessary polarities between which our creativity can spark like a dialectic. Only then does the necessity for interdependence become unthreatening."[43] The intimate repetition of the ideas out of the mind and mouth of a family member with whom she frequently interacted became less and less a socialization of what Laralynne was to value, and who she was to be. Instead, more and more, she recognized and embraced them as ideas and ideals she opposed. In her willingness to learn and explore the words to do so, then acting on the risk to challenge, she helped to create a space safe enough for additional progressive family voices to be expressed. This fostered in her mother the worth, willingness, and risk to join Laralynne in a justice-affirming resistance, valuing the known other enough to explore the possibilities of an equitable humanity within and between them, herself, and others.

Yet another expression of calling among Reconstruction's othermothers is the more traditional "reciprocities of Good Works" in the sacred exchange sense of Christian mission.[44–46] A steady volunteer in the Fight for Lifers program, Doris demonstrates this in linking her current volunteer efforts with Reconstruction to the faith she has known since childhood:

> [I was] raised in the church all my life. Both grandmothers were Christian women who didn't just talk about it. They walked it. At the age of 28 was when I experienced my transformation for real and been walking with the Lord ever since and glad about it. And me just going and sharing the word of God with some of the men, their lives have been changed....[Recently] I was impressed by God to write individual letters to them. The inmates couldn't believe that I had taken time to write individual letters and personalized them out of what I had written down on paper [after prison visits] and what I could remember of each individual. And they sent me a message since I been here to let me know they're praying for me.... And to keep at it because if you can save one or two lives, then you've done something good. That's the work that helps me live. (Personal Communication, n.d.)

Some Reconstruction women began with an early childhood resistance to verbal bigotries, while others engaged in a formative fellowship with imprisoned persons as their calling of justice. Some are motivated by love, and others express their calling as a duty of religious faith, valuing these men as prodigal sons (as reflected in The Bible, King James Version, Luke 15:11). "For the prodigal son...a full reentry into the family [means] taking on the mind of the father with such a deep appreciation for his love that he...[experiences] an interior surrender of all components of the person—thought, emotion, will, behavior, relationships and soul functioning, made to the transforming presence of Christ."[47] Consistent with Moon, many Reconstruction women express their calling by nurturing their individual spiritual direction; their expression of pedagogy of principled transformation as they share these directions and transformations with others.

Centerwomen: Leadership Strategies, Transformative Outcomes

Some Othermothers have made contributions of special note. Those of greatest value include collaborators, with a rich set of relationships they bring together to serve common justice ends; workplace innovators, engaging in strategies of risk and resilience to challenge more and less overt oppressions within and beyond their workplace(s); and women of exceptional balance, who navigate challenges and contradictions with an intellectual grace and forthright strength. Three special affiliates were, and remain, at the center of the organization. Together, they reflect three distinct demonstrations of the importance of women to the achievement of the organization's mission. In these all too brief profiles below, their vision, caring, and craftwork demonstrate how and why they are "centerwomen"; that is, women whose decisions and actions of vision, leadership, and an ethic of caring have been shared with such depth and richness that few words other than phenomenal can be used to describe them. As Patricia Hill Collins (1991) has stated, "Certain women in these overlapping community and workplace networks became 'centerwomen.' The skills centerwomen gained from their centrality in their families enabled them to keep people together, ensure that obligations were fulfilled, and maintain group consensus."[48–52] Just as Black women's mothering tradition emerged as a powerful foundation in the union-organizing drive "for [that] particular effort at institutional transformation."[53] Reconstruction has benefitted from women as a similar force for change through its various initiatives and affiliations across the years. Centerwomen of the organization conjure the title, energy, and final stanzas from Maya Angelou's (1995) precious poem, *Phenomenal Woman:*[54]

Now you understand
Just why my head's not bowed.
I don't shout or jump about
Or have to talk real loud.

When you see me passing
It ought to make you proud.
I say

It's in the click of my heels,
The bend of my hair,
the palm of my hand,
The need of my care,
'Cause I'm a woman
Phenomenally.
Phenomenal woman,
That's me.

Barbara Moffett, Phyllis Jones-Carter, and Lucinda Hudson are three phenomenal women who have shaped and molded Reconstruction Inc. and have done so with a passionate commitment, high quality ethic of caring, and focused excellence in their leadership that can only begin to be put into words. They are, in many respects, the epitome of what the organization's capacity-building mission has been, is, and can ever be. A brief biography of each is below.

Barbara Moffett

Barbara Moffett was a visionary leader. The Director of the American Friends Service Committee's (AFSC) Community Relations Division, Ms. Moffett passed away in October 1994. Throughout her personal and professional life, Barbara Moffett was "an important strategist and steadfast supporter of racial and economic justice throughout the United States."[55] Like any such brevity, describing a person of scope, depth, and decades so briefly is a woeful underestimation of the "how" of her craft and compassion, and it only begins to account for her wholeness. As noted in chapter 3, in their formation in AFSC, Ms. Moffett was essential to the formative stages of Reconstruction. So much so that it is safe to write that whatever Reconstruction might have become without her is a nearly impossible hypothetical to imagine, and it isn't worth speaking about because of all of who she was and all that she did. The Ancestors saw fit to have Ms. Moffett be the first organizational contact William Goldsby was introduced to after Mary Norris caringly responded to his call to action and opportunity at the AFSC–sponsored MOVE Memorial event in May 1988.

From summer 1988 and throughout the final six years of her life, William and Barbara engaged in a reciprocity of the most precious kind: spiritually anchored, passionate, grounded in a willingness of shared commitment, with all of these and many more characteristics of common mission caringly repeated and often remaining almost entirely unspoken. Consistent with its mission and Reconstruction as an organization itself, the reciprocity between Barbara and William was consistent with and extended from "a true revolution of values" as Rev. Dr. Martin Luther King Jr. stated and nurtured the term in his April 1967 "Beyond Vietnam" speech. This true revolution of values was reflected in her lengthy tenure with AFSC that began in 1947 and continued until her passing in October 1994. Her introduction of William (along with William Meek) to Mr. Virden Seybould led directly to the funding of a feasibility study and to the formative idea of Reconstruction becoming a program of AFSC's Middle Atlantic Region. In 1990, at a critical moment of the organization's early growth, Ms. Moffett strategized with William to secure internal AFSC support from Birthright Quakers (i.e., those born into the faith) when many others within the organization were in the process of furthering the marginalization of the program viewed by many as problematic and "too radical"—even for an organization "based on the Quaker belief in the worth of every person, and faith in the power of love to overcome violence and injustice."[56]

Ms. Moffett was willing to risk reputation and career to broaden the boundaries of Reconstruction's radical inclusion into AFSC's Middle Atlantic Region. This—and so many other thoughtful decisions and principled actions too numerous to list here—was among Ms. Moffett's most frequent repetitions. Described as "incorrigibly compassionate, tough-minded, [and] in the forefront of the historic movements for civil rights...and many other movements,"[57] she was the first centerwoman of the organization, even before it had its name. For Reconstruction and so many other justice initiatives, Barbara Moffett was the guiding lighthouse of support and safety, allowing the justice journey of these efforts to continue enriched by and beyond the possibilities of her incomparable touch.

Phyllis Jones-Carter

The first historical analysis of what would soon become Reconstruction Inc. was completed by Lucas Ford in March 1990. In it, Phyllis Jones-Carter's name is not mentioned. However, across its history of more than two decades, this first-year document is probably the final historical record that is not a direct extension of Ms. Jones-Carter's consistent leadership. When William Goldsby was moving the formative AFSC program forward, he extended his outreach for various social service supports and participations, meeting with several agency heads and related leadership. In the summer of 1990, Ms. Jones-Carter was called into one such meeting between William and the director of a social service agency with which she worked. From that moment forward, she was among the very first critical links uniting social service agency participation with the mission of Reconstruction. She was the first and longest tenured president of Reconstruction's Board of Directors, beginning her term before the organization formally existed on the first interim board in November 1990. A few months later in April 1991 Ms. Jones-Carter was one of three persons to sign the Articles of Incorporation establishing Reconstruction as an independent, nonprofit organization. Her commitment to, attendance at, and participation in board meetings throughout the formative years of the organization's history enriched a stability and possibility that had as much or more symbolic utility for realizing Reconstruction's capacity-building potential as any strategic action of leadership from which Reconstruction has ever benefitted.

A woman of egalitarian commitment and stern character, Ms. Jones-Carter has exhibited a creativity and sense of joy that has been a very special spiritual presence within the organization. This has been demonstrated in many ways, including having proposed that a bus trip (from Philadelphia) to New York City to collectively watch and discuss a stage play be used as an organizational fundraiser. Using the old school road trip model, merging the arts with critical awareness in a conscientized communion and valuing the wholeness of joy's possibilities among former felons, their families, and interested others are reflected in this and so many other of her many leadership touches.

Her attention to detail and vigilant adherence to an ethic of caring are also reflected in her many other Reconstruction activities. At meeting after meeting during the fragile, early days, Phyllis consistently provided fruit and other food for meetings. This simple act of willingness was both symbolic and literal in its leadership contribution. It, like so many other choices Phyllis made, enriched a "homespace" sensibility within the meetings and the organization so consistent with the powers often centered around—while being profoundly more than—a metaphorical kitchen table reflected in Black women's work.[58–61] The ways of her leadership are also reflected in her substantive critiques, flexibility, and timely responsiveness. In the formative stages of developing a within-prison curriculum for the first cohort of soon-to-be-released Graterford affiliate men, the program committee was critiqued as follows: "Women's presence in the curriculum is inadequate; Treatment department has criticized it for this." These kinds of concerns—how must these men in this type of organization experience the presence of women in the curriculum?—are the types of programmatic assessments Ms. Jones-Carter provided. And in summer 2009 when a recent call was extended on very short notice for a group of women in the organization to fellowship and reflect on their Reconstruction experiences, Phyllis not only showed up she was early, patient in allowing others to arrive as they did, and maintained a sense of sharing equity within the focus group. This, despite her having the longest and most substantive tenure among all those in attendance.

Perhaps her leadership actions of greatest value have come in the ways Ms. Jones-Carter has thoughtfully balanced a career of social service—including decades as a Department of Corrections employee of multiple Pennsylvania prisons—with an unwavering dedication to an organization seeking to dismantle and "delete the reasons for" the very prisons from which she recently retired. This caring contradiction, that is, apparent dialectics, proactively lived to serve a larger end,[62–65] is one among the many similar contradictions Reconstruction has navigated from its origin to now. Through her consistent and comfortable merge of these two seemingly dissonant affiliations, Phyllis demonstrated that working for systemic change within the very system of one's career not only can occur but perhaps must occur. When recently asked for her definition of justice she emphasized "a system [of] clearly defined issues, fair and impartial discussion and fair treatment for individuals." Her defining justice emphasis on a balanced equity is what and how she has lived her life and how she has contributed as a centerwoman of Reconstruction Inc.

Lucinda Hudson
On January 22, 1997, the Board of Reconstruction Inc. met and seven people attended. Three women and four men. One of those women was Lucinda Hudson. Minutes from the meeting show that William asked each board member to "speak to where they are in respect of commitment to the Board." Each person provided a reflection, addressing various issues and concerns. Challenging life circumstances. Pending moves. Feeling disconnected or cautious regarding sustaining their board participation. Lucinda's response? That she is "in it for the long haul. Very committed." Those words—clear, focused, and strong—have been true since the first time she touched Reconstruction's soil to seed its mission. And those words continue to be true today, 18 years after her affiliation began, as she continues her work with Reconstruction's newest initiatives of committee development and organizational collaborations. As with Ms. Moffett and Ms. Jones-Carter, Lucinda's centerwoman contributions to Reconstruction

are diverse and are rooted in the words that have been used before. Dedicated. Consistent. Passionately engaged. Unwavering. Strong. Principled. All of these and more reflect the elements of her willingness to use so much of her time and caring to further this work. As one early example, when a documentary about the organization was completed in 1995 (led by the craft and efforts of Patrick Murray with the support of Scribe Video; see chapter 5), Lucinda partnered with William and Patrick to secure showings of it at a local café as a fundraiser. From site planning and outreach, to outlining aspects of the breakfast dialogue to follow, her focus on funding the organization and its mission was matched by other aspects of her diverse skill set. This skill set includes engaging in respectful opposition to an organizational policy or practice with which she disagreed, without devolving into alienating imposition. This is reflected in the 1997 board meeting moment considering overnight stays of daughters when their fathers were residing in the Phase II residential reentry space of the organization and in many other moments like it across her affiliation.

Perhaps most critically, Lucinda has used her principled, numbers-oriented sensibility to assist with the most consistent challenge across the organization's history: an uncertain financial footing. She has prepared reports, paid bills, assisted in the preparation of grants, processed check requests, managed the uneven and often small donations, helped with the organization's taxes, and been of profound service in sustaining whatever meaning Reconstruction has been able to give to fiscal solvency. And due to her sustained encouragement, Lucinda experienced her Reconstruction affiliation as a family affair for many years. In addition to having a son who was an important presence in a program-building initiative that will be considered later (see chapter 6), she has and continues to exhibit her passionate commitment and clarity of mission so important for a grassroots organization to keep its doors open. She is now and will forever be, one of Reconstruction's most precious centerwomen.

Women-Centered Challenges

Women in Reconstruction Inc. exemplify the praxis of beneficial tensions. Yes, the organization is grounded in and built upon a worldview of holistic equity in every expression of the term. Yes, women were, and remain, central to both the founding and long-term progress of the organization. Yes, the community capacity-building resources of the centerwomen and othermothers considered above do summarize the vital, long-standing presence of and contributions to the organization made by women. Yes, as Kay states previously, Reconstruction is unique among grassroots organizations in its ability to be consistent in its articulation—and expression—of the values this holistic equity worldview demands, maintaining a far too uncommon reciprocity between these two aspects of organizational praxis. Yes, true to the chapter's title, it is very difficult, if not impossible, to imagine Reconstruction's existence, much less its progress across the years, without the essential participation of women considered in the pages above and in every chapter of this book. Yes. Yet many women-centered challenges within the organization remain. The four that most consistently emerged were (1) therapeutic alienations (2) critical mass (3) participation versus perception and (4) an uncertain future.

Therapeutic Alienations

Reconstruction Inc. is a multidimensional, capacity-building organization with three core programs—Alumni Ex-Offenders Association, Fight for Lifers, and Leadership, Education, Advocacy and Development—and has established and maintains a rich set of collaborative allies (see chapter 8). The values Ivy and other women emphasize are central to the organization and its curriculum, both past and present, prioritizing the development of leadership while making "a tireless effort toward the discovery of curative and regenerating processes, and unfaltering faith that there is a treasure ...in the heart of every man."[66] After extended observation, these "curative and regenerative processes" result from bringing together three therapeutic models: the Sanctuary Model of Relational Resilience,[67–70] the Culture-Centered Healing Model,[71–73] and a Therapy of Liberation.[74–78] The therapeutic approach that informs both the support meetings of AEA and every meeting the organization holds is likely to be experienced differently by different persons. And women have been the members who have most frequently expressed discomfort with its potentially alienating processes. As Tamika and Déjà reflect on their reintroduction and introduction to the support meetings:

> To be honest with you, I had so many [issues] I'm not even sure what specifically we were talking about that night. I remember feeling like I was on the defensive. Rather than feeling like I was being assisted, I felt like I was being antagonized. My ethics, my morals and my worth as a woman was being questioned, and I didn't bring whatever that situation was to the table for that result. I feel like I've always been open and honest about what my shit was. I went to AEA with [the children/CPS situation], and by me bringing it to Reconstruction, I was expecting more and I got less. I don't know if this is because this is the only system they're used to. Or because they have more knowledge of it than I do. Or if it's just because of how they view people who are in this situation, why I didn't get the response I was needing or the support that I was

looking for. I don't know. But I felt alienated and so I alienated myself [from the organization]. From everyone and everything. (Tamika, Personal Communication, n.d.)

I went to AEA, and it was...was...I really wanted to focus on what was goin' on with me. But it was good, because when I listened to everybody tell their story, and then, they get feedback. I was like, "Eeeoooo-wuh!" And everybody accepted [their feedback]. Deal with that. Handle that. 'Cause it was straight at you! And can you really handle that ... I was sayin' somethin', and the guy said, "Well, this is not the time for that." And [I thought] if this is not the time, than when IS the time?...You put [your issues] out there on the table and the responses that you get might not always necessarily be the ones that you were looking for. The question is, can you handle it. You have to be thick-skinned to handle that type of constructive criticism. (Déjà, Personal Communication, n.d.)

Both Tamika and Déjà spoke of being alienated from the AEA program and from the entire organization. By the type and amount of critique. By the depth of collective intrusion presented in multiple voices. And by the demanding elements of challenging the role of victim and emphasizing individual and collective agency that could bring about change. This sense of alienation was experienced by a small number of women (and a few men); persons who place priority on voice as both a decision to participate and a process of fellowship often feel unintentionally othered within Reconstruction, leading them to distance themselves from the organization. This manifests as a gendered paradox of Reconstruction's therapeutic Sanctuary Model primacy on a "socially responsive, emotionally intelligent community that fosters growth and change"[79] and egalitarian inclusion. In the engagement of intended support, alienation still occurs. The demand for simultaneously being that vulnerable and that strong in that way led both these women to feel as if they were being attacked and responded to abusively rather than supportively. This difference appears to, at least in part, be organizational outcomes of what some see as characteristic differences between female and male ways of knowing,[80,81] a paradox given the testament to Reconstruction's nurturing of women's power and voice shared by Jamilla. Paradox or no, the cost of a resulting distance from the organization is especially detrimental given the second, women-centered challenge of critical mass.

Critical Mass

For Reconstruction, or any other grassroots organization, social justice, and women's experiences of and contributions to its realization, is much more than a numbers game. Yet numbers do matter. How they matter is because group size, the number of active members of a group, can inform a wide range of intra-organization dynamics, intergroup relations, and other possibilities.[82] Organizational capacity is understood by many to be heavily determined by size and the achievement of capacity-building ends,[83,84] and Reconstruction's relationship to all of these numbers issues is informed by gender. So how numbers matter is a critical challenge for the presence of women in achieving its organizational mission. To illustrate these challenges, one member commented:

> People were coming together and saying, "Fight for Lifers has been really good for me because I know that I'm not alone in the suffering [and] that I feel for having my loved one incarcerated." It's disappointing to see that those people aren't around now. So, are they finding some other way that provides that support for those struggles? Or are they dealing with them on their own? So again, just wishing and knowing that we need to have stronger outreach to bring those people back to the table, back to our living rooms. (Personal Communication, n.d.)

Another member stated the following paradox:

> Men can and will be involved, naturally. They can be the out front people, very effectively and [more frequently] say, "We're committed to women's issues." I think it can happen. But it's going to lead back to, "Where are the women you say you're so concerned about?" (Personal Communication, n.d.)

And another member reflected on geographic, institutional constraints:

> I work, as I know William does, with people in Graterford and Chester. Which are men's prisons. We don't have a women's state prison or federal prison in close proximity. So in local jails, just because of higher turnover and things, it's more difficult to have a stable group that one works within the jail setting than in the prison setting. (Personal Communication, n.d.)

Where are the women? There are challenges of sustained engagement even after a sense of isolation has been muted. There are challenges of visibility even after statements and actions of commitment are expressed. There are challenges of immediate access for within-prison volunteering because of the absence of a women's state prison near the city. Where are women? No, those critical centerwomen of leadership are not figureheads in any way. They are, in fact, central to the past and present functioning of the organization. No, women members are not framed within any Afrocentric version of the Madonna-whore myth of ideal-typing of women in an off-putting imposition. Without even a hint of superficial tokenism, and with gender, sexual identity, and all domains of individual and group difference inclusively engaged, Reconstruction values everyday expressions of the Audre Lorde (1984) truism that "tolerance is not enough."[85] No, an environment of sexism, visible or less visible, does not pervade organizational dynamics at every turn. No, the family-first focus of the organization is not in any way mistaken nor misleading. No. Yet the sustained, inclusion of women remains an uncertain challenge. Whether it's the challenges of sustaining engaged affiliation after "church effect" appreciations wear thin, or the contradiction of truly inclusionary men stating and restating commitment to women without the consequential and visible presence of women in outreach, or the difficulties of institutional proximity negatively impacting potential institutional outreach.

As a result, dynamics of diminishing return, variations in perceived social incentives, and the reality that intrinsic rewards are most often the only compensation provided by the entirely volunteer organization lead the women's margin to be thin and thinner still. It is difficult to have a "free rider" problem (i.e., diminishing investment in collective contribution as group size increases) when the number of persons who actually consistently participate in any one initiative is extremely small. As Marwell and Oliver (1993) state: "When groups are heterogeneous, group size tends to have a positive effect on the provision of jointly supplied collective goods."[86] For Reconstruction, operating with such a small critical mass of very few dedicated affiliates, and a thin margin for the "provision of collective goods," any alienations become magnified. This is all the more the case when geography and other place-informed factors intersect to impose still further on the potential for sustaining a larger critical mass of women.

Participation and Perception

In addition to the therapeutic model and fellowship style of the organization, and the numbers shaping its definition and praxis, women's experiences in Reconstruction are also challenged by a literal and symbolic distance between the perception many have of the organization and its actual participants. As one member stated:

> There are women in leadership positions in Reconstruction. On the board. And have been all along...certainly women have been encouraged and supported to be full participants and spokespeople. Which again is one of the things I really value about every encounter I've had with Reconstruction. It's very egalitarian in a full sense....At the same time when I think of Reconstruction, I think of mostly men. [Even though] I know that's not true. I do think of them too [women in leadership]. But in terms of the on-the-ground, doing the work day-to-day [I think of men]. And that's not entirely true either. But with Reconstruction, I do tend to think of the men. (Personal Communication, n.d.)

This distinction between perception and (the leadership and egalitarian praxis of) participation has been true since very early on in the history of the organization, and it was expressed in a variety of ways by most women affiliates with whom we spoke. Women perceive the organization as a men's only domain—even when they know that not to be true—which then nurtures the prediction of it as a men's only space and then causes women to be less willing to participate in an unwelcome space. Thus, leading it to remain male-dominated. Between this perception and men not doing enough consistently enough to act against the unspoken comforts of a "men's club" context, challenges remain in creating a gender-balanced organization.

Thus, Reconstruction's public perception is likely to remain such for the foreseeable future. Given the apparent contradictions that are revealed when men are repeatedly the face of attempts at women's inclusion as reflected in the critical mass discussion above, this perception will likely continue. It is all the more likely, given the set of other misperceptions commonly associated—and perhaps intentionally re-created in the mass media—with the practices of mass incarceration (e.g., economic restructuring, global human rights violations, health-wellness disparities, the global economy; see chapter 9).

An Uncertain Future

> Women are the cornerstone. It if weren't for us, there would BE no male population because they have to come out of us in order for them to even be here. If we can begin to strengthen our women. To have a different and a better resolve about who [we] are as individuals, then that can begin to strengthen our communities. We'll be better mothers. Raising better children. Having men who feel better about themselves. And then it can create a different, more productive, healthier cycle. (Jackie, Personal Communication, n.d.)

Jackie's comment is a hopeful reflection for a possible future and is consistent with the title of this chapter. The chapter's title is borrowed from a speech of Mrs. Lela Spratlen, a pastor's wife, and the grandmother of the book's first author. Speaking to a southern Baptist organization in 1936, what she stated then remains true today: "There is no progress without a woman in it." So, what's next? A more complete consideration of this question is presented in chapter 9. How these women-centered challenges considered above are to be proactively addressed is a part of Reconstruction's uncertain future. What should the organization do? According to Eden (1992), "A key to the willingness to commit oneself to a highly demanding undertaking is one's belief in one's capacity to mobilize the physical, intellectual, and emotional resources needed to succeed."[87] Though far easier words to write than to live, following from the literature, this capacity to mobilize is the fuel for all organizational progress. And capacity-building begins with the assets already present within, and accessible to, individuals, families, collaborators, and all other organization affiliates. That is as true in Reconstruction addressing these women-centered challenges as it is for all other tasks and processes of change. Whatever its future, Reconstruction is informed by the truism of Prof. John Henrik Clarke that "*history is a current event.*" And Reconstruction's proud history has been touched by, and will continue to be centered in, the excellence of many women whose voices and contributions are reflected, and reflected on, above.

Conclusion

As demonstrated in the analysis above, women of Reconstruction Inc. nurture justice by contributing to community capacity-building outcomes in many ways. When asked to define justice, their responses reflected a spectrum of diverse meanings since justice can take many forms. This included a detailed specification of four types of justice: exchange, distributive, social, and retributive. Within this justice spectrum, their less formal, more personal definitions of justice included:

1. Engaging in a righteous battle (i.e., "the fight for what is right").
2. A system of fairness ("a system...where issues are clearly defined to make a fair and impartial discussion [of] fair treatment").
3. Equitable access ("Everyone should have an equal opportunity provided they are qualified").
4. Victory of truth ("laws carried out in a righteous way...and the truth has prevailed").
5. Equity in moral judgment ("moral rightness in general...something given for worthy behavior...or penalizing misbehavior").

Like their varying relationships to the organization, their definitions of justice also reflect a diversity that enhances the "intentional community" character within the organization.

Within and Beyond an Organization's Praxis of Gender-Informed Justice
Like their perceptions of justice, these women live multiple and varied reciprocities, that is, how they engage in sacred exchange and with whom. Their reciprocities are diverse patterns and relationships of formal and informal exchange deeply rooted in a sense of collective investment. Value is placed on

exploring what the sacred is in thought and action and how those patterns and relationships of exchange can change individuals, and by doing so, enrich the interdependent capacities of individual members, their and other families, interested others, organization collaborators, and the larger community. This chapter explored the experiences of many women who have affiliated with Reconstruction and its mission. Yet the phrase itself "women in Reconstruction Inc." is a paradox. On the one hand, it would be both intellectually and historically dishonest to ignore any form of difference and raise questions regarding how that form has impacted the organization. Aspects of sex and gender have mattered in a variety of ways. And here we've considered many among them. On the other hand, the organization places great value on and engages equity in every part of its foundations, motives, actions and outcomes. And to specify women and raise questions regarding their unique (and non-unique) organizational experiences, to some, may suggest a "set aside" perspective of unintended othering quite inconsistent with the principled equity of the organization.

Because Reconstruction Inc. is an equity-based, affiliation member organization and is not a charity-motive service model organization, individual, familial, organizational, and communal principled transformations extends from the Reconstruction mission. The women in the organization constantly demonstrate the "how" of this, including the temporal, emotional, and spiritual toll associated with this type of civic engagement. Along with some of the necessary strategies of self-protection and "spiritual insulation" necessary, given all that this work demands of those volunteers willing to step forward and do it (well). How are we to continue to see, seek, and manifest possibility? How are we to do so while the prison industrial complex seeks to re-create itself in this current era of economic constraint? These women's experiences provide partial and highly beneficial answers to these and related questions, extending from their participation in nurturing the Reconstruction mission. There will be no progress without them as the organization continues to refine its future. Now.

Endnotes Toward Principled Transformation

Extending from the rich, communal contributions made by women in Reconstruction, three possibilities toward principled transformation emerge:

- Transformative Trainings—The work of organizations would be enhanced by focusing on (1) the historical struggles of women; (2) the distinctions between women's interests and women's leadership to understand how women's leadership can sometimes perpetuate oppressive outcomes; (3) subtle sexisms that can unintentionally alienate women's participation; and (4) the long-silenced voices of poor and working-class women too often rendered invisible.

- Resolving Rage—Actions toward the resolution of rage include being "radical inclusionists" when it comes to women's voices and vision. Meaning organizations would benefit from the necessary struggle to proactively facilitate an egalitarian organizational model, where women's voices consistently contribute in all public forums and all settings in which decisions are being made.

- A New Justice—Nurturing a new justice paradigm demands various transformative sacrifices, including (1) men no longer hiding behind a perceived need to protect women, and by doing so, legitimating a desire to kill one another; and (2) men abandoning the abusive dominion of male only decision-making spaces regarding the military, prisons, allocation of money, and public education.

A Pedagogy of Progress: Nurturing Community, 1993–1998

> You cannot lock everybody up forever. No way we can put everybody away. So we've got to come up with another plan. I still believe in the ability of people to change and turn their lives around....The best thing that Reconstruction contributed is hope. And also the opportunity [for inmates] to look at themselves and see what they could do to grab hold of the information so that when they left [prison] there were instruments and tools that they could use to maintain a life in the community. A helpful, hopeful life.
>
> Ms. Bessie Williams, Reconstruction Liaison, Unit Manager (ret.),
> Graterford Prison, August 2009

Collaboration among diverse people living the helpful, hopeful lives Ms. Bessie Williams speaks of above has been and remains at the core of the mission of Reconstruction Inc. To strengthen that foundation of help and hope, former felons, their family members, and interested others—inside and outside of prisons—used the second 5 years of the organization to further a vital set of principled transformations. With its arrival, 1993 brought many changes. This included fundamental refinements in its capacity-building pedagogy of principled transformation, in other words, how organization strategies of action were guided by its Afrocentric and egalitarian values to nurture the praxis of its mission to "*change [oneself] to change the world*." This mission is a global goal grounded in the gradual process of change resting in each individual's contributions to themselves, their families, and the local and global community, especially those most directly touched by the prison system and its many collateral consequences. And changing oneself and the world is a product of cultural action. In 1993, and throughout the second 5 years of the organization, Reconstruction engaged in a rich diversity of cultural actions. Paulo Freire (1970) suggested that the first element of dialogical cultural action is cooperation.[1] And, through formal and less formal collaborations, reciprocity between dialogue and other actions is one among the more valuable and transferable means by which hope for the emancipation of the oppressed can transform social reality.[2–5]

Goodman and his colleagues (1998) suggest that building community capacity is a central concern in grassroots community organizational development and implementation.[6] Community capacity-building is "the interaction of human capital, organizational resources and social capital within a given community that can be leveraged to solve collective problems and improve or maintain the well-being of a given community."[7,8] From its origin through its first five

years, Reconstruction Inc. nurtured the assets of individual affiliates, their families, and the other organizations with which it interacted. This capacity-building
model extends from several interdisciplinary strands, including the "local
movement center" concept from social movements. Local movement centers
are "a dynamic form of social organization...[that] vary in their degree of organization [and] their capacity to produce and sustain protest" and other valued
aspects of social change.[9–11] A dialogue between critical pedagogy, local movement centers, and community capacity-building is both conceptual and practical
and is demonstrated throughout the history of Reconstruction Inc. This chapter
explores this pedagogy of progress from 1993 to 1998, the second 5 years of the
organization.

Critical Cooperation

From its origin, Reconstruction Inc. has been guided by curricula documenting
its pedagogy of principled transformation (see chapter 2). For its pedagogy to
nurture desired transformations, many diverse dialogues must be established
and sustained. These include institutional collaborations it has caringly nurtured
over the prior five years (1988–1992). During the final board meeting in December 1992, one board membership was revoked due to a sustained lack of
participation, and the addition of a new board member, Hakim Ali, was confirmed. A number of diverse resource partnerships were at play, including William Goldsby, Executive Director, and other board leadership having recently
met with faculty members at Philadelphia's Lincoln University. Together, they
considered what types of university supports would be most helpful in furthering Lincoln University's contributions to Reconstruction's organizational mission. More directly related to capacity-building access, a supportive community
member was considering renting out a house she owned for Reconstruction
affiliates to live in during their post-prison, residential reentry Phase II. And
rentable office space to house Reconstruction at the AFSC Friends Center
would not be available until sometime early in the year. Thus, the start of Reconstruction's second 5 years presented many changes and resource collaborations. Not unlike many Thursdays across the previous year, Thursday, January
21, 1993, was time for another Reconstruction board meeting. As 1993 began,
William Goldsby's official title became Executive Director. What he was the
executive director of would be given greater meaning and take greater shape in
the coming 5 years.

The positive momentum for Graterford was moving forward with a favorable yet volatile uncertainty. After William met with the Superintendent of Prisons in Harrisburg, Pennsylvania (see chapter 3), a set of relationships were steadily nurtured, as familiarity with William, his voice, and his vision progressed beyond the immediate circle of AFSC and the city of Philadelphia. Steps toward initiating Phase I, the intense, within-prison, transformative reentry program, were progressing well. This within-prison program of the first Reconstruction curriculum was the vital, early transformative pedagogy. It was guided by the goal of readying these soon-to-be former felons for their next steps out of prison and back into the community. One Reconstruction board meeting in late 1992 reflects these intersecting momentums:

> Phyllis [Jones-Carter], Lori [Pompa], and William met today with Stachelek, Williams, and DiGugliamo at Graterford. The prison administrators were very supportive of the project and gave Reconstruction the OK to start classes January 19th [1993], as planned. A [prison] classroom was guaranteed to the project for three full days per week. Remuneration to participants was set at 25 cents per hour...The administrators recommended that we include the applicants...not chosen...possibly offering special workshops or trainings for them.[12]

The director of inmate treatment services (Stachelek) supported Reconstruction's effort so much that Graterford Superintendent Donald Vaughn insisted that if unanimous (overt) support was not demonstrated by the prison staff for the Reconstruction program, it could not proceed in Graterford. The within-prison support of the mission, process, and intended outcomes of Reconstruction's program was so well respected that—prior to its initiation in any form (i.e., with no track record of success)—Mr. Stachelek and his staff were already recommending that those not selected into the first cohort should be presented with an alternative form of exposure to the program. Here is where the paradox of shared intent mixed with the lived demonstration of desired outcome in ways that furthered the mission of both. The paradox of shared intent was that, consistent with Ms. Williams's words above, by 1993, Reconstruction was already recognized for sharing in the rehabilitative ideal of the prison staffers who valued that over whatever punitive dimension the institution may (also) have. The paradox was in the mixture of traditional and more "radical" goals of what this rehabilitative ideal actually was and how an organization like Reconstruction might contribute to its achievement. The lived demonstration of a desired outcome was William himself—one who valued his own journey as a former felon enough to embrace a sense of reciprocity; giving and receiving a principled transformation in himself and others who were also bearing the mark of "violent offender" with the powerful possibilities the mixture of rage and resilience allowed.

This mixture was also reflected in the organization's board of directors. Ms. Jones-Carter was Board Chair. Ms. Pompa was an active board member, whose early dedication to the Reconstruction mission was matched only by her skill sets in grant writing and other forms of fundraising. She used them both in many helpful ways, including having been instrumental in securing much of the early funding for the organization. Within Reconstruction the leadership structure was set, with the executive director and board members in place. Despite some turnover, a consistent critical mass had developed that was deeply enriched by the arrival and new presence of Hakim Ali on the board. The bylaws of the organization were being drafted and by May would be completed and approved. And the board's five-committee structure (Executive, Program, Housing, Funding, and Public Relations) was also established, with multiple members on each committee and specific committee leadership who had stepped forward. A rich diversity of race, class, gender, sexual identity, sociopolitical worldview, and other aspects of individual and group difference were reflected among the nine persons attending the January 1993 board meeting, the five board members unable to attend, and the other affiliates who made up the domains of capacity-building that were engaged throughout the meeting.

Yet in this rich demonstration of organizational progress, the grassroots truths of Reconstruction's justice mission were also apparent. Five of the thirteen board members were not in attendance for a mixture of reasons, yes. Still, a 38% absenteeism level was a marker of concern. How strong is a collective leadership when nearly two-fifths of the collective don't show up? Two $5,000 grants had been completed and submitted but were not funded. Yet when a service model and personnel infrastructure for the organization would soon be (conservatively) budgeted at nearly $100,000 per year, how were these nonrenewable, one-time grants to be understood? How cohesive is a leadership when a board membership is revoked, thus being removed from the board, in two consecutive board meetings to end and begin the New Year? What is the meaning of capacity-building in the midst of fragile footing? These questions reflect the challenges of having an all-volunteer board and a virtually unpaid staff of one and a half persons, for an organization that had yet to establish a solid funding foundation. Reconstruction continued to answer these questions, even as it solidified its unsteady yet consistent progress.

Collaborative Contradictions:Reconstruction's First Graterford Cohort

I would like to see a program of that type remain in Graterford—and all other facilities—because I am very big on reentry. And I see the need for programs like Reconstruction...the Lifers [those serving life sentences in the first cohort of participants] were unique people. They wanted to say to the other inmates who had an opportunity to return to the community, "Don't get yourself into the situation that we're in. We don't know when we'll ever get out again. So think about what you're doing." [Lifers] served as a deterrent to inmates who...still had an opportunity to return to the community. (Ms. Bessie Williams, Personal Communcation, n.d.)

From early in the African past, value has been placed on the unity between family and community and the presence and possibilities of unexpected alliances to mobilize important sources of support. Emphasis on collective survival, interdependence, and responsibility to others were central to the process and practice of all forms of fellowship.[13–16] These values, perceptions, and strategies of action were especially critical in all rites of passage settings, or settings of intentional, focused transformation, to move persons from one understanding of self, family, group, and community to another.[17–20] This Afrocentric emphasis on collective survival, interdependence, and responsibility, in partnership with a mobilized unity between family, community, and unexpected allies, was central to the process and pedagogy of Reconstruction's first cohort of participants in its within-prison reentry and reintegration readiness program. In virtually every element of organizational affiliation and participant engagement, a pedagogy of principled transformation guided the decision and actions of all affiliates of this layered and multidimensional process. As one critical example of how the trust and respect Ms. Bessie Williams refers to in the opening quote, which William Goldsby had established in communion with the Graterford prison administration, contradictions in prison policy were addressed and resolved collaboratively.

There is a long-held, standing prison rule that no prisoners should in any way be directly involved in the decision making related to any other prisoner. Yet in direct opposition to this rule, the Graterford administration agreed to allow inmate participation in the recruitment, application, evaluation, selection, and sustained participation in virtually every aspect of Reconstruction's within-prison decision making. A small group of lifers and other inmates formed an Internal Advisory Committee (IAC) as a leadership collective, which then joined the process and provided essential input. These men guided the internal outreach to other inmates, unit managers, and other prison staffers open to the potential for this program of possible transformation. They had met with the

Reconstruction Program Committee and had worked with William and the committee for more than a year to specify and refine the primary components of the formative curriculum. Guided by William and informed consultants volunteering their time, in 1992, a series of tolerance discussions were held on Saturdays for both the IAC and the board members. These moments and processes of collaborative contradiction enriched every affiliate who came into contact with the Reconstruction mission within Graterford at that time. On Tuesday, January 19, 1993, as a product of a capacity-building process where many assets were brought together, Reconstruction's first Graterford cohort began.

The Beginning

It was clear from the very beginning that inmates must be involved at every level of development of the program and how the program would be facilitated. The selection process of the IAC was complete, and a group of 24 men were selected. All those selected by the IAC had been approved by the Graterford administration. From day one in Graterford, perhaps the two most prominent, engaged capacity-building dimensions (Goodman et al. 1998) were leadership and networks of trust. Guided by the same subcommittee structure of Reconstruction's board, the IAC prepared bylaws pertaining to the structure of IAC and its relationship to Reconstruction. They also completed practices and procedures that established a creative momentum within the prison, which included meeting weekly with William so that a regular Reconstruction presence continued developing the IAC program. These men helped design their brochure, held discussions about persons at risk for a misconduct while participating, helped Reconstruction prepare for its meetings with the Parole Board, and engaged in a host of other activities. These leadership strategies of action enriched a multilayered network of trust among and between persons, roles, units, and relationships that would likely otherwise be understood and engaged in adversarial or even contradictory terms. Yet guided by the praxis of its transformative mission to *"change [oneself] to change the world,"* the IAC was a vital component in the collaborative practice of Reconstruction's pedagogy of principled transformation.

An Early Challenge

The formative steps of an organization's new alliances are among the most challenging and enriching processes in which the organization could possibly participate. Generally, the more unsettled the organization's infrastructure and the smaller its membership, the more fragile any new alliance becomes. All the more so, when one of the participating partners is a total institution, symbolically and literally reinforcing a society's rule of law. Such was the case when Reconstruction Inc. established a service-oriented alliance with the State Correctional Institution at Graterford (SCI-Graterford). Just over a month after Reconstruction's first Graterford cohort had begun, events took place that threatened the organization, the cohort, and all elements of the formative within-prison network of trust that had taken well over a year to establish.

On February 23, 1993, *The Philadelphia Inquirer* reported that a Graterford inmate had been stabbed to death while watching a group of others play basketball. "Michael Keaton, 20, of [local address] was stabbed with a homemade knife, or 'shank,' at about 8:30 a.m. as 150 inmates worked out in the field house of the [prison]."[21] The 4,200-inmate prison, operating at 60% over what the prison was built to accommodate, was then put on lockdown. No one was allowed to exit his cell for any reason, visiting times were suspended, and service delivery of virtually every kind, save meals, was halted. The lockdown lasted three days and "was gradually brought to an end as prisoners were allowed out of their cells ...and permitted in the dining halls...[after] one inmate told investigators that he saw the stabbing from a balcony in the field house and identified Kevin Johnson as the killer."[22] Mr. Johnson was then arrested, placed in solitary confinement, and would soon be moved to another prison.

The Reconstruction program was informed by and extended from unity between family, community, and unexpected alliances to mobilize important sources of support. Ironically, the dispute between the two men was informed by family and community and was at least indirectly a product of Mr. Johnson having mobilized important sources of support to complete the murder. Institutionally, it was a demonstration of what can happen when the institution has no program addressing rage through the lens of historical conditioning. Individually, it was a demonstration of what happens when the absence of principled transformation is mixed with an unfiltered rage and is expressed as an individual act of vengeance. Apparently, the killing was a consequence of one of Mr. Keaton's cousins having killed one of Mr. Johnson's brothers. A prison official remarked that Johnson would "never be allowed back out among the prisoners because his presence would give rise to concerns about security and safety [as] there are other family members in the prison."[23] Yet in true capacity-building fashion, like all events in participants' lives, the murder and its individual and institutional aftermath gave Reconstruction a glimpse of resources hidden behind the emotion of rage.

No, neither of the men was a participant in Reconstruction's program. A prevailing hope is that if both of them had been, the taking of one inmate's life by another would not have taken place regardless of the challenging emotions. Whatever the accuracy of this hope, all of the participants of the IAC, the first cohort, and all administrators and staff members had to call on and use all available resources this setback demanded. After missing three weeks of classes, Reconstruction's work continued despite the murder, the lockdown, and the subsequent chilling effect all imposed on the prison and inmates. The Graterford administration considered the option of being able to make up the missed time by holding classes five days a week instead of the previously approved three days per week. Within this time, a letter was sent to Mr. Stachelek in response to his letter "listing dates for all upcoming meetings/events, including update[d] committee work."[24]

As the post-lockdown progress continued, the IAC continued to refine its role. The very credibility, the ability to meet, even the IAC's opportunity to simply continue to exist, was called into question in the aftermath of the lockdown. But they continued to move forward with the support of the Graterford administration. Again, given that most of the IAC were lifers or men with many years yet to be lived out in prison, what should their role be for a group of other fellow inmates within 18 months of their scheduled release? The vital dialogue of cooperation that answered this question was grounded in the sustained leadership of Tyrone Werts and Brian Wallace. These two men and all the men of IAC sustained their efforts to answer this and its related questions. Per May 20, 1993, Board meeting minutes (BMM), the IAC submitted a proposal to the Reconstruction board "for their teaching role in the classes and involvement in program development."[25]

At nearly the same time this internal inclusion of the IAC was being refined, two other critical strands of program development were also taking place. For one, further enriching the network of trust reflected in the prison support of the program, the Graterford administration asked for a program evaluation. Less than four months of lockdown-interrupted engagement within the prison had taken place and already a call for assessment was being made. But caringly, truer to a dialogue of allies in a shared mission rather than a top-down imposition of untimely critique, the administrative request of Reconstruction was far more of a request for an update than it was for a point-specific exploration. Board Meeting Minutes from May 20, 1993 reflect that by this time, Mr. Donald Vaughn, the prison superintendent, had "heard some very good things about Reconstruction." When meeting with William, Mr. Vaughn stated that other programs were very anxious to come into the prison, "but [these other programs] have been turned down because the administration [was] waiting to see how this program [would do]."[26] What principles and methods are actually used in the classroom? How might these pedagogical strategies be replicated in one or more ways for the general population of inmates? Using "results" of Reconstruction's choosing, how effectively are these strategies—and their intended outcomes—starting to be assessed? No specific list of questions. No survey or other instrument to be administered. No testimonials to be compiled. But some demonstration of contribution that could help Graterford better understand the possibilities for programmatic intervention, if only to further nurture discipline in the rehabilitative dimension of its prison mission.

In addition, informed by the set of cooperative relationships he had established and sustained with a diverse set of Pennsylvania Department of Corrections staff members and administrators, William met with Mr. Alan Castor, Chairman of the State Parole Board. Within two years, Mr. Castor would be ousted from his job after overseeing a questionable prison release of another inmate in a different prison. But at that time, he made a set of beneficial contributions to the procedural aspects of the cohort members' progress. How to best navigate required urinalyses, manage inmate-specific information access through a Release of Information form, and maintain consistency of comparable protocol were among the procedures William and Mr. Castor discussed. Programmatic consistency was improved even more when Mr. Castor agreed to assign a single parole officer to all participants.

Both within and beyond the prison's walls, the Graterford process could not have occurred without the diligence and follow-through of many women. At the time of the first Graterford cohort, Bessie Williams was named by Graterford Superintendent Donald Vaughn as the liaison between Graterford and Reconstruction. Ms. Williams assisted the program in running smoothly. Early on, Kathy Sheppard volunteered her craft for more than half of first-year cohort experience. Ms. Sheppard came into the classroom for about six months and helped the men create journaled autobiographies complete with pictures and their personal reflections. And at a turning point of possible tension within the curriculum, a women-focused weeklong workshop revealed to the participants a better gender, sexuality, and family awareness. For the men, one of the most important lessons from this workshop was its inclusiveness. Women from all walks of life were on the panel: different races, sexual identities, and class backgrounds. These participations of women were across a wide diversity of roles and contributions. In addition to the panel, Ms. Sheppard, Ms. Williams,

and Dr. Welmina Johnson led a workshop, "Releasing Our Arrested Development." Her thorough curriculum encouraged the men to open up and recognize
many dialectics, including the many strengths in their vulnerabilities. This included one cohort member who shared a deeply held secret about his family
and his arrest with the other men in the group. Resources of resilience and con-
scientious caring so many women shared with the program moved the Graterford experience well beyond what it would have otherwise achieved. Yet as
these within-prison successes mounted, questions about a space for the next
step of transformation did as well: their reentry into the community. Where
would the program's Phase II take place? What kind of living space would define this essential transition?

Homeplace and a Sacred Circle

Like leadership and networks of trust, resources are another core dimension of
community capacity-building identified by Goodman and his colleagues
(1998).[27] As the progress in Graterford continued, participants were changing
with each session of a visitor, panel discussion, or other activity of the curriculum; with each role-play of principled communication and quality listening; with
each newly revealed element of self. As these personal, familial, and organizational transformations continued, both intimate and political, two essential resources were being developed and refined: (1) a Sacred Circle of outside
support and (2) a reentry homeplace to establish transitional footing for a life
outside the prison walls. These resources were multidimensional, engaging a
number of forms of capacity-building simultaneously and made simple and profound contributions to the organization and to these men.

Sacred Circles
In order to realize Reconstruction's intended mission within the Graterford
cohort, its pedagogy of principled transformation was built around a process of
nurturing sacred circles. The circle, "the African spiritual symbol par excellence,
tak[ing] on its full meaning as it stands for the constant renewal of Life," represents a symmetry and equity of all within it, sharing to further whatever is collectively valued among those it contains.[28,29]   These patterns of information
exchange were critical and constant. The traditional symbolic circle "incorpo-
rates spiritual beliefs, harmony, and the belief that life occurs within a series of
circular movements that govern relationships...reality is conceptualized as process, the movement of life through wholeness, connectedness, and balance

[guided by a] process pedagogy as healing [in] the three phases of belonging, understanding and critical reflection."[30–32]

Informed by its dialogue among Afrocentricity, capacity-building, and critical pedagogy, circles of support and information exchange were central to the first Graterford cohort and throughout the organization. The process of uncovering the causes of the men's rage and getting a better understanding of what personal and environmental issues were behind their offenses guided them in their transformations. The capacity they demonstrated to listen to each other's experiences was subtle yet apparent (i.e., empathy). The norms were for them to make a call or write their family and inquire about their children, or their parents (i.e., intimate outreach), or for them to talk about immediate issues and circumstances that either they or their families were facing (i.e., awareness and introspection). When possible, the workshops and various activities took place in a circle and were informed by a guided equity of information sharing (i.e., balance and reciprocity). For example, panel discussions took place with panelists sharing in the circle of all rather than sitting behind the barrier of a desk or at a set-aside kiosk at a distance.

Circles of support, two outside volunteers for each of the 24 participants, began to meet with them. Marked by reciprocity of two-way fellowship, the circle of support met and got to know the Graterford participants. Like many spiritual, healing, and leadership scholars, Reconstruction Inc. founder William Goldsby often uses the metaphor of peeling an onion.[33–35] This metaphor symbolically represents the layers and stages of introspection and discovery of where one is arrested in one's development and how that then may influence various decisions and actions. The circles of support were yet another means of engaging in this process. They frequently led to the discovery that securing SSI or another form of support may be necessary for a few of the Graterford men, as their level of psychosocial wellness made seeking work an inappropriate option in immediate reentry. They developed a resume and began to assist the cohort member with job opportunities in the community. During the last three months of the in-prison Phase I, prospective employment interviews were arranged, health appointments were made, and, when relevant, drug and alcohol treatment facilities were prioritized. These circles of support, or sacred circles of a reintegrated life, were vital resources in the principled transformations of these men and laid the foundation for reestablishing a post-prison sense of home.

1808

As previously noted, community is both place and process made up of members in a location who feel and share bonds or a sense of attachment in some way. Community members share in patterns of exchange they value and that reinforce the bonds of fellowship to one another and to place. *Homeplace* is about "the construction of a safe place where Black people [can] affirm one another and by so doing heal many...wounds."[36–39] Race is one of many characteristics that inform these valuable safe places. And the mix of these individual and group differences provides useful tensions and other resources. The resilience and healing of the Graterford cohort as it transitioned to its next steps of a new freedom needed to be in a transitional space of some kind; a homeplace of collective value for the organization and the prospective residents alike. Tensions in acquiring this homeplace were a process that reflected the potential utilities of intracommunity conflict.[40] As a community capacity-building organization, Reconstruction Inc. nurtures resources to maximize the assets of individual, familial, institutional (e.g., schools), and other constituent members of its community. This includes furthering an environment of collaboration among various local organizations, assisting them in the maximization of their assets as Reconstruction nurtures its own (see chapter 8).

What are the utilities of intracommunity conflict in capacity-building outcomes? Research has demonstrated that engaging in interpersonal communication and contributing to various mutual obligations can enhance a sense of self-esteem, value, a feeling of being cared about, and can have a powerful, protective effect on well-being and various quality of life outcomes.[41–43] We also know that "'communicative action' offers possibilities for...stakeholders in the [capacity-building] process to have their voice heard."[44–46] This includes those within the community who share a different, perhaps oppositional, view of what forms of inclusion principled transformation can and should value and engage in and thus who is included—and excluded—from the community. An early test in realizing a potential symmetry between intracommunity opposition regarding Reconstruction's reintegration mission occurred with the acquisition of a transitional space for reentry to continue the principled transformations outside the prison walls.

The May 20, 1993, Board Meeting Minutes read, "Ms. Emma Ward agreed to donate her apartment building at 1808 Tioga to Reconstruction. It has six units, and all but one of them is currently occupied....We will arrange a meeting to transfer [title]. Mr. John Wilkens is advising us to get the building appraised and to have a city building inspector look at the property."[47] Mrs. Emma Ward was a longtime Tioga neighborhood resident who had heard about Reconstruction and its program working with currently incarcerated, two-time violent offenders seeking to reenter the community. Due to some formative publicity the program received, Mrs. Ward was aware that board members were actively searching various sites and properties in North Philadelphia. When a different, suitable location had been identified, the process of acquiring this alternative property began. This included meetings of the Funding and Housing Committees of the Reconstruction Board to develop a strategy of exploration and acquisition. All this on an avenue whose Tioga name is rich with historical echoes as an especially strategic location for First Nation peoples and others as "a natural watchtown where rivers and trails converged."[48,49] This place name history understood as a pathway to new and unknown spaces, rich with uncertainty and opportunity, was named after a First Nation ethnic group known as a people who gave special priority to "knocking the rust off of the chain of friendship." to enrich alliances within their group, and between their group and others in hopes of enhancing a possible future.[50] Ms. Ward's choice was very much in keeping with the historical legacies and Ancestral expressions her decision affirmed.

The neighborhood reaction to this news was mixed at best. Reflecting the capacity-building paradox of intracommunity opposition, when hearing of having to move with the change of building ownership, current residents of the property exhibited a range of reactions from being nearly neutral to hostile opposition. Who were these new folks who may have misrepresented themselves to Mrs. Ward and tricked her into giving her building away (they were a group of criminals, remember)? And if Reconstruction was to have a new landlord, what kinds of changes might this demand in the decisions and actions of the tenants? Many surrounding neighbors also reacted with that sense of hostile curiosity. The potential for a group of violent offenders residing a very few blocks away—or perhaps even next door—led a number of residents in the neighborhood to actively protest the prospect of Reconstruction moving into the neighborhood. At the time, William had lived in the neighborhood for less than four years, in a community in which many residents had lived there for all or nearly all of their six, seven, or more decades of life. Was he an interloper or an ally? One older woman neighbor carried a picket sign saying, "Where I was born is NOT a place for Criminals!" Having been born many years before in one of the 1808 units, she was offended that it would now house violent criminals. Hers was one among many loud voices of local opposition.

In addition, many times when William would walk the two and a half blocks between his home and 1808, leaders and participants of other organizations in the neighborhood approached him. Some with veiled hostility, others with a more overt sense of envy mixed with angered surprise. They all shared with him that they had been in the neighborhood for many years longer than he had and had never received anything close to this level of commitment and resource support. They therefore expressed doubts about Reconstruction's actual mission. Perhaps it was yet another nonprofit organization fronting some sort of hostile and gentrifying corporate acquisition. Perhaps it was an organization with a desire to mask the criminal actions of its "unredeemable" criminal constituency. Perhaps it was a deceptive action of a nearby university, using a grassroots organizing narrative and structure to impose further hardship on an already marginalized community. Perhaps Reconstruction was an organizational hypocrite, who actually sought to spy and increase the levels of disproportionate incarceration among African Americans and working-class people, turning that portion of Nicetown into a new prison. Perhaps. These and many other alternatives became the organizing symbols around which a vocal opposition mounted. So, phone calls were made to insure that Reconstruction was actually an independent, nonprofit organization. Calls were made to insure that a programmatic alliance had been established with Graterford prison and that actual work with current inmates was taking place. More calls were made to see if Reconstruction and its leadership had a large sum of money and were planning to buy up and displace longtime neighbors. With all these calls, a loosely organized opposition gained power. An already marginalized neighborhood, Nicetown/Tioga was thus marked by the stigma of Black racial predominance and the declining presence of any multiclass mix that used to be the hallmark of many similar neighborhoods in generations past.[51,52] Residents in the neighborhood sought to prevent what many understandably viewed as an even further marginalization in the form of a visible criminalization at 1808. Yet during this time of opposition, other voices emerged as well.

Allies Emerge

Father Paul M. Washington was an Episcopal minister, community activist, and a man of profound character. He passed away in 2002 at the age of 81. Fittingly, there now is a small foundation in his name affiliated with Friends for Change.[53] In 1962, Father Paul was made rector at the Church of the Advocate. During the generation of his leadership, the Church of the Advocate was at the forefront of virtually every cause for justice and a broader voice and opportunity for those whom society most often marginalizes. Serving as the Episcopal Chaplain at Eastern State Penitentiary in Philadelphia, Father Paul's causes of justice advocacy included incarcerated persons, formerly incarcerated persons and their families, and community members. This led him to serve on the Reconstruction Advisory Board, where he collaborated with several other ministers from local churches, and he hosted a number of community meetings to support Reconstruction and its intended mission. In addition, a neighborhood analysis led by Patrick Murray and Phyllis Jones-Carter found that approximately one in seven neighborhood households had a family member either currently incarcerated or who had recently been released. After the report was shared, and from these community meetings, it became even clearer that many of the neighbors voicing the strongest opposition actually had family members who were incarcerated and would soon be coming home. Given the reach of the prison system, in working-class, African American neighborhoods, a substantial proportion of households would potentially benefit at least indirectly from Reconstruction's presence in the neighborhood.

In addition to these community meetings and information sharing, hearings organized by a staff member of the local City Council representative were held in an effort to mediate this dispute. The only person to consistently show up for these legal proceedings was the one young resident living in 1808, who, along with a majority of the other tenants, was many months behind on his rent. Community meetings, coupled with improved awareness of what the organization was, whom it sought to share servant-leadership with, and the support of many local ministers, reduced the opposition. They moved in after paying Mrs. Ward $1.00 for the building for her tax benefit. A few neighborhood residents were also brought into a new voice and understanding of themselves as community leaders when they stood in support of Reconstruction. Various forms of tempered inclusion were associated with the move into the neighborhood across a range of sustained reaction. Some neighbors valued the organization as a beneficial addition, a value-added resource that could garner useful resources that might not otherwise be a part of the neighborhood. There were also beliefs and actions toward the other extreme, all the way to one neighbor who actively organized others near her for more than 15 years to be hostile toward or outright oppose every organizational initiative of any kind from the acquisition and move into 1808 forward. Grassroots community development is seldom clean, that is, void of tensions of various kinds. Similar to the use-value of rage as a critical fuel for beneficial change, the tensions associated with the move into

1808 were also helpful in strengthening Reconstruction's organizational resolve and transforming opposition into allegiance and other strategic assets.

Over the next few years, 1808 was the site of a sustained momentum to further principled transformation. It was also the site of paradoxical, often unpleasant situations that, despite their challenging circumstances, contributed, if only dialectically, to the realization and renewal of Reconstruction's mission. This included a rich mixture of both hopeful and less hopeful activities and outcomes and responding to profound levels of alienation from family among some Reconstruction affiliates, and the beneficial introspections of self, family, and collective that this demanded. It also included impromptu moments of fellowship of shared music and fish frying, dance, and of unplanned overlaps in family visits. A probation violating "hot" urine and the subsequent return to jail for the probation violation for one of the earliest reentering residents, and the sustained sobriety of many other residents who adhered to their parole officer relationship and demands with self-respecting consistency. It included the drug overdose of one resident, and the overdose, and consequent death of another. These outreach efforts for fellowship among the residents were mixed with the isolation of active addiction in the stunted transformations of a few. This rich mixture showed how grassroots community capacity-building is an uncertain—and necessary—process. Just because they entered the program, all persons would not be saved or even helped. The much-feared criminalization of the neighborhood never occurred. Amid this recognition of contributions and limitations, an opportunity to document the process of Reconstruction's growth was pursued.

Challenges of Maintaining Momentum

The successful acquisition, resulting controversies of neighborhood hostility and civic engagement, and sustained maintenance of the 1808 building beginning in 1993 were a profound triumph in the early history of Reconstruction Inc. They were also symbolic of an ongoing paradox common to grassroots organizational development. William Goldsby's vision and actions, combined with those of a small critical mass of interested others he had brought together, had successfully co-created an organization marked by many assets, including:

1. A quality mission
2. Effective strategies of institutional and community engagement
3. Strong leadership
4. Consistent board membership

5. A small but loyal network of shared vision and collaboration
6. Some capital resources (i.e., a building for the reentry Phase II of the program)

However, these assets were combined with a (nearly) unpaid executive director and no paid staff, the fiscal uncertainty of having no budget to speak of and a very limited, volunteer-only means to secure an improved funding base, and a primary constituency of current and former felons socialized and institutionalized out of a collective identity for engaged actions on their own and related other groups' behalf. While the in-prison, Phase I of the program had engendered principled transformation on the part of most, if not all, participants, Reconstruction could only partially act against the individualized, institutional reentry process. Uneven and small-scale returns from grant pursuits, small-scale donation drives and other limited fundraisers, the sustained willingness of William Goldsby to use his slender resources to further the mission, and a small and devoted group of volunteers have all been vital to Reconstruction keeping its doors open. These challenges were rendered most visible when the process of reentry began in earnest and after a second within-prison cohort had begun to be screened.

In an August 4, 1994, memo to the board, Executive Director William Goldsby stated, "we must focus the rest of our time raising money and electing new board members to replace us. We need to bring on new board members to carry on our stated mission, and raise money to pay a good staff to carry out the daily functions of the program."[54] At this point the first cohort was progressing toward the completion of their first-year, within-prison Phase I of the program, and the prospects for their staggered release times across the cohort were progressing well. The 1808 property was secured. And with volunteer efforts and donated resources coordinated by the design and craftsmanship of Patrick Murray, and assisted by other members of the Housing Committee, converting it to a rooming house model was already over budget and understaffed. During that same August 1994 board meeting, the organization's program operation was budgeted at $175,000, a fiscally conservative estimate, given the multiple domains of organizational engagement. One month later at the September 1994 board meeting, the *actual* organizational balance was reported at $4,036.00.[55] Where would the other $171,000 come from?

Outreach to neighborhood churches seeking their sponsorship of one reentry program participant for a seemingly nominal amount (e.g., $5–10 per day) was met with very limited success. In marginalized neighborhoods, local area churches typically navigate their own struggles of financial solvency, especially those without a substantial commuter base of persons sustaining affiliation with their family church, or the church they grew up in.[56] As a result, it was highly unlikely that any of them would take on a primary or even tertiary support role or even make a substantial one-time donation to an organization supporting the principled transformation of two-time violent felons. Grants continued to be submitted in an increasingly scattered, piecemeal fashion. Efforts to hire a grant-writing consultant had very limited success, even as small-scale funding initiatives continued. A shared bus trip to Atlantic City here, soliciting donations, or even loans, from "friendly" organizations there. These efforts were coupled with the absolute denial of any possible consideration for funding from several sources due to not having the proper, formalized financial documentation (e.g., Board Meeting Minutes from November 17, 1994 reflect, "Black United Fund will not consider our proposal because they will only accept a true audit, and we do not have a current Charitable Organization Certificate."[57] Reconstruction Inc. was the proverbial "doughnut hole" grassroots organization: a ring made up of the above-listed assets, guided by a small, dedicated critical mass of committed few—with no financial center of any kind. A rich sweat equity of in-kind work and a set of just-in-time emergency donations have been vital resources to its success beyond survival. And despite these many challenges, organizational progress continued. It was fueled by a few people's strong commitment to realizing the organization's mission, faith in the valued contributions Reconstruction continued making beyond hardships, and the shared harvest of hope.

1995: More Triumphs, More Strain

As 1995 began, the process of preparing for Phase II, with reentry participants residing at 1808, continued. Despite the lack of funding, a group of sometimes unsteady support persons in the Phase I participants' sacred circles, and an in-prison program that required supreme effort on William Goldsby's part to maintain, uncertain progress continued. This included the organization hiring its first paid staff member. Bruce Oxford had previously worked at Hospitality House, a halfway-back residential facility for persons who had violated their parole but were not returned to jail or prison. A very gentle man deeply committed to his work, Bruce brought stability to the work of the organization and security to the men housed in 1808. Working just eight hours per week, he did individual casework and worked with the Community Advisory Committee, a short-lived group of neighborhood residents who took a more active role in nurturing formal and informal ties to the residents of 1808. The Community Relations Division (CRD) at the national office of AFSC continued to provide in-kind services, including phone access, postage for Reconstruction's mail, printing, and some copying. Other community involvements included a planned outreach to local private industry for support and their possible consideration of some form of innovative affiliation with the organization. Perhaps most ambitiously, Reconstruction was creating a documentary of these formative years.

A Lens of Contested Reflection

The Reconstruction documentary was tentatively initiated in late 1993, with the completed documentary copyrighted in 1995. The process began when William Goldsby spoke with Mr. Louis Messiah, founder and executive director of Scribe Video, a media arts organization that provides low-cost workshops and various online editing and other support services for documentary filmmaking. Through its Community Visions initiative, in the mid-1990s and into today, Scribe "teaches documentary video-making skills to members of community organizations in Philadelphia...[as] a part of Scribe's mission to explore, develop, and advance the use of [these resources and skills] as artistic tools and as tools for progressive social change."[58] Led by the efforts of Patrick Murray, with the assistance of Hakim Hudson, Lamar Rozier, and a few others, the whole two years was a teaching moment for all involved. In the process of its completion, new spaces of understanding were developed among the documentary-making volunteers. For example, many of the young Black men had never worked with "out" affirming lesbians. As in many other times, tolerance building and learning to navigate differences informed by nurturing a caring respect allowed these young men to deal with and, for many, overcome their group prejudices. Others with Scribe and from within Reconstruction had never before entered a prison. A group of neighborhood young men developed the soundtrack for the 17-minute documentary and navigated the sound-image editing process online. This was one among many ways in which simply learning to use the equipment was consistent with Reconstruction's pedagogy of principled transformation and its consistent growth as a learning organization.

> The documentary was promotional. Also, Channel 12 [public television] bought it, and aired it for about a year. [It was] for any educational setting. Any activity that deals with sociological questions about halfway houses. Crime. Incarceration. (Patrick Murray, Personal Communication, n.d.)

Described by Patrick as "far more organic and developmental, than organized, story boarded and linear," the videography and other steps were informed by Scribe's guidance and direction. And this again led to some beneficial tensions in furthering the intended contributions of the completed film. The most consistent disagreement between Reconstruction's volunteers and Scribe guidance was in site selections and "controversial" representations. How best to represent living the mission to "change [them]selves to change the world" among a primary affiliation of two-conviction, violent felons primarily from predominantly Black neighborhoods of Philadelphia? What does honest representation require? Scribe guidance advised against what many Reconstruction volunteers viewed as primary answers to these questions. No date stones on inner-city schools to reflect the contradiction of 19th-century schools being used to prepare persons for 21st-century lives. No images to conjure the federal investigation of corrupt Philadelphia police officers (who were eventually indicted for various crimes) that was ongoing at the time of the filming. No rundown houses so as not to reinforce the stereotype of them being the only thing in the ghetto. No singular White people on screen as they appear too out of place with the otherwise all-Black representatives of the Afrocentric organization.

> The context for the problems that you find in the 'hood is at least as important as personal, individual responsibility, for making your life choices. At *least* as responsible. And it's probably *more* important. Because that's society that first sets up the situation to be as it is. And maintains it through denial of any responsibility. It's just. It's *criminal.* That's the point I would have made more strongly. Leaning on *social* responsibility for the way things are. That you can't just lock people up, who are just doing what anyone would do in an unbearable situation. It's not right. It's just not right. (Patrick Murray, Personal Communication, n.d.)

Beyond the disagreements about what should and should not be taped, what should and should not be added as supplementary footage, who should and should not be presented on screen, and so on, these differences fueled the process, leading to a mediated consensus outcome that is in keeping with the whole of Reconstruction's mission. Scribe paid for it all. Various homes, rundown and otherwise, are in the video. The urban messaging of graffiti images is in the video. News footage of the MOVE tragedy from 1985 is in the video. And consistent with the holistic truths of an Afrocentric mission, Brother Joe Dudek, who is White and was a longtime board member and one of the most vital voices in nurturing the Reconstruction mission, is presented onscreen in the video. For the sake of integrity and honesty, the documentary had to be real. Yet still, on an intensity scale of representation and inclusion of the rich dialectics of oppression and libratory, or at least empowered content, Patrick stated, "On a scale of 1 to 10 [with 10 being the most intense], in the final content and cut, we got to a 6. Maybe to a 7."

Learning all the while, the documentary experience was yet another one of struggles and successes. Arguing and admissions. Disagreements and laughter. And so much more. The drawings and tagging on public walls; the beauty, politics, and culture they symbolize and nurture. The documentary took place in the midst of marked organizational changes. It stands as a valuable reflection of a profound moment of triumph in Reconstruction's second five years, even as its formative foundation furthered a slow, steady organizational implosion.

Unsettled Moments and a National Disgrace

The impact of Reconstruction's many organizational challenges listed above were combined with a local and national environment of increased hostility as the "war on drugs" was emboldened by a series of federal, state, and local legislative acts (e.g., the 1986 Anti-Drug Abuse Act and Drug Trafficking Act). The federal acts instituted mandatory minimum sentences, severely racialized the cocaine quantity ratio, and further magnified the already severe racial disproportionality of mass incarceration. They had multiple, local trickle down effects, made all the more challenging in a city and neighborhood marked by increasing hostilities in the drug trade, combined with mass corruption in street-level law enforcement.

> By the mid-1990s, the Mafia in some cities, most notably Philadelphia, had become its own worst enemy. A mob war that broke out in the City of Brotherly Love in the 1990s left several Mafia members dead...[and] seriously weakened the local La Cosa Nostra. Evidence of how the mob had changed was the fact that...John Stanfa, the Philadelphia godfather, was unable to control the young members of his gang from going on a killing rampage and triggering a senseless gang war.[59]

These heightened hostilities in organized crime also manifested in the drug trade and everyday life of African American neighborhoods, including the area Reconstruction called home. Police corruption added to this mix of federal and local legislation, high stakes, and organized crime. Perhaps the most visible example was a group of police officers in the 39th precinct. They planted drugs and other incriminating evidence in the homes, cars, and clothing of many persons, stole more than $100,000 from drug dealers, and "sent many innocent people to prison."[60] Their convictions led to more than 60 overturned cases.

During this same period, one national story captured the imagination of the media, and it was quickly translated from an individual tragedy to a symbolic rationale for increased repression. Len Bias, a University of Maryland basketball star, had recently been drafted into the National Basketball Association by the Boston Celtics, the signature franchise of the NBA. On June 19, 1986, while celebrating having been drafted and being positioned for NBA stardom, he consumed cocaine in a teammate's dorm room. That same night Len Bias died of a drug overdose. This sequence was the fuel on a "war on drugs" fire that was already more than ten years old. This literal and symbolic death "triggered a (possibly unintentional) near-genocidal attack on the African American population of the United States. Or at the very least, the systematic disenfranchisement of African American males."[61] Bias's overdose death occurred a few miles away from Philadelphia and two years prior to the formation of Reconstruction as an AFSC program. Yet because of the intersecting visibilities associated with Bias's death this triggering impacted Reconstruction Inc. in several ways.

On the heels of the Len Bias tragedy and the aftermath of the federal anti-drug and drug trafficking legislation, many oppressive collateral consequences followed. In May 1995, the U.S. Sentencing Commission released a report acknowledging the racial sentencing disparities for powder cocaine, typically associated with Whites, compared to crack cocaine, typically associated with African Americans (i.e., the crack penalty being 100 times more severe). The Sentencing Commission then recommended a severe reduction in the discrepancy.[62] Then, for the first time in U.S. history, the post-1994 Contract with America Congress overrode the Sentencing Commission's recommendation for discrepancy reduction—an override that went unchallenged by the conciliatory Clinton administration. Nearly ten years in the making, suggestions to reduce these outcomes were systematically and repeatedly ignored.[63] In the wake of Len Bias's hypervisible death, the consequences of the legislative activities that followed were varied and severe. They mixed with the Philadelphia-centered realities of the heightened challenges of intensified hostilities in organized crime, repetitions of police corruption, and the many diverse dynamics of everyday racial and socioeconomic exclusion in the City of Brotherly Love. This was the middle and late 1990s moment of Reconstruction's effort to sustain its mission of principled transformation among a small group of former felons, their family members, and a critical mass of interested others inside and outside of prison walls.

Dormancy Is Not Death

Organizations are processes and dynamic structures with many moving parts that change over time. And learning organizations are, by definition, agents of change. Their primary function is to gain new information and incorporate that information into their organizational strategies of action to more effectively engage their intended mission.[64,65] These changes are in many ways made more pronounced in small organizations, with little critical mass to absorb the shocks of even minor changes in role, strategy, or structure. They are made still more challenging within a grassroots, social movement organization seeking to build capacity on multiple levels centered in what many see as one of the most unsympathetic groups: felons with a history of multiple violent offenses. As Reconstruction Inc. moved through and grew during its second 5 years, these dynamics of organizational change included many vital victories (e.g., successful entry into Graterford prison, acquisition of a residential reentry property, completing a documentary on its formative history). But how much can a small, grassroots, reentry organization take on? What minimum infrastructure is necessary in order for it to sustain one primary initiative (i.e., within-prison reentry preparation) as it attempts to establish and manage two others (a second in-prison cohort and a reentry transitional program upon release)? All this, with virtually no paid staff, without any steady funding, and informed by controversies and collaborative tensions, both large and small. Whatever the necessary minimum infrastructure threshold of organizational efficiency might be,[66,67] Reconstruction did not have it. Being a resource-constrained organization, its constraints included being limited in its capacity for self-promotion and other forms of solicitation for financial support.

Yes, Philadelphia was perhaps the perfect site for this formative reentry movement to be initiated in 1988—the birthplace of the U.S. prison system and of the Quaker questioning of penal social control.[68,69] Yes, 1988 was a valuable time for this process to begin, just after a set of legislative actions that exploded mass incarceration and more than a decade before any department of corrections conducted any research identifying key needs of former felons upon their release.[70,71] Yes, it is difficult to doubt that this effort being initiated by a former felon motivated by the echoes of the 1985 MOVE tragedy, and realizing his vision in collaboration with a Quaker organization (AFSC) was an Ancestrally informed intersection of time, space, and mission. Yes, to these truths and many more. Quality leadership, engaging a quality mission, with a critical mass of a few committed others, is a great deal. But it was not enough. Reconstruction Inc. had collectively reached beyond its grasp. Thus, as 1995 ended and 1996 began, a more pronounced change than anything that had previously occurred began. It would, in effect, be a movement into organizational dormancy.

Markers of Decline

Dormancy is a process that occurs regularly in nature. Bears hibernate. Caterpillars build cocoons in order to transform. And in the healing process and growth for plants and animals alike, forms of dormancy naturally occur. In community development and grassroots organization building, a similar social movement process takes place as change over time in community-based organizations is seldom linear. Lofland (1979) suggested, "white-hot mobilization is self-terminating.[72] Members grow weary" as the ebb and flow in the projects, pace, and levels of mobilization vary over time.[73,74] "Timelines for...activities must be flexible, [since] unexpected developments can either enhance or thwart plans, [and] bursts of activity around a given project may be followed by periods of dormancy."[75–77] This was occurring as the successes and challenges of 1995 came to the year's end.

In December of 1995, William Goldsby journaled about a set of factors—both personal and political—informing Reconstruction and his and others' relationship to its mission. These included his reflections on the Million Man March of October 1995 and the theme of atonement that informed Min. Louis Farrakhan's keynote speech and the fact that no organization emerged to galvanize the justice possibilities of that moment of mobilization.[78,79] Closer to home, Mazie Abu-Jamal, the son of political prisoner and death row inmate Mumia Abu-Jamal, had worked in the Reconstruction office earlier that summer, which returned William to links between the MOVE tragedy and his original motive for coming to Philadelphia with the family consequences of the prison industrial complex. And just as Reconstruction was being recognized in *The Philadelphia Inquirer* and *EBONY* magazine, one of the organization's central figures was rearrested for a felonious crime and sentenced to ten years. "Time, space and silence," he wrote, "must be addressed, dealt with, understood and rethought" (Personal journal, December 24, 1995).[80] This was followed up on January 31, 1996, with the thought, "Our people are held hostage with the idea that survival is more important than liberation."[81]

The social justice organization member weariness that Lofland (1979), Olney (2005), and others write of is a product of many things. A large mission, dialectically driven capacity-building engaged by a small and smaller number of sustained affiliates, is difficult to sustain.[82,83] Another indicator of Reconstruction's movement toward dormancy is reflected in the ten-year count pattern in the organization's more than 100 archival documents that have survived (see Table 5.1). The consistency of documented activities among the board, executive committee, and organizational programs is reflected in the newly incorporated organization, with 1992 (the year following incorporation) being the most active. With the development and refinement of the organization's institutional collaboration with Graterford prison under-way, 1993 was also a very active period. Then what followed was a marked decline of 50% or more in the following two years and a more than 50% decline thereafter. With so few doing so much, perhaps some form of decline was predictable, if not impossible to avoid.

Table 5.1 Count of Archive Documents by Year

1989	1990	1991	1992	1993	1994	1995	1996	1997	1998
0	2	6	33	28	10	14	5	3	0

Across these years of decline, there were fewer references to grants in development, recently submitted, or currently under review in the board meeting minutes. Fewer and fewer planning activities were taking place, and informal, small-scale fund-raisers were also reported less frequently (e.g., shared bus trips, exhibiting the Reconstruction documentary for coffee shop discussion and donations). References to committee work reflected an increasing strategic ambiguity, and they were increasingly centered in the decisions and actions of the executive director and less and less in the progress of (the all-volunteer) committee initiatives. This was followed by fewer meetings and less attendance at meetings that did take place. As a result, intensification in the oligarchic character of organizational leadership occurred and reduced leadership diffusion and collective accountability. And a tension arose between William Goldsby and Graterford administration after William made a comment about the purpose of prison and the potential for various transformations during a Fight for Lifers event. His comments were viewed as inflammatory and anti-administration. Consequently, he, individually, and Reconstruction as an organization were banned from Graterford for more than a year.

Three committee reports from the final Board meeting minutes prior to dormancy, March 26, 1997, are a telling record and moment of the Reconstruction mission.

Housing: Patrick and Joe reported that the big question is what to do with the house for it not to be a financial liability. One interim thing to do is lease the property to PUT (People United Together). Also Laurali Wade, an associate of Arthur Clark in association with New Directions would like to lease the property but would like it for long term. No decision was made. Suggestion was made to stop spending money on 1808 West Tioga, except only to run the office with voice mail. Patrick made a proposal to contract Bahiya and Shafik to do a PATH for Reconstruction. Everyone was in favor of this plan which entails setting a goal and mapping out a focused visual plan that would get us there. This is an excellent ideal if we stay on track. The date for this PATH to take place is May 3, 1997 at 1808.

Financial: Lucinda reported that the past due utilities total [is] in the range of $4,000.00. We have less than $1,000.00 in the bank. The gas and electric are the most delinquent bills. We also need to get insurance on the property.

Fund-Raising: Bahiya reported that she had spoken to Millie Bernstein of the Public Welfare Foundation and that it did not look promising [for] the proposal...she had submitted. Millie said that it would be hard to sell us to the foundation because we have not been able to maintain staff; we do not seem solvent. Also they have funded us for two years and we cannot show that we can secure other funds to match....Millie gave a list of other funding sources which may be helpful....Bob discussed building a mailing list. He...also reported that there are two proposals he has submitted. One to Bread & Roses for $10,000.00 and The William Penn Foundation for $15,000.00. We should have an answer from both of these proposals the first week in April.

Next Meeting: Wednesday, April 23, 1997 @ 1808 W. Tioga @ 6 pm.[84]

Neither the Bread and Roses grant nor the William Penn Foundation grant was funded. Yes, what has been and remains at the core of the mission of Reconstruction Inc. is nurturing collaboration among diverse people living the helpful, hopeful lives that Ms. Bessie Williams spoke of to begin this chapter. Yes, the organization's second 5 years furthered a vital set of principled transformations to strengthen that foundation among former felons, their families, and a critical mass of interested others both inside and outside of prisons. Yes, William Goldsby's vision and actions, combined with those of a few others he brought together and that gravitated to Reconstruction, had successfully co-created an organization marked by many assets. Still, from the spring of 1997 to the summer of 2001, there are no surviving archival records of any kind. No board meeting minutes. No minutes from the Executive, Housing, or Fund-Raising committees. No flyers of participation in community events of any kind. By 1998, Reconstruction Inc. had truly entered a period of organizational dormancy.

Maintaining Mission as an Organization Changes

Dormancy, like the paradox of intracommunity conflict as discussed previously, was also a dialectical capacity-building resource. Njia and Ma'at are the consciousness and strategies of action of victorious thought.[85,86] Yet the specifics of their grassroots organizational expression are in formation, and their relationships to and with dynamics of momentum toward growth and "organizational efficiency" is an uncertain process. This analysis of Reconstruction's second 5 years explored the how and how much of these dynamics and demonstrated a living, grassroots pedagogy for 21st-century Black urban struggle. One essential element of this pedagogy is how youth are engaged in it and by it. Before considering the bridge of time from the dormancy of the late 1990s to the organization's current best practices (see chapter 7), we assess Reconstruction's youth program in the next chapter, LEAD (Leadership, Education, Advocacy and Development). By doing so, we'll show how Reconstruction has also engaged a pedagogy of principled transformation to further its mission by helping youth impacted by mass incarceration live helpful, hopeful lives.

Endnotes Toward Principled Transformation

Extending from the collaborative contradictions of Reconstruction's second 5 years, three possibilities toward principled transformation emerge:

- Transformative Trainings—It would be beneficial for transformative trainings to focus on the many-layered connections between spirituality, social justice, and methods for self- and organizational criticism. Developing human spiritual potential, both independent of and informed by religious influences, is essential.

- Resolving Rage—Actions toward the resolution of rage include individual and collective demonstrations of the human and spiritual resources always available with or without foundation or government funds. Peace building beyond the mediation of tensions often requires little more than time, caring patience, therapeutic craft, and a safe space.

- A New Justice—Nurturing a new justice paradigm invites prioritizing policies for sustainable, diverse, and egalitarian resource sharing among different communities and classes of people. Spiritually, materially, and communally we have what we need to build on history, heal, and live this new justice.

Part II, Chapter Six

"And a Little Child Shall Lead Them"

Active participation of youth is essential to reenergizing and sustaining the civic spirit of communities. Through skill development in the areas of collaboration and leadership, and the application of these capacities to meaningful roles in community, youth...play a fundamental role in addressing the social issues that...impact their lives and those of future generations.

Michael Hancock

African American youth are not passive victims of social neglect. Many find remarkable ways to struggle collectively to improve the quality of their lives...community spaces [must] foster revolutionary hope and radical imaginations for African American youth...increasingly neighborhood-based organizations...recognize the role care, healing and justice play in developing young people as well as fostering strong vibrant community life.

Shawn A. Ginwright

Organizational development, including entering a dormant period and reestablishing activities thereafter, is seldom, if ever, linear. Both in terms of the self-concept of individual members and the organizational culture and grassroots movement dynamics, the ebb and flow of change is interactive and uncertain as is the means that momentum sometimes provides.[1,2] As 1997 ended, Reconstruction was an organization in name, guided by the unpaid leadership of its founder and former executive director, though there was no board and there were no officers. In need of income, William began to work at Hospitality House, a halfway-back facility for men who had violated their probation or parole but were not sent back to prison. Yet, without an organizational infrastructure of any kind, William remained steadfast in his desire to establish and sustain initiatives to enrich a sense of caring and collective ownership in the neighborhood. Children and young adults are an invaluable resource in the capacity-building process, and their radical imaginations are among the most valued assets in Reconstruction Inc. From early in the organization's history, Reconstruction has consistently included youth. The organization creates and sustains leadership roles through which their contributions are respected in an environment of intergenerational equity. In Reconstruction, youth nurtures the organization's mission both inside and outside of their families, which are at the core of the organization. And, most fundamentally, Reconstruction Inc. is a family-centered, capacity-building organization. Somewhat less clear in the preceding chapters is how Reconstruction engages (in) an intergenerational dialogue to nurture the present and future of children and young adults' imaginings of hope in a possible future resting within each person who has ever had any contact with the organization for any length of time. To do so, Reconstruction places great value in the active participation of youth.

Like all organizations, Reconstruction is informed by its contexts, both large and small. It operates in a challenging neighborhood, marked by troubling characteristics that have come to define the lived experience of the urban core of Philadelphia and many other cities. Yet, true to much community capacity-building, that same neighborhood is also rich with assets and the means to empower them to improve local quality of life, as well as those beyond it. This spatial tension between challenges and assets, present troubles and collective empowerment, is also an essential part of the resources and tensions of placing youth at the center of any intergenerational dialogue. The local, lived experience of this dialogue is reflected in the strained neighborhood environments of social disorder and unsupervised youth. It is also reflected in the many ways youths come together to enrich social order in an environment of collaborative excellence. In Reconstruction, youth are neither "passive victims of social neglect" nor passive recipients of older adult decision making and patterns of engagement.[3] Rather, youth are critical agents of change, central to enriching the organization's mission. By exploring its history of youth-oriented initiatives, this chapter details the strategies of action shaping how the care and healing necessary for young people's voices and visions to be heard and valued are expressed within and beyond the years of the organization's five youth initiatives.

A Youth Focus Begins

> I want to speak on the word "ostracize." Most of us are very shocked walking the streets when we see a young Black man. White people. They move over when they see a young Black man. A lot of people in here would do the same thing. We talk about hatred. And we say don't harbor hatred. I'm angry. And unfortunately or fortunately, I've learned how to deal with my hatred. I've learned how to deal with my anger. But, for the most part, young Black men have not. At this point, I want to offer us a *solution*. (William Goldsby, Personal Communication, n.d.)

In his May 1988 call to action at the American Friends Service Committee's MOVE Memorial Event, William Goldsby recognized the developmental process of life-course marginalization and verbal and behavioral fear-as-disrespect in the taken-for-granted behaviors in public space. Writing about a "cosmopolitan canopy" on the same theme, Elijah Anderson (2011) explores the urban core of Philadelphia, and what continues to be a primary means of interracial engagement and impositions of stigma in public space that are often compounded by youth. "Beyond the ghetto racial inequalities that persist in less visible but nonetheless potent forms...racial profiling is a routine occurrence for black males, and black females are often insulted in racially degrading terms. The stigma of blackness, compounded by the contagion of ghetto stereotypes" continue to inform the behavior of many, shaping race, rage, respect, and civility in everyday life.[4] Consistent with William's call to action, early in Reconstruction's history focus was given to the question: How can an environment of opportunities be nurtured to respond (well) to the challenges of race, youth, and stigma within and beyond public space? Within the answer to that question: How can rage be a valued asset for the capacity-building development and principled transformation of the young? The organization's answers to these questions actually began years before dormancy with its first youth initiative in 1994.

On June 2, 1994, the Executive Committee of Reconstruction Inc. held its regular meeting at 1501 Cherry Street at the Friends Center. At this meeting early in their fourth year of independent incorporation, the small group of volunteers representing each of the standing committees of the organization (Executive, Funding, Program, Housing, and Public Relations) was on the agenda to report on the present level of progress of each. The charge of the Program Committee was to address everything from the development of a personnel policy for the soon-to-be-hired staff members Funding Committee resources would allow to be hired, to the design and development of resource partnerships with other organizations and social service agencies to assist affiliates in successfully navigating their parole, treatment, and the related activities necessary for a sober and sane tempo of reentry to be successfully established. Consistent with the organizational emphasis on structure, the agenda was followed as the Program Committee was third and, as scheduled, provided the third report, including a youth project as Item C.

The Executive Committee's goal for this youth project was to formalize a means of bringing youth together, to provide youth-initiated project development and the creation of valued, sustained means of formal and informal fellowship (i.e., preventive), and to create youth-oriented alternatives for young persons who had entered into the criminal justice system (i.e., juvenile justice reentry). These goals were organized with Nicetown-Tioga neighborhood youth in mind, along with any other local youths who might also value a new opportunity: nurturing a vision of themselves as agents of social change. When the entire board met on August 4 of that year, Hakim Hudson, then 22 years old noted, "We're working to establish a support group for young African American men with children. I'm also working on video production with [Patrick] Murray, Steplight, James, and two facilitators."[5] These first steps began an initiative that would bridge the dormancy period of the organization, Reconstruction's first, formal youth initiative, Brothers Strengthening Families (BSF).

From the moment members of the first Graterford cohort began sharing their backgrounds and present concerns, engaging with their families became a critical request and requirement for their continued participation within the program (see chapter 5). There was an early recognition of living within and beyond whatever shame, reticence, or other emotions of immobility may have been informing their real and imagined child-related hesitations. It was essential for them to place greater value on their recognition that they were not the only persons bearing the consequences of past actions that had led to their incarceration. Their families were as well. And with all but two of the first cohort members having one or more children, the intergenerational realities of their situations and the organizational mission of principled transformation became more vivid as they progressed in the Reconstruction curriculum. With that recognition, furthered by Hakim Hudson's willingness with BSF, the Program Committee began the formative steps toward a sustained youth initiative.

Leadership

For Reconstruction, demonstrating leadership in organizing children and young adults began well before the formal youth program was launched. The "servant-leader" is the leadership model in each of Reconstruction's programs. "It is the leader who models service by humbly serving the led, rather than expecting to be served by them.[6,7] Therein is the paradox of servant-leadership. Leader-modeled service...tends to be contagious so that followers of servant-leaders are inspired to pass on the gift."[8] In effect, to serve is to lead, when the individuals engaging in the activity understand themselves first as a servant to and in a process with others to further the ongoing exchange between individual, familial, organizational, and communal goals. Driven by a willingness to engage in principled actions, leadership is the art of mobilizing with others in shared struggle to achieve shared ends.[9] Grounded in this model, a youth initiative began.

Like many good ideas for fellowship, Brothers Strengthening Families (BSF) began with a general goal rich with potential and complexities resting beyond the goal's simple core. Within the Tioga neighborhood, William and Hakim realized that there were many young men with one or more children. When dealt with individually, the everyday tasks and challenges of relating to the equally young mothers and assisting in the rearing of these children was sometimes leading to problematic interactions and outcomes. To navigate the challenges of young fatherhood more creatively, a collective of these young men began to meet. From defining masculinities to "creepin'" and sexual fidelity.

From relationship building with maternal grandmothers to the politics of reentry employment. BSF provided an outlet for these young men to know themselves and each other better. BSF encouraged them to come to an understanding of their places of vulnerability and challenge, disappointments and triumph alike, and how all of these fit into an understanding of self, of BSF, and how the approximately 25 members related to the larger mission of Reconstruction. On any given Friday night at their meetings, six to fourteen Black fathers, from 17 to 25 years old, would meet at the Reconstruction office for fellowship. At the same time that BSF began, the documentary for Reconstruction was being developed. In the footage that was being compiled, the consults and assistance from Scribe Video, the blocking of coverage, and the influences both in front of and behind the camera, youth were an important part of every dimension of the documentary's capacity-building progress. Then the second step in the progress of youth leadership was the formation of the 20W Club.

20W Club and Divas With Attitude
Reconstruction clarified what and how engagement with youth might continue as a formal program or other initiative. As William recently recounted, "I was there and grinding on my block...I was being led by my Ancestors and the God of my knowing to move forward, talk with, and organize the youth on the block by giving what I had. And Patrick was willing to do the same. This was the genesis of these groups." During this time, these youth allied with others from a nearby neighborhood and formed what they named the 20W Club, with 20th Street and Westmoreland Avenue being a nearby intersection of their north-central Philadelphia neighborhoods. It was a break dancing and affirming fellowship that came together and developed into still other initiatives. These included young girls seeking to affirm their voices and visions, forming Divas With Attitude.

The 20W Club and Divas With Attitude then collaborated to develop and self-publish a newsletter of their writings and reporting, based on activities and events that were taking place in their lives both local and beyond. What began with a willingness to meet a group of young males where they were, developed into a momentum of diverse expressions of youth community capacity-building. William and Patrick soon recognized that for nearly two years they were babysitting these youth on Saturday mornings, including serving them breakfast. From this, William realized that for a youth-centered initiative to succeed, parents must be involved in the process of neighborhood and personal property revitalization. In board meeting minutes of January 13, 2002, Board Member

Butch Cottman "asked that [the organization] develop a plan for work with Uber Street youth in the next few months, which he suggested could be characterized as our 'Spring Offensive.' Our plans might include getting tickets for the kids to the Sixers' games, drug and alcohol seminar for kids, or participation in repairing all the distressed porches on Uber Street."[10] Leisure, health-wellness and prevention, and civic engagement alternatives were being considered. A year earlier, in 2001, William had recommended to the newly reformed Board of Directors the opportunity to take on these youth-oriented successes as a formally sponsored organization initiative. As William recounted,

> I presented the idea of this initiative, along with the newsletter 20W and DWA had produced. It was harshly shot down. I quietly and personally realized how much I didn't fight for what I really wanted...[At that time] I was in a deep depression because I didn't know what I was doing with Reconstruction. And those around me didn't know how to rescue me...[Too often] we submit to the loudest voice in a group; the two members on the board who opposed exploring this project. Others on the board didn't express their voices. These same two members were well-versed in Roberts Rules of Order, which gave them even more power and control over me in running the organization. (William Goldsby, Personal Communication, n.d.)

And with that decision of the newly formed Reconstruction board, a moment and momentum of youth-oriented organizing was lost. Yet this was still a moment of profound resilience in the Reconstruction mission. Personal resilience, when William's willingness progressed beyond the personal challenge of the board choosing not to support this effort and his disappointment in himself for not fighting harder for what he then felt mattered most. Community resilience was beyond the uncertainty of parental oversight and limited parental participation throughout the 20W and DWA activities. Still, the youth collective continued its progress for a time, despite the lack of support as it transitioned into a second vision of itself. Organizational resilience was beyond the absence of a larger adult infrastructure to help guide youth actions and foster broader opportunities. Beyond the internal rejection of the board of these initiatives as an idea worthy of their support, in that act the newly formed board did assert a voice and gave itself a renewed sense of investment in organizational leadership. In spite of this decision, a multilevel resilience occurred, enriching a new expression of youth-oriented participation. What soon followed was the collective construction of the Club House.

The Club House
The third youth-oriented initiative in Reconstruction began when a chance observation became a means of structuring youth energy and effort. One day in the winter of 2001, William saw a group of young boys from the neighborhood searching for

old plywood. Rather than scolding them in the moment or, worse yet, scolding them and then reporting what he had seen to a parent or guardian, he engaged them about their motives and intended use of the wood. A vital dimension of nurturing sanctuary is meeting a rich diversity of persons where they are, complete with their motives and actions. William learned that their goal was to build a fort—one among the more universal boyhood activities that exists. William then suggested a couple of alternatives for the boys to consider: other wood they could secure, other means to secure it, and other ways they could collectively achieve their fort-building goal. And with those alternatives, before any formal organizing, began a youth-oriented initiative under the guidance of Reconstruction. Patrick Murray, an Ivy League-trained, master's degree architect, contractor, and master carpenter, is an original and longtime Reconstruction member. As Patrick recalls,

> [The Club House] evolved by the kids themselves. They were tearing boards off of vacant houses to make a Club House. And William stopped them and said, "No. Let's do this [instead]. Let's make a Club House. But you've got to get organized [first]." So William used it as an opportunity to teach organization skills. How to show up. How to organize [them]selves. How to run a meeting. How to let everybody give their input, and so forth. (Patrick Murray, Personal Communication, n.d.)

The Club House (circa 2004).
Photo Credit: Patrick Murray

Structure. Collaboration. Access to voicing one's vision in an equitable environment. A set of strategies for generating additional resources. Dedication to
follow through, guided by a framework of reciprocity, and the collective
achievement these shared assets of process and protocol created. All of these
and more—all, central pillars in the foundation of relational resilience in Reconstruction and its mission, from its AFSC origins through this period of dormancy and beyond—were on display in this youth-led construction project.

The youth learned how to select officers, keep notes, save their money, and
struggle with difficult decisions. The learned lessons of unexpected allies, when
the neighbor they thought would be most sensitive to their cause was not, and
another neighbor who expressed little liking for them and their efforts had no
problem with them building the Club House adjacent to her home. William ran
their meetings for two hours each Saturday morning. Patrick guided their building progress, which was also for two hours each Saturday. These two project
domains continued for more than two years. Both by accident (i.e., William observing the youth as they were collecting plywood) and by design, a set of decisions and some unintended actions of near-neighbors led the site of the fort to
be right next door to William and Patrick's home. Goal specified. Location decision made. A process for securing materials developed. A structure of leadership established. Design decisions begun. All the while, it was principled
leadership that was actually the truest "product" under construction. Patrick,
the building skillset mentor and unofficial project manager, continued:

> So, we structured it together. They set up a formal [organizational] structure. President.
> Vice-president. Treasurer. Even in meetings, William makes sure that everybody has
> their say. So, in the design, we did the same thing. First we talked about what everyone
> thought the Club House should be. And then we had them draw a picture of what they
> wanted the Club House to look like. And we [built consensus,] taking all of their ideas
> and making them into one thing. And then we built a model of the design, so that they
> could get an idea of what they were building, what it was going to look like when it was
> done. And then, we built it. And they actually did most of the work, except for the
> roof....I was just sort of helping them. The youngest of them was probably nine. I
> think the oldest was thirteen or fourteen....I think it worked because they started out
> with motivation. It was THEIR project. That's what they wanted to do. (Patrick
> Murray, Personal Communication, n.d.)

From development to construction, each necessary skillset was modeled
and engaged. This included Patrick showing the youths how to build a complete
model of the physical space using Popsicle sticks, rice paper, and glue. The Club
House, which still stands today, represents a critical triumph in demonstrating

the capacity-building process at the core of Reconstruction's mission. As Patrick notes, "The Lifers (i.e., the Fight for Lifers program of Reconstruction) donated a bunch of framing lumber. That's where we got most of the wood. The rest of it, we bought. And one of the guys on the block donated the Plexiglas for the windows, because he worked at a Plexiglas place." Sharing the initiative's diffusion, Patrick and the Club House group boarded up the windows of vacant houses on the block. Then other neighbors bought paint and drew pictures of curtains and flowers on the plywood nailed in the windows. An outreach for collective participation engaging neighbors in new and caring ways. Fundraising. Intergenerational collaboration. Yes, an organization anchored in the process of reentry and reintegration and the dynamics of mass incarceration. And also keenly aware of the ways in which the formal and the informal can be brought together within and across generations.

All the while, each of the young boys participating in the Club House initiative was also regularly being approached. And some were pulled into the drug trade. Still, the initiative stands as a lived experience of how terms such as "social disorder," and "unsupervised youth" can be responded to with the forthright praxis of youth civic engagement and collective efficacy. In a process they define, young persons can be nurtured to achieve collective success, creating and using an iconic symbol of youth: a fort; a sanctuary. Built of their sweat equity, in their own name. After it was completed, they held youth-serving block parties in the space, charging and collecting admission, and renting it out for other gatherings. They turned it into a means of still more skill development in collective property management. In every dimension of its definition, the Club House was high quality, youth-driven capacity-building, and it served as a spark for still more Reconstruction-sponsored youth initiatives.

Education

After leadership, education is the second major domain informing youth-oriented initiatives within Reconstruction. Similar to that of the larger organization, Reconstruction's youth-oriented initiatives have also been defined by its pedagogy of principled transformation. How does its spiritually grounded, egalitarian exchange of information enrich an individual, familial, and organizational culture of resilience? And here, we consider children and young adults. The examples of the leadership domain of Brothers Strengthening Families, 20W Club, Divas with Attitude, and the Club House collective also exemplify the educational priorities that inform youth outreach and engagement and were the precursors to the organization's fourth youth program: Leadership, Education, Advocacy and Development (LEAD).

A Group Begins

As William continued his work with Hospitality House, the Alumni Ex-Offenders Association (AEA) began. Founded in 1998, AEA first met in Hospitality House, as many of these men were former House residents. Meeting there was a step forward for them, recognizing that these former residents were returning to this place of secondary incarceration voluntarily, rather than having been sent there by the court system, to help move them from reentry to reintegration. And the men currently in Hospitality House were also taking a step forward, as they were regularly exposed to a valued group of men who had very recently been in the role and place they currently were and who had successfully completed the Hospitality House program. They began to understand better what the process of a sustained, sober reentry was, and what moving from reentry to reintegration was actually going to demand of them and of their families.

As AEA continued to grow, a first group of young adults, 20 to 25 years old, began to attend AEA meetings at about the same time. They had each been incarcerated for three to five years in state prisons or boot camp, and as they participated in AEA, they valued how their experiences and reentry priorities were both similar to and different from those of older AEA members. These young women and men from diverse family backgrounds, and with different criminal histories and reintegration challenges, had come to AEA through various pathways and helped refine Reconstruction's mission. They began to establish a distinct sense of a young adult collective identity that was in line with that of the larger AEA goals, yes. Yet they were informed by a different purpose. As they continued participating in AEA, they reflected on their own recent movement out of adolescence and into early adulthood, which led them to begin thinking and talking about a more preventive mission. Leadership, Education, Advocacy and Development (LEAD) tied together a set of leadership strands that had been developing for many years. The original mission of LEAD was to enhance members' facilitation skills by running groups whose criminal justice pipeline participation had begun, which covered court preparation and how to make their time serve them, rather than them serving time, regardless of where in the system they were placed.

From their early affiliation forward, these first LEAD members and those who would follow them later were informed by the larger Reconstruction mission and its focus on the reciprocity between individual and global change. They were taught that to facilitate a group with an agenda is the same as facilitating one's life. And that facilitating one's life means that, like a meeting, a day should have a plan. That plan should be informed by an intended outcome, should follow that plan toward the achievement of that outcome, should have some endpoint review period of assessment, and some sort of specification for follow up and follow through in preparing for the next interval. Whether that interval is the next meeting of the group, or the next day in one's life, it should be defined by purpose, with the plan helping to fulfill that purpose. The name itself, defined by these young former offenders, LEAD, was guided by their goal to have each of the four components—leadership, education, advocacy, and development—be realized and internalized by each person who came into any contact with LEAD. Whether that contact was for a single hour, a single meeting, or years of sustained affiliation in multiple roles, the goal of these original members was for the depth and detail of exposure to vary, even as the method and mission remained the same. Once that happens, the individual's, their families, and the community's capacities are enhanced. Established with the first group of eight young adults, this plan and purpose has remained consistent throughout LEAD's history.

> The main focus of the L.E.A.D. project is to prevent young people from entering into the adult prison system by training them in political and life skills that can motivate them to organize in their communities. [To do so] L.E.A.D. facilitators also do in-service training. These young adults put their skills to use in service of the organization and individuals with whom [the organization] works.[11]

To do so, in 2002, these young adults in AEA were contracted to facilitate life skills and court preparation classes at the Northeast Treatment Center (NET), a juvenile detention facility. And less than one year later in 2003, first six, then eight, then nine core members of this new collective decided to call themselves LEAD. With this name, the group began to establish and sustain an identity and self-understanding of how its membership, mission, and intended contributions did and did not overlap with that of AEA. With LEAD now underway, they developed a curriculum for the young men at the NET. As they first entered, and then continued their NET participation, their understanding of the potential for their contributions, along with a more complete sense of independence, grew. In a decision that both affirmed their individual and collective authority and autonomy, while simultaneously undermining their commitment to LEAD's mission and to the larger organization, the contract with the NET led them to be both LEAD members and paid employee consultants facilitating

these courses for the 10- to 17-year-old clients housed at the NET. This partici-
pation-for-pay consultant arrangement occurred prior to any of them providing
any substantive investment of unpaid sweat equity into the formative program.
And as their commitment to compensation remained, their interest in nurturing
the LEAD mission waned. But the consult role did enrich a number of capacity-
building components within the fledgling LEAD program.

From a resource and outreach standpoint, this included renewal of LEAD's
NET contract and the administrative skill-building that was associated with the
management of those resources. They entered into a contract with the University of Pennsylvania's Neighborhood Youth Network (NYN) to facilitate leadership development workshops (an adaptation of their NET curriculum) at
three of UPenn's Youth Opportunity Centers. Thus, it included an expansion
of the youth curriculum these formerly incarcerated young adults had developed, under the guidance of William and the older AEA membership. Part social learning and prevention. Part therapeutic and emotional intelligence. Part
legal process and critical awareness. This multidimensional, prevention-oriented
curriculum would now be presented to a larger number of youth.

The hope was to help move these adjudicated youth from the "cradle to
prison pipeline" they were beginning to be vested in into an alternative, capacity-building pipeline of civic socialization, progressively nurturing their individual and collective possibilities for a new justice. Affiliation with the
Neighborhood Youth Network brought LEAD into contact with a coalition of
youth programs, who's "mission is to ensure that those who wish to offer youth
workforce development services are efficiently connected with the youth that
can make the best use of those services."[12] However, when the funding access
of these LEAD members outpaced their establishment of a leadership infrastructure and was greater than their clear and collective resource management
protocol and moved beyond their mechanisms for resource renewal, task follow
through lessened, participation willingness reduced, and membership waned.
Consistency in the fulfillment of their first contract with the NET, much less
the much newer NYN contract, declined, and the first group of LEAD members was nearing its end. Yet in the persons and process of this decline, the
seeds for a new season were being planted.

Advocacy

To advocate is to act on behalf of a person, group, or idea in order to further
change. As within the larger organization, within LEAD, for leadership to be

valued and education as "the practice of freedom" to be engaged, advocacy is essential, in other words, participating as a political actor, motivated by values of principled change, to help realize new and more just interpersonal and institutional outcomes. Advocacy is an especially vital resource for principled transformation, especially when organizing youth. From its origin to now, as the first group of LEAD members recognized, advocacy is a valuable means of nurturing a shared sense of the possible in the achievement of the LEAD mission. Focusing on the "critical social capital" central to the capacity-building process, Ginwright (2007) states:

> Critical social capital is facilitated by intergenerational advocacy that challenges negative concepts about Black youth; it is developed by building a collective racial and cultural identity, and sustained by cultivating an understanding of personal challenges as political issues. [It] departs from traditional notions of social capital by placing a greater focus on the collective dimensions of community change, and it centers on how ... political awareness serve[s] as [an] important community and social resource for youth.[13]

As demonstrated in the examples presented, LEAD did, and continues to, engage in initiatives that do much more than (just) challenge negative concepts about Black youth and narrowly engage in individual and collective identity enrichment. And advocacy cannot be and has never been solely, or even primarily, a conceptual exploration nor an idealized strategy of action. In Reconstruction and LEAD, advocacy is a spiritual invitation, a process, or demand of affiliation. Enter. Grow. Lead. Learn. Transform. These are the words of practice that inform how all affiliates, including youth and young adults, are civically engaged within and beyond the organization, to both contribute to and benefit from the program's critical social capital.

To facilitate the growth portion of this process, the recognition that advocacy is ever present is key. Consistent with a cultural, critical pedagogy and reflected in the organization's core curriculum and in LEAD's young adult-led initiatives, advocacy is MUCH more than organizing a media campaign or public speaking or leafleting on the street. Rather, it follows in the Freirian tradition of "education [as] the practice of freedom, the means by which men and women deal critically and creatively with reality and discover how to participate in the transformation of their world."[14] And from this, a group of young people came into LEAD, providing it with new vigor and a renewed sense of mission. With this, the transformation in which Freire and other critical pedagogues center the process of education was aptly reflected in the formation of LEAD's second membership group.

Broadening Inclusion

In 2004, as the participation of the first LEAD group waned, five of those core members continued to express interest in and contribute to realizing still more of the potential they and others saw in LEAD. From within the organization under the recently re-formed board, along with the Alumni Ex-Offenders Association and Fight for Lifers, LEAD became one of Reconstruction's three primary programs. Other young people continued to come through the doors of 1808. Increasingly, persons seeking simply to participate in a justice mission who had no criminal or incarceration background began to participate. This included neighborhood youth who had participated in the Club House collective and were now aging into their late teens, youth from the greater Philadelphia area who had heard about one or another program or activity of the organization, former offenders, and college students from Penn State University interested in participating in off-campus activism.

The means by which they heard about Reconstruction and LEAD varied greatly. Some were friends of friends from the neighborhood. Others had an extended family member who had participated in one of the short-term LEAD interventions at the NET. Some had parents who had friends in the Church of the Advocate, which Father Paul Washington led for many years and had served on the original Advisory Board of Reconstruction years earlier. Still others had become aware of Reconstruction through the struggle to establish the residential transition space at 1808 more than a decade before, when they were very small children at the time and had grown to a place of appreciation of Reconstruction's mission and longevity. A few new persons. Many different pathways. What they shared was age similarity and a willingness to first understand, grow to appreciate, and live with and through the four terms that made up this youth-oriented program of Reconstruction Inc. In this second membership group, the primary focus was to learn how to establish agendas, how to facilitate groups, and host political discussions. This work was less focused on the first group's consultant model and more on the development of an organizational praxis of advocacy, that is, reciprocity and conceptual clarity and the actions of change these concepts demanded. This capacity-building praxis was executed in four critical ways. First, this group of young people recognized the value of building bonds across the penal divide, when members of the original core befriended and organizationally engaged with persons of shared mission, many of whom had not had any contact with the criminal justice system. This broadened inclusion provided a new richness from which the collective could draw and progress.

Second, this group refined a process of social justice collaboration with other young people's organizations. This included a new collaboration with Geo-Clan, which, in 2004, was a fledging initiative of young people who shared information in new and nontraditional ways, outside of the mainstream media, and organized for social change. Consistent with the larger Reconstruction mission and the focus of LEAD both then and now, as their current Web site specifies, GeoClan.com declared its commitment "to bringing fresh voices to the forefront." They state on their Web site:

> In a world of deafening mainstream media silence, we decided to cover our news by ourselves for ourselves. We're building a hub of information for and by people of every ethnic and cultural background. Joining the GeoClan.com World Family means the opportunity to share your creativity, opinions, and thoughts with an international audience. The GeoClan.com World Family is in the business of "Uploading Change."…. We are transmitting information to incite hope and inspire people! Joining the Geo-Clan.com World Family is to tap into your creativity and use it to change the world.[15]

The shared recognition of youth coming together in valued ways to exchange quality information to further progressive initiatives designed of, by, and for youth and young adults was the bond that furthered their collaboration. Differences that arose were addressed through consensus, which then included the exploration of how and why consensus building was the most valued strategy for collective engagement and the nurturing of justice outcomes. With the alliance of GeoClan, this second LEAD group developed and carried out the third of its three core strategies of capacity-building praxis by creating and completing a leadership training institute.

Through the institute, LEAD brought together local and nonlocal leaders alike, who had been engaging in social justice activism in various roles through diverse organizations and structures for decades or longer. The teach-in framework borrowed from and built on some of the best mechanisms for radical change used during the local area expression of the Civil Rights Movement. And everything about the institute—from the facilitator-speaker choices to the agenda, from the primary themes to the format of engagement, from the organizational representation to specification of post-institute next steps—was developed of, by, and for young persons. Also, their sustained affiliation with the NET was enriched when they reached out to and incorporated the participation of mothers who had lost loved ones to violence. In continuing to respect and move beyond the life-skill building and court preparation information, these mothers sharing again merged capacity-building motives in powerful ways. LEAD members furthered their facilitation and leadership skills. The youths in the NET, many of whom were currently there serving juvenile sentences for violent offenses, received a restoratively framed understanding of the harm their actions had caused to the mothers and families of the victims. And the mothers were afforded the opportunity to begin to share and heal from their loss. The institute's success, as an event, a resource, and a call to action, was a direct result of the quality of LEAD's leadership, education, and advocacy.

The fourth and final praxis of LEAD's second membership group was organizing to provide daycare so that a broader group of persons could attend and fully participate in a Fight for Lifers Conference. In May 2005, more than 400 persons came to this conference sponsored by Fight For Lifers [FFL] to focus on and further a movement seeking to abolish the sentence of life without the possibility of parole. The collective view was that this sentence represents a punishment that is cruel and unusual. LEAD members gave leadership in various areas of the FFL conference. In addition to their daycare activities, they provided security and facilitated panels and plenary discussions. Here, LEAD exhibited both internal and external collaboration within and between programs of the larger organization, and within and between other organizations as well. By doing so, this LEAD group linked the servant-leader role to an intergenerational information sharing process to allow others to further a shared mission of advocacy for persons who may never know life outside of prison walls. As key group members returned to college, began work schedules that were in too much conflict with LEAD meeting times, moved on to participate in AEA activities, or simply experienced decline in their level of interest in furthering the LEAD mission, there was turnover once more, and another group of LEAD came to an uncertain closure. Yet this time as before, these successes served as a quality foundation for the next group of young voices.

In 2005, the next LEAD membership group involved a near-complete turnover of participants. Though the persons were quite different, this new group, in effect, returned to an expression of the first LEAD group. This time a young, energetic public school teacher who was a member of the Fight for Lifers Steering Committee facilitated a political workshop with LEAD. In her school, as she encountered students who had some form of political analysis she would recommend them to LEAD. As she gradually invested more time in leadership, she brought still more students into the program, including some of her younger family members. When one of the students then spoke of his early LEAD experiences to a second teacher at the same school, that teacher brought in two of his students. And with that, a new LEAD membership group began. Like the first, they soon reached out to fund a new initiative. As participating board members in LEAD, William and Lucinda applied for and received a $1,000 grant from Philadelphia Activities Fund Inc. (PAF). As presented recently, PAF is a nonprofit corporation established "to foster and promote educational values of sportsmanship, the arts, and health to individuals ... [and give] support to programs and organizations that encourage the instruction and education of individuals which will train, develop and improve their capabilities." Consistent with its capacity-building mission, pursuing and securing this grant again broadened LEAD's network of organizational interactions. Now guided by two teachers and made up primarily of teenaged participants with no history of criminal justice participation, this group of LEAD members again developed a set of grant-seeking and administrative skills in an effort to create resources for their formative initiatives.

In an effort to sustain a more coherent and consistent leadership, a new advisory structure was used. The Reconstruction Board structure changed, requiring that board members participate in one or more programs of the organization. Two Board members participated with LEAD: William as Chair and Treasurer Lucinda Hudson. Under their guidance, LEAD successfully organized their second leadership conference, again held at the Vernon House. Motivated by the exploration of distinct leadership styles and structures, they began to move toward a collective leadership framed in the millennia-old, continental African-based village council model, which was anchored in consensus building and egalitarian decision making. For the first time in LEAD's history, this group included members who were very young. Can all the messages be heard and understood as well? Can the roles and rules continue to shape the group's effort to meet each member where they are? Similar to the Club House collective that was a vital precursor to the establishment of LEAD, 8- and 9-year-old children became valued members of the group. This period was also marked by a range of collaborations. These included reestablishing ties with the Uber Street Youth Club (which had been formed out of the Club House collective), establishing for the first time a resource-sharing relationship with the Gerome Brown Community Center computer program project, and co-sponsoring a trip to NYC with YHEP to have fun while also furthering their capacity-building through exposure to a different city's patterns of youth engagement. All this, while still sustaining a (much more sporadic, yet) steady consult relationship with the NET juvenile detention facility. This group even held several exploration meetings that focused on the collaboration between the American Friends Service Committee's Youth Spirituality Project to explore ways in which social justice themes of interest to them might be linked with more-formal, faith-informed activities.

As they identified what they wanted to do over the summer months of 2006, the group engaged in an exploration of culture, history, and both the benefits and challenges of a more collective structure. Enriching the resource partnerships of LEAD and Reconstruction, they met every other week at the public library and also met at Parkside Association a local nonprofit assisting low- and moderate-income persons to improve access to affordable housing. Their meeting regularity led them to develop and participate in a summer leadership institute on the history of LEAD, and it was coupled with the formative development of a new vision statement and work plan. These efforts, though well intended, had both the asset and limitation of being anchored in the formal guidance of the two public school teachers. As the school year began, both teachers simply stopped coming. Informed by the fragile participation of the very young and without a clear youth-led directive and without the teachers who had led them to this opportunity this group of LEAD quickly ended.

A 2006 program summary report listed nearly 20 young persons—all of whom were noted as "current but in-active members" of LEAD. This same document stated the following:

> LEAD has dealt with many kinds of situations. [Including] The death of newborn babies. Those who've ran from other states seeking refuge in Philadelphia. The 13 year old brother of one participant died because he was born with a hole in his heart. [That member] decided to attend LEAD's group rather than her brother's funeral because she knew [if she had gone to the funeral] that she and her sister would fight. LEAD decided to have a service there for her brother. LEAD has dealt with various types of abuse and has a protocol for dealing [with] these types of issues.[16]

In addition to leadership and education, these life circumstances informed the "revolutionary hope and radical imaginations"[17] for the youth in LEAD and the challenges and triumphs of their advocacy within Reconstruction. They were guided by a consistent mission and fellowship structure, with shared therapeutic interventions directly linked to context and circumstances beyond the individual, as the priority of every meeting. This framework has allowed LEAD to progress with and beyond participant turnover and other challenges.

Development

For Reconstruction's youth work, and especially for LEAD, the umbrella process informing all of its initiatives and activities is reflected in the last of the four words describing its youth-oriented program: Development. Individually, famil-ially, organizationally, and communally growing within and beyond each of these interdependent levels. Development, by engaging in the strategies of ac-tion to actualize one's "radical imagination" and realize progressive possibilities within oneself and others.[18] Valuing one's own questions and nurturing an envi-ronment of support in fellowship with others who are doing the same.

> I came into LEAD thinking about those two [music industry] businesses. Thinkin' that I had to do somethin' with my life and get them off the ground. 'Cause [at the time] I was just...livin'. And I just wanted to do something...I wanted to be a part of doing that. But, now that I'm the LEAD Coordinator, I'll tell you where that direction went. The struggle is my life. Been in a struggle my whole life. Jus' always wanted to do somethin' about it. I felt like I had a lot of why questions. And so, when I started beings and deal-ings with Reconstruction, and Will [William Goldsby], and he started to answer those questions. And if he couldn't, we had a network base of people that could. And he could call them. Like, especially Yumi [Odom]; call him a "walking encyclopedia"... and he could jus' run it down for you. And [I] just became part of the family. And with my creative skills. Just puttin' my ideas out, and not being hushed at all because of my age. And it's mostly older people in Reconstruction. And it's just being comfortable here, that allows us [youth] to really see how creative we can be. Who we really are, actually. So, [I] LOVE Reconstruction. It's like, definitely don't need any therapy sessions. 'Cause we handle it all. And there's a whole base of different people, that can assist you on several things. [I'm] starting to get into grant writing. And we have someone with those skills. Leaders. Facilitators. Organizers. A whole variety of people among Recon-struction. And LEAD is a valued part of all that. (Deion F., 22 years old, Personal Communication, n.d.)

With a mother who is a former board member and neighbor of William, a father who, upon his release, was a central figure in the establishment of the AEA program growing out of the Hospitality House period, and with an older brother who was a member of an earlier generation of LEAD, Deion was a child of Reconstruction. His reflections above in 2008 demonstrate the diverse ways in which development can, and does, occur among those young people strong enough and curious enough and willing enough to value their own strug-gle and their own possibilities while valuing the same in others, as they enrich that strength, curiosity, and willingness to "do something with" their lives, with LEAD as a valuable means to do so.

"We Are the Ones We've Been Waiting For"
A fourth LEAD membership group was bridged by children from the previous group, whose new membership was 12 to 18 years old.[19] Then in 2007, the par-ticipation of ten core members began. This group was a mix of young people,

including persons with and without a criminal history; persons with and without parents who were in active addiction; persons with and without parents who had previously participated in some aspect of Reconstruction in prior years; persons with and without some college training, in preparation for and onto four-year college campuses; persons who were and were not working regularly, some of whom had enough independent income to be of financial assistance to their family household. This rich mixture included persons from 12 to 22 years old. As their collective sense grew so too did their aspirations. In an initiative funded by Sparkplug, LEAD met regularly with other youth in the nearby Logan Neighborhood Youth Center as they continued to nurture both the social justice and therapeutic LEAD missions. The social justice LEAD mission includes training youth to avoid entering the adult system. It includes political and life skills that can motivate organizing in their communities and advocate for themselves. And the therapeutic LEAD mission is to engage (in) the relational resilience of collective support, active listening, and service to others as they serve the best of themselves. Consistent with Deion F.'s reflections, this generation of LEAD thoughtfully and creatively merged these two missions in new and engaging ways.

This included outlining a new training course intended to educate other young people in their communities, develop local youth leadership, and increase their membership. The course outline focused on three main areas facing young people in many of Philadelphia's poorest neighborhoods: family crisis intervention, economic and credit restoration, and political education. This curriculum was to further LEAD's development, which brought together leadership, education, and advocacy. Guided by it, participants would be motivated to join LEAD, continue facilitating this training with other youth using a training-the-trainer model of skill building, initiate activities, and organize projects to address the (personal, family, and community) issues raised in the sessions (e.g., starting their own businesses as peer counselors or credit restorers). This framing and strategy is consistent with the sentiment of the late June Jordan's 1980 poem to South African women that *"We are the ones we've been waiting for."*[20] The model was one in which the dilemmas of record or situations to be considered were volunteered by the participants themselves to affirm their own voices and give primacy to their lives as both text and context for capacity-building and change.

They then enriched this foundation, seeking out and participating in an internal collaboration for mutual benefit. LEAD leadership reached out to William and Hakim (Ali) to explore how to best understand and respond to a contradiction that was consistently arising in each of their lives: crisis. They quickly said that their goal was less about crisis management, which they viewed as an inaccurate understatement that misrepresented both the content and growth potential resting inside a challenging event, interaction, or ongoing process. Instead, they wanted to better explore less the asset-limitation dichotomy associated with it and more the continuum of challenges and opportunities associated with the particular circumstance. Bringing together both the social justice and therapeutic missions of LEAD, led their own life experiences to be the lessons of the curricular overview they were designing and would teach from.

The meetings of LEAD members with William and Hakim took place during yet another critical period of membership transition. Critical, in that the prior LEAD group had just experienced a profound challenge of family, follow through, and organizational mission. A female LEAD member's teenage daughter alleged that she had been sexually assaulted by that member's partner. Choosing not to believe her daughter's allegations, the mother aggressively challenged her daughter. This included a counter-allegation by the mother that, even if the events had occurred as the daughter was alleging, the daughter had encouraged the actions of sexual impropriety and that the daughter's intent was to keep the mother from being able to "ever be happy" in maintaining a stable relationship with a man. Since both daughter and mother were LEAD members, the family dynamics, program consequences, and organizational pedagogy of principled transformation each experienced this moment of profound tension. Transitioning from this situation and its outcomes, LEAD members, now squarely anchored in a women-centered leadership, insisted that William and Hakim meet with them, as William states, "to give them some history on both the LEAD program, Reconstruction as an organization, and the interdependent missions of both."

From this series of long and layered meetings, informed by William's crisis management training, Hakim's abiding Muslim faith and his unyielding commitment to the relational resilience within and beyond Reconstruction's organizational mission, these young adults of LEAD created a curriculum that best fit their experiences, informed by the iterations of LEAD membership that had preceded them. Through their curriculum-building activities, they specified and explored numerous thoughtful and creative clarifications that were both conceptual and practical, in other words, they were true to the praxis of Reconstruction's mission. At the macro level, these included distinctions between cultural and historical situations, analyzing aspects of similarity and difference

between them. At the family level, they included patterns of overlap and independence between sibling rivalry, (more temporally bounded) crises within a
family, and more long-standing dysfunctional family patterns. By doing so, they
enriched both the therapeutic and social justice missions of LEAD.

As William recently recalled, "We met with them weekly and ascertained
from their experiences and the contribution of the other LEAD groups before
them, that they recognized that all situations required proper management skills.
[Informed by] this, along with my background, we agreed on the title 'Situation
Management,' and designed the skill set of this pillar." Situation Management
not only became one of the three pillars of the revised curriculum in the LEAD
program, it also was incorporated into the Reconstruction curriculum. Here
again, true to Deion's words, not only were young people "not being hushed at
all because of [their] age," but their voices and visions were respected and amplified as the innovative facilitators of change for the entire organization that
they (also) were for themselves.

Now and Then

Shortly after LEAD's fourth membership group discussed above was recognized for its innovative contributions at Reconstruction's 2008 annual meeting,
some form of a collective crisis of faith occurred among the leadership's core.
Across it, only one consistent presence was willing to participate in a commu-
nity-university partnership. In an upper-level undergraduate course developed
and taught by this book's first author, the interdisciplinary theme of building
community capacity was explored through the lens of students' sociological
imagination. Small groups were required to first affiliate and volunteer with a
nonprofit organization. They then completed a capacity-building assessment,
exploring the primary assets and areas of possible change associated with the
organization. Reconstruction's LEAD program was one of the organizations
participating in the winter quarter of 2009. William Goldsby and Deion F. Morrison traveled to Columbus, Ohio, and interacted with students in the course—
those completing the small group assessment of LEAD, as well as the others.
Throughout the quarter, there was limited participation among Philadelphia
LEAD members in the multiple conference calls to Philadelphia, and incomplete participation on the part of students in the course. While the process was
instructive for both the students and for the organization, the limitations of
engagement and follow through—on both sides of the university-community
partnership—reflect the benefits and challenges associated with capacity-
building youth in a university's service-learning framework. This, even when

those youth are being graded on their performance, informed by participation and follow through.

On the Philadelphia side of the partnership, what instigated this latest LEAD leadership crisis was a combination of challenged trust, a less steady commitment, an uneven meeting follow through, and an eroding intimacy. As this group of mainly 20-somethings increasingly retreated to individualistic responses to challenges both unique and widely held, the shared and the collectively committed declined as the unspoken and the unmet increased. And as with all other aspects of Reconstruction, because the critical mass of leadership is so small, the consequences of any collective ripple are magnified. The group thus faded with one member staying on, followed by a brief dormancy, and the gradual addition of persons, some of whom were entirely new to the organization while others had participated in one form or another for many years. This, along with a couple persons resting in between these two extremes, re-created yet another group of LEAD.

Sampson, a longtime LEAD member, returned, just as Teon, a new member began participating. Another new member was referred from a young women's halfway-back program, as another young man joined Patrick's return and bridged LEAD's current struggles with its past. This fifth formation agreed to be the LEAD Program Development Committee. In this role, the group further developed the mission that exists on the newly developed Reconstruction Web site.[21] This included putting in place an ongoing training for each curriculum theme. They secured the commitment of Tania Talbo, a Reconstruction affiliate and financial planner, to donate quality time when needed to conduct workshops on the politics of economics.

They reached out to Jerry Hawthorne, founder of Continuing Opportunity for Family Education Enrichment (COFFEE) and longtime collaborator with Reconstruction, who committed to running trainings with LEAD participants using the COFFEE (systems) Family Therapy Model. And they secured the commitment of Butch Cottman to facilitate the Leadership Awareness curriculum component, a new session of which is now underway. As of this writing, two LEAD members are now in their 18th week guided by Mr. Cottman's steady hand. In their program development committee role, they are enriching the organization's collaborative strategy of action by inviting other groups working on youth issues to join LEAD as a coalition. These various activities have also led this fifth membership group to clearly define youth membership in LEAD as being either under 18 years of age, or 18 and older. They have also engaged the therapeutic mission in new and creative ways to better deal with

LEAD members who become intimate. Here, the goal is to effectively address personal issues that may surface in the program in a way that does not result in persons leaving the program, the organization, and this critical work.

This fifth LEAD membership group is building upon the rich legacy of the groups that preceded it while also creating a new exploration of leadership and structure for themselves. This critical mass of ten members—with one teenager and no others younger than 22 years old—was asked en masse to join the Reconstruction Board. Could this enrich their program investment? Would this improve consistency? This group brought the awareness, borne of both necessity and possibility, that youth in the organization is 18 years old and older. This group, together with AEA and FFL program leadership collectives, became the Reconstruction Board Program Development Committee. This group, like each of the generations before them, is also informed by the critical contradiction of the uncertainty and sometimes complete absence of a strong, *sustained* leadership that can carry on these many tasks of its merged mission. True for all of the organization's programs, this is especially true for LEAD. As in every collective leadership structure, some form of a more complete check and balance system would likely help. Yet in the midst of current challenges, growth continues.

Capacity-Building With Youth and Hope

Reconstruction's youth work takes place within the larger societal context. Relevant statistics and their consistency across recent history are jarring. An African American young man has a 1–in–3 chance of going to prison in his lifetime compared to a 1–in–17 chance for his White male counterpart. Homicides among African American young men 15–19 years old are one of their leading causes of death. And three out of every five Black men who dropped out of high school—an increasing trend—have one or more prison numbers.[22,23] African American young women are a fast-growing incarcerated population, being more than three times as likely to be in jail or prison compared to their White counterparts.[24] In 2008 in California, for example, though they are no more likely to have committed a crime, the arrest rate for Black young women was 49 out of every 1,000; more than three times the rate of Latinas and nearly six times the rate for Whites.[25] In short, mass incarceration for African American and other young women of color is also troubling. Beyond the depersonalized glare of such comparisons—and the many persons, families, and communities adversely impacted by such statistics—youth are being challenged in many ways. Yet against this challenging backdrop, simple, local intimacies of access and safe space across generations remain.

Often, former members and affiliates of the organization will drop by William's home. Just as the Reconstruction office is at 1808, his home is also a safe space. Of pleasant reminders and unresolved moments. Of faith and fellowship. Of conjure and caring. Sometimes the motive for doing so is simply to share a brief hello with William as they move from one part of the city to the next. Sometimes doing so after months or perhaps even years away from the organization and one's earlier participation in it. Other times, the motive for the visit is more intentional and directly related to Reconstruction's justice mission. Recently, Kaleeja, a former member of Divas With Attitude when she was a child, stopped by William's house without calling or contacting him beforehand. Arriving with mixed motives, Kaleeja came with her boyfriend, Jaleel. And as with most visits to William's house, her visit was unexpected but welcome. As William soon learned, Jaleel was in urgent need of addressing his probation by completing some form of community service. In need of accruing many service hours in a very short period of time, he was very interested in securing a letter to his parole officer noting that Reconstruction Inc. could serve as his outlet for demonstrated community service and that he had completed the 30 hours of service necessary, though the deadline to do so was now just days away. By way of faith, other Reconstruction board members were also visiting William's house the day Kaleeja and Jaleel came by. And true to the collective engagement of Reconstruction's mission, they too were included in this impromptu subgroup meeting. Collectively, with the complete and equal participation of Kaleeja and Jaleel, all in attendance collectively developed a plan of action to assist Jaleel. As William recently noted,

> We did not entertain any unprincipled participation in a misrepresented letter for any amount of money. Instead, we offered him an orientation [to introduce him to the organization]. We gave Jaleel two weeks to call once he got the letter to inform us whether or not he wanted to join us in this work. During those two weeks he went through a great deal of personal, internal struggle. [Despite his struggles,] after the two weeks, he called to say, "I am in." (William Goldsby, Personal Communication, n.d.)

In the few months since, Jaleel has made consistent, high-quality contributions to LEAD and Reconstruction as a whole. Having also brought a friend of his into the organization, Jaleel, formerly homeless and uncertain, is now renting a room in a home owned by a Reconstruction affiliate, and both he and his friend are now receiving the well-deserved praise from their judge and parole officers for their participation and the ways they have productively changed their lives. This type of transformative moment regularly occurs as the total number of young people's lives that have been touched by the organization now reaches well into the hundreds, if not more. And no doubt William's doorbell will be ringing again. Very soon.

Despite these many leadership groups over a rather short time, and the substantial turnover that too often occurs in grassroots youth organizing, in many respects each LEAD membership group built on the previous one. The personal challenges of each individual member fed the capacities of the program and organization. In these youth formations, each personal issue was talked about. The causes and connections related to it were explored. And the personal-as-political realities associated with it in the young person's life were collectively and respectfully engaged, then debriefed. What meanings can young people give to the presence and processes associated with "the personal is political"? What illustrations are there that they value, of young people organizing around growth-promoting initiatives, expressing the gifts they are and possess? How are grassroots organizations enriching opportunities for young people to gather together within and beyond the diversities their gatherings possess, valuing their differences to help build community capacity, both for themselves and for others?

From the historical works of Stack (1974), Aron (1974), Gottlieb and Heinsohn (1973), and others to the more recent works of Ginwright and his colleagues (2002, 2007, 2010), Ager and colleagues (2008), Bradley and colleagues (2004), and many others, questions remain regarding how best to organizationally build capacity practices that assist youth in their development.[26–31] And where are their individual and collective places of rage in their coming of age? "Young people are mobilizing resources around issues; organizing groups for social action; planning programs at the local level; and advocating their interests in public agencies. They are raising consciousness and educating others about their common concerns, and providing services of their own choosing. No single strategy characterizes all [their] approaches to practice."[32]

Conclusion

Across the years, Reconstruction Inc.'s youth initiatives have touched thousands of lives, contributing in countless ways to the proactive development of children and young adults in its North Philadelphia neighborhood, throughout the greater Philadelphia area, across the state of Pennsylvania and beyond, through the Internet's global reach. Specifying the metrics of the impact of grassroots organizational initiatives is always difficult, all the more due to the uneven trajectories of youth development. Researchers struggle to assess effects with the specification of, and distinctions between, community mobilization, community activation, and individual and group outcomes.[33,34] This is made still more difficult when the intended contributions are more than specific service provision outcomes or specific, bounded, short-term information sharing or behavioral changes.

Metrics That Matter

The contributions of Reconstruction's youth initiatives are many, with most being difficult, if not impossible, to accurately measure. Yet despite these measurement challenges in quantity and quality, many youth capacity-building contributions of Reconstruction are worthy of note. These include:

1. The hundreds of youths serving juvenile sentences, or who are awaiting adjudication, processed through the Northeast Treatment Center who have participated in LEAD workshops and have been presented with components of the LEAD curriculum.
2. Those who have attended LEAD leadership institutes at the Vernon House along with other educational outreach events throughout the city.
3. The many youths who have attended multiple LEAD meetings; (4) youths who have participated in various events LEAD has organized and sponsored in partnership with GeoClan and other organizational collaborators.
4. The neighborhood children who participated in the 20W Club, Divas With Attitude, and Club House collectives.
5. The teenage and young adult fathers who developed and sustained Brothers Strengthening Families, which bridged the years of Reconstruction's dormancy.

As challenging as the impact of these primary contacts are to measure, secondary and tertiary contacts are still more challenging, given the many informal and indirect interactions with the larger youth mission of Reconstruction that many other youths have had. Though uneven, the impact has been substantial.

Many current and former youth affiliates of the organization are exhibiting their leadership, education, advocacy, and development skills through the establishment of retail businesses, clothing design, contracting, and other urban redevelopment work. Some are using their appreciation of spiritual enrichment and critical pedagogy to affiliate with other social justice initiatives, including the UNIA of the Marcus Garvey legacy and Black Student Unions. Some are participating in economic development initiatives, including labor organizing. Many current and former Reconstruction youth affiliates are college graduates or are currently taking college courses, including several graduates of Temple University across the years and a LEAD member who is currently attending an Ivy League university. Others are participating in one or more political initiatives in more traditional lobbying and electoral campaigns. Still others are refining their grant writing skills or furthering other civic development activities. And many others are mentoring a next generation of youth in numerous formal and less formal ways.

As reflected here, many challenges are associated with the development and refinement of an organizational praxis of youth civic engagement. And many triumphs. And all are informed by and occurring in the midst of "the cradle to prison pipeline." Reconstruction's intent to change the image, the context, and the lives of youth was severely hindered by the lack of resources and multiple expressions of miseducation that too often interrupted this goal. Like many grassroots efforts, too often LEAD could simply not compete effectively with the effects of poverty and challenges of limited funds. As previously noted, each of the young boys participating in the Club House initiative was regularly being approached and pulled into the drug trade. Now, years later, all but one of those boys are in jail, with two serving life sentences. Multiple DWA affiliates are now dead while many others are young single mothers. A LEAD member who participated during the time LEAD helped Fight for Lifers organize its successful 2005 conference was killed. Having come to LEAD as an early, young member of AEA, through Reconstruction he secured his first job with the Youth Health and Empowerment Project teaching other youth about safer sex practices. Along with other members, he sponsored a trip to New York City, chaperoning still younger children from the neighborhood. Yet in the midst of these positive activities, he was approached and asked to take a ride in a car. After having been driven a few blocks, he was shot in the head. This was preceded by the shooting death of another neighborhood youth in fewer than 30 days. Yes, LEAD is changing the lives of many youths, in ways both large and small. Yet the so-called "war on drugs"—complete with its painfully real collateral consequences in the urban core—remains, along with the rest of the social context of the intersections of concentrated poverty, highly accessible violence, and the absence of enough collective welfare amid these many constraints to engage enough youth in productive activities. In short, all the oppressive reinforcements of societal margins remain.

In his important and chilling 2005 book, *No Place for Children: Voices From Juvenile Detention,* photographer Steven Liss put together a coffee-table book of children engaged in the criminal justice process.[35] This series of photos raises a set of questions regarding how children are perceived in society in general and, more specifically, the role they play in the current era of mass incarceration through the individual, familial, and societal destructive pipeline that is highly selective regarding who is and who is not most likely to be funneled into it. The images, both individually and taken together, speak to the paradox of systemic inclusion. If there are times and places for all youth to be, what circumstances of support, social context, and marginalization could possibly have led these many youths to be there in the moment the photograph was taken? And what in the world is to be taken from this answer of the role that grassroots community organizations might play as one of many valued forces of change in the lives of young people? This chapter provides a set of answers to these and other related questions. We explored the organization's history of youth initiatives, thoughtfully engaging its mission in youth-led ways. Reconstruction Inc. has influenced the lives of many, many youths across the years in ways that are apparent and in far more other ways more difficult to measure. Yet the mobilization outcomes are certainly there. Together, how these triumphs and challenges inform us in the present and into a possible future is up to the ongoing efforts within and beyond the capacity-building pipeline of progressive socialization that Reconstruction Inc. continues to develop and refine in its now generation-old organizational praxis of youth civic engagement.

Endnotes Toward Principled Transformation

Extending from the rich, communal contributions made by youth affiliated with Reconstruction, three possibilities toward principled transformation emerge:

- Transformative Trainings—The transformative training of youth must have them understand that power lies when and where decisions are made. They should emphasize how to make efficient and important decisions, build consensus, and develop and sustain progressive support systems.

- Resolving Rage—Actions toward the resolution of rage among youth rest in resisting all forms of developmental "othering" and youth alienations by nurturing environments of intergenerational respect. Strategies can include enriching peace-building collectives for social justice study (e.g., the Club House), multi-organization collaborations, and a skill-building, resource vision for youth owning land.

- A New Justice—Nurturing a new justice paradigm demands revisions of all policies that solidify marginalizing racks among youth (e.g., race-informed applications of zero tolerance policies). Educating youth for critical awareness should include their active input in curriculum building and them understanding the contradictions regarding how middle-class persons and others benefit from keeping the poor where they are.

Part III
Capacity-Building

Building the Bridge Between Them, 1998–2007

> For capacity building to be successful, it was understood that communities need to have pertinent information readily available to them, fair and just processes in which to participate and develop, and clearly defined goals that benefit the common good.
>
> Dr. Brian Steels

> William, [James Barnes], a couple other guys and I. We just sat down one night, and it was really just a brainstorm. We [asked], "What can we do to try to help some of the [reentry] guys that are going out there, that are struggling?" We incorporated an alumni meeting where people could come back and tell us what was going on outside, since we left Hospitality House. And it started kickin' off real good. Everybody was coming back.
>
> Cameron Glenn; Co-founder, Alumni Ex-Offenders Association, November 2009

The second decade of Reconstruction was a vital bridge between a period of organizational dormancy to current collaborations, new leadership in both persons and structure, and best practices. The foundation for these most recent years is marked by a range of diverse activities, triumphs, and challenges, borne of redemption and a strong organizational resolve. The years 1998 to 2007 were a focused, renewed effort to grow with and beyond the limitations of organizational oligarchy and a small critical mass so common to grassroots organizing to its current place of more consistent collective leadership and an increasing affiliate willingness to engage the servant-leader role within multiple programs and initiatives.[1,2] In a praxis partnership between culture and community (i.e., a reciprocal exchange between the concept and actions extending from both), capacity-building was essential to the possibilities during these years of the bridge between.

Capacity-building occurs when culture and community come together as local area assets of individuals, families, organizations, and others are brought together and maximized to collectively nurture and improve the quality of life within and beyond that local area.[3,4,5] Consistent with Steels's (2007) emphasis,[6] during this second decade of Reconstruction Inc., the ways in which pertinent information was shared among members and Tioga community neighbors was expanded. The ways that fair and just participation in the organization and in its relationship to the local area were more clearly defined, along with the processes and mechanisms for their diverse expression among and between members. And the organization's capacity-building strategies were enriched to more effectively engage its mission to *"change ourselves to change the world,"* guided by collectively specified work plans—both programmatic and role-specific—and more clearly defined and diversified goals that benefitted the common good.

By doing so, Reconstruction Inc. gradually became what it remains today: a small, spiritually grounded, multiple-program, reentry and reintegration organization that continues changing the lives of those it touches in diverse, progressive ways. It is an enterprising Sanctuary for former felons, their family members, and others interested in nurturing a new justice paradigm. Here we use *Sanctuary* not in the religious nor spatially set aside retreat sense of the term, but in the everyday, spiritual praxis sense of shared spaces of a principled transformation. Consistent with the earliest forms of these capacity-building, education and action collectives of African civilizations,[7,8] to more recent expressions from Danish history into today,[9,10] from its second decade forward, Reconstruction built individual, family, organizational, and local-area capacities by being a learning sanctuary. And each of these capacity-building dimensions of a learning sanctuary will be explored in this chapter.

Growth During Dormancy

From its origin to the present, members of Reconstruction Inc. do much more than "just" limited skill-building for successful reentry and sustained desistance. Former felons, their family members, and a wide range of interested others come together to engage in conscientization toward living a new justice paradigm; in other words, "developing [individual and collective] consciousness that is understood to have the power to transform [their own lives, as well as] reality [itself]."[11] As discussed earlier, across its first ten years of growth from a spiritually grounded collective in William Goldsby's vision, to its years as an American Friends Service Committee program, into an autonomous, 501(c)3 nonprofit organization, by 1997 Reconstruction had grown into a place of reaching beyond its grasp. The day-to-day processes of organizational maintenance were far more than what William could have expected of himself as the sole, consistent leadership presence. The small, dedicated working board had been worked too often and too much. And most board members began to maintain an understandable organizational distance. The weak funding foundation was now even weaker. And the still unhired, still unpaid staff was now even further from being either hired or paid. As William recently recalled:

> I remember sitting in the office at 1808 struggling and trying to complete the organization's tax returns [and] dealing with all of the other administrative issues, as well as the

personal needs of the residents [of 1808]. It was apparent that I did not have the abilities to manage all of this. It became overwhelming. (Personal Communication, n.d.)

Sociologically, be it from a systems view or an alternative paradigm, organizations are processes with many moving parts that change in many ways over time. And learning organizations are, by definition, agents of change. Their primary function is to gain new information and incorporate that information into their strategies of action to more effectively engage their intended mission.[12,13] As Reconstruction Inc. began its second decade, these dynamics of organizational change did not end even as its dormancy began. With an overworked board of directors that was no longer meeting, with no steady funding or staff, and informed by controversies and collaborative tensions both large and small the organization did not have the necessary minimum infrastructure of organizational efficiency.[14,15] Yet the Reconstruction mission still grew.

Alumni Ex-Offenders Association Begins
William Goldsby began working at Hospitality House in February 1997 to incorporate an adapted Reconstruction curriculum and practice into it. After its successful revision to be consistent with the six-month, rolling residence structure to better serve these clients, a few of them moved beyond the requirements of sustaining their Hospitality House residence in good standing. They approached William to explore the possibility of creating something more.

> We incorporated an alumni meeting where people could come back and tell us what was going on outside since we left [had] Hospitality House....We had agendas and a structure. We talked about what was tough for us. How were we making out? How were we employed, or lookin' for work? How was our family life going? Stuff to see where we were at. What were we doing now that we were outside the Hospitality House doors? Were we continuing to be supportive of family members that had looked out for us while we had [been in prison]? What we were striving for. Just basic stuff. (Cameron, Personal Communication, n.d.)

This small group of men came together and quickly recognized that by building and sharing in a collective intimacy, they increased their individual and collective strength and furthered their potential for moving from reintegration to sustaining a principled transformation. By doing so, consistent with the Reconstruction mission, these men engaged in "the practice of freedom [as a] quest for human completion," coming together to transform themselves and the environments around them.[16] These men valued their own quests while valuing and sharing in the quests of others.

Despite its organizational dormancy, with that autumn 1997 meeting, the Reconstruction mission continued to grow as a learning sanctuary. Together, they learned how to build consensus when they deliberated on what to name their group. Guided by the adapted Reconstruction curriculum and influenced by their own personal transformations, they collectively decided they were alumni from penal institutions. Like college graduates being alumni of their educational institutions, these men were also institutional alumni. AEA meetings in Hospitality House helped the men move from reentry to reintegration as both groups understood better what the process of a sustained, sober, post-incarceration life actually was and what principled transformation demanded of them and of their families.

Refining the Method of Mission

Because of the respect he had earned across his years of organizational development and innovative leadership, at Hospitality House William had the flexibility to create the curriculum and teach his curriculum his way. Unlike the captive constraints of the Graterford prison setting, this was a six-month residential program for halfway-back parole or probation violators. Thus, the screening and program participation would have a different structure. And the methods and meaning of participatory leadership among the men would also have to change. William was allowed to bring in guest speakers from all walks of life. The director and other staff members respected his request to respond to his work (as with all work in the facility) as sacred; that is, understood as extending from a space of greatest good, ancestrally respectful, and intending to nurture expressions of both within and among Hospitality House residents.

As a result, no others were allowed into his sessions without prior notice, and this was especially critical for participants' parole officers. Could they explore expressions of their sacred selves and the vulnerable and sometimes volatile places within themselves and others that sacred search demanded, in a fellowship of caring respect and without the fear of procedural or co-resident reprisals that could initiate further criminal justice troubles? Yes, largely because of the procedural safeguards William established and that the Hospitality House leadership and fellow staffers heeded. But perhaps what worked best during William's years there was the openness and willingness the participants exhibited and the diffusion of the Reconstruction curriculum; in other words, the ways that collective leadership was shared within the house and their families. Two former residents during that time recently reflected on those years.

I actually started attending William's group...through Hospitality House. I may have even facilitated a few of those meetings. Will started definitely getting my feet wet with that work....I may have been working different jobs outside...but I was always connected. Whenever the support group meetings would meet, I would be there either to help facilitate or be amongst the group. (Deion, Personal Communication, n.d.)

So, once I got to Hospitality House, met up with William and a couple of the guys, it seems like it just took off for me. It was, "Okay. That [prison past] is behind me. I can move forward now".... I [made and] sold clothes while I was at the house. I was very active. I [started] school; going to community college. Once I got there, I got very much into it [and] that really started my recovery process....I also got involved in local political organizing, [and] was voted in as a committee person, [12th] ward, [9th] division. All this came through Hospitality House [and] getting myself together. (Cameron, Personal Communication, n.d.)

In addition, the families of all those who came into contact with William's program became more involved in the wellness of the men. Many, for the first time. This included immediate and extended family members and was amplified when William created a couples group. In it, the spouses, girlfriends, or partners came into the Hospitality House setting in fellowship with other couples, and were given the latitude to speak with rigorous honesty about the dynamics of rebuilding intimate relationships. In their interviews, Deion and Cameron spoke of the many ways in which the collective leadership of William's curriculum and the entire Hospitality House structure shaped their principled transformations in the whole of their lives. It was expressed through diverse participations and leadership in William's groups, in the house as a whole, as well as through their economic creativity, educational participation, and political and other civic engagements. William described the intent and focus of the curriculum as having been "designed with precision to direct participants to learn how to like and love themselves. Once the participants see themselves as worthy, then it becomes easier for them to begin to grow." With Hospitality House's structure and resident flow being a 30-person house and a six-month program, and with William having worked there for more than six years, Cameron and Deion were two among the hundreds of men who were exposed to this revised form of the Reconstruction curriculum and mission. And in this environment, added complexities were recognized and addressed. These included asking and answering the "What next?" question, moving from the reentry of halfway back, to the reintegration of being all the way back as principled men.

All of this built upon a moment when a two-time violent former felon working as a staff counselor in a halfway house for persons who had violated their probation or parole sat down with a handful of other former felons then living in the halfway-back facility. It was a moment of organizational (re-) development, and precursor to founding the Alumni Ex-Offenders Association (AEA) just a few months later. Building capacity, the many assets of each Hospitality House resident was now being given a—strictly voluntary— environment of support in which to further their social supports, communication and leadership skills, sense of community, and means of engaging in critical reflection of their lives, the social circumstances of society within and beyond the Hospitality House walls, the larger criminal justice system, and the patterns and relationships within and between each. It was a formative moment of furthering conscientization and sanctuary; that is, reflecting the simple ways in which the lived praxis of a pedagogy of principled transformation could inform the daily walk of these men seeking and building change. Within themselves. Within their families. And within the communities in which they continued interacting during their time in Hospitality House.

What Intimate Defiance Demanded
During this same period, because of the moment of organizational crisis, William called a board meeting. In the ongoing mix between intimacy and bureaucracy central to Reconstruction and all grassroots organizing, the meeting took place in his living room. Four or five board members gradually arrived, and as they did the meeting took on an increasingly somber feeling. Something had to change—with what, how, and how much being the three critical questions of the meeting's agenda. And beginning in the early 1990s, a national environment was increasingly defined by three strikes laws requiring longer prison sentences on repeat offenders and in some states, life sentences for three felony "career criminals." Special attention was given to repeat violent offenders, beginning with the 1993 state legislation in Washington (Initiative 593), and California's 1994 Proposition 184. Symbolizing the current mood, the California proposition passed with 72% support. And by 2004, 26 states and the federal government had laws satisfying the general criteria for three strikes statutes.[17,18] The 1994 election of Tom Ridge as governor, who ran on a Contract with America, "get tough on crime" platform, led Pennsylvania's parole statutes to quickly become more stringent. The consequences were especially true for two-time violent offenders in Reconstruction's program at Graterford Prison. Eligibility for parole was denied to the *entire* second Graterford cohort. The possibility for nurturing an organizational momentum toward its justice mission, or even for the organization to simply survive, seemed unlikely.

In this 1997 moment of organizational pressures that were at once national, local, and highly personal, William had gone more than a year without an organizational salary of any kind. The fund-raising committee had grown weary after many months of unsuccessful grant solicitations, followed by less and less fund-raising of any kind and no operating funds coming into the organization. The Graterford denials magnified the fiscal crisis with no persons eligible to enter Phase II of the Reconstruction program and to then move into 1808 to maintain it as transitional housing for men. All the while, the bills for the property mounted, as did the unpaid rent. This was the moment of that board meeting. As William recalled,

> I remember that meeting. I was told to destroy the [corporate] seal for Reconstruction. It felt like I was having an out-of-body experience....I was participating, but it felt like I was somewhere else thinking about my next move. My mind and Spirit were not here. It wasn't as painful as it was without emotional attachment....It is relatively easy to be hired to direct, coordinate, or facilitate an organization that exists already, and that has a board of directors responsible for hiring and firing staff and managing all of the IRS reporting requirements. However, it is more than a notion to be expected to provide the vision, [and the] programs, as well as execute them. When I was asked to destroy the seal, none of these issues were dealt with. This and a lot more was hard and I withdrew within. (Personal Communication, n.d.)

A longtime and highly supportive board member recommended that the corporate seal for Reconstruction be destroyed to, in effect, end the organization. This same board member also recommended that, before doing so, the organization should offset its debt to William for his high-quality and entirely unpaid leadership by deeding the 1808 property over to him. Throughout the meeting, the other attending board members remained virtually silent. With little dialogue, William's deep sense of an othering distance grew, even as everyone sat there in his living room. For an organization grounded in consensus building, the honest expression of various perspectives, and the rich dialogue so consistent with its mission, the near-silence furthered the distance as the two recommendations were collectively, tacitly approved. And with their approval, the meeting ended as the mood moved from somber to sorrowful.

William never destroyed the seal. The board member's understandable, though problematic decision and recommendation had grown out of a partially principled decision-making process. How could his many unseen practices of principled leadership, the undervalued hours of time, and the unrecognized actions of vision and spirit be so quickly torn asunder? To destroy the seal would be to validate each of these denials, something William was unwilling to do.

Where was a place for valuing how the organization's brief but meaningful historical memory could lead to a place of caring resolve and nurture opportunities still to come? Both personally and organizationally, how did they get to here? Though the future was uncertain, there was plenty of reason to believe Reconstruction had one to look forward to and to help rebuild. Again, to destroy the seal would be to validate this absence of memory, this muting of organizational resolve. From 1997 to 2003, William sustained his quarterly 990 filings with the IRS, each (accurately) declaring no income and no organizational activity. This kept Reconstruction in good standing and was allowed largely because William was the founder, and his address and social security number were on all the legal documents. And so the seal and the organization remained. William gave priority to his organizational memory and bridged it with his ancestral memory as his spiritual appreciations and possibilities continued to grow.

Opening to the Echoes of Sacred Exchange

In this moment of Reconstruction's uncertainty, William enriched his spirit in the repetitions of culture and community by affiliating with two collectives: the village of Kum Bah Yah and the New African Voices Alliance. As William recalls, "I was strongly engaged in the village at this time, learning what it meant to village, collectify resources, and understand specifically how the personal is political and the political is personal." Within weeks of the organization meeting of intimate defiance discussed above, a man who was the leader of both collectives passed away. On September 5, 1997, surrounded by family and friends, Shafik Asante's heart stopped beating and he drew his last breath. Born and raised in west Philadelphia, Asante was an ordained minister who had been reared in an environment of human rights activism going back in his family for generations. He used his adult life to create and maintain such environments through organizational development and social justice organizing in Philadelphia. He was a man who had a clear understanding of and spiritually embraced "the personal is political" as a lived calling. A cancer survivor for more than 20 years, he "did not just talk the talk, he walked the walk by nurturing community in his everyday life."[19]

At the memorial service, Butch Cottman, a colleague and close friend of Asante, spoke, raising essential questions about the lessons of Asante's life. His words of passion and purpose spoke of the visible and familiar aspects of a well-lived life of justice leadership. He also spoke of contradictions and many elements of the hidden and less well known. He spoke of how both could serve as important expressions of how anyone valuing the life and memory they were there to celebrate might explore the myths, meanings, and messages reflected in a more holistic appreciation of Shafik Asante's legacy. As William recently wrote:

> [Butch] was most powerful. He talked about how Shafik was a contradiction and how we in the Village needed to evaluate Shafik's leadership. This was awesome. Although none of the others really wanted to hear that, it was refreshing to me. Also, I found it strange that we never got to evaluate Shafik's leadership....Though extremely painful, yet radical and progressive, meeting Butch was one of the best events of my life. As a result of the Village, meeting Butch, asking members of the Village to assist me with Reconstruction; [all] had a profound effect on me and the curriculum. The involvement of these Village members [in Reconstruction] brought with it more understanding of the personal being political, and an actual process for self and organizational critique. (Personal Communication, n.d.)

These were vital lessons in rebuilding and sustaining a spiritually grounded, capacity-building, learning organization. Lessons that William heard, respected, and internalized. Coupled with the passing of Shafik Asante, William had never given himself the opportunity to truly grieve the passing of Reconstruction's centerwoman Barbara Moffett three years earlier. Nor had he allowed himself to grieve the passing of Bill Meek a year later, whose profound gifts of consciousness and caring had been "centerwoman-worthy" through his board participation, insight, and dedicated contributions. Now with Shafik Asante's passing, a third critical inspiration for and contributor to Reconstruction as both an organization and a mission was gone. This moment of profound grief was followed by necessary action. This moment demonstrated how the personal process of principled transformation so central to the organization could be influenced by someone's passing and by the Ancestral echoes that follow.

A Cultural Tempo of Capacity Building

Goodman and his colleagues (1998) and Chaskin and his colleagues (2001) have presented two of the most valued and widely cited lists of community capacity-building domains with an understandable amount of overlap between them, including leadership, resources, and a sense of community.[20,21] Lacking from these listings, or perhaps implicit within them both, is timing and the symmetries of participation associated with it. Both of these are central to nurturing the achievement of the capacity-building goals of maximizing shared and un-shared assets in an effort to improve individual and collective quality of life outcomes. Culture and community are brought together through the valued resources of timing and symmetry to further an individual's growth and enriching a grassroots capacity-building organization's possibilities. Such was the case when William's individual growth led him to engage three learning sanctuaries. In the same period, he was an active member of the New African Voices Alliance (NAVA), the village of Kum Bah Yah, while working at Hospitality House. All this, as Reconstruction moved from dormancy to revitalization. This moment brought together the characteristics, functions, and strategies of action with leadership, social networks, and community values to create a cultural tempo of capacity-building.[22,23] In effect, Reconstruction was experiencing a principled transformation while dormant because of the changes and growth William was experiencing and because of the reciprocities of change and growth occurring in the individuals and collectives with which he was affiliating.

NAVA brought together African American community organizers to function as a grassroots leadership collective. Part study group, part creative arts coalition, part political organizing cooperative, and ALL inclusionary advocate for capacity-building as a praxis, NAVA was a weaver of multiple alliances. The village of Kum Bah Yah was first and foremost informed by living the noun as a verb: to village. To village begins with wanting one. It continues by actions that nurture caring affiliation, which across many cultures is often anchored in food: "Bake some food, make it free, and they will come. At the gathering, talk about your real needs and concerns. Share beautiful stories about yourselves and your family. Develop a plan to resolve whatever needs to be resolved … [and insure] that children grow up knowing that, in addition to their parents, there are people committed to their comfort and development."[24] Despite its many layers, and less visible complexities of personality and purpose, the village of Kum Bah Yah was a group of primarily African ancestry persons living in and around the greater Philadelphia area who were guided by these simple villaging principles and the values and actions extending from them.

Among the elements of craft and personhood fundamental to William Goldsby are his love of fellowship and food. True to his deeply southern roots and sensibilities, it was this aspect of the villaging process that resonated most strongly with him, and it grew stronger still, through and with his participation in both NAVA and the village of Kum Bah Yah. As if kneading dough in the process of making another batch of his biscuits, during this time William was also kneading the rituals of his cultural collectives, refining both the Reconstruction mission and the curriculum reflecting that mission. The "flour" of sacred space was mixed with the "eggs" of collective leadership, the "milk" of participant openness and willingness, mixed with the salted TLC of honesty and caring, along with the strength and bravery that only shared vulnerabilities can discover. These were some of the resources William mixed and kneaded together, as the organization's renewal took shape within and beyond the Hospitality House walls.

Maintaining Momentum

In spite of these truths, as AEA grew stronger, this collaboration of space and resources became strained. As more and more AEA members were nonresidents, fewer and fewer current residents chose to attend. Again by consensus, AEA chose to have membership be exclusively voluntary, leading to only non-mandated persons to attend. Given the other mandatory groups residents had to attend, this voluntary alternative became one fewer and fewer residents chose. This then led the Hospitality House Board to raise an essential, utilitarian question of its own well-being: Why should they use their slender resources in support of a formative organization that is not theirs and in which few residents participate? Their answer was to gradually withdraw various forms of AEA support. The decision was made to no longer pay William to host AEA meetings. Then, any and all on-site resources (e.g., office supplies) used to further AEA and its mission were off limits. Then still other resources, both large and small, also declined. In 1999 and 2000, AEA developed and successfully conducted its first two leadership retreats held at the Vernon House, a community housing collective. This growing autonomy and off-site retreat success further strained the relationship between AEA and Hospitality House.

William's work continued to be supported by grants he wrote in partnership with selected board members. Further demonstrating the independent resources for program funding, unlike William's work, the supervision of the residents was being funded by the Pennsylvania Parole Board. A critical tension resulted when the Parole Board reduced the program from eight weeks to one week—while expecting similar, if not better, results. And what was defined as *results* was also different. As William noted, "The only thing they wanted to see was men participating in drug and alcohol programs. Also, they wanted more results for their dollar. So the number of participants doubled" with only a small increase in funding to support the participation of these added persons. These various changes in process and protocol ended up having a variety of negative effects on both staff members and residents alike.

Finally, in 2004, AEA began to meet in the community at the Vernon House. Vernon House Inc. is a nonprofit, member-managed housing community committed to "remain[ing] a diverse community...[and having a] membership of different races and ethnicities, of different ages, income levels, and sexual orientations, and of people with differing physical abilities...[also] re-flected in its governing committees and Board of Directors" (Bylaws, Art. II, Sec. 2, p. 1). With this move, AEA's membership continued to grow in new and unanticipated ways. Counselors at Hospitality House, Hannah House (a women's halfway-back facility), and juvenile boot camps continued referring their clients to AEA. Other processes beyond its growth also took place. The founding of AEA and vital 2001 to 2004 turning points that quickly followed were essential. Together, timing and strategy mixed with culture, community, and capacity-building to end Reconstruction's dormancy.

Reconstructing Reconstruction

On July 8, 2001, a newly established board for Reconstruction Inc. met at the Vernon House. Seven persons joined William in the meeting. As William noted, he and Patrick Murray were the only carryover persons also on the board at the previous archived meeting in March 1997, and everyone who agreed to serve on this new board had a political analysis and was passionate about political and social change. Two prior meetings are referenced in these minutes: a general meeting on May 6, 2000, and a special meeting on May 30, 2001. Two meetings one year, three weeks apart. Yet these meetings do not reflect the diverse ways in which the organization's mission was being reengaged in William's Hospital-ity House work, the founding of AEA, and his villaging activities. Also, beyond these meetings, some form of collective communication had recently taken place among a subset of the newly established board members because refer-ence is made to the return of their questionnaires from a January 2001 ex-change.

The July 2001 meeting demonstrates the ways in which the organization was again in board-led operation. "Reconstruction Inc. CDC" appears at the top of the minutes. This acronym for "community development corporation" illustrates the shift in focus in the collective leadership. No longer would Re-construction be understood as a (primarily) single-issue, service-oriented reentry organization. Instead, with this new board, Reconstruction would be a member-ship-driven, community capacity-building organization guided by a CDC model of engagement. "Characterized by an IRS 501(c)(3) nonprofit tax-exempt status, a volunteer board, and an emphasis on physical redevelopment, CDCs have taken on the heroic task of trying to rebuild communities devastated by capital-ist disinvestment...[when] debt-weary governments at all levels withdrew from the pressing problem of urban poverty."[25-27] This CDC focus was driven by both local and global factors. But perhaps the primary driver was the recently announced Blight Initiative of Philadelphia Mayor John Street. Following from the well-documented "broken windows" spiral-of-decline thesis and the role of social and physical disorder as both an intermediate process of, and outcome in, urban decline,[28–30] the Blight Initiative was an effort by Mayor Street to move from talk to action. "In April 2001, Mayor John F. Street unveiled his Neighborhood Transformation Initiative (NTI)...to combat blight in Philadelphia...[by] generat[ing] $250 million from the sale of general obligation bonds to address the physical consequences of long-term disinvestment and population loss."[31] Reflecting the local public sentiment at the time, an open letter to the editor by Rev. D. David Royster directed at Mayor Street was published in *The Philadelphia Inquirer* on January 21, 2001. It read:

> Philadelphia, sadly, may be the national capital of abandoned buildings and broken windows. On street after street, on block after block, the message to the decent citizens of our city is very clear: Yours is a blighted community, perhaps beyond repair and revitalization. The message to criminals is also clear: This is a place ideally suited, hideouts and rent-free shelter galore, for illegal activity. It's more than public safety. These thousands of abandoned buildings must be demolished to create sites for large-scale redevelopment of all kinds.[32]

This top-down frame of reference reflected in the pastor's letter is demonstrated by the ways in which possible strategies of action to address long-term, intentioned urban disinvestment rest outside of the residents of the urban core and that "large-scale redevelopment" is the goal such external initiatives are seeking to achieve. These views are consistent with the initiative proposed and partially carried out by Mayor Street. They are also consistent with "urban-renewal-as-urban-removal" displacements of low- and middle-income residents from the targeted neighborhoods of these types of initiatives and the highly selective pattern of their engagement. These have typically led to mass-market profiteering and architects, builders, and contractors who most often do not live in these neighborhoods, have no interests in them beyond financial gain, and are seeking to engage in highly concentrated, situational gentrification for their profit. All too typically, residents of these targeted areas are—if they are in a position to continue living in the neighborhood at all—left still further away from the ability to own their homes. Consistent with how such initiatives unfold by intended design to reinforce expressions of "American Apartheid,"[33] the politely worded McGovern (2006) conclusion was that, in Philadelphia, "NTI did not promote equitable development...[and] the result was a watered-down effort that...has fallen short of what might have been accomplished."[34]

The main focus of the July 2001 board meeting was to discuss a recent blight meeting of the Neighborhood Transformation Initiative office (NTO) and what the Blight Initiative protocol was likely to be as funds were made available. Tioga was one of the targeted neighborhoods in Mayor Street's original specifications. In 2000 it had a sizably overrepresented proportion of dilapidated, abandoned, or unoccupied homes relative to the city as a whole and a proportion of persons with completed 4-year college degrees nearly 67% below that of the city of Philadelphia. It also had a median income 31% less than and a poverty rate 38% higher than the city as a whole.[35] Quite understandably, Board member Butch Cottman thought Reconstruction should "figure out how to utilize the Blight Initiative to [our] advantage because Patrick [Murray] needs Reconstruction to help apply pressure to the Mayor's office, re: industrial and residential property cleaning and sealing in the Tioga area, and that we should tell NTO to host a meeting we can attend as an informed organization in the community" (Personal Communication, n.d.).

Another board member who had attended the most recent NTO meeting reported having "found out the hidden agendas of some of the churches in the area, [seeing] no need to meet again." Another member said she was "not convinced that the representatives from the NTO office are serious." As Reconstruction refined its CDC plan for participating in the Initiative, board members critiqued the hidden agendas they saw in how other neighborhood collectives were doing the same, and they questioned the seriousness of public representatives who were intermediaries in the Blight Initiative's implementation. Specific board member assignments were given. Another special meeting was scheduled to address organizational matters, along with the next board meeting having been scheduled for two months later in September. With this meeting, a focal issue had been defined, a new critical mass of board leadership came together, with related organization-building meetings and information sharing having also taken place before and outside of the board meeting, Reconstruction Inc. was itself reconstructed as a collectively led, grassroots, capacity-building organization.

From 2001 Forward:
An Organizational Odyssey of Culture, Politics, and Purpose

When culture and community come together, opportunities for capacity-building improve. This truth is sometimes most vivid when the communities in question are in a culture quite different from one's own. Such was the case when William traveled to South Africa in early September 2001. As William wrote to a friend:

> I saw American racism on another level traveling with a group of young and older Quakers. It was revealing. Being able to speak with people who had experienced Apartheid firsthand...who fought to dismantle Apartheid ... who had struggled in the middle of that revolution, was incredible. They were not prepared for what happened afterward. The generals in the revolutionary army were cared for. But the foot soldiers were left without any political, emotional, or financial support. It took me seeing what prisons were in South Africa to get a real understanding just how much people who are locked up in this country are confined in these bricks and steal wallets constructed in the back pockets of urban America. I see [that] the people behind the walls are currency laying in these folds the same as they did in the ships during the Atlantic Slave Trade. I had a rude awakening that we are all precious commodities. We are still being sold at the auction block; [whether in] sports, [as] a celebrity, or a prisoner. (Written Personal Communication).

Though unplanned, William and his Quaker travel companions were in South Africa at the same time the 2001 World Conference Against Racism, Racial Discrimination, Xenophobia, and Related Intolerance was taking place in Durban, South Africa. And just days after their return to the United States, the bombing of the towers of the World Trade Center took place on September 11. Among its members, Reconstruction was successful in drawing a correlation between the bombing of the towers and the topics of concern at the World Conference Against Racism. This was moved further forward as details of the American reaction to the profound tragedy of the bombing and the ways that victimization, blame, innocence, and priorities in the use of public funds were defined and portrayed informed Reconstruction; what its mission was and should be and what strategies of action are most beneficial to its achievement were deeply explored among its members. What explorations surrounding the many related why questions associated with bombing—those that were asked, the many that remained unanswered, and those that were never asked at all— and related othering dynamics of individual and group difference were vital in shaping the recently restructured leadership and all other members. All of this impacted the compassion and urgency that informed William as Reconstruction continued its transition into a community capacity-building organization.

"Glocal" Ties That Bind

As 2001 ended, the new leadership was completing its various assignments. Framed in both the short- and the long-term, the tasks of board members included detailed assessments of the history, current quality, and ownership of local properties; securing a clean copy of the now-outdated bylaws of the organization from 1994; approaching other local organizations to explore what aspects of shared mission might inform the potential for resource sharing and collaboration; and other activities that helped renew the expression of the mission in day-to-day, week-to-week expressions. These were the everyday capacity-building actions their leadership invited them to complete. And these experiences were taking place in a recently post-9/11 United States and a much larger changing climate of local, national, and international understanding—and lack of understanding. In keeping with the model of other learning sanctuaries, or "intentional communities," the Reconstruction leadership increasingly recognized the value of combining "local sustainability with global sustainability...[operating] locally, and being mindful of global responsibilities as citizens of the world. [Both organization and other] community members [were] deeply concerned about the world...translating this concern into their local practice."[36–38] Here again, as before, the goal of the Reconstruction leadership was not to engage in set-aside moments and exchanges, in set-aside places of protection and distance. Instead, the goal and mission were to share in the values and practices of how principled transformations were improving the quality of the lives of many, including persons who did not interact directly and regularly with Reconstruction. These were Reconstruction's glocal ties that bind.

In 2002, after exploring the meanings and consequences of successfully drawing a correlation between the Durban, South Africa Conference on Racism's themes, and the actions, outcomes, and aftermath of 9/11, the organization's glocal ties linked Mayor Street's Blight Initiative and targeting of Tioga with the intergenerational lessons of social justice organizing in creating the youth-led Club House initiative. Both were lessons in land use, skill-building, collective resources, and related politics of urban place. Then longtime charter Reconstruction member Patrick Murray's organizational commitment and architectural and contracting skillset led him to be point person both in the Club House and the CDC assessment of neighborhood properties. As related tasks of engaging formal pedagogy, he also guided a community collective of Reconstruction members and interested others in a focused study of Massey and Denton's (1993) seminal work, *American Apartheid.*[39] Like Patrick's diverse contributions to the neighborhood and organization, the awareness of new information and what to do with it was anchored in the book's first two pages:

> Most Americans vaguely realize that urban America is still a residentially segregated society, but few appreciate the depth of black segregation or the degree to which it is maintained by ongoing institutional arrangements and contemporary individual actions.

They view segregation as an unfortunate holdover from a racist past, one that is fading progressively over time. If racial residential segregation persists, they reason, it is only because civil rights laws passed during the 1960s have not had enough time to work or because many blacks still prefer to live in black neighborhoods....[However] this extreme racial isolation did not just happen; it was manufactured by whites through a series of self-conscious actions and purposeful institutional arrangements that continue today.

Meeting, discussing, and exploring the what, how, and how much of this book's relevance to the neighborhood, the organization, and their family lives, this group of Reconstruction members and interested others came together regularly for months in an effort to move from historically informed understanding, to the realities of what they see and live every day, and to possible strategies of action to shape a more just future. Building on the New African Voices Alliance (NAVA) praxis model of information sharing and collective action, the group used its growing familiarity with the process and practices of residential segregation to be more informed participants in Blight Initiative activities. As with this and every study group, like NAVA, engaging in study groups taught affiliates how to be disciplined, structured, and focused. True to its praxis, their sustained affiliation increased their willingness to take responsibility for change at the core of their personal and collective principled transformation. This group and work continued as the board progressed in the renewal of its leadership. Their efforts included sustaining the property cleanup days in the neighborhood, furthering housing development plans through loan agreements with local donors and financial institutions, and making collaboration appeals to various organizations: private and public, religious and secular, local Mom and Pop outlets and larger-scale nonlocal landholders. Always, the goal was to engage in a range of appeals and foster potential resource collaborations of various kinds.

As 2003 began, the organization again had a primary leadership built from a small critical mass of only the most committed volunteers. Again in a space where the 1808 property was a far more consistent resource taker than funds producer, and William was again running multiple programs that met in various places throughout the city. A rather chaotic time, it was also a time of renewed possibilities. William recently recalled:

All of this influenced the Reconstruction curriculum...having asked [an] intense [mix of] people with extreme personalities to serve on the board....Board meeting dialogue certainly didn't focus on reentry. Rather, it focused more on governance.....The best of this period was that a year was spent developing a set of bylaws to govern more political work than providing services like [we] had in the beginning....Developing and deciding on the bylaws got people frustrated, and they began wanting a program. But the diversity of opinions was too great to decide. This group too didn't meet for a while. Then I called them back together and asked them to govern the three programs I had been running on my own [and] they agreed to govern the three programs. (Personal Communication, n.d.)

An intense mix of strong personalities was now on the newly re-reconstructed board. A focus on governance in its work resulted in clearer, more appropriate bylaws and a trio of programs—Alumni Ex-Offenders Association (AEA), Leadership, Education, Advocacy, and Development (LEAD), and Fight for Lifers (FFL)—to test drive the new governance, reestablish a consistent expression of demonstrated, organizational mission, and sustain a renewed momentum. The organization guided by revised, program-specific curricula and grounded in a pedagogy of principled transformation had itself been principally transformed. And all the while, the one constant during this period of change was FFL. From before, it was a Reconstruction program, and throughout the organization's dormancy and transformation, FFL continued to enter Pennsylvania prisons. Originally founded by a group of life-sentenced individuals, consistent with Pennsylvania state law, these persons were without the possibility of parole. The FFL goal is to challenge the current system and to create the possibility for parole for life-sentenced persons. Before, during, and since the period of dormancy, FFL provided its unique mixture of personal and family advocacy, legal study group, political education, artistic expression, and the principled leadership fundamental to every Reconstruction affiliation.

Fighting for Life

Whose lives are worth fighting for? Before, during, and since Reconstruction's brief dormancy, FFL has been actively asking and answering this question. A continuous, functioning collective since 1993, and a program of Reconstruction Inc. since 2002, FFL formed "in response to the long recognized need for a statewide political action organization devoted strictly to the issues of life-sentenced prisoners, a group of [them] at SCI-Graterford and concerned citizens formed a planning committee...[and] created Fight for Lifers Inc."[40] Perhaps most critically, FFL challenges simple us-them dichotomies of whose lives have worth, with persons serving life sentences as the central figures of FFL advocacy. But to define FFL as purely an advocacy organization is to misrepresent its mission.

> The mission of Fight for Lifers is to educate the public about the realities of serving a
> life sentence in the Commonwealth of Pennsylvania and the necessity for consideration
> of parole review for life sentenced prisoners on a case by case basis; to provide support
> throughout the commutation process for individual lifers who have proven their merit;
> to provide information, support and guidance for their loved ones, and to advocate for
> their special needs and the quality of life issues facing lifers and their families.[41]

As reflected in these words from their newsletter, Fight for Lifers is unique. It offers multiple domains of focus through diverse efforts to nurture a broader, truer justice. True to being a program in an organization guided by a pedagogy of principled transformation, the first domain is education. FFL promotes legal awareness so that persons are informed consumers of the legal process and the means by which they can assert their rights under the law when engaged in the criminal justice system in any way. They "struggle to publish four times a year" the Fight for Lifers newsletter, "The Magnifying Glass."[42] The summer 1999 issue illustrates this domain. The feature article of the six-page newsletter is by a lawyer, Gregory H. Knight, Esq., titled, "My Perspective on the Impact of the Bergoll Decision."[43] This United States Supreme Court decision of June 15, 1999, focused on the right of anyone charged with a crime to face the accuser and the complexities of doing so when the victim is a child. It was a concern at the time because of its applicability to capital cases where a life sentence is an option before the court. It discusses the constitutionality of a November 1995 ballot initiative found to have been improperly presented to voters since it is against the law to address more than one issue within a single ballot initiative. This required voters to make multiple decisions simultaneously, in violation of Article XI, Section 1 of the Pennsylvania State Constitution.

Political advocacy and opposition to the life sentence without the possibility of parole is Fight for Lifer's second domain. A central focus of FFL's message is the injustices associated with this sentence, and over the years, FFL continues participating in various legislative and other political activities in order to have this sentence changed so that the possibility of parole exists. In a state where life-sentenced persons must remain in prison until their final breath, and which has more juvenile lifers than any other state (by a wide margin), the possibility for parole becomes especially critical. As William Goldsby recently stated, "If we believe in change, then we need to put in place that lifers change and deserve a chance to demonstrate that change" with the opportunity to live a life beyond penal confinement (Personal Communication, n.d.).

FFL advocates *with*, rather than on behalf of, a set of interdependent subgroups. They advocate for and with all those connected to incarcerated persons

serving life who must keep their spirit and wits about them, even as they navigate the many challenges of sustaining family support. This includes dealing
with overpriced phone charges to stay in phone contact with their incarcerated
loved one. Through *The Magnifying Glass* newsletter, they advocate on behalf of
lifers by promoting books they have published (e.g., John Griffin's 2002 *A Letter to My Father*), sharing research on lifer's extremely low recidivism rates for
those able to secure release, publishing creative writing, open letters, criminal
justice critiques, and editorials. They advocate for youth who have been treated
as adults within the system, despite the realities of their chronological age and
sometimes still more limited maturity levels. And above all, in a state where life
means life, Anita Colon, May Hadley, Donna Pfender, and others advocate for
and with family members and other loved ones of lifers in the meeting-by-
meeting, event-by-event, shared fellowship of a common bond of caring struggle to deal with the legal, economic, and spiritual challenges associated with the
process of a life sentence.

    To further these education and advocacy domains, a third Fight for Lifers
domain is its provision of direct legal support. This is focused primarily on the
commutation process and what is involved in applying for it. Commutation,
"the conversion of a legal obligation or entitlement into another form," is typically understood as a process by which a governor releases a formerly incarcerated person due to current circumstances. The application for commutation is
an act of voice and vision. In Pennsylvania, commutation is too often determined by political atmosphere rather than by the applicants' merits (e.g., accomplishments, community support, remorse for the victim, or spiritual
change). Through its newsletter, meetings, rallies, and communication with local
and state politicians, Fight for Lifers provides legal assistance and engages in
advocacy for changing the Pennsylvania commutation process.

    A fourth domain of Fight for Lifers is to promote social and cultural
change, which takes various forms. In their newsletter, *The Magnifying Glass*,
there are one or more poems in every issue. Many of the poets are themselves
currently serving life sentences in a Pennsylvania prison, with all readers outside
of the prison walls being in a position to be an audience of many beyond the
end of the writer's pen. Social change can be promoted in visual and artistic
terms. The summer 1999 FFL newsletter had on its cover a picture of a very
long corridor of the Eastern State Penitentiary that had by that time been closed
and was serving as a museum. In the corridor were 132 T-shirts hung on
clotheslines strung in a sequence of diagonal lines moving from one corridor
wall to the other, at different heights, for as far as the camera's lens could cap-

ture. "An exhibit of 132 T-shirts with the names painted on them of the 132 women currently serving life without [the possibility of] parole were hung...and will remain on display until the end of October [1999]."[44] The article accompanying the photo goes on to discuss that many of the women so charged were "battered women who struck back." It recognized that "the t-shirts also represent all (at that time) 3,400 life-sentenced individuals in the state [including] men who committed fatal acts while suffering from post-traumatic stress induced while on military duty." Art. Engagement in feminist discourse. Activism. The politics of symbolic exchange. The Fight for Lifers display and the discussion of it were all of these and more. The display and the related event also spoke to the collaborative nature of all Reconstruction's work, as the above message accompanying the t-shirt display was signed by Amnesty International, the American Friends Service Committee, the Pennsylvania Prison Society, and other attending groups. The display was the product of a multi-organization meeting of these and other organizations that had been initiated on March 8 of that year, International Women's Day.

Another merge of activism and art is the Photo Wall. Discussed in the fall 2002 issue of the newsletter, the Photo Wall is "comprised of seven panels and over 350 photographs of Pennsylvania Lifers. [It] was set up at the forum and attendees found it powerful as they viewed the many faces….[This included] prison-taken portraits, photos of themselves with family members, [and] letters from Lifers."[45] It provided a human face to lifers during a FFL forum on forgiveness, challenging unjust silences in Fight for Lifers' daily walk. This forum on forgiveness demonstrated the FFL engagement of yet another of its diverse domains: exploring spirituality in individual and collective transformation. In the fall 2002 issue of the newsletter, the previous spring's Forgiveness Forum was celebrated. The Photo Wall had been displayed at the forum (panels of it have since been displayed at various Reconstruction fundraising events and other activities throughout the years. The panels are displayed daily in the Reconstruction office at 1808 Tioga). Discussed primarily from a religious perspective, the core of the Forum was a panel of faith leaders including a Muslim imam, a Catholic priest, a Jewish rabbi, a Baptist pastor, and a Mennonite faith leader. While faith engagements during incarceration and in the process of reentry are one of the growing segments in reentry and reintegration research,[46–48] less well known are the ways in which faith in the possibilities of diverse transformations both within and beyond the criminal justice system—be they individual, familial, organizational, communal, or broader still—are, in fact, intertwined.[49,50] This FFL forum explored these themes in a dialogue that went beyond religious engagement, into considerations of ethics, values, spiritual growth, and how forgiveness can be understood as a diverse praxis of ideas, dialogue, and various actions for change.

Families First

On April 17, 2005, William Goldsby responded to an e-mail from Townsand Price-Spratlen with the following:

> The goal of the statewide conference that we have planned for May 21st is to organize family members of life-sentenced prisoners to abolish the life-without-parole and/or add life with parole in Pennsylvania. The attached program does not include the follow-up which will be to facilitate several debates in various locations in Pennsylvania. The debates will focus on some of the same topics from the conference. The follow-up also will be to involve the Legislative Black Caucus to join us in this work and adopt the concept "To abolish life-without-parole is not political suicide. Rather, it is a career" (Personal Communication).

Consistent with William's plan-of-action just over 30 days prior to the event, on May 21, 2005, more than 400 persons came to this Fight for Lifers Conference on the Temple University campus from all over Pennsylvania, the tri-state area, and beyond. They did so to further a movement seeking this sentence-abolition goal. In a post-conference e-mail exchange between the book's co-authors on July 7, 2005, William stated:

> The conference went very well. We had a beautiful turnout of mostly family members [of lifers]. That is what we were aiming for. The topics of discussion were well-received because they were topics that regular working class people [typically] don't take the time to discuss. We are now beginning to organize our post-conference projects....It is interesting reading about your family roots because my nephew is digging up our family legacies....We have discovered that my great-great-grandad was an [Alabama] legislator during the Reconstruction Era.

Reconstructing Reconstruction by nurturing family ties within and across generations. And this conference was yet another successful contribution to this progress. The collective view of conference organizers was that the life without parole sentence represents cruel and unusual punishment in view of the hardships and dehumanizing practices associated with it. As political prisoner and Pennsylvania Death Row inmate Mumia Abu-Jamal stated in his taped speech prepared for the conference, a life sentence without parole "is a half-life on Life Row. It is a lifeless life. It differs from the death penalty only in degree, with time as the executioner."[51] With each of the FFL program domains discussed above reflected in the events of the day, the conference provided a rich mixture of arts and advocacy, critical education and proposed legislation, historically informed foundations and plans for present and future action. The dynamic speakers and many breakout sessions allowed all persons to be heard and valued. These included reflections from prior meetings with then-governor Ed Rendell, gains and limitations of a bill prepared by attorneys Ernie Preate and Angus Love, and a discussion on "The Complexities of Victimhood."

Theatrical performances and letters from lifers read by their family members reinforced the day-to-day lived experience of the life sentence in Pennsylvania prisons. The stage performances were done by Tova, a performance collective that seeks to further social justice. As described by Donna Pfender, president of Fight for Lifers-West,

> Tova means good in Hebrew. It is also the name of a performance arts organization in Philadelphia that seeks to tackle social justice issues through the telling of stories. The people telling the stories are the people who experienced them. None are actors....[I] witnessed the opening night of "Beyond the Walls: The Road to Redemption." This "Theatre of Witness" piece is both an elegy and a call for peace performed by and created with family members that have lost loved ones to murder, to prison and/or to the streets, former offenders who are working to transform their communities, and children who are living in the midst of the violence. Y'all! This piece was so powerful. (Written Personal Communication, 2005)

Nurturing what is spiritually good. Celebrating the arts as political praxis. Acknowledging the tensions between pain and progress. Refining and redefining the complexities of victimhood and the many legal and public policy questions they raise. Valuing the therapeutic worth of dialogue as others empathetically listen to the telling of one's stories. Exploring redemption, atonement, forgiveness, and letting go. All in the midst of a quality performance in a quality conference as Fight for Lifers furthered its own mission, as well as that of Reconstruction.

An informed critique of the commutation process and historical trends in lifers' legislation added to the keynote address of Butch Cottman on "The Prevailing Contradictions in Criminal Justice." With input and active engagement from LEAD and AEA, as well as the members of Fight for Lifers in both the Philadelphia and Pittsburgh chapters, all three Reconstruction programs participated in the conference. Speaking to the quality of collaborations the new board and entire organization had nurtured, many organizations were active in the conference, including Bread and Roses, Mott Foundation-CTAC, Resist Foundation, Whole Foods, Lou Restaurant, and the Pennsylvania Lifers Association; many individuals also made generous donations. And throughout the day, food was provided by the Human Rights Coalition, which monitors abuse in the Pennsylvania Department of Corrections.

Consistent with the tone and focus of the conference, Murder Victims' Families for Reconciliation (MVFR) is a national organization founded in 1976. It is made up of "[a] geographically, racially and economically diverse [group of] family members of victims of both homicide and executions who oppose the death penalty in all cases, [and] includes people of many different perspectives."[52] MVFR stands against all forms of cruel and harsh punishment for all persons, especially and including the murderer of their loved one. Like MVFR, FFL believes that the life sentence without the possibility for parole is too often held in place not by the family members of victims but instead by politicians, using it as a resource for their gain. The success of the 2005 Fight for Lifers Conference was a result of a coalition of many willing to give and share principled leadership in the service of building the capacity of the families of lifers, and changing the law and the commutation process in and beyond Pennsylvania.

Neighboring Intimate Empathy

Later in 2005, the Philadelphia Department of Behavioral Health and Human Services (DBHHS) awarded $10,000 to Reconstruction Inc. With it, a van was purchased that allowed for more participation by elder parents of lifers, which increased the FFL membership. In addition, using the villaging principle discussed earlier, FFL began to sponsor living-room discussions on the issues raised during the conference. At one such event, a family that invited FFL into their living room also invited a near neighbor to join them. During the discussion, the host family and its near neighbor learned for the first time that they both had sons serving life sentences. They had been neighbors for more than 15 years and had never before discussed their shared truth. This realization was a moment to behold. Sometimes members change themselves to change the world, one living room at a time. The surprise, support, awe, and more brought tears to the eyes of many who attended and demonstrates the victories of caring and change in the grassroots process of engaging Reconstruction's intimate mission.

The Philadelphia DBHHS funds were also used to sponsor a set of workshops facilitated by Continuing Opportunity for Family Education Enrichment (COFFEE). COFFEE uses a very progressive therapeutic model for dealing with family issues and behaviors often at the core of crimes, violent and otherwise. The capacity-building intent of these workshops was that through the transformative potential within individuals and families they nurture, the likelihood of crimes resulting in life sentences without the possibility of parole can decline. Whether guided by the intimacy of a neighbor's living room or newfound therapeutic resources for responding to personal or family challenges, after the conference, Reconstruction continued to build and grow.

Continuing to Build

Once the "church effect" feel-good echoes of the Fight for Lifers conference had faded, the work of Reconstruction continued. At this time, the work involved "the entire neighborhood, with a special focus on youth and unemployed adults, particularly ex-offenders."[53] This was a critical period of the organization, refining the meanings and processes of being a member-driven, community, capacity-building organization. This included securing the help of the Community Training Assistance Center (CTAC). Over the next two years, CTAC helped Reconstruction in two critical ways: initiative and program refinement and work plan development. As William recently recalled,

> During their first year of working with us, we dealt with helping the board and each program to trim down all of the many ideas we had on our plate. They made it painfully clear that we [again] did not have the capacity to manage all of our lofty ideas. Instead, we had to focus on our membership, recruitment, and provide whatever support and training we needed to keep members engaged in their families and in the work. (Personal Communication, n.d.)

This first-year refinement process was then followed by a second year that was just as intrusive and challenging. During year 2, CTAC focused only on the Reconstruction work plan. What goes into it. How a work plan is a map for the organization and its membership. And how that map might best be followed to effectively build the organization's capacity for achievement and nurture the same within each of its individual and family members. This second-year focus led Reconstruction to struggle to determine which of several different models and ideas it should use for the work plan. The board decided to organize itself and the three programs (AEA, FFL, and LEAD) into three interdependent areas: internal development, public relations and outreach, and research development. These same three areas are the map that guides each program, and it provides the time and life management protocol all members are encouraged to use.

This critical period of organizational refinement also included making a clear distinction—to its own leadership and membership, as well as to all prospective affiliates and organizational collaborators—the ways in which Reconstruction's engagement in the CDC process would differ from how CDCs are typically understood. This included working with community residents as equal partners, meeting neighbors where they are and supporting them in their own personal struggles, focusing on family preservation and the building of better (spousal, intergenerational, and other) relationships, having board members continue to do much of the work of the organization, and prioritizing layered reciprocities, including training neighbors in the skills they need to be experts at making their own community work well, and work better.

In the interests of applying the cultural lessons of self-criticism William had brought from his time with New African Voices Alliance and the village of Kum Bah Yah, and the utilities of transparency in information sharing within and beyond the organization, capacity-building challenges were listed for each of the organization's three programs in the annual report.[54] And their listing demonstrates the strategies of organizational action that were being prioritized within each program. "AEA must systematically develop its access [to] men and women transitioning out of penal institutions so that we may communicate and develop the AEA message and recruit membership." The institutional partnership with Graterford was no longer functional. The service framing of the organization with the first Graterford cohorts was now gone, and a new model was under construction. This included a recognition of "the need to build an emergency response protocol" in collaboration with other service organizations, with a formal follow-up process to ensure that resources have been effectively accessed and delivered for beneficial outcome. Direct co-counseling-modeled therapeutic support[55,56] was recognized with the reported recommendation that

> AEA must reenergize the support group; organize new groups at new sites; prepare more members to facilitate support groups, and develop media that promotes the AEA support group[s]....[This includes] developing a certification training regimen for ex-offenders, community activists, and social workers and others who can benefit from an all-around grounding in the issues both clinical, political, and economic that face ex-offenders, their families, and communities every day.

These same themes of standardized development, systematic outreach, work plan projections, and the patterns of relationships between educational, therapeutic, skill-building, resource, and economic development domains were the capacity-building challenges of LEAD. As expected, coming out of the conference success, the Fight for Lifers' work plan and challenges were highly domain-and task-specific. The work plan emphasized:

1. Continuing *The Magnifying Glass* newsletter.

2. Collaborating toward the development of a faith-based lifers support system.
3. Sharing information with other similar groups to identify specific inmates for selected advocacy for parole or commutation campaigns.
4. Co-authoring a statewide resolution that would promote parole and/or a fair commutation process for lifers.
5. Systematically sharing justice critiques of the meanings of being judged "by a jury of one's peers" to inform public sentiment and further legislative and public policy campaigns.[57]

The capacity-building challenges extended directly from each of these work plan points of emphasis, and added improving youth and student involvement and fundraising to FFL's capacity-building priorities.

By the mid-fiscal year report of December 2006, the weight of grassroots organizing and its associated challenges were again reflected in the organization's update. The office was receiving 30 or more calls a month from lifers from throughout the state of Pennsylvania and across the country. Many more calls came from non-lifers returning to the community, interested in furthering their reentry and reintegration. Reconstruction was serving in a "boundary spanner" role of bridging persons with other organizations in entirely other capacity-building domains, including referring many persons each semester to Temple University's Pan-African Studies Community Education Program. Near daily referrals to various job sites and other organizations that assisted in resume development and employment referral was taking place. All this, in addition to regular housing referrals, frequent transportation support to various meetings, responding to family crises and other emergencies, and providing detailed, legal advice multiple times a week. The following paragraph from the December 2006 update characterized both the 2006 calendar year that had just ended, 2007 that was soon to begin, and the entire organization's history, including these bridge years between:

> Reconstruction's ability to sustain its work through community organizing and direct services needs a lot more technical and financial support. Reconstruction envisions a time when the constituency understands and internalizes the principle of reciprocity where they are not only consuming services, [but are also] provid[ing] services and advocacy for each other. To that end, Reconstruction recognizes that our membership needs a lot of training in drug and alcohol addiction, family therapy, conflict resolution, [and] economic and political development before we reach that point.[58]

Building Beyond the Bridge's End

Small critical mass. Uncertain, shoestring budgets. Passionate leadership. Clarity of mission. Many people who have touched and been touched by the organization. All of these sustained and prevailing truths, with few and fewer willing to maintain affiliation for any length of time to further the strategies of action for sustained social change, the sacred exchange of ancestral echoes, and the choice to value Reconstruction's pedagogy of principled transformation in their daily walk. As William recently noted when reflecting on the organization's second decade:

> The forces and power of poverty [are] really horrific. This is so especially when people have been marginalized and disenfranchised and conditioned to accept and perpetuate their blighted existence.... Reconstruction created an environment where people understand that within them is the potential for progressive and radical change, and that this change occurs when we are structured, disciplined, and focused. At this point, we begin to educate anyone and especially our members. This also counters oppression and the family ceases to erode. (Personal Communication, n.d.)

These are some among the challenges of sustaining a capacity-building organization in this era of mass incarceration and, by doing so, build beyond the bridge's end. Reconstruction's second decade came to an end with the arrival of 2007, which proved to be an especially active organizational year. The challenges reflected in the events of 2006 had created the need to move from organizational structure and protocol development, and return to refining the curriculum for the organization and within each of its three programs. In 2007, the "Reconstruction Community Organizing Curriculum" for the entire organization was drafted. And revised. And redrafted. And revised. And...this six-and-more-page, single-spaced document was the resource of exchange for the members of the Alumni Ex-Offender Association's Internal Development Committee who took on, and engaged in, the tasks to assess and redefine. With all things Reconstruction, the process of exchange was prioritized as an opportunity to dialogue and a libratory resource for personal and interpersonal transformation. Exploratory. Engaging. Labor intensive. Both intellectually and spiritually rigorous.

This curriculum refinement process was a values-driven, detailed exploration of the lived experiences of (political and cultural) alienation, arrested development, co-dependency, and individualism, and their intended, capacity-building polar opposites (community, self-determination, reciprocity, and collectivism, respectively). And it was a detailed exploration of how Reconstruction as one grassroots organization could best nurture a process of principled transformation; in other words, furthering capacity-building as a life praxis through the frequent expression of these beneficial opposites, and the ability to assist others through equitable exchange to do the same. This process informed the entire organization's progress in more and less direct ways, as multiple dynamics of everyday actions were scrutinized in new and different ways.

Throughout, the work plan structure of the new Reconstruction remained its most effective organizational strategy. During the Blight Initiative period and the most redevelopment-centered portion of the CDC process from 2001 to 2004, Reconstruction was making progress informed by the resource contributions of the Community Training Assistance Center (CTAC). The work plan structure extended from CTAC's assistance. It was (and continues to be) used for personal, familial, communal, and organizational clarity. It helps to compartmentalize and manage situations more efficiently. This multilevel work plan process informed the refinement of the curriculum (organizationally), and the manner and content of collective exchange regarding an organization member's substance use (personally). It also suggested interventions for responding to interpersonal and family challenges (familially), and was the foundation for Reconstruction's various local area participations, including the neighborhood study group on American Apartheid, the Club House initiative, and neighborhood cleanup days (communally). As 2007 progressed, the multilevel work plan process again was a vital resource in maintaining a quality pace of organizational progress.

When Media Attention Comes Their Way
While the Reconstruction curriculum was going through its cycles of detailed revision and the day-to-day referrals, phone calls, event planning, legal consults, and other resource exchanges of the organization's office continued, perhaps the most externally noteworthy organizational event was a story on Reconstruction published in the *Philadelphia City Paper* in July 2007. The article, "... And Stays Out: Hakim Ali's Using His Years Inside to Help Ex-Cons Stay on the Up and Up," was a feature piece on former staff member and longtime board and committee member Hakim Ali.[59] It described Reconstruction's current priorities and strategies of action. Attention was also given to what is perhaps the single most valuable organizational statistic from Reconstruction's original Graterford Prison cohort: "Only four of the [original] 25 went back for parole violations and only one was re-arrested for another crime. [This is] a remarkable success considering that the Bureau of Justice reported a 67 percent re-arrest rate at that

time. But success was not enough to keep [the program] afloat."[60] The Alumni Ex-Offenders Association emphasized its priority on family involvement in the reentry process, along with the learning sanctuary mentoring model used in that program and throughout the organization. AEA "offers practical advice and emotional support to individuals seeking to reenter society, and counsel[s] their families on how best to help their loved ones through this difficult time. All of the volunteer counselors are ex-offenders, and so [personally] know the difficulties people face upon release." In the article, Tania Falbo is briefly profiled as having "started attending meetings when one of her son's childhood friends was released from prison, [and] says those counselors are one of the program's greatest strengths. 'I think it helps to have ex-offenders who are now helping others. I think that's a good role model.'"[61]

With resources having been secured to briefly hire him into a much needed, half-time office manager position at the time, Hakim charted responses to the article in the weeks that followed. Responses to articles are only made by a very small number of the persons who actually read and value the article and represents an uncertain percentage of all article readers. Beyond those who may have read the article and visited the Reconstruction Web site, or who may have called off-hours and chosen not to leave a message, in the week that followed, ten documented responses came via the Reconstruction office phone. This included persons who received lengthy, detailed case consults on their pending legal circumstances, those who visited the office, others who then completed an initial orientation, others who attended a meeting, and others whose parole officer or other justice system representative interacted with the organization. This included friends or family members of persons in some kind of legal trouble, and persons across a wide spectrum of age, race, gender, and class affiliations. In short, many persons took notice, and a few of them chose to respond.

Conclusion

Reciprocity, the process of sacred exchange, is a challenge in grassroots organizing. The second decade of Reconstruction made challenges associated with centering reciprocity as a learning organization's praxis. When resources are limited, new contacts are relied upon to understand and then to act on moving from a service model client, to a skill-building affiliate of a collective. For one person in particular, both Hakim and William provided extensive information and support. This was an acquaintance of one of the key leadership group members of the organization's LEAD program. Having seen the article, they valued the information. They were then attempting to minimize their current situation and chose not to follow up. When a routine traffic stop quickly redefined their sense of urgency, they called the Reconstruction office. This began with a lengthy initial call with Hakim. Hakim then consulted with William, then returned to the inquiry call, and then all three persons shared a conference call. Like much of Reconstruction's actions of its intimate justice mission, that first call was many things at once. Part allaying fears as a counselor would. Part clarifying legal standing and prior case circumstances as a representative of the court would. Part sharing laughter about the circuitous means of the person finally getting in touch with the organization as a friend would. All sharing quality information in the interests of nurturing a new justice paradigm as the founder and longtime Reconstruction member would and do in their daily walk.

Over the next several weeks, fellowship with this person included multiple service-oriented interactions, including consults with his court representative, both electronically and by phone. Yet, at the point at which it came time for this person to participate more fully in a reciprocal engagement with the organization, they made several promises of participation on which they never followed through. This type of contact—initial contact in search of short-term service, while not seeking to understand or participate in the reciprocal portion of the member-driven, capacity-building process—occurs with a near-uncountable frequency. The challenge in the past and into today remains keeping the doors open, the phone lines funded, and persons willing to engage the mission ready at a moment's notice. True to the servant-leader role in principled transformation to be of service. To support a stranger well beyond the distances the charity model maintains. To, in whatever ways a single situation can do so, help to nurture a new justice. Through it all, the visibility of the article provided some valuable exposure and led a number of persons to be aware, who might not have otherwise known of Reconstruction Inc. And that alone has value. And true to the Reconstruction mission, those persons, as well as those they may be in fellowship with, know that there is an organization that can assist them in recognizing that they themselves are the capacity-building resource that can change their particular circumstance. And that by doing so, they can change the world.

The Personal Is Political

In 2001, shortly before his trip to South Africa, William was diagnosed with perspective glaucoma. In 2003, as the community development corporation process, American Apartheid study group, and collective response to the Blight

Initiative progressed under the new board's leadership, William was diagnosed with a progressive form of glaucoma. By 2005, while planning for and carrying out the successful Fight for Lifers conference, William had lost more than 95% of his vision and was declared legally blind. A year later in May 2006, his eldest sister passed away, and the following year his father passed. Still other personal challenges soon followed, including the uncertain grief of having another family member lost at sea. All of these and other personal issues were placed in the organization's check in—a vital, introductory portion to every meeting, in which every person in attendance shares a brief statement about how they are doing. The collective decision was that placing William's personal concerns there would best allow him to continue giving principled leadership to the organization. He was expected to disclose his personal issues, including turning over to AEA the decision of whether or not he should have corrective surgery. Against William's own personal wishes, AEA decided he would have the surgery. Some members chose to not participate in that meeting who did not want to be responsible in any way for any negative results of the surgery. Beyond his individual health challenges, each of William's family tragedies was also put forth for collective feedback.

These public privacies informed how other members trusted—or were alienated from—the process and the Reconstruction mission. Whether sharing a personal profile in the City Paper, bringing to light an empathy of shared struggle among neighbors, or dealing with the most personal health and family challenges, "*changing ourselves to change the world*" is much more than a slogan. Rather, it is a means of valuing how the personal is political. It is a strategy of action. In fact, it is a way of life, guiding the members and families of the organization, moving it and them across the dormancy years into a new period of possibility. All the way across and beyond the bridge between them.

Endnotes Toward Principled Transformation

Extending from the capacity-building of Reconstruction's second decade, three possibilities toward principled transformation emerge:

- Transformative Trainings—Quality skill-building within an organization demands multiple strategies for connecting spirituality with the organization's mission—in its pedagogy, leadership, economics, and actions. An understanding of relationships between power, equity, and justice are central to the actions of this transformative spirituality in living the organization's mission in one's daily walk.

- Resolving Rage—Actions toward the resolution of rage are a product of realizing one is an agent of change. Angers of injustice (i.e., one expression of sacred rage) are the fuel for transformation. These angers can be beneficially nurtured when the local and global poor rise beyond being colonized, when land is acquired and managed justly, and when an equitable collective efficacy guides the exchange of resources.

- A New Justice—Nurturing a new justice paradigm demands fundamental redistributions of wealth and the many resources related to wealth. Economically, policies that move us much closer to a tax structure of the 1960s, for example, would be a libratory step toward that new justice. Institutionally, expanding access of former felons to reenter prisons would enrich their spiritual leadership, and that of currently incarcerated citizens with whom they interact, as well.

More Than a Moment's Notice: Reconstruction's Recent Best Practices

It's truly amazing to me, the selflessness of the participating individuals of Reconstruction. I haven't run across anything [else] like that, Townsand. The ability to pull together and assist in any way possible. To just give....If Reconstruction put in any time or effort with an individual, they only ask that the individual they put in time with, come back and do something likewise that was given to them....That's the expectation. If you were given assistance, support, make yourself available to do the same for the next person coming through the doors. Just being an example of...a principled individual.

Deion Morrison, longtime Reconstruction affiliate, November 2009

Our prison system has become the chief means of warehousing redundant labor, the unemployed, the unskilled and the poor.... Social transformation along the contemporary boundaries of color and class will require new kinds of strategies, new approaches and new thinking. We must assist the development of community-based initiatives that have the capacity to educate and mobilize those who suffer most from racial oppression. Through this effort, we may make an important contribution toward the reconfiguration of American democracy itself, which could conceivably, one day, include all of us.

Dr. Manning Marable. United Nations World Conference on Racism,
Durban, South Africa, September 5, 2001

Throughout its history, Reconstruction Inc. has been and remains an affirmation and exploration of the lived experiences and contradictions when reciprocity is the central value in a small, well-led, grassroots collective. Perhaps by necessity, when reciprocity is at the center, so many resources including and beyond dollars and cents anchor an organization's currency. The former felons, their families, and the interested others who are the persons demonstrating the "selflessness of participating individuals" to which Deion Morrison referred during his 2009 interview, simultaneously engage shared sacrifice; a sometimes uncertain, often uneven "sell," especially in the most recent years of substantial economic constraint. Yet that sensibility informs and is expressed through the values, motives, and strategies of action central to Reconstruction, both as a mission and an organization. Consistent with the words of the late Professor Manning Marable in his 2001 speech at the World Conference on Racism,[1] our description and analysis of the organization in these chapters extends from the view that Reconstruction is one among the "community-based initiatives [with] the capacity to educate and mobilize" in addressing the current challenges of mass incarceration and its many allied oppressions. What follows is a discussion of best practices reflected in the organization's current initiatives and structure to demonstrate how it is educating and mobilizing those who suffer most, by also educating and mobilizing persons, families, and allied organizations that experience these oppressions quite differently. By doing so, we demonstrate both the contemporary lived experiences of Mr. Morrison's selflessness comment and how Reconstruction responds to Professor Marable's important mobilizing call to action.

Building on the Recent Past

Affiliating with an organization guided by a pedagogy of principled transformation demands critical awareness. Beyond the bridge from organizational dormancy to the most recent years, a best practice momentum was nurtured by that critical awareness. In October 2007, Butch Cottman shared a news item with family, friends, and affiliates of Reconstruction Inc. The Associated Press article documented that, in just three years (2003–2005), more than 2,000 persons died while in police custody.[2] That is a pace and regularity of death at the hands of law enforcement that should give us pause: a pace of almost two such deaths every day in the United States. The author, Ms. Hope Yen, pointed out that to focus on high-profile incidents in a single city, like those of Abner Louima or Amadou Diallo of New York City, is to misrepresent both the geographic and numerical prevalence of this process. To place these deaths in the context of more than 12 million arrests per year makes them rare events. The fact that just one of every six of the suspects fought with, or otherwise hit police, makes the vast majority of them something other than retaliatory, and far fewer still as a result of the officer's life being threatened in any way. For African Americans to experience these deaths at nearly three times their proportion in the general population, and Latinos at nearly twice their proportion, renders them racially and ethnically informed, if not motivated. The article was sent by a longtime affiliate and shared without comment with other affiliates of a capacity-building organization seeking to nurture a broader justice, as a best practice momentum progressed.

Six weeks later, in December 2007, William Goldsby circulated a spreadsheet that listed 15 foundations of varying sizes and funding bases that might respectfully consider a grant submitted by Reconstruction. The list of persons with primary responsibility for completing grant follow-ups for these potential funders included seven members. No member was listed fewer than four times, and at least two names were listed for each of the fifteen possible funders. This structure and plan of action reflected a division of labor and participatory leadership to help move toward a more stable financial base. However, soon after the spreadsheet was circulated and a meeting had been held to begin the grant preparation process, a member who had been brought onto the board and had expressed excitement about giving primary leadership to this funding process almost completely withdrew. This member first significantly reduced their availability and participation, and then did not follow through on a set of next step tasks toward grant preparation. One among these included facilitating a set of grant writing workshops for skill building among a group of learned and willing persons with uneven grant preparation histories. In the end, only two of the grants were prepared and submitted, with one of them being funded.

Another effort toward a broadening of financial resources for the organization was less successful than board members had hoped. Again the primary challenge was the very small size of the organization's critical mass and the necessary reliance on a few persons to do labor-intensive tasks voluntarily. If their lives or priorities changed in a critical moment, the result of that personal change often has substantial organizational consequences. As 2008 began, consistent with the restricted financial capacity of most small grassroots organizations, Reconstruction's continuing struggle for a resource base to allow both its reach and grasp to be more in line with one another remained.

Then, in January 2008, two articles were circulated among the Alumni Ex-Offender Association membership to begin their political discussion. The two brief articles were titled, "The Suffering of the Poor is the Life Blood of Capitalism," and "How to Destroy the Public Schools: When the Rich Pay No Taxes." The first of these, written by Butch Cottman, is a one-page overview and invitation to the role of political study for informed civic engagement, the definition of capitalism, and how an understanding of both political study and capitalism are valued tools in the practice of principled criticism and social action.[3] The second of these is a January 17, 2008, op-ed essay by Paul A. Moore, a teacher in the Miami-Dade County (Florida) school district, and it demonstrates what happened to the funding for Florida schools due to changes in state and other tax policy under the governorship of Jeb Bush.[4] These articles were the first two topics for discussion among the Internal Development Committee of AEA, the core of the study group membership within Reconstruction at the time.

The first of these capacity-building examples was an electronic dialogue about life-taking in point-of-contact, law enforcement practices directly related to—and that help fuel—mass incarceration. The second was a renewed effort toward developing a balanced, collective process for organizational funding. And the third was the use of accessible technologies to organize a study group to further pedagogy as "the practice of freedom" among the Reconstruction membership. Leadership. Resources. Citizen participation. Interorganizational networks. The meaning and mechanisms of community power. Strategies for enriching critical reflection. These are among the most valued dimensions in the process of community capacity-building.[5–9] The most recent years have continued to both mirror many of the ongoing challenges of grassroots social organizing and simultaneously enrich Reconstruction's capacity-building core. These dimensions were a part of the everyday exchanges in "the selflessness of participating individuals" to which Deion refers previously. And each of them continues to be a valuable part of this new beginning for Reconstruction Inc.

Current Best Practices

Recent research on the reentry and reintegration of former felons has identified programmatic suggestions for the present and future of the large number of former felons now returning to their communities from prisons and jails.[10–16] Generally, the focus of this work is how departments of corrections (DOCs) can most effectively prepare currently incarcerated persons for their transition, and the role of jobs readiness or state-sponsored jobs programs associated with such state-level DOC programming. With a few exceptions,[17] what this best practices research generally does not include is the assessment of programming in communities for persons already outside institutional settings. What is entirely lacking is any detailed consideration of grassroots, former felon-led, community organizations. Thus, we know little about how such an organization has helped former felons move beyond desistance (i.e., sustaining a crime-free life) by having met and valued other former felons where they are, in a family-centered fashion. We know little about how it nurtured critical awareness and civic engagement toward their spiritual and principled transformation. To help move us further toward the society that Dr. Manning Marable called for, where best practices flourish, we consider six strategies of action used in Reconstruction to enrich and share its ongoing mission of *"changing ourselves to change the world."*

Best Practice #1: Cultivating Innovation
In any attempt to build success beyond survival, innovation is essential. Innovation is "the successful introduction of means or ends into an applied situation...[to] bring something new into use."[18] Its expression in community

organizing is perhaps most visible in the ways in which timely creativity for the sake of more effectively engaging the organization's mission has occurred. With a mission grounded in change at multiple levels, Reconstruction Inc. has cultivated innovation as a strategy of action across its history, and it continues to do so today. Below, we share three innovative examples.

First, with the growth of various social media, Reconstruction has continued to adapt the role of technology in contemporary social organizing. The LEAD program for youth organizing has a "Friends" page on Facebook, and two LEAD members regularly update the page and engage with those who've come upon it, allowing followers to stay abreast of various programs and organizational initiatives. And, as presented in the examples above, e-mail is the most widely used resource within the organization, allowing all members in the organization's network to be made aware of various activities.

The organization's Web site is one component of the Public Relations and Outreach domain of the organization's three-domain work plan (see chapter 7). Consistent with Reconstruction's capacity-building, in a series of workshops, the Web designer of Gypsy Lane Technologies has trained and works with three other affiliates to maintain the Web site. In this way, the implementation and sustained use of technology becomes another opportunity for skill-building as a shared asset within the collective; in other words, using technology to cultivate still more innovation. All the while, the organization's pedagogy of principled transformation is never far from any domain or initiative. The first item of the Web site's third dropdown "Programs" menu is Community Capacity-building, where the organization's Three Pillar Curriculum is presented. The guiding paragraph of curricular implementation includes the following: "In the interest of promoting faith and collective wellness, and in providing only a concise overview, the above...series of concepts can be effectively tailored to specific groups and their specific missions." The capacity-building curriculum is viewed on the Web site and is guided by the organization's collective interest in "promoting faith and collective wellness" among individuals, families, and organizations that might benefit from furthering their specific mission.[19]

Beyond the use of technology, Reconstruction also cultivates innovation with programming creativity, including the recent creation of its Reentry Assistance Program (RAP). RAP provides pre-release planning, and immediate transitional services to assist soon-to-be reentering citizens with a direct pathway of change, assisting them with the planning and management of service access for the last few months of their prison sentence, and the first few weeks of their reentry transition. RAP began when Reconstruction became aware of a recent change in Pennsylvania state law where longtime inmates in Restricted Housing Units were "aging out" of their sentence. The law was directed at persons imprisoned for nonviolent offenses, who had been imprisoned for more than 12 years on their most recent sentence, and who were at or approaching their 60th birthday. The "graying" of the prison population is one among several forthcoming trends that will shape mass incarceration for the foreseeable future.[20–23] And this trend will directly impact Reconstruction and other similar organizations for many years to come. RAP provides family-centered support, informed by the expectation of reciprocity described earlier by Deion Morrison. A recent RAP meeting excerpt follows.[24]

A RAP Meeting Moment

Arthur: I think that before going up there [to the prison], we ought to have in hand a list of things that we want out of a relationship with [the prison administrator]. So that in conversation with her we can gauge whether or not those things are going to be possible. And then see what it is that she is looking for [from us], and see if that is something we're willing to give up.

William: What I would recommend in addition to coming up with a strategy for that meeting is that, Bro. Thomas. When the two of you e-mail her, are we all on that e-mail?

Thomas: Some of them. But no, not on everything. Most of them, I believe.

William: Is her supervisor on them? Does he get cc'd those e-mails?

Thomas: No. He does not [at present]. Are you suggesting—?

William: What I'm suggesting is that we e-mail [the supervisor and the administrator] after we identify who's going up there. The workers are our best friends. Whether they have a problem with some of our workers or not. They are our best friends. So, we have to really win them over and unite with them.

Thomas: Or our worst enemies.

William: They could be both depending on how we approach them. So, I am suggesting that this coalition create a positive relationship with [Ms. Hamilton]. And her supervisor. We do that by having a communication with both of them via e-mail. Does that make sense?

Thomas: Yes, it does.

The organization's recent interactions with two former felons and their families further illustrate many of the challenges associated with the RAP innovation. Comparing the circumstances of the two men in the fall of 2009, William Goldsby stated the following:

The two common things [between the two former felons] is, one, they both were re- leased from RHU, and two, they both were not particularly honest when it comes to their family support. Mr. [Lombard] does not have anywhere near the level of [family] support compared to Mr. [Bailey]. Mr. Lombard's wife made it very clear that he could only stay there that night [his first night after release]. And the rest of his family has not reached out to him at all. In terms of class, they might have equal amount of resources available to them. For Mr. Bailey, it's obvious that, the contradiction here is that, when [Arthur] talked to the elder sister, whose house we went to, she was adamant that hav- ing him come there would run other family members away. But today [when Recon- struction's RAP initiative facilitated a restorative, family "sacred circle" and discussion], it was completely opposite of that. It didn't show any of that. (Personal Communica- tion)

While collaborating with a member of the Human Rights Coalition (HRC) various RAP affiliates received from these two men vague, noncommittal, and/or inaccurate information about the level and nature of family support they had, or anticipated having, upon release. When the family space is unwelcom- ing, that rejection often has material, spiritual, and emotional consequences, each of which has to be addressed. These issues were addressed interdepen- dently through multiple one-on-one, family member, and social service interac- tions and inquiries with various Reconstruction members.

So [we discussed] hypotheses regarding what happened. How it happened. What's the change? As we were debriefing in the ride from Mr. Bailey's sister's home. We were able to use Jerry's model. I asked Hakim, what was the seating arrangement....The pro- gressive part about COFFEE's method is that there's no dysfunctional family. There are crises within them. But there's no dysfunctional family....Jerry helps us look at hy- potheses and raise questions to explore [and possibly] dismiss those hypotheses....So, when we went through that, it was an amazingly transparent situation. (William Goldsby, Personal Communication, n.d.)

Here, Reconstruction cultivates innovation by incorporating a therapeutic model into their family-centered, reentry process. By doing so, multiple do- mains of a principled transformation are both accessible and understood by as many family and nonfamily members as possible. Jerry Hawthorne is a clinical and family therapist and founder of Continuing Opportunity for Family Educa- tion Enrichment (COFFEE). COFFEE is a progressive organization engaged in a form of therapy of liberation[25–27] built from a systems theory of participant interdependence, used to analyze the situational dynamics that inform all inter- actions.[28] Reconstruction has collaborated with COFFEE in a variety of ways over the years, including this use of the COFFEE model to engage in a more principled reentry. By doing so, this innovation is an effort to better understand how personal, familial, institutional, and community histories inform the patterns of family interaction within and across various life stages, and how the actions from this awareness encourage the potential for spiritual and principled transformation to unfold. William summarized the innovative experience of RAP, noting:

> As we build our capacity, we recognize when and where we should and should not include the family if there are any. In the case of Mr. Bailey, his sister participated in his first introduction meeting to the organization. The assessment unfolded the fact that it was not good having her there for several reasons. His prison reputation was one we didn't have permission to speak about while she was there...It was imperative to address this and to offer him support to change the behavior that kept him stuck....Our own assessment disclosed more data that helped improve our practice. (Personal Communication, n.d.)

From the creative use of current technologies, to therapeutic creativity to nurture individual, familial, and organizational transformations, or any number of other patterns and strategies of action (e.g., broadening the secular Community Development Corporation model for resident-led neighborhood revitalization, revising the villaging strategy to explore new organizational collaborations), cultivating innovation is an important better practice of Reconstruction Inc.

Best Practice #2: Nurturing Leadership
Leadership is a central resource in the process of community capacity-building,[29–31] and it is recognized as being fundamental to organizational effectiveness.[32,33] Whether interacting with Department of Corrections staff during the first cohorts of the Graterford years before the Alumni Ex-Offenders Association began (see chapter 3), or assisting a current life-sentenced inmate in their application for commutation through Fight for Lifers, principled and collective leadership are two of the most central themes in how Reconstruction prioritizes reciprocity in its organizational decisions and actions. Leadership has been defined as the ability to influence the direction and structure of participation, facilitate activities and the acquisition of resources, further alliances, and manage meaning and the means of achieving the intended mission within a program, strategy, or any other organizational initiative.[34–36]

Reconstruction's nurturing of leadership was displayed in 2009 through the collective securing of resources for longtime Fight for Lifers leader Anita Colon to speak at and actively participate in the International Human Rights Convention in Geneva, Switzerland. Ms. Colon was an invited speaker on a panel discussion concerning the Convention for the Rights of the Child. This global diffusion of the organization's mission was focused on Ms. Colon's expertise and family experience with the Pennsylvania law allowing juvenile accessories to the taking of a life to be sentenced to life without the possibility of parole. Combining the local critique and work against the law, with the global fellowship of persons advocating for the rights of youth around the world, Reconstruction's "glocal" leadership is a valuable asset in fighting for the present and future of youth's lives and opportunities.

A second example of this best practice is in refining the current role of LEAD in the organization's mission in Germantown High School and in the juvenile justice facility, NorthEast Treatment Center (NET). "The 'Youth Social Justice and Peace Engagement Project' invited [Germantown Friends] Meeting members to lecture on Peace Issues at Germantown High School to senior social science classes."[37] This project's original intent was broadened with the inclusion of Reconstruction and LEAD. It is collaboration with the Germantown Monthly Meeting (GMM, of Quakers) and the high school. When William was invited to be a respondent to a GMM affiliate's presentation on Michelle Alexander's (2010) book, *The New Jim Crow*, he agreed to do so on two conditions: that a program be collectively created, and that within that program, young people facilitate the discussion(s). Guided by that shared agreement, the program was launched.

The urban corridor of Germantown Avenue is adjacent to the portion of Nicetown-Tioga in which Reconstruction is located. Illustrating the racial and class makeup of the neighborhood and school, while the zip code in which this public high school is located is 81% African American and 15% White, the high school's student body is 97% African American, and 93% of the students are eligible for discounted or free lunches.[38] Realizing the leadership potential resting in reciprocities of risk, two LEAD members who are quite literally at-risk (i.e., marginally housed and homeless, marginally employed and jobless, familially estranged former felons) ran the six-week discussion series guided by Reconstruction's Situation Management pillar of the current curriculum (see chapter 2). As presented in an internal memo, the introductory session held in April 2011 included fewer students than anticipated because:

> …there had been a riot the day before, which reduced the number of students who attended this first session. After an introduction of the LEAD facilitators, a clip from [one of] Michelle Alexander's presentation[s] discussing mass incarceration was shown.…[Students] were asked what they thought of the information/clip. There were several comments like, "That's crazy." Many of the students appeared and expressed concerns that the system was not right. There were a few voices that said that the sys-

tem was fair. The facilitators asked the students to state why they took their positions. Some said that children know better; they know what they are getting into before they get into trouble....[Others stated] that children are not developed enough to understand many of the decisions they are faced with. There were students who had [prior] arrests, and one student's mother was a police officer. Though none were without an encounter with the police....[They were then] asked what could be done about the unfairness of the system.[39]

Reconstruction nurtures leadership by engaging the facilitators and the students in a pedagogy of principled transformation. In an informed discussion of a possible justice. In a rich reciprocity of shared and unshared risks. "In addition to raising larger social and political questions, [an administrator] asked that [these workshops] assist the students in communicating better, without arguing."[40] After various GMM affiliates had made a series of presentations on peace, Reconstruction was called on by a GMM Friend to broaden the scope and content of these interactions. This inquiry and consequent collaboration is a product of Reconstruction's principled leadership of sustaining long-term, shared respect with Quakers and other peacemaking collectives, including the American Friends Service Committee (AFSC).

To share the potential for this effort in diffusing leadership both with and beyond LEAD's core, two new young men were asked and agreed to assist in designing and realizing this initiative's potential. One of these young men was Jaleel, who appeared at William Goldsby's front door one day, seeking to do community service to complete a compulsory commitment of his parole. Today, Jaleel's participation and life circumstances, informed both by triumph and challenges, have become an important part of the collective leadership of this youth peace initiative. LEAD members have fostered a more engaged, praxis-oriented leadership among the Germantown High School students to develop "a process where youth will be given an opportunity to identify social issues, understand the reasons behind them, and organize to change these issues ... [while also] assisting the students to communicate better, without arguing."[41]

A second LEAD initiative to nurture leadership was also organized in 2011 at the NorthEast Treatment Center (NET), a youth penal institution. Reconstruction has returned to and re-established a strong presence in the NET with court preparation, critical awareness, skill building, and more. As Teon, a LEAD member and facilitator of this initiative, recently stated,

[Reconstruction's] and LEAD's curriculum [deals with] family dynamics, economics, emotional awareness, learning how to organize, how to facilitate meetings, how to build consensus, learning how to be a better mentor....The reason I choose to be a part of

LEAD is because I feel as though the mission needs to be addressed to the youth at a younger age before they do go down that road and become lifers or criminals or dead ....[So we're] beginning to go into the NET with our curriculum....And just not as an organization. But as a mini-community. (Personal Communication, n.d.)

In partnership with LEAD, AEA is providing court preparation for the youth. This includes connecting with the attorneys representing the young women and men in the NET, asking the judge to decide favorably when the youth is sanctioned, and inquiring whether their sanction can include community service with Reconstruction. AEA member Michael Grant, a licensed barber, goes to the NET each week to give haircuts to the young persons heading to court that week. Fight for Lifers members facilitate discussions on the life sentence, which, in Pennsylvania, means life without the possibility of parole. As the book goes to press, longtime FFL member Mae Hadley and her grandson are preparing to facilitate an intergenerational dialogue. This FFL participation at the NET takes on still greater meaning, given that the fathers of more than half of the young men with whom Reconstruction is currently working are now serving life sentences in Pennsylvania. These many children of lifers will soon also be in fellowship with a former felon whose life sentence was recently commuted by Governor Ed Rendell. This former lifer has agreed to join Reconstruction and assist in this initiative.

These, along with many other examples too numerous to explore here, extend from Leadership Development being the first and primary pillar of Reconstruction's capacity-building curriculum. From effective engagement with current technologies, and being a voice and presence in the global fellowship for youth justice, to facilitating an informed dialogue for the local exploration of justice themes with youth currently being adjudicated, nurturing leadership is a best practice in Reconstruction Inc.

Best Practice #3—Prioritizing Collaborative Capacity

For individuals and organizations alike, there are cost-benefit assessments associated with any activity or initiative. For a small, values-driven, grassroots organization like Reconstruction, one among them is the circumstances in which the benefits of collective investments and shared resources toward a social justice outcome are understood as being prospectively greater than the "costs" associated with acting independently to achieve the same or similar ends. Collaboration is perhaps best understood as collective participation to further "horizontal solidarity"[42] of values, strategies of action, and desired outcomes. And for an organization that prioritizes consensus building as its most valued

strategy for virtually any activity, collaboration is a vital best practice for furthering the Reconstruction mission. Well established in the social science literature
is the fact that the many challenges "of community revitalization and the goal of
creating an ongoing community capacity to address it generally [are] beyond the
ability of any single organization to address."[43] Sharing resources for collective
gain to create community capacity grounds the three examples demonstrating
how collaboration is one among Reconstruction's core best practices.

First, virtually from its moment of origin, Reconstruction has situationally
affiliated with one or more organizations to address an urgent challenge. As one
recent example, when a LEAD member's brother was incarcerated, the LEAD
member took in his 15-year-old niece. He then asked the organization for help
when he got a call from his niece's school saying that she was acting out and
that they had proof that she had been sexually active. He was barely able to
manage his rage without doing harm to himself, his niece, and the family. This
stress was coupled with additional health challenges, limited income, and difficulties with the mother of his own child. Reconstruction called on COFFEE
and Nurturing Hearts and Minds to assist in managing this set of situations, and
various resources were exchanged between the organizations. Perhaps most
critically, again using the villaging praxis so important to Reconstruction, several
four- to six-hour sessions were held in the comfort of private homes with the
teenager, her uncle, and members of all three organizations. Through this collaboration, no city bureaucracy was imposed. No additional financial burden
was incurred. And the intimate interactions strengthened each participating individual, the family at the center of the villaged moment, the organizations, and
the community. It was a situational collaboration independent of the state,
which furthered a set of interdependent capacity-building outcomes for all.

Second, beginning Brothers Strengthening Families and 20W Club in its
earlier years (see chapter 6), Reconstruction has participated in various forms of
organizational mentoring from its origin to now. This includes currently being
the fiscal sponsor of YASP (Youth Art and Self-Empowerment Project).[44] And,
perhaps this is best exemplified in its current relationship with EXIT-US, a
"non-profit community capacity-building organization which supports returning
citizens in [their] transition from penal institutions to "design their own freedom."[45] Its founder, Thomas Ford, after sustained membership and a high-
quality depth of participation in the organization over four years, was recently
elected by consensus to be the Executive Secretary of the Reconstruction
Board. Like all other sponsored groups, EXIT-US is expected to have representation on a Reconstruction committee or on the Board, and it now facilitates

the Reentry Assistance Project (RAP) described earlier. Among the many assets of this collaboration are the energy, commitment, and knowledge that Thomas Ford in particular has shared with members of both organizations, along with increased access to job opportunities due to his affiliations. Also, EXIT-US has been especially helpful in assisting with the completion of multiple Reconstruction grant applications, one of which was funded.

The third collaboration example is Reconstruction's participation in a multi-organization collective currently organizing the Prisoner Advocacy Summit (PAS), scheduled to take place in summer 2012. Thomas Ford of EXIT-US and Reconstruction was selected as the coordinator of the Summit planning committee. And Angus Love, Executive Director of the Pennsylvania Institutional Law Project, applied for and received a substantial financial commitment from Pennsylvania State Senator Shirley Kitchen to host the event. At the time the original call was widely distributed for the first summit planning meeting, Reconstruction Inc. was joined by 13 other organizations in making a commitment to this project. Virtually from that first planning meeting forward, Reconstruction provided the structure for the content, prioritizing, and flow of subsequent meetings to further progress toward the summit. To simultaneously bridge multiple disparate organizations (sacred-secular, national-local, youth- and later life-focused, civilly disobedient cooperative, and organizations with both long histories and recent startups), Reconstruction prioritizes collaborative capacity as a best practice in many diverse ways.

Best Practice #4—*Valuing History as a Current Event (Strategic Maturation)*
Within organizations that keep their doors open for any length of time, there are various kinds of unpredictable undulations—changes of mission, focus, priority, or of something else. Depending on how leadership and members respond to them, these undulations can sometimes lead to the premature—or necessary—abandonment of strategies of action that have not yet had the chance to fully mature or flourish. For a grassroots, capacity-building organization, these dynamics of change and healing are a part of its culture,[46–49] and they inform how learning takes place, individually, interpersonally, and organizationally. Informed by a small, critical mass of participants, simply sustaining what works well is difficult. And it is these learning organization dynamics that leads the maturation of earlier strategies of action to be one among Reconstruction's better practices. Regular organizational self-criticism, assessments at the conclusion of every meeting, and the patterns of critique and information sharing regarding what has worked more and less well in the past, allow for the

recognition of what organizational strategies are working best. These strategies are then returned both as valued ritual and as a means of transformation, using them to make valued contributions to the *current* achievement of the organization's intended mission.

In addition to the Leadership Best Practice example discussed above regarding LEAD's return to the NET, Reconstruction's sponsorship of the Gathering of Men and Community (GOMAC) is a second example of this best practice. GOMAC is an organization initiated by men incarcerated in the State Correctional Institution at Chester, Pennsylvania. GOMAC took place at SCI-Chester as a result of the shared efforts of their leadership working with Phyllis Jones-Carter, Reconstruction's first board chair and organization centerwoman. In 2009 Ms. Jones-Carter, a high-level prison administrator, was among the growing number of DOC affiliates who recognize the short- and long-term dangers of mass incarceration, and the value of enriching opportunities for those currently incarcerated to build their reentry and reintegration capacity to increase the likelihood for sustained desistance upon their release. It was also a product of SCI-Chester having been opened in 1998 as the state's first recovery prison, designed to treat inmates with substance abuse problems. Reconstruction's spiritual pedagogy of principled transformation was viewed as supportive of the "spiritual experience" of sustained recovery. Their reestablishment of the grassroots organization–penal institution partnership was similar to the Graterford years as GOMAC began.

This was a strategic elaboration beyond mere renewal, in many respects (i.e., moving beyond that which had come before it), including:

1. Using the organization's Three-Pillar Capacity-Building curriculum, which had not yet been developed at the time of the Graterford cohorts

2. Emphasizing the first Leadership Development pillar to ensure a thorough understanding of the four principled transformations (see Appendix)

3. More consistently and intentionally nurturing the organization building skills of the men inside guided by a strong, yet flexible structure and curriculum

4. Encouraging a partnered facilitation process in every meeting to place more emphasis on the necessary investments for collective ownership toward sustaining GOMAC's success

5. Using every opportunity to meet the men where they are while still exploring the complexities of the sometimes difficult concepts and strategies.

Due to a combination of factors including retirements and administrative changes, ideological discord regarding approved conceptual content, and uncertain motive by particular administrators, GOMAC came to an abrupt and premature end. This, despite its demonstrated successes reflected in the responsiveness and increased quality of participation among the men after little more than 18 months of consistent prison entry. Challenges associated with the GOMAC initiative were many and too frequent to consider in detail here. Through them all, the maturation of this long-held organization strategy was both a return to Reconstruction's origins of an institutional partnership and a maturing movement well beyond that point of origin.

Best Practice #5—Leveraging Spiritual and Social Ties (Enriching Sacred Space)
Reconstruction's origin in Philadelphia was geographically and spiritually informed. There are "places that have been identified that foster spirituality. Subsequent [groups] have used the same [special] places to enhance their beliefs.... Potential lessons can be learned from these places through cultural review. New technologies and contemporary experiences may be able to help rediscover the [spiritual] nature of these sites."[50] Special places are informed by the current actions of both material and spiritual intention. And Reconstruction Inc., in structure, place and process, is a product of a set of intersecting spiritual sites. After completing multiple Peace Corps assignments in Central America, William Goldsby sought out the city as a place to understand the possibilities of contributing to a new justice in a place where a recent expression of injustice had occurred.

Reconstruction began in a moment of Calling when a set of faith-led leaderships intersected:

1. The MOVE organization engaged the urban Sacred.[51-53] This challenged others, leading them to be bombed in 1985 with the mayor's approval, and an inner-city neighborhood burned
2. A sacred space endured the flames of urban fire
3. As a faith-affirming organization, AFSC memorialized the MOVE bombing on its grounds and within other Quaker meeting spaces. Though very different in makeup and membership, a spiritual bond of

empathy informed their choice to spiritually explore the lessons of this curious injustice

4. Shortly thereafter, what would become Reconstruction began as an AFSC program. Less than two years after its incorporation, Reconstruction was gifted a building as an act both of charity and reciprocity; the engagement of sacred exchange

5. The gifted building is on a street named for First Nation peoples: *Tioga*, a word of the Seneca Nation meaning gateway, or the meeting of two rivers, "where many important...trails converged"[54,55] (see chapter 1).

Preceding the Reconstruction mission by centuries, yet similar in their expression, the Tioga were known for being helpful to others to enrich alliances among members of their group and among themselves and other groups, to enhance a possible, shared future. Given these and other spiritual intersections that inform the organization, it is little wonder why enriching sacred space is an essential better practice of the organization. Two additional examples, one symbolic, the other strategic, are briefly considered.

Symbolically, several images adorn the walls of the Reconstruction office. The presence of new growth is reflected in an image of a sunflower. The legacies of the Civil Rights Movement are embodied in a quote of Angela Davis. Pathways and patterns of organizational change are presented in a "mind map" of the organization's possible progress, drawn a few years ago. And multiple 4 feet by 5 feet framed poster boards, the Photo Wall of life-sentenced persons in the state of Pennsylvania are always in the southeast corner. These many Polaroid images remind all who enter the office of one subgroup of Reconstruction affiliates who are unsilenced as the work of Fight for Lifers and each of the organization's programs continues. And on the eastern wall is a copy of a newspaper article originally published in 1857.

The 1857 article announces the U.S. Supreme Court decision of *Dred Scott v. John F. A. Sanford*. The Supreme Court refused to grant Mr. Scott's petition for freedom from slavery after he moved with his owner from St. Louis, Missouri, to the free state of Illinois. This decision was the culmination of a set of legal actions Mr. Scott had taken more than a decade before, in 1846. It was also the culmination of a much lengthier dialogue regarding citizenship and the legalities of slavery dating back to the 1787 Constitutional Convention in Philadelphia, Pennsylvania. The sons of Dred Scott's original owner, Peter Blow, financially supported his claim to freedom. Mr. Scott did not win his case as lengthy residence on free soil did not make him free, and the decision—and the case's larger questions—directly inform the Reconstruction mission. "The question is simply this: Can a negro, whose ancestors were imported into the country and sold as slaves, become a member of the political community...[and be] entitled to all rights and privileges...[of] a citizen? We think they are not...included, and were not intended to be included, under the word 'citizen' in the Constitution."[56] What is freedom? In what places is there access to freedom? Who is "entitled to all rights and privileges" of a citizen? More than a mere vocabulary of expression, freedom is perhaps the most Sacred capacity-building resource.[57,58] The opportunity of self-governance in attitude, affect, action, and outcome. The Dred Scott Decision article on the office wall provides a constant reminder of all that. Consistent with its many historical echoes of African, African American, and First Nation humanity and patterns of fellowship, freedom, citizenship, and all things that affirm their just expression, Reconstruction enriches each in its daily work.

Because, as noted by Prof. John Henrik Clark, *history is a current event*, the urban sacred is much more than (just) symbolic echoes of a sacred legacy or the meanings attached to a legal decision of centuries past. As a result, strategically, Reconstruction enriches sacred space in many ways. The Club House initiative brought young men together to learn about place and property as they constructed something of special value to share with one another. In addition to the Club House, whatever its location, every meeting of every program within the organization begins with a moment of silence. This is done to nurture a sense of Greatest Good within all those participating in that moment's fellowship and unite in spirit with the many, many more beyond that (Sacred) circle with whom similar values are shared. And also, the organization has renewed its affiliation with Tioga United. Building on the traditional CDC model for community reinvestment, Tioga United is a community nonprofit organization guided by the Mission Statement, "Rebuilding Our Community One Step at a Time."[59] This shared effort, leveraging spiritual ties to the local area is, the Sacred familiar. The Sacred familiar has been reestablished in an effort to educate local residents about collective investment and the process of home ownership, enhance the forms and frequency of beneficial economic and noneconomic interactions in the neighborhood, and use the CDC process to improve local control and increase the number of owner-occupied homes in the area.

As Hild (2006) notes, "A sense of place provides a feeling of well-being. The honoring of such locations is part of the respect and regard...[where] reciprocity occurs in the physical closeness and the benefits derived at these locations."[60] In a neighborhood in which the poverty rate is 38% above that of the

city of Philadelphia as a whole, home ownership that is 6% below that of Philadelphia's median, with a median home sale price that is almost 50% of that of
the city of Philadelphia,[61] this collaboration can help change these patterns. The
diverse formal and informal neighborhood investments extending from this
shared initiative are acts of faith in the possibilities of the neighborhood's future. In collaboration with Tioga United, and consistent with the organization's
better practice, Reconstruction is helping to enhance the neighborhood's sacred
and secular sense of place—one neighborhood cleanup, home ownership workshop, abandoned property inquiry, or one of any other capacity-building act at a
time. Consistent with Belk and colleagues (1989), Hild (2006), Shiner (1972),
and others, as Reconstruction's membership acquires, renovates, and owns
land, this collectively owned land becomes sacred space and will sustain future
work.[62-64] Both symbolically and strategically, these are among the ways in
which Reconstruction enriches sacred space.

Best Practice #6—Work Plan for Managing Uncertainties
True to any learning organization, perhaps the greatest challenge is the management of uncertainty. This is especially true for a small grassroots organization like Reconstruction. Many of the uncertainties identified in earlier chapters
and earlier periods of the organization's history remain true today. As the critical mass of the organization experiences a slow, steady growth, as younger
members grow more stable and consistent and as a new leadership, in both persons and structure, continues to emerge, these uncertainties are being anticipated more quickly, addressed more effectively, and managed from a more
refined resource foundation. One ongoing uncertainty is the absence of consistent financial resources. Earlier efforts to bring to the board a person with high-
level grant-writing skills has been replaced with the priority of developing that
skill set from among its primary constituency. Grant announcements and peri-
odic grant-writing workshops are held so that all who choose to attend are
aware of the mechanics of grant building, and the potential transferability of
these grant-writing skills. An open invitation consistently invites others to take
collective ownership of the organization through sustained investment. This is
being done increasingly, by a broader set of voices and visions, in the ongoing
growing pains of managing financial uncertainty.

An uncertain leadership future also remains. As its primary leadership ages,
who will be next to lead grows more salient. A revision in the leadership structure of the organization and of each program within it was recently instituted. A
critical mass of four to six persons from each of the three programs (AEA, FFL

and LEAD) were invited to be steering committee members for that program. And each steering committee was then invited to the Board of Directors, solidifying the leadership of each program and strengthening the leadership of the entire organization. Still, difficulties remain. Individual and family stresses. Navigating stigma, marginal employability in a weak economy, and the related emotional and spiritual strains. So, uneven participations extending from the material and related challenges continue to influence the organization, even as its leadership future grows brighter and more possible.

A third uncertainty common to all organizations that Reconstruction manages is the ongoing relationship between its reach and its grasp. Managing the diffusion of its mission, what it can initiate is different from what it can effectively maintain. Efforts were put into growing a Fight for Lifers chapter in Harrisburg, Pennsylvania, to partner with FFL-West in Pittsburgh and FFL-East in Philadelphia. Its central location would broaden membership. But small numbers, communication breakdowns, and difficulties of making time for a new commitment in the lives of family members of local lifers led to its fragile closure soon after it was begun. Similar challenges have occurred in efforts to establish a Reconstruction Two chapter in Columbus, Ohio. Various resources toward training a small, critical mass of persons willing to grow the leadership of a new out-of-state chapter have not resulted in any sustained affiliates, due to many of the challenges listed above. Outreach efforts in both Harrisburg and Columbus continue.

These uncertainties are as old as fellowship itself. And like many other organizations before it, Reconstruction Inc. continues to manage them while also experiencing many meaningful successes. All the while, the organization continues to reconstruct rage—one program, one initiative, one member at a time. "There comes a moment when we must bracket that rage and consciously turn, difficult though it may be, to the [space within fellowship and within ourselves] of love and praise and the liturgy of acceptance and belonging."[64] And principled transformation. To manage with and beyond uncertainties, Reconstruction continues to grow within and beyond these brackets of rage, these challenging circumstances, material, emotional, and otherwise. These best practices help the organization grow from them to continue nurturing healthy, principled change. With and beyond the many uncertainties of grassroots organizing to help build a new justice paradigm.

Conclusion

Virtually every example of Reconstruction's initiatives and strategies of action could have been used to exemplify one or more of the other best practices explored above. Yes, LEAD's new initiative at the NET nurtures leadership. It is also a strategic maturation, growing the origin of its youth-oriented program from nearly two decades ago. Working with Tioga United on the process and politics of home is both an initiative grounded in a sense of the sacred that can rest in local secular settings, and it is a collaboration sharing resources with another nonprofit organization. All of them, each of them, are among the many moving parts in the process and engagement of grassroots community capacity-building. In addition, like each of the best practices themselves, each of the examples of the practices is multidimensional. The tentacles of community capacity-building are long, with each dimension furthering a strategy of action that assists the organization in using that best practice to further the organization's mission. Above all, true to the Reconstruction mission, each of these best practices is nurturing a new justice. A new justice very different from the one we now live in is a realizable goal. And each of us can play a role in nurturing that new justice. Not as some myopic and outlandish mirage of distant impossibility. But, instead, as a best practices possibility for our increasingly glocal future.

Visioning Reconstruction's Possibilities
What if the urban revitalization process was increasingly built on an equity-driven foundation of capital enrichment for collective profit? What if this selective reinvestment toward multi-income ownership in "sustainable communities" was prioritized instead of constantly renewing the spatial "rape" model of external acquisition and absentee profiteering? Then Reconstruction Inc. and other similarly situated organizations could experience a very different financial and institutional environment of support toward reconstructing spatial rage.

What if educational innovations were inclusively engaged so that a practice of freedom was the prioritized praxis in classrooms urban and otherwise? What if this led to the steady improvement of our schools, informed by strategic, state-supported challenges to the abusively privatized boundary elaborations, to move (well) beyond local area property tax funding adherence? What if these changes were marked by greater resource sharing across space and were much more inclusive of service learning engagements, the Highlander weekend community schools model of justice pedagogy that flourished during the Civil Rights Movement, and other strategies and structures to minimize alienations of many kinds? What if students were nurtured from when and where they entered? Then Reconstruction Inc. and other similarly situated organizations could experience a very different cradle-to-excellence-and-possibilities-pipeline and environment of support toward reconstructing the rage of educational inequalities.

What if the Sacred-secular reciprocity, both symbolically and strategically, was empowered with and through spirituality? And what if these various alliances enriched a far stronger dialogue? Not in pursuit of faith profiteering and building the next unneeded megachurch. But instead as an equitable dialogue between libratory and public theologies, libratory and collective therapeutic engagements, simultaneously inclusive of churches and grassroots capacity-building organizations alike. Here, church-sponsored CDCs could, for example, nurture nondenominational labor organizing of low-wage workers and linking fair wages and faith, to reduce health disparities while enriching diverse civic engagements. Then, Reconstruction Inc. and other similarly situated organizations could experience a very different, affirming, and collaborative social justice environment of support toward reconstructing religious rage.

What if the prison system was defined as obsolete and the subtle and unsubtle nuances of the cradle-to-prison pipeline were well understood and shutting it down entirely was a global priority. What if an equity pipeline of principled transformation, or an equity-and-access pipeline of global prosperities, was consistently empowered to take its place. Then, Reconstruction Inc. and other similarly situated organizations could experience a very different, affirming, environment of support toward reconstructing the rage of mass incarceration.

What if hoarding was understood differently? On television, there are shows about hoarders, where individual persons prioritize the acquisition of things piled in problematic, cluttered private spaces. Hoarding is understood as an individual sickness, an obsessive-compulsive disorder. These persons are distractingly and repetitively presented as individually "crazy," even as the most substantial hoarding of wealth as magnified inequalities has taken place during the last generation within the United States. Within the center of global empire. And this hoarding, along with its allied practice of mass incarceration, is being done all too quietly. Actually, quite loudly, as the margins of the marginalized grow wider, and the wealth-grab continues virtually without comment. If hoarding were understood and responded to differently, then Reconstruction Inc. and other similarly situated organizations could experience a very different framework of societal awareness and caring as an environment of support toward reconstructing the rage of local and global resource inequalities.

What if media and arts innovations allowed a show titled *Libratory Praxis* with the title being explained and explored through a wide diversity of voices and life experiences to get—and *remain*—on the air for a profitable run? Each episode would illustrate a diverse set of one or more multidimensional reciprocities and move its featured characters or reality show participants well beyond the charity model of response to systemic inequality outcomes (e.g., *Extreme Makeover* of individualized rebuilds, leading the made-over house to be well in excess of the median housing value of the block it is on). Such a show would figuratively move them and the everyday public's awareness to a more balanced, capacity-building equity model of shared resources. Then Reconstruction Inc. and other similarly situated organizations could experience a very different framework of civic engagement and a libratory environment of support toward reconstructing the rage of media misrepresentations.

What if the centrality of a dialogue about what community capacity-building was, is, and can be, along with what its role in the process and structure of politics was, is, and can be, were as much a part of the public consciousness as these issues—seemed to be—during the campaign and eventual election of President Barack Obama? When the realization of a community organizing past became a respected, valued resource and foundation upon which diverse expressions of the personal as political and its reverse are the everyday, rather than some out-of-nowhere anomaly. Where the faith-affirming repetitions of villaging in its truest sense were valued. Not as some *Mayberry, R.F.D.* television fiction, or any other historic, small-town idealized memory. But, rather, as a current, possible, *urban* and rural present of informal and shared local area prosperity. Then Reconstruction Inc. and other similarly situated organizations could experience a steady, more visible progress toward realizing a new justice paradigm, even in our current uncertain environment of support.

What if...

Endnotes Toward Principled Transformation

Extending from Reconstruction's current best practices, three policy possibilities emerge:

- Transformative Trainings—Enriching social justice collaborations could be advanced by assessment strategies to recognize social "battle wounds" in the organization and in its members. Giving priority to spiritual, emotional, and social well-being will allow the leadership of grassroots organizations and nonprofits to learn how to use collaboration as a structure and strategy to work beyond burnout and continue to grow the movement.

- Resolving Rage—The collaborative resolution of rage must build upon the collective leadership of interdependent missions as diverse organizations with little or no resources continue coming together and learning how to build consensus and sustain collective leadership. As the contradictions and illusions of interdependent industrial complexes (prison, military, media, pharmaceutical) are being collectively challenged, reconstructed rage can continue fueling many principled transformations.

- The spiritual seeding of a New Justice Paradigm demands sentencing reform to leave room for compassion and transformation. Various kinds of citizen-driven boards (e.g., judge report cards, community justice panels) and such boards having a legal connection to commutation decision making would increase accountability and civic engagement. Policy initiatives that more visibly and honesty link mass incarceration with environmental justice and the social degradation of American corporations are long overdue.

Part III, Chapter Nine

Transformative Collaborations Toward a People's Democracy

Quite literally, Reconstruction kept me out of the penitentiary. I can say that for a fact. And AEA [the Alumni Ex-Offenders Association] was the primary source. Our support group concept. The intimate relationship developed with members of AEA. The trust level that was developed. The respect over the years that was developed. That grouping of people were able to sort of harness me when the main thing that I have problems with surfaces. Which was my rage. At times [it] was uncontrollable...and [I] put myself in some really, really volatile situations that would have been damaging to someone else or damaging to me. The fact that this organization was in my life and I had an avenue to vent and I allowed them to challenge me...based on the respect I have. The trust that had been established. All of those things being in place...There were other things too...But the most clear benefit was that I was able to stay out here.

Mr. Hakim Ali, longtime Reconstruction affiliate, November 2009

Penal warehousing, which combines physical immobilization with political disenfranchisement, has become the state's solution to the "surplus populations" left behind. This solution is part of a broader shift from the welfare state to the "law and order" state.... Hence the well-documented transfer of public spending from education, health and welfare, to policing and prisons.... The transnational prison-industrial complex is not just about surplus labor, it is also...about surplus land...[and] has woven mass incarceration into the fabric of the global economy.

Professor Julia Sudbury, 2004

The consistent, yet unsteady history of Reconstruction Inc. is the foundation for its strong and flexible present and promising future. What possibilities are there for others to experience what Hakim Ali and many returning citizens like him have experienced before? How might Reconstruction and other grassroots initiatives continue to help keep former felons out of the penitentiary and living lives of principled transformation? These and many similar questions are especially important to ask and answer. Reentry is going to happen for most of those incarcerated today and in the days to come. Moreover, it is becoming increasingly apparent that current policies of mass incarceration are unsustainable. Court-sanctioned releases to reduce prison overcrowding are enforcing unplanned and expedient returns of former felons to unprepared families and unready communities. Costly extended confinement from "three strikes" and other callously conceived rules is severely straining many state social service budgets. These realities along with other evidence that the current system is badly broken point to the urgency of a needed shift toward planned reentry.

We appeal to and challenge those making decisions about how and how well reentry is to be managed at the institutional, community, and national levels to understand and adapt what has been learned from the Reconstruction experience. In doing so, major transformations can occur in how penal policies and practices are developed and implemented. Major strides can be made toward the goals of ending mass incarceration and moving toward a more humane and just society. Current policies too often put such transformations out of reach. The United States imprisons more of its population than any other nation in the world. Consistent with Sudbury, "the state's solution to the 'surplus populations' left behind" in the widening wealth gaps of the global economy extends from the history of U.S. imprisonment—a history that began with intentional targeting by race, class, and caste. According to Teeters and Shearer (1957) the very first person admitted to a U.S. penitentiary was "a light-skinned Negro…born of a degraded and depressed race, and had never experienced anything but indifference and harshness."[1] Today, we live with the symbolic and material, both the distant and more recent history and current consequences of this long-standing practice.

As chronicled here and elsewhere, beginning in the late 1970s, there has been an explosive expansion in the U.S. prison population. Like the institutional origins that preceded it, this era of mass incarceration over the last generation has been highly disproportionate by race and class, and it has magnified many enduring local and national inequalities. Through both omission and commission, our nation has arrived at a place in which the label "prison nation" fits all too well.[2-7] "In the past three decades, incarceration has become an increasingly powerful force for reproducing and reinforcing social inequalities…in the labor market, educational attainment, health, families, and the intergenerational transmission of inequality."[8] According to the 2009 Pew Center on the States report, for the first time in American history and in all of recorded history, a nation is locking up more than 1% of its adult citizens. And more than 1 in every 31 U.S. adults (3.2%) is incarcerated or otherwise "on paper" (i.e., on probation or parole). For African Americans the numbers are even more alarming. Comprising just 12% of the U.S. population, they are nearly 40% of the 2009 total prison and jail population, with 1 of every 11 adult Blacks incarcerated and a still higher rate in many inner-city, high-crime neighborhoods.[9] The cumulative consequences of historical oppressions now combine with the collateral consequences of racialized mass incarceration of the *"New Jim Crow."*[10] For justice to be done, the present prison system must be fundamentally and principally transformed.

This alarming rate of current institutional control is, in effect, an endpoint of an equally alarming pattern of economic change: a more than 400% increase in the amount of money the 50 states spent on corrections since the Baby Boom generation. Spending increased from $11 billion in the late 1970s to nearly $50 billion in 2008! Yet this huge increase in spending is associated with a declining impact on crime (i.e., a diminishing return). Some states now spend more on locking people up than educating them. Spending on prisons is causing financial hardships in such states as California, Texas, and Kansas. Many other states are soon to follow if current patterns and priorities do not change. Quickly. Because at least 95% of all state prisoners will be released from prison at some point, mass incarceration has created a large and growing pool of released felons; a trend that is then coupled with them most often returning to neighborhoods marked by high poverty and crime concentrations in the most densely populated urban areas.[11–14] Thus, for the foreseeable future, the reentry and reintegration of persons returning from jails and prisons will disproportionately impact poor and working-class African American communities. Yet, how grassroots organizing matters in these and other similar communities is not well understood.

Currently, there is little research analyzing reentry in systematic and longitudinal terms at the organizational level. This study begins to fill this gap in our understanding of how grassroots, community capacity-building organizations interact with and influence the individual, familial, and communal levels of reentry and sustained reintegration. These experiences are also important because they represent organizations that are neither state funded nor faith-based. This book moves our thinking toward multimethod, longitudinal analyses of organizational influences on "life course transitions and cognitive factors that contribute to desistance from crime [which] can provide useful information for post-onset interventions."[15]

Reconstruction Inc. was founded in the city of the U.S. penitentiary's birth, in a neighborhood that was and continues to be severely challenged by mass incarceration. Since 1988, it has consistently contributed to the successful desistance of individuals by working collaboratively with others to resist the collateral bondage of being in an "imprisoned community."[16] Its curriculum, structure, and strategies of action have allowed a culturally centered, spiritually grounded organization and membership to exist for a generation, experience success beyond survival, and continue contributing to improved quality of life outcomes among many within and beyond the North Philadelphia neighborhood in which it is located. As explored in the preceding chapters, assets of returning citizens at the core of its membership are nurtured in diverse and pro-vocative ways. With and through the past and present intimate challenges Ha-kim Ali refers to at the beginning of this chapter, and guided by its current best practices, these many organizational assets are nurtured—culturally, commun-ally, and in terms of improved capacity for principled transformation. To what end? Answers to this question follow, extending from the three parts of the book: Culture, Community, and Capacity-building.

The Three C's: Toward Transformative Collaborations and a Broader Justice

Any organization is much more than simply the engagement of its symbolic and material components (culture), the place and process of its repetitions of fel-lowship and resource sharing (community), and the maximization of assets to further quality of life outcomes (capacity-building). For Reconstruction, these are the means in service of a broader mission, a praxis toward transformative collaborations and a broader justice by changing themselves to change the world. Chapter 8 explored Reconstruction's current best practices and their re-lated challenges. Their use and regular evaluation is making beneficial contribu-tions to their effectiveness and possible suggestions extending from them toward a new justice paradigm. For both economic and humane reasons, an increasing number of Americans agree that far too many of our citizens are in-carcerated. Contributing to the principled transformation of former felons, their families, and interested others in a variety of ways is one strategy to challenge our societal addiction to mass incarceration and its related processes. By doing so in the communities in which they live and work, Reconstruction members are furthering cultural, communal, and capacity-building practices of a new jus-tice.

For its part, Reconstruction Inc. is driven by the mission of *"changing our-selves to change the world, by uniting [with] the many to defeat the few."* To effectively engage this mission, it is built upon a faith-affirming, cultural foundation to fur-ther the "practice of freedom" in the exchange of information among members, their families, their neighbors, and with other organizations and institutions, in an effort to further openness toward and the praxis of equity-based, justice-affirming change. In other words, it is guided by a spiritual pedagogy of princi-pled transformation that informs its decisions and actions. These are challeng-ing words to write and still more challenging to live. Words demonstrated in the actions and outcomes stated in the opening by Hakim Ali and to a greater or lesser degree by every other past and present affiliate of the organization interviewed for this book. By doing so, the organization and its members' goal begins with—at the very least—substantially reducing the entire infrastructure of mass incarceration by transforming our commitment to penal warehousing; a commitment that is politically, economically, and institutionally grounded in a centuries-old history of American penology. And it is our sincere hope and intent that prior chapters have made a quality contribution to that transformation. Reflected in the best practices and "what if" possibilities of the prior chapter and throughout the entire text, we recognize that these principled transformations must occur at many different levels, in various places, and in various ways.

We emphasize going forward that mass incarceration must end—and in the foreseeable future. Prison populations must shrink substantially to those whose criminal severity renders them to be a danger to themselves and others. What will this ending look like? How could it come about? At the grassroots level, how should organizations respond? How will the overarching themes of culture, community, and capacity-building be adapted or implemented? And beyond the dynamics of a single organization, what are other examples of principled transformation toward realizing this societal and global goal? Further, as mass incarceration is reduced, what is next for small towns and rural areas in which most prisons are located? What is next for the urban neighborhoods to which former felons typically return? What is next for the media and additional promoters of us-them perspectives of othered images and socialization? What is next for the political capital of mass incarceration promoting "get tough on crime" narratives for political gain? What is next for criminology and penology in their analyses of phenomena related to these changes? Earlier chapters have explored these in terms of program and curriculum development, organizational structure and collaborations, group affiliation and therapeutic dynamics, and historical changes in all of the above over time. And all in the Culture, Community, and Capacity-Building praxis of Reconstruction. First, organizationally anchored examples will be considered, followed by a larger, more glocal example. Then, one or more illustrations from prior research will be presented to further demonstrate the presence of a current momentum that is enriching culture, nurturing community, and building capacity toward the realization of a new justice paradigm.

Resilience and Transformative Collaborations

Natasha Frost and Todd Clear (2009) suggest that the "grand social experiment" of the "Punishment Imperative" of mass incarceration has failed.[17] While

experimental metaphors are always risky when their structural reality and institutional consequences are so real, they go on to suggest that two possible story
lines from it extend into the future. The first is more of the same, with the recent past as prologue. More unsustainable "get tough" political narratives and
public sentiment. More racialized application of law. More abusive prison overcrowding. More post-release, collateral consequences. And all with damaging
and unjustifiable costs to communities and to society as a whole. More of the
same. In the second possible storyline, "a weary public becomes alarmed by
mass incarceration, and a political will develops to change its course....Undoing
the damage that has been done [will] take more than the repealing of a few of
the more draconian policy initiatives. [It will] require...a new grand social experiment." The outlines of this grand design are clear. Desistance-oriented reintegration informed by effective planning, social supports, and grassroots
capacity building. These, coupled with individuals, families, and communities
prepared to reintegrate transformed returning citizens with the skills and supports needed to make desistance work. These, coupled with substantial progress
toward many of the "what if" societal transformations at the end of chapter 8.
Taken together, these changes will clearly require massive changes within and
beyond the entire prison industrial complex. More broadly, it will require a new
justice paradigm. Help in getting our society from here to there can begin with a
more accurate representation of public sentiment toward redemptive resilience.

Based on public polling this new grand social experiment appears to be
overdue.[18] Among U.S. voters, nearly nine out of ten are in favor of rehabilitative services for prisoners, compared to a punishment-only system. Seven out
of ten felt that reentry planning should begin no later than one year prior to
release, with almost half of American voters believing it should begin at the
same time one's sentence begins. Nearly eight of ten are in support of legislation allocating federal money to prison reentry, with nearly half of the polled
voters expressing strong support for this reentry legislation. And more than two
of three feel that reentry and rehabilitative services should be available to incarcerated persons while they are in *and* after they are released from prison.[19] In
short, there is strong public belief in the rehabilitative expression of resilience
and strong public support for penal reform. Transformative collaborations are a
critical means to move toward these and other reforms.

Transformative collaboration is nurturing profound change through collective decisions and actions of a shared mission. Here, we use transformation to
mean profound change; in other words, "praxis in the context of communion...[as] shared cultural action for freedom characterized by dialogue"[20] and in

opposition to unjust structures and the actions of others that perpetuate them.[21–23] Collaboration is "exchanging information, altering activities, sharing resources and enhancing the capacity of another for mutual benefit and to achieve a common purpose."[24] Transformative collaboration has been described in each of the preceding chapters analyzing what and how Reconstruction Inc. has engaged its organizational mission. Reconstruction in the Tioga community of North Philadelphia is an example of transformative collaboration in the urban core. Not as a well-intended, external imposition. Nor as any short-term programmatic intervention. Instead, Reconstruction was founded as, and remains, a local, resident-run, reentry and reintegration capacity-building collaborative. It is indicative of what can occur in new and different ways to align with public support for penal reform and strengthen the foundation for a new justice paradigm. Through culture, community, and capacity building, consistent with the levels of public support to do so, future initiatives should promote various forms of this process.

Understanding Culture and Embracing Cultural Change

When Audre Lorde (1984) wrote of the "fund of necessary polarities" to allow for change to spark like a dialectic among like-minded others in a group or setting, she aptly described the process of understanding culture and embracing its change: valuing the resources that only shared differences can provide.[25] This is what Reconstruction has done and continues to do and how a similar process can occur in other capacity-building initiatives, both inside and outside of reentry and reintegration. One, longtime (White, middle-class) Reconstruction affiliate with no criminal history and with empathy for persons different from herself stated:

> One of the things that has kept me interested in supporting Reconstruction over the years is the clarity of the values and the nature of those values ... that [are] respectful of others and recognizes diversity in every sense. That respects the personhood of everybody involved…[grounded in a] radical humanity…[a] commitment to working with others, to work collaboratively, to have every voice count, to be fully respectful of all involved. Whether that's youth. Whether that's women. Regardless of the race or ethnicity. Prior incarceration, whatever it is. And, of course, to be in solidarity with those who have been most oppressed and to work in [equity-affirming] ways that are empowering. (Anonymous, Personal Communication, n.d.)

These are the values at the cultural core of the organization. And it is these same values that are highly transferable and applicable in any setting, toward any cultural end. Just as this affiliate has done and continues to do to serve a justice end, well beyond Reconstruction's reach, persons can challenge their

understandings and associations of groups different from themselves—
especially regarding former felons—then act with radical humanity to serve that
broader justice. Here, the struggle is against the systematic condition from being
voiceless to being an egalitarian affiliate, where each voice is developed, expressed, and heard. All the while operating with enough commitment, honesty,
and trust to risk and actively participate in the sometimes difficult discussions
this radical humanity demands is vital in making the most of the cultural fund
of differences Audre Lorde wrote of. Within Reconstruction, and true of any
collective, among the most essential values are selflessness and reciprocity. As
noted in chapter 8, the words of Deion Morrison reflect this well:

> It's truly amazing to me, the selflessness of the participating individuals of Reconstruc-
> tion. I haven't run across anything [else] like that, Townsand. The ability to pull to-
> gether and assist in any way possible. To just give….If Reconstruction put in any time
> or effort with an individual, they only ask that the individual they put in time with,
> come back and do something likewise that was given to them….That's the expectation.
> If you were given assistance, support, make yourself available to do the same for the
> next person coming through the doors. Just being an example of…a principled indi-
> vidual. (Personal Communication, n.d.)

And what this process is has been labeled many things including a "Culture
of Healing" and "Culture of Peace," "Relational Resilience," "Cultures of Non-
violence, Growth and Change" of the Sanctuary Model, and the "Politics of a
Critical Pedagogy.[26–29] Whatever the label and related nuances associated with it,
using culture to further transformative collaboration in both structure and strategy builds upon these and other similar values; to build upon spiritual life lessons of affiliation, assist all in living more positive, fulfilling lives, and further
the many potential benefits that an embrace of culture and cultural change can
provide. Whether one is a policymaker in the federal government, a former
felon, an administrator in the Department of Corrections, a survivor of crime,
or the family member of someone currently incarcerated for a crime, this cultural core can be a living praxis, shaping one's decisions and actions. As one
Department of Corrections administrator and probation officer put it, "We
went through a culture changing process to review the values and mission of
our agency. We invested in strategic planning, training, and rewriting our staff
performance expectations and reward system before moving ahead with major
program development."[30] This was done to have the probation officer training,
skill-building, and evaluation system at the county level of a Midwestern state
better reflect a level of humanity in managing their caseload. These actions "resulted in improved operations in each core functional area" of the larger DOC

unit.[31] These are among the action outcomes with culture as a resource in transformative collaboration.

Many other organizations enrich cultural domains of their own to provide a rich resource for reducing the entire infrastructure of mass incarceration and help transform our societal commitment to penal warehousing. As mass incarceration shrinks, what is next for the economy of the small towns and rural areas where prisons are typically located, where they are perceived to provide the most stable local employment alternatives? A diverse set of transformative collaborations will be required in these areas. "Workforce transformation and real economic development opportunities turn out to be key to prison population reduction [since] the so-called keeper must be figured into the equation."[32] As one example of progress, Milk Not Jails in New York State is an organization dedicated to nurturing rural culture and economic development. It notes that "over 350 rural towns across the nation are home to a prison [and] over 75% of New York's prisons are located in rural areas." For this organization, mobilizing residents to support the dairy industry and the long-term sustainability of the rural economy enriches the culture and history of these rural areas and "is a political campaign to advocate for criminal justice and agricultural policy reform that will bring about positive economic growth. Milk Not Jails insists that bad criminal justice policy should not be the primary economic development plan for rural New York."[33] The sole answer to rural economic redevelopment? Likely not. An answer that is true to the culture and regional roots of these areas? Certainly.[34]

To demonstrate a related role for criminology and penology in addressing this concern, researchers have (2004) explored the impact of prisons on employment growth.[35] They analyzed data "on all existing and new prisons in the United States since 1960 [to] examine...in U.S. countries.[36] They evaluated three periods between 1969 and 1994 and found that in rural areas—where the majority of prisons have been built—"established prisons are *negatively* related to total employment growth in urban areas [and] *there is no evidence* that prisons have provided a boost [in rural areas]. Neither established nor newly built prisons made a significant contribution to employment growth in rural counties" (italics added). So even during the period of sizeable prison buildup, there is evidence to suggest that prison growth did not provide a net economic benefit even to the areas in which the prisons were built.

Also the Rural Economic Development Center at the University of North Carolina provides a set of case study examples of how this question can be addressed. Professor William Lambe and his colleagues are exploring how economic development innovations in small town clusters in North Carolina and Missouri are being culturally and economically redefined.[37] Farming is a cultural staple of small-town and rural America. The organizational creativity of Milk Not Jails can enrich the alternatives for sustained quality of life so that bad criminal policy will not be the misguided plan for rural economic development. This can be a model for other initiatives throughout the United States that are also informed by the myths and realities of the rural prison build-up.

Nurturing Community

Transformative collaboration occurs in and across locations (place) and is relational (process). "Relational coordination is an emerging theory for understanding the relational underpinnings of collaboration."[38] Community is also both place and process. A community is made up of members in a location, who feel and share bonds or a sense of attachment in some way, and who share in patterns of exchange those members value and that reinforce the bonds of fellowship, both to one another and to place. To help further a reduction in penal warehousing and all processes and practices associated with it, Reconstruction nurtures community by engaging in a spiritual pedagogy of principled transformation. In this practice of freedom in the traditions of Paulo Freire, Ida B. Wells Barnett, and others, consensus building and unity in all manner of interpersonal exchange are prioritized, with reciprocity being the primary pattern of engagement.

In its collaborations, Reconstruction regularly looks to share resources to further collective ends (e.g., use of the COFFEE model of therapeutic intervention in its Re-Entry Assistance Program, partnering with Germantown High School and the Germantown Friends Meeting to establish a communal fellowship of faith-secular-social justice resource exchange). Among Reconstruction's membership, civic engagement is very seldom used as a phrase, yet it is a valued repetition of expected and (tacitly) "required" affiliations beyond the organization alone.[39,40] Members' political participations, service work among those members affiliated with 12-step organizations, and the many ways that various members are of informal service to others within and outside of the network are a few of the many examples of this place-informed process of communal priority.

Within Reconstruction, community is also understood in and through the lived experience of empathy. This is consistent with work exploring the relationships among community, justice, and responses to social breakdown.[41,42] As an organization, Reconstruction struggles to facilitate an egalitarian model in its structure and strategies of participation. Its members make room and time for translations as the need arises based on language differences, and for the least vocal members, collaborators, or visitors to understand and express themselves. Trainings are held and priority is placed on having the patience to listen to differences and incorporate new ideas as well as struggle to build consensus. Here, consistent with Matthew 21:16 (King James Version), "Out of the mouth of babes and sucklings thou hast perfected praise?" listening to the voices of the youngest persons in a given meeting is given importance in word and deed by the meeting facilitator and all others. Here, listening to the voices of women around the table amplifies what each person in attendance has missed in their lives, as too often women's voices have existed in our personal lives but have not been respected in the public forum. Trainings that develop human spiritual potential, both in association with—and entirely void of—religious influences often take place.

This extends from the organization's placing importance on learning how to reduce distances between others—be they geographic, emotional, spiritual, or otherwise. The prison system imposes distances between families counter to any humane sense of community for both the inmate population and the community in which the prison is built. Whatever the form of these distances, Reconstruction prioritizes developing effective and progressive support systems that nurture persons holistically. And it extends from the organization's history that time and again has shown that, both individually and communally, a place and process was made for the arrival of "just enough." Just enough courage for William to speak among strangers and spark the organization's Philadelphia presence and initial collaboration with the American Friends Service Committee. Just enough openness on the part of George Stehalek, Donald Vaughan, and other Department of Corrections officials to be respectful toward a former felon-led collective seeking fellowship with current Graterford inmates. Just enough willingness of local Tioga residents to not hinder the location of reentry transition housing in their neighborhood. Just enough collective leadership for current best practices to help one more youth at NorthEast Treatment Center know themselves, dealing with the life sentence of their father, challenges associated with their sustained investment in a socialized pipeline stunting the realization of their communal and spiritual potential. Just enough shared respect to value the development of trainings where the quiet voices of women who are not middle class, who have carried their families, and have too often not been mentioned in media and in the public consciousness outside of pejorative bigotries. From the valuable voices of these women in Reconstruction and elsewhere in community rest many answers too often unseen and unheard, but for the too loud voices of the educated and of men. Just enough, and more.

These many organization-specific examples are in symmetry with other examples of how nurturing community contributes to transformative collaborations and is acting for justice by acting against the physical immobilization and political disenfranchisement of mass incarceration. Beyond the many local collaborations discussed in prior chapters, the work of Pattillo (1998), Clear (2007),[43,44] and others are growing the evidence in support of various forms of community justice. Narrowly defined, community justice is "all variants of crime prevention and justice activities that explicitly include the community in their processes and set the enhancement of community quality of life as an explicit goal" (Clear 2007:191).[45] Its emphasis is on restoration, successful post-prison reintegration, and (if sanctions are warranted) for new crimes or probation-parole violations, favoring ameliorative sanctions such as community service and forms of skill-building fellowship. However systemically ingrained and allied with formal social control they may be, David Kennedy's Ceasefire Project in Boston (2002), the Safer Foundation's Safe Return Project, and California's Community-Based Reintegration program for parolees are three among a growing number of illustrations of progress in using community as a resource in transformative collaborations to help silence the too-loud sounds of mass incarceration.[46]

Burnett and Maruna (2006) move this work further by using a strengths-based approach to reentry and reintegration. Their case study focuses on the strengths of former felons who voluntarily participated with other local area citizens who were not former felons on a Citizen Advice Bureau (CAB) in Great Britain. CABs are not counseling services but instead are British "registered charities...which provide training in the use of a computerized information systems [to] provide free, confidential and impartial advice ...[on] matters relating to housing, debt, employment disputes, welfare provision and legislation." Taken together, these are informed interactions in community, with former felons being the "experts" or information providers, interacting with other local citizens in collective fellowship to improve the quality of life of both CAB service providers and recipients. Such "strengths-based resettlement" has shown to be, in effect, an exchange of strengths, reduction of stigmas associated with the label "former felon," and a furthering of shared investments in community.[47]

The Healing Communities Initiative is a faith-based example here in the United States, with congregational participants in Michigan and affiliates in other states as well.[48–51] Healing Communities reject and actively work to dissolve any shame or stigma perceived or felt by returning citizens, their family members, and others in the community. Their goal is continued membership in a neighborhood and the gifts returning citizens possess and can share with others in environments of reconciliation and equity. As in Reconstruction, in this congregational collective forgiveness and reconciliation are a faith-informed reciprocity, demonstrated in and through everything from group labels and language, to a movement toward an engaged empathy and diverse resource exchanges. Healing Communities strives to grow beyond the charity model through people, congregations, patterns of interaction, and the values that are the foundation for creating "stations of hope"; that is, part place, part process in service of transformative collaborations and a broader justice. Across these examples, be they secular or religious, justice-oriented or service-focused, in partnership with formal social control or more autonomous, a growing variety of initiatives are demonstrating the various ways in which the nurturing of community—often from the grassroots forward—is being used to reduce the reach, level, and patterns of participation in the prison industrial complex.

Building Capacity

Capacity-building is maximizing local area assets of individuals, families, organizations, and others to collectively nurture an improved quality of life within that local area.[52–54] And the lessons this process teaches can benefit those individuals, families, organizations, and others who live within and well beyond its borders. Entering into a capacity-building fellowship with others (especially when salient group differences exist) is a long-practiced and critically important strategy. It often begins with a single, simple moment of being at the right place, at the right time, with the right willingness and availability to then act with conviction and calling. For Reconstruction, capacity-building as civic engagement is demonstrated by members sharing a need, an urgency, and nurturing related reciprocities of shared engagement to help others, organizational members or otherwise. The organization's capacity-building is linked with using rage as a vital resource for principled transformation. Its members build within themselves and their collaborators "a progressive politics of rage [that demands that members collectively, and] responsibly invest rage to harvest emancipatory returns…[as] a major tool for creating justice."[55] Healing rests beyond the rage. Wellness rests beyond the rage. "There comes a moment when we must bracket that rage and consciously turn…to the [pedagogy] of love and praise and to the liturgy of acceptance and belonging."[56] Many assets within oneself and shared in fellowship with others rest beyond the rage, where a collective excellence and human rights do as well. And it is toward these ends that Reconstruction builds capacity in reconstructing rage.

It's training for its board, its (largely unpaid) staff, and the whole of its membership develop skills that help them connect spirituality with the organization's mission. Not as a religious practice. But as a means of sharpening the spiritual leadership skills of all affiliates to better understand connections among economics, spirituality, and the many demands of changing oneself to change the world.[57] The trainings, guided by their spiritual pedagogy of principled transformation, teach assessment and evaluation: of self and others, of actions and outcomes, of individual and institutional actions both large and small. All this, toward building a rich diversity of unexpected alliances. All toward improving the ability of returning citizens, their families, and interested others to work collectively, in equitable fellowship as the poor rise beyond their marginalized caste and acquire and own land. To the point where they put in place collective initiatives that are a product of the consensus building and other assets extending from the culture and community components discussed above. Reflected in the comments of Hakim Ali at the start of the chapter, this is occurring with little or no resources and is removing the mental shackles of internalized oppression toward the creation of an increasingly diverse collective leadership.

Again, as with culture and community, beyond Reconstruction's organizational reach and collaborations are other examples of how capacity-building is actively dismantling the prison industrial complex. And again, social science is playing a role through the documentation and exploration of various examples of the transformative growth of individual and collective assets. And family members of returning citizens are among the most critical. Much recent research has demonstrated the roles and importance of one's family and supportive others as a vital asset in the capacity-building process of reentry, increasing the likelihood of sustained reintegration.[58–65]

Beyond family, focusing on capacity building in the post-prison reentry process, perhaps the most comprehensive capacity-building assessment was the 30-program comparative, "Evaluation of the Prisoner Re-Entry Initiative."[66] Evaluating the Taxman and colleagues (2004) Prisoner Re-Entry Framework, these well-funded, two-year programs used a set of formal mentoring initiatives, analyzing data on program development, participation, and (primarily) employment and recidivist outcomes. Program participants were more likely to obtain jobs and remain employed after exiting their program. They had substantially lower two-year recidivism rates compared with similarly sentenced other former felons, with less than 10% being rearrested for a new crime or being reincarcerated for a technical violation. This top-down version of capacity-building was an agency-defined, service-oriented, mentor-led, hierarchical model of multi-million-dollar intervention that showed promise.

In addition, more creative, egalitarian capacity building is demanding a strengthening of the links between the reduction of penal warehousing, urban transformation, and the global economy. In effect, glocal transformation is occurring, with a simultaneous revision of both the carceral state and the living environments to which former felons are returning. Unless gentrification is well underway, these are neighborhoods that most others living elsewhere too often choose to selectively and intentionally ignore. "The reconstruction in this post-war environment begged for something other than a return to what many felt were dehumanizing structures and spaces not designed to promote human interaction and development."[67] Unlike the post-World War II European cities that Fasenfest uses as historical referents, in many respects, early 21st-century U.S. urban capacity-building warrants a similar Marshall Plan. After the so-called war on drugs, and consistent with the Reconstruction model of organizational leadership, substantial reinvestment in the urban core can and should be guided by the persons currently living there. The quiet, too often ignored voices and visions of poor and working-class women and men and the former felons and their families anchor the assets of reciprocal initiatives toward a new, more equitable quality of life for all.

Examples of urban gardening in inner-city Detroit, Chicago, and northern Indiana demonstrate the extreme circumstances in which concentrated redevelopment initiatives—when locally sponsored, locally organized, locally managed, and where the benefits of which are shared inside-out from the local area—are experiencing small and promising results.[68,69] These initiatives are not urban experiments. They are a return to the lessons history provides, nurturing the best of local, collective investment, both within and beyond corporate constraints. The potential for local gardening as a replacement activity after the decline of the manufacturing base of the urban core rests in focusing on food production to augment the nutritional intake of poor residents, and engaging in related commercial activities to deepen the dollar turnover within the neighborhoods. In Detroit and elsewhere, urban gardening "resonates with similar local-food-by-local-grower initiatives around the country. They point to new models...[and] are likely to generate new economic and political realities...[and] the need for more responsive and representative local government."[70] Like European city outcomes at World War II's end, all are powerful possibilities amid the collateral consequences of contemporary mass incarceration that has ravaged the U.S. urban core. No bombs were dropped there. The severe systemic inequalities of the war on drugs and its related dynamics imposed the shrapnel's symbolic and material remains. And here as elsewhere, the personal is political.

> Local efforts, however valiant, must be tied to political processes ... [and] constituent pressures to come to the fore...if we hope to grapple with the global forces arrayed that define and limit local outcomes. Global economic and political forces create and overwhelm local realities on the ground and national politics plays a critical role in making this possible—if only because national politics are an integral part of global affairs ...[yet, still bring] hope to a population eager for change that would speak to local conditions and put an end to many of the ravages of this global economy.[71]

These are some among the means through which assets are being maximized as persons, families, and communities are being transformed in principled ways. Whether one considers therapeutic strategies toward the effective management of emotional challenges, training, and skill building for the sake of organizational development or placing value on family, collective efficacy, and social support in the reentry process, capacity-building within and beyond Reconstruction Inc. is making powerful contributions toward change. Whether one considers comparative service delivery among reentry programs, or the role of urban gardening in strengthening neighborhood nutrition and economies, the links between post-prison reintegration and the glocal process of urban redevelopment are growing stronger, and capacity-building is a valuable component in the progress toward bleeding mass incarceration and feeding a more equitable quality of life for all. Persons most directly impacted by mass incarceration—former felons, their family members, and others interested in nurturing a more just future—are gathering together more frequently, in numbers both large and small, and crafting that future. Whether it be All of Us or None in Oakland, California, the Critical Resistance conferences and chapters across the United States, the Children's Defense Fund taking on the cradle-to-prison pipeline as its primary concern, or others, many are refining mission and exploring the most useful strategies of action for change. And all the while, steadily enriching and sharing assets like the quiet consistency of Reconstruction Inc.

For 24 years, Reconstruction has been "finding a way to create a durable, interracial, bottom-up coalition for social and economic justice...[by] cultivating an ethic of genuine care, compassion, and concern for every human being."[72] Centered in a reentry and reintegration process, it has done so through the praxis of its pedagogy of principled transformation, the structure of its three programs (AEA, FFL, and LEAD), the repetitions of the three pillars of its capacity-building curriculum (see chapter 2, and Appendix), the rituals of and emphasis on its family-focused foundations, and its constant emphasis on the four primary transformations through which its affiliates manifest the organization's mission. Reconstruction has touched and contributed to the transformation of thousands of lives.

Michelle Alexander (2010) and others note, "We must face the realities of the new caste system, [challenge] the flawed public consensus that lies at its core...embrace those who are most oppressed by it, [and move beyond] traditional approaches to racial justice advocacy, if we hope to end the new Jim Crow."[73–77] Toward ending the new Jim Crow, Reconstruction faces these realities. It has been organized and collectively led by the vision of William Goldsby in fellowship with a small, critical mass of persons allied with the organizational mission. Former felons, their family members, and interested others—on both sides of the prison walls—continue to collaborate both in reform work and in movement building since "reform work *is* the work of movement building, provided that it is done consciously as movement-building work."[78] By doing so, Reconstruction Inc. and its transformative collaborators are doing much more than reform alone. Collectively, they are building capacity to move beyond prisons and nurture a new justice paradigm.

Visioning the Better Future for Reentry and Beyond

In this book and, more critically, in all its organizational actions of transformative collaboration with other persons, organizations, and institutions, Reconstruction Inc. is visioning a better future beyond reentry. However, a new justice paradigm suggests the redistribution of wealth, reversing the current trend of more and more in the hands of fewer and fewer. With such redistribution, we can begin to rebuild our personal and spiritual lives, rebuild our homes, and acquire and rebuild new and old spaces and structures. In small, rural towns. In densely settled urban neighborhoods. And in the institutional and symbolic bridges that bond them to one another. A new justice paradigm means building on what already exists but (also) opening the processes so that the distribution of political, economic, educational, and other institutional resources can be more equitably shared. A new justice paradigm would recognize that our criminal background, drug history, profession, or any other characteristic of our intersectionality are not necessarily reasons for our inclusion or exclusion. Instead, they are "the fund of necessary polarities" vital to realizing this new justice.[79] In nurturing its possibility, foundations and other entities that fund grassroots organizations would likely benefit from more training on the necessities of supporting systemic changes beyond two-year periods, or whatever their funding cycle demands. When we speak of "systemic change," the needs and what causes the oppressions the grassroots organization is addressing took much longer than a single funding cycle to create. And it is most certainly going to take much more than a single funding cycle for an organization to move toward the desired systemic change. And every sector of society can play a role in enriching this vision.

For scholars, innovative social science contributions are warranted on both macro and micro levels and at various scales. Perhaps even necessary. At the macro level, across multiple outcome domains, researchers might explore what happens when a state intentionally shrinks its prison system, with Kansas, California, and Texas being among the first to try to reverse mass imprisonment's fiscal and human rights nightmare. And how institutional uses of a restorative justice, amends-making framework are diffusing within and across various settings and for what outcomes they are contributing as best practices could be helpful. Such work could be all the more useful, since some of these restorative diffusions are taking place in environments of selective drug decriminalization (e.g., medical marijuana), and where disenfranchisement laws are being revisited. At the (individual and organizational) micro level, how are personal intersections of the drug war, recovery, and the process of reentry interacting with environments of health disparity and faith-led and secular interventions in each of these interdependent challenges? What strong and fragile collaborations are most useful in nurturing well-being, diverse faith affiliations, and sustained reintegration? The answers to these and other related questions will help us better understand the resource partnerships most beneficial to challenging penal warehousing and nurturing principled transformation.

For policymakers, a principled transformation in focus and outcome are warranted. As a research partnership between a department of corrections administrator and a lawyer and law professor has suggested, what is called for is a three-condition approach to "drive the reentry movement as a sustainable force for change in corrections and the criminal justice system."[80] The three conditions: (1) have successful reentry by "the core mission of corrections"; (2) establish—and sustain—a "dramatic commitment" to in-prison reentry programming that is linked directly to organizations, agencies, and the social networks in the neighborhoods to which former felons return; and (3) legislator priority on "comprehensive sentencing reforms" that focus on and strengthen returning citizen community ownership.[81–83] These policy recommendations are useful steps toward dismantling the entire apparatus of the prison system.

And for all these, whatever one's life station or current place, interested in knowing and nurturing a new justice substantially more equitable than what has historically been, and what currently exists, we invite your creativity to experiment with new and unexpected "modes of organizing that challenge the conventional civil rights organizing...[and] be willing to make mistakes."[84] In that spirit, we hope that you risk thoughtfully as William did in challenging hundreds of strangers in 1988 to begin this justice journey. We hope that you enter unexpected alliances as Donald Vaughan did in seeing an unknown yet possible value in inviting Reconstruction into Graterford Prison in 1993. We hope that you sustain innovative commitments as Phyllis Jones-Carter, Anita Colon, Lucinda Hudson, Hakim Ali, Patrick Murray, May Hadley, and others have across their years of caring commitment and affiliation with Reconstruction, and their abiding faith in its organizational possibilities. And we hope that you reconstruct your own (out)rage toward realizing a new and very different justice from what we know today.

Beyond legal reform, urban interventions, and social science and policy innovation, with history being a current event and an important teacher of lessons for what may soon take place, we can once again look to it to provide us with a better sense of what may lie ahead. Following the Civil War, the 19th-century era of Reconstruction has been defined as "America's Unfinished Revolution."[85,86] It was a profoundly incomplete transformation of a society in desperate need of significant change after ending North versus South battle lines and bloodshed. Still today, sometimes overwhelming echoes of those prior battle lines and bloodshed remain. Now, we too face a set of challenges not unlike that of our 19th century ancestors. As the second decade of the 21st-century progresses on the clock, what other forms of progress might also be brought into being? We are answering that question now.

On March 25, 1965, a speech was given in the city that gave birth to the modern Civil Rights Movement. On the steps of the Alabama State Capitol, speaking to a group of persons gathered there to help nurture a new justice, Reverend Dr. Martin Luther King Jr. said:

> I know you are asking today, "How long will it take?" I come to say to you this afternoon, however difficult the moment, however frustrating the hour, it will not be long. Because truth crushed to earth will rise again. How long? Not long. Because no lie can live forever. How long? Not long. Because you shall reap what you sow. How long? Not long. Because the arc of the moral universe is long. But it bends toward justice.[87]

Having said these words for the first time in 1961, Rev. Dr. King was using them again, a month after the assassination of Min. El-Hajj Malik El-Shabazz (Malcolm X). And each time he used them, he was paraphrasing a 19th-century Unitarian minister, Rev. Theodore Parker, from a sermon he gave in 1853. A critical metaphor of spiritual leadership and community organizing bridged the 112 years between the two speeches. Two generations after Rev. Parker's sermon, and more than two generations before Rev. Dr. King's speech, Dr. W. E. B. Du Bois wrote in 1903, "It is a hard thing to live haunted by the ghosts of an untrue dream."[88] The arc of the moral universe bending toward justice is an idea. Now, nearly two generations since Rev. Dr. King's important words, such an arc does exist. Being haunted by ghosts of an untrue dream is a metaphor. Yet, with history being a current event, many such ghosts haunt us still.

While late-20th and early-21st century mass incarceration may not be an "equal" moral imperative to that of chattel slavery, or the years immediately following the 1896 *Plessy v. Ferguson* "separate but equal" Supreme Court decision, or the modern Civil Rights Movement, whether it is or not, similar sentiments are called for now. Simply put, "both sound fiscal policy and increased public safety are best achieved by coordinating and strengthening the efforts of those organizations and individuals committed to the goal of reducing our prison populations and investing in community."[89] For nearly a generation, Reconstruction Inc. is a grassroots organization that has been guided by the goal of reducing our prison populations through principled transformation, and it has invested in community in many ways, both large and small.

If we are to nurture the direction in which the arc of the moral universe bends, our efforts in responding to the many painful realities of the untrue dream of mass incarceration and its collateral consequences must be resisted in new and creative ways. These communities will be made safer and more whole through a set of sometimes simple, sometimes layered, yet necessary principled transformations being furthered by Reconstruction Inc. and organizations like it throughout the United States and the world. Informed by the sentiments of these spiritual leaders, both religious and secular, and the truths they spoke of in 1853, 1903, 1965, and today, the decisions and actions to nurture a new justice rest before us. Both now and into a possible future, may we make them and perform them well.

Epilogue

Dr. Edward Rhine

Dr. Rhine is past president of the International Association of Reentry (IAR) and is the Deputy Director of the Ohio Department of Rehabilitation and Corrections.

The unprecedented growth of mass incarceration has served as a catalyst for the emergence of a remarkable and ever-widening commitment to prisoner reentry across correctional systems in the United States. While the former grew to prominence substantially expanding the net of confinement beginning in the early 1970s, then accelerating thereafter, the latter has appeared only recently, mainly since the turn of the twenty-first century. It shows, however, promising signs of resiliency, if not long-term durability. Each of these trends requires brief elaboration as they form the dramatic backdrop and colliding contexts for understanding the unique journey and important lessons that reflect the birth and vital work of Reconstruction today.

Mass Incarceration in the United States

It is indisputable that the United States has experienced unparalleled prison population growth for the past four decades. Eclipsing other nations, the country's rate of incarceration places it as the global leader in the proportion of citizens it confines. Standing at five percent of the world's population, America locks up roughly twenty-five percent of prison inmates around the globe.[1] In 2008, for the first time in the nation's history, one in one-hundred adults were housed in prisons and jails across the land.[2] The overall number of incarcerated adults now stands at over 2.4 million.

A more recent report shows that the number of state prisoners declined slightly for the first time since mass incarceration began its steady ascent. However, the total prison population increased because the number of offenders under the jurisdiction of the Federal Bureau of Prisons jumped up. While the state prison population has declined, ever so modestly, there is a notable variation in this trend. In 26 states, the population dropped with some states showing substantial reductions, several by 5% or more. Yet, in 24 states, the number of prisoners grew, in several states very significantly.[3]

Whether this portends a turning point in prison population increases, especially at the state level, or a momentary respite, a retributive narrative will continue to exert an influence over the landscape of punishment in the years ahead. But the leverage it exerts will be muted to some extent as fiscal pressures in a growing number of states are triggering calls for sentencing and correctional reforms that did not enjoy a political foothold during the most active decades of the prison buildup. In fact, there has been a pronounced dissipation (though not elimination) of budgetary support for further increases in prison capacity given the diminishing economic and social benefits attached to such an expansion.[4,5] This evolving context has created promising soil for the expansion of the prisoner reentry movement that is already well underway.

The Prisoner Reentry Movement in Corrections

For the past decade and more, an impressive energy and correctional focus has developed targeting returning citizens. To a significant extent, the exponential growth of mass incarceration in the U.S. eventually seeded what has now become a reentry movement in corrections when the recognition settled in that the vast majority of those sentenced to prison all come back, as Travis (2005) states, in his "Iron law of Imprisonment."[6] The sustained growth of prison populations has created an ever-larger pool of released felons with nearly 750,000 individuals released annually. Many of them return home ill-prepared and all too often insufficiently equipped to navigate the transition from confinement to the community.

Gaining momentum, this embrace of reentry is beginning to show signs of a promising resiliency across the field. This resiliency comes from the ways in which it has become embedded in the infrastructure and discourse of corrections at the federal, state, and local level. At the national level, there has been bipartisan support for prisoner reentry since President Bush urged Congress to give ex-offenders a "second chance" in his 2004 State of the Union address.[7] This gave way to the passage of the Second Chance Act (SCA) in 2007 with funding appropriated in the years since to support prisoner reentry initiatives, and importantly, the creation of a National Reentry Resource Center. Recently, a Cabinet-level Federal Reentry Policy Council was formed to coordinate and target barriers and challenges to ex-offender reentry.[8]

A sizable number of states have moved towards prisoner reentry altering their policies, programs, operational practices, and information technologies to support implementation efforts. They have adopted a framework and increasingly evidence-based strategies for addressing reentry that are qualitatively different than in years past. The view of reentry in these jurisdictions is broad and holistic extending far beyond prison walls. In some instances, there is an acknowledgment that community investment and ownership in reentry is critical to the successful transition of offenders post-release.

The vibrancy of the reentry conversation now under way was highlighted in a recent event convened in Washington, D.C., in December 2011 called a "State Leaders' National Forum on Reentry and Recidivism."[9] Every state correctional system was represented at this forum. Sponsored by the Justice Center of The Council of State Governments, the PEW Center on the States, the Public Welfare Foundation, and the Bureau of Justice Assistance within the U.S. Department of Justice, the attendees discussed national and state trends in recidivism, and the complementary roles different levels of government, reentry organizations and advocates must play in this process.

Before Prisoner Reentry: The Story of Reconstruction

It is against the backdrop of mass incarceration and prisoner reentry that the story of Reconstruction comes to the fore as a unique organization and compelling ethnographic narrative. The monograph by Price-Spratlen and Goldsby offers a revealing longitudinal window into the evolution and reach of an organization that has remained steadfastly committed in its mission to meeting and assisting ex-offenders "where they are." Their work, the result of a productive collaboration between a sociologist and the architect of Reconstruction, presents an in-depth accounting of the struggles, negotiations, and accomplishments of an organization that was founded on a principled commitment to openly acknowledge and find productive solutions to the stigma, exclusion, and rage experienced by black men.

Reconstruction was seeded in supportive collaboration with the American Friends Service Committee (and later the Pennsylvania Prison Society) following a special commemoration of the tragic MOVE bombing in 1988. It became incorporated in 1991. Rooted in one North Philadelphia neighborhood in the urban center of Philadelphia, Reconstruction has now existed for over twenty years. Throughout this period, as an Afrocentric organization, it has actively sought to address the myriad issues associated with prisoner reentry, and reintegration within a bolder vision seeking to challenge and respond to the reach of mass incarceration.

Reconstruction experienced its formative growth and continued organizational maturation alongside the rapid-fire increase in prison populations throughout the country. It took path breaking and risky steps to address prisoner reentry long before the importance of this issue was recognized at the federal, state, or local level. As a small, culture and community capacity-building organization, it has at all times endeavored to create a different model of justice.

It has done so by adopting a pedagogical framework that is inclusive of ex-offenders as individuals, their families, their local neighborhoods and others who wish to participate, in association with a relatively limited, but highly engaged cluster of affiliates.

The trajectory of Reconstruction, like other grassroots organizations that are found at a local level, has not been one of linear growth. Rather, it has experienced over several decades intersecting and unpredictable moments of organizational progress, periods of dormancy, and ongoing financial uncertainty. It has also witnessed continuous transitions in leadership and membership relative to its Board of Directors, and its core programs, inclusive of the Alumni of Ex-Offenders Association (AEA), Leadership, Education, Advocacy and Development (LEAD), and Fight for Lifers (FLF). Across time, Reconstruction has demonstrated a complex mix of fragility and resiliency.

The history and present work of Reconstruction show what can be achieved relative to engaging and mobilizing the energy and knowledge of ex-offenders. Yet, its story also highlights how sobering the prospects are for managing successfully the visible, as well as invisible barriers associated with offenders transitioning home from prison. The long-term experience of Reconstruction offers revealing and timely insights that may be fruitfully applied in addressing the competing dynamics informing prisoner reentry and mass incarceration today. These are insights that have relevance to those states, advocacy organizations, communities, neighborhoods *and* individuals interested in moving the reentry agenda forward in ways that contribute tangibly to public safety and an enhanced quality of neighborhood and community life.

Ex-Felons' Organizational Interaction With Correctional Systems: The Need for Mutual Accommodation

The early and ongoing work of Reconstruction offers valuable instruction on the importance of establishing relationships of mutual trust and support with the leadership and staff of correctional systems, if an effective and sustained commitment to prisoner programming and advocacy is to be maintained. Yet, these early efforts also reveal how difficult it is to negotiate and maintain relationships that remain mutually productive and supportive.

One of the more impressive accomplishments of Reconstruction was the design and adoption of a reentry program curriculum at Graterford Prison, near Philadelphia. The first set of meetings with the Superintendent and Deputy of Treatment took place in 1991. Thereafter, the initial phase of what was to become an intense within-prison, transformative reentry program curriculum began inside the walls. The prison administration reached a startlingly unique agreement permitting the formation of an Internal Advisory Committee (IAC) composed of inmates serving life sentences or long terms of incarceration. The IAC, in turn, participated in every aspect of the development of the curriculum and, eventually, the selection of 24 men who were within eighteen months of release as the initial cohort of participants. These individuals had at least two violent felony convictions. The curriculum was rolled out with this cohort of inmates in January 1993.

The multi-year effort to craft a reentry curriculum to be delivered inside the prison involved the shared collaborations and steady efforts of a cross-section of inmates, prison officials, and Reconstruction. Despite the enormous investment made by the various parties, throughout the design of the curriculum and after the implementation of the program, tensions emerged within an environment that revealed an ever present and volatile uncertainty. Eventually, the program was suspended for a year. Even more, when the program resumed and the next cohort of inmates went through the program, *none* of the graduates were granted parole eligibility by the Parole Board. Many years later, in 2009, at SCI-Chester, a disconnect occurred relative to internal administrative support undermining a reentry-based program before it really got off the ground after discussions that lasted nearly one and one-half years.

The breakdowns in communication, and the suspension of Reconstruction at Graterford demonstrate how critical it is to achieve ongoing accommodations that foster binding and trusting relationships between an ex-felons' organization and the staff within a correctional setting. It is also worth noting that the launching of the Graterford reentry curriculum was undertaken long before the reentry movement appeared in corrections. There is now a greater receptivity on the part of correctional systems in a growing number of states to forge such opportunities by making the walls of confinement more porous to programs and efforts that start inside, but continue into the community post-release. This is inclusive of community-based organizations, faith volunteers, and others, as well as felon-led organizations to assist those about to be released prepare for their transition.

The Value of Mobilizing Ex-Felons in Reentry Preparation and Post-Release Support

The trend in corrections toward embracing prisoner reentry offers the promise of a different kind of dialogue centering on returning citizens. By emphasizing comprehensive reentry planning, programming and transitional services during and following release, there is often a presumption that what is provided will meet the needs of offenders returning home. However, in most correctional systems presently, with few exceptions, the individuals seated around the table determining and responding to such needs have not systematically included those of ex-offenders or organizations led by ex-felons.

Reconstruction began as an ex-felon led initiative motivated by the desire to deconstruct and reconstruct black rage as a capacity-building resource and emancipating force for principled change. The organization asked how it, alongside other key affiliates, might provide meaningful guidance to men leaving prison such that they would be better equipped to negotiate the demands of reentry and reintegration, while living lives of principled transformation.

One of the key answers that emerged relative to the transition from prison to post-release was the formation of the Ex-Offender Alumni Association (AEA). This group began at Hospitality House in Philadelphia, in 1998. With a desire to form a support group for ex-offenders, a small group of men, mainly former residents of the halfway house who had violated the conditions of their parole, met and planned for two years. They sought to define and address what ex-offenders needed to move through and beyond the initial boundaries of re-entry to a sustained, successful reintegration into their family lives and communities. Now a core program under the auspices of Reconstruction, AEA's original and continuing goal is to help formerly incarcerated persons, their families, and the community at large better understand the struggles confronting individuals leaving prison, while offering a learning environment that nurtures and refines their capacity-building skills.

Over time, the participants come to better understand what the process of a sustained, sober reentry requires, and what engaging in the critical transition from reentry to reintegration actually demands of them. Within a context of what is referred to as "Sacred Space," the rage that convicted ex-felons feel is openly addressed and actively considered through group discussions that encourage the cultivation of relational resilience and the personal capacity to become a "servant leader" and agent of change. All AEA and Reconstruction ask is that those who are the recipients of their investment likewise respond by giving back to those who follow in the program.

The forum provided by AEA, and its felon-sponsored leadership and dialogue offer a meaningful venue for its members who are regarded as valued participants. Its very existence is premised on the respectful recognition that each individual brings intellectual and creative abilities and other assets that enhance the capacity of AEA to collectively accomplish its work more effectively. Its continued growth over many years demonstrates the value of mobilizing the expertise of ex-offenders in shaping the curriculum and content of programming, and in providing peer-to-peer mentoring during the months and years following incarceration.

Recognizing All Reentry Is Embedded Within a Social Ecology of Local Relations

Though there is a good deal of research that speaks to the importance and efficacy of evidence-based programs, some of the most promising work on prisoner reentry may be found in correctional agencies that share a holistic vision; one that is systems-oriented, interdisciplinary in reach and inclusive of other state and local agencies, community organizations and partners, and engaged citizens.[10,11] In more than a dozen states, unique collaborations have been established at the local level through the formation of prisoner reentry task forces or councils. Their growth is grounded in a recognition that correctional systems are much better positioned to effect and sustain effective reentry practice by nurturing partnerships, especially at the local level, that foster more expansive community ownership of those returning from prison.

The most promising innovations being tested around the country deploy multifaceted models tied to the social ecology of local relations to which offenders return. These models seek to establish an approach that is largely community-centered. They embrace the need to create coalitions of community organizations to provide support for individuals returning from prison, while drawing on social service agencies as boundary spanning organizations that facilitate reaching beyond prison walls. Additionally, they endeavor to form active partnerships with corrections and parole drawing on their capacity to broker institutional arrangements. Within this approach, offenders exiting prison are provided with meaningful pathways to address and move away from antisocial attitudes and behavior.[12]

Reconstruction's overarching approach acknowledges the nuance, and complexity of dealing with the sobering prospects ex-offenders face as they confront the myriad challenges associated with the transition from prison. Its pedagogy has consistently incorporated an ecological focus in addressing the culture and community context within which individuals often struggle, yet must navigate post-release. The organization across its curricula and "best practices" places an emphasis on productively re-immersing and connecting ex-offenders to the local ecology of social relations to which they are returning at the neighborhood level. Consistent with its overarching philosophy, Reconstruction has done so not as a well-intentioned, yet external imposition, nor as a short-term programmatic intervention. Rather, it has listened responsively to the voices of those most affected steadfastly remaining a local-resident run, re-entry and reintegration capacity-building collaborative.

The history of Reconstruction reflects a long-term commitment to maximizing the assets of individuals, families, organizations and others that when brought together collectively contribute to an improved quality of life locally. Its lessons and experiences may prove particularly instructive in those states where correctional departments have created partnerships aimed at forming and sustaining a local infrastructure of prisoner reentry coalitions. Whatever distances are imposed during or after incarceration, between those who are released, their families and the neighborhood to which they return, dealing effectively at the level of social ecology requires developing local support systems that nurture persons holistically.

Conclusion: Reconstruction's Critical Pedagogy and the Shifting Dialogue on Punishment

Scholars have begun to take note of the escalating impact of mass incarceration arguing that it is appropriate to use such terms as the "punitive state" or "prison state" as a description of its boundaries.[13–23] Though it is a dramatic, if not normative term, as Weisberg and Petersilia (2010) point out, it is evident from this literature that mass incarceration has itself become a social problem with far-reaching implications for offenders, families, and communities (Simon, 2012).[24,25] It now functions as an increasingly powerful force for reproducing and reinforcing structural changes in the nation's social, economic and familial life.[26]

Reconstruction is premised on a critical pedagogy that is committed to unraveling the presence and adverse consequences that attend mass incarceration, especially on the lives of poor and working class African American communities who are disproportionately affected. It has long since secured its presence and has consistently honored its praxis by operating "1808," its residential center, in a marginalized neighborhood where one in seven households had a family member either currently incarcerated, or who had recently been released. As an Afrocentric organization, Reconstruction brings attention to the critical importance of situating race not in a race-neutral context, but within a framework that places it at the center in addressing prisoner reentry and the impact of mass incarceration.[27-29]

There are very few, if any, organizations comparable to Reconstruction. Its inclusive pedagogy is premised on "valuing the resources that only shared differences can provide" tied to a spiritual call for principled transformations grounded in a larger commitment to change oneself in order to change the world. The story it reveals serves to showcase the breadth of its efforts across time, from curriculum and program development, to the delivery of reentry programming involving two cohorts of inmates at Graterford Prison. It is notable that the first cohort to go through the program at Graterford later graduated demonstrating impressive success years after their release. Of the original group, as of 2007, only one was returned for a parole violation, while one other was re-arrested for another crime.

The reach of Reconstruction's efforts, which are also inclusive of the provision of transitional services, coupled with residential and post-release support groups, highlight how far its work has cascaded out over the course of several decades. It is not just the remarkable scale of such activities, but the pedagogical content of the learning combined with a driving commitment to provide tangible, long-term guidance and support that meets the needs of formerly incarcerated persons, their families, and their communities on their terms.

The continuing vitality of Reconstruction underscores how critical it is that those who are committed to the mission of reentry and reintegration forge connections—systemically tied together, but rooted locally—that actively engage the voices, experiences, and organizations of ex-felons. Doing so will enrich the larger commitment to reentry. Even more, by virtue of the sustained collaboration and mutual respect that such efforts require, it will also enhance the prospects for producing lasting outcomes that contribute to the quality of life, especially for those individuals and in those locales most affected by the sobering realities associated with mass incarceration.

Appendix

Reconstruction Community Capacity-building Curriculum (6/2009)

Reconstruction's curriculum is designed for individuals, families, and community groups in and outside of institutions. We believe that each human being is sacred and is valuable to themselves, the family, the community, and to society. Each of us needs to be critical thinkers, be good decision makers, and give principled leadership to our family and eventually change the world. This curriculum has three pillars, is interactive, and transformative.

The Curriculum Concept

Pillar I. The Leadership Development entails understanding the principles and practices of four themes: from alienation to building community, from arrested development to self-determination, from co-dependency to reciprocity, and from individualism to collectivism. This pillar enhances the ability to recognize behaviors that keep one from transforming. It enhances economic and political awareness as well as builds potential to make necessary personal, economic, and political analysis.

Pillar II. Situation Management builds on the previous pillar and shows how to understand the differences between crises, ongoing drama, dysfunctional family versus crises within the family. This pillar helps with interpersonal and group conflicts, and identifies existing skills as well as develops new problem-solving skills. An individual's ability to effectively participate and coordinate Emergency Response Systems is heightened.

Pillar III. Support Group Development trains how to create and facilitate support groups and systems. Members learn how to build personal and group working agendas that address any needs of the participants, and develop the skills that produce principled solutions to the various issues.

Reconstruction recognizes the phenomenon of intellectual licensing as well as the need to promote faith and collective wellness. To that end, the above concepts do not include style of facilitation, suggested text, activity protocol, nor does it include coalition building. It is simply a series of concepts to be tailored to specific groups with specific missions.

The art of development is
changing ourselves to change the world and
uniting the many to defeat the few.

Themes Reflection:

A. Alienation versus Community/Self Knowledge
1. What does it mean to be cut off from family, friends, society, and oneself?
2. What are the ramifications for continued self-alienation?

B. Arrested Development versus Self-Determination
1. How can being "stuck" in a particular frame of mind or period in your life effect positive growth?
2. What are the benefits in shedding misinformed or misguided ways of thinking and negative behavior?

C. Co-Dependence versus Reciprocity
1. In what ways has co-dependent behavior impacted your life?
2. How can the idea of overcoming the LUST for personal gain enhance building the village?

D. Individualism versus Collectivism
1. Me, Myself, and I
2. What are the benefits of operating for the betterment of someone or something other than self?

The art of development is
changing ourselves to change the world and
uniting the many to defeat the few.

Notes

Prologue

1. McCoy, C. (2010, May 9). 25 years later: Lessons of the MOVE tragedy. *The Philadelphia Inquirer*, pp. B1, B5.
2. Goldsby, W. (1988, May). *Commemoration event at American Friends Service Committee event of the 1985 MOVE tragedy*. Philadelphia, PA.
3. Bradbury, J. [1819]. *Travels in the Interior of America in the Years 1809, 1810, and 1811*. Lincoln: University of Nebraska Press.

Chapter One: Echoes of Rage: AEA, Resilience, and Healing

1. U.S. Department of Justice, Office of Justice Programs, Bureau of Justice Statistics. (2009, December). *Prisoners in 2008*. (NCJ Publication No. 228417). [Rev. 2010, June 10]. Retrieved from http://bjs.ojp.usdoj.gov/content/ pub/pdf/p08.pdf
2. Alexander, M. (2010). *The new Jim Crow: Mass incarceration in the age of colorblindness*. New York: Free Press. p2.
3. Dash, M.I.N., Jackson, J., & Rasor, S.C. (1997). *Hidden wholeness: An African American spirituality for individuals and communities*. Cleveland: United Church Press.
4. Churchill, W. (1910, July 20). *Address to Parliament, in 2 Winston S. Churchill: His complete speeches, 1897–1963*. New York, London: Chelsea House Publishers.
5. Garvin, D. (1993). Building a learning organization. *Harvard Business Review, 71*, 79–91.
6. Clear, T. (2007). *Imprisoning communities: How mass incarceration makes disadvantaged neighborhoods worse*. Oxford: Oxford University Press.
7. Kazemian, L. (2007). Desistance from crime: Theoretical, empirical, methodological and policy considerations. *Journal of Contemporary Criminal Justice, 23*, 5–27.
8. Mills, A., & Codd, H. (2008). Prisoner's families and offender management: Mobilizing social capital. *Probation Journal, 55*, 2–24.
9. Visher, C. A. & Travis, J. (2003). Transitions from prison to community: Understanding individual pathways. *Annual Review of Sociology, 29*, 89–113.
10. Beam, J. (poet). (1989). In *Tongues Untied* [Documentary Motion Picture]. United States: Frameline.
11. Grier, W. H., & Cobbs, P. M. (1968). *Black rage*. New York: Basic Books.
12. hooks, b. (1996). *Killing rage: Ending racism*. New York: Henry Holt.
13. Williams, S. T. (2007). *Blue rage, black redemption: A memoir*. New York: Touchstone.
14. Ibid. p217.
15. Andrews, D. P. (2002). *Practical theology for black churches: Bridging black theology and African American folk religion*. Louisville, KY: Westminster John Knox Press. p82.
16. Alexander, M. (2010). *The new Jim Crow: Mass incarceration in the age of colorblindness*. New York: Free Press. p2.
17. Wenning, M. (2009). The return of rage. *Parrhesia, 8*, 89–99.
18. Ibid. p97.
19. Staples, J. S. (2000). Violence in schools: Rage against a broken world. *Annals of the Association of American Political and Social Science, 567*, 30–41.

20. Walsh, F. (2003). Crisis, trauma, and challenges: A relational resilience approach for healing, transformation and growth. *Smith College Studies in Social Work*, *74*, 49–72.

21. Wenning, M. (2009). *The return of rage*. Parrhesia, *8*, 94–97.

22. Randel, W. P. (1939). *The place names of Tioga county, Pennsylvania*. American Speech, *14*, 181–190.

23. Murray, L. W. (1921). *Aboriginal sites in and near Teaoga, now Athens, Pennsylvania*. American Anthropologist, *23*(2), 184–214.

24. Ganter, G. (2007). *Red jacket and the decolonization of republican virtue*. American Indian Quarterly, *31*(4), 559–581.

25. Asante, M. K. (1980). *Afrocentricity: The theory of social change*. Buffalo: Amulefi.

26. Goh, S. C. (1998). Toward a learning organization: The strategic building blocks. *SAM Advanced Management Journal, 63*,16.

Chapter Two: When Love is the Cultural Core: A Curriculum of Race and Rage

1. Garvin, D. A. (1993). Building a learning organization. *Harvard Business Review, 71*, 78–91.

2. Chaskin, R. J. (2008). Resilience, community, and resilient communities: Conditioning contexts and collective action. *Child Care in Practice, 14*, 65–74.

3. Fletcher, L. E. & Weinstein, H. M. (2002). Violence and social repair: Rethinking the contribution of justice to reconciliation. *Human Rights Quarterly, 24*, 573–639.

4. Fry, L. W. (2003). Toward a theory of spiritual leadership. *Leadership Quarterly 14*, 695.

5. Walsh, F. (2003). Crisis, trauma, and challenges: A relational resilience approach for healing, transformation, and growth. *Smith College Studies in Social Work, 74*, 49.

6. Freire, P. (1970). *Pedagogy of the oppressed*. New York: Continuum. p15.

7. University of California, Berkley. National Abandoned Infants Assistance Resource Center. (2006). *Spirituality: A powerful force in women's recovery*. Retrieved from: http://aia.berkeley.edu/media/pdf/spirituality_issue_brief.pdf

8. Fellowship of Intentional Communities. (1959). *The intentional communities: 1959 yearbook of the Fellowship of Intentional Communities*. Yellow Springs, OH: Fellowship of Intentional Communities.

9. Cumbrie, S. A. (2001). The integration of mind-body-soul and the practice of humanistic nursing. *Holistic Nursing Practice, 15*, 56–62.

10. Chaskin, R. J., Brown, P., Venkatesh, S. & Vidal, A. (2001). *Building community capacity*. New York: Aldine de Gruyter. p180.

11. Du Bois, W. E. B. (1969). *The souls of Black folk*. New York: Signet Books. (Original work published 1903) p46.

12. Fry, L. W., & Cohen, M. P. (2009). Spiritual leadership as a paradigm for organizational transformation and recovery from extended work hours cultures. *Journal of Business Ethics, 84*, 265–278.

13. Bellah, R. N., Madsen, R., Sullivan, W., Swidler, A., & Tipton, S.M. (1985). *Habits of the heart: Individualism and commitment in American life*. Berkeley: University of California Press.

14. Freire, P. (1970). *Pedagogy of the oppressed*. New York: Continuum. p34.

15. Ibid. p19.

16. Trauffer, H. C. V., Bekker, C., Bocarnea, M., & Winston, B. E. (2010). Towards an understanding of discernment: A conceptual paper. *Leadership & Organization Development Journal, 31*, 177.

17. O'Connor, J. (1987). *The meaning of crisis.* New York: Basil Blackwell.

18. Turner, B. A. (1976). The organizational and intergenerational development of disasters. *Administrative Science Quarterly, 21*, 378–397.

19. Pearson, C. M., & Clair, J. A. (1998). Reframing crisis management. *Academy of Management Review, 23*, p64.

20. De Leon, G. (2000). *The therapeutic community: Theory, model, and method.* New York: Springer Publishing Co. p330–31.

21. Combahee River Collective. 1981. A Black feminist statement. In C. Moraga & G. Anzaldua (Eds.), *This Bridge Called My Back: Writings by Radical Women of Color.* London: Persephone Press. p210–218.

22. Freire, P. (1970). *Pedagogy of the oppressed.* New York: Continuum.

23. Dillard, C. B. (2006). *On spiritual strivings: Transforming an African American woman's academic life.* Albany: State University of New York Press.

24. Dillard, C., Tyson, C. A., & Abdur-Rashid, D. (2000). My soul is a witness: Affirming pedagogies of the spirit." *International Journal of Qualitative Studies in Education, 13*, 447–462.

25. Hanna, F. J., Talley, W. B., & Guindon, M. H. (2000). The power of perception: Toward a model of cultural oppression and liberation. *Journal of Counseling and Development, 78*, 430–441.

26. hooks,b. (1993). *Sisters of the yam: Black Women and self-recovery.* Boston: South End Press.

27. Hunn, L. M. (2004). Africentric philosophy: A remedy for Eurocentric dominance. *New Directions for Adult and Continuing Education, 102*, 65–74.

28. McLaren, P. (1999). A pedagogy of possibility: Reflecting upon Paulo Freire's politics of education. *Educational Researcher, 28*, 49–54, 56.

29. Snow, D. A., & Phillips, C. L. (1980). The Lofland-Stark Conversion Model: A critical reassessment. *Social Problems, 27*, p433.

30. hooks, b. (1990). *Yearning: Race, gender, and cultural politics.* Boston: South End Press.

31. hooks,b. (1993). *Sisters of the yam: Black women and self-recovery.* Boston: South End Press.

32. Dillard, C. B. (2006). *On spiritual strivings: Transforming an African American woman's academic life.* Albany: State University of New York Press.

33. Drake, S. C., & Cayton, H. R. (1962). *Black metropolis: A study of Negro life in a northern city* (2nd ed.). New York: Harper Torchbooks. p62.

34. Hamma, R. M. (1999). *Landscapes of the soul: A spirituality of place.* Notre Dame, IN: Ave Maria Press. p99.

35. Haymes, S. N. (1995). *Race, culture, and the city: A pedagogy for Black urban struggle.* Albany: State University of New York Press.

36. Maruna, S. (2001). *Making good: How ex-convicts reform and rebuild their lives.* Washington, DC: American Psychological Association.

37. Maruna, S., LeBel, T. P., Mitchell, N., & Naples, M. (2004). Pygmalion in the reintegration process: Desistance from crime through the looking glass. *Psychology, Crime & Law, 10*, 271–281.

38. Taylor, P. V. (1993). *The texts of Paulo Freire.* Buckingham, England: Open University Press. p52.

39. Freire, P. (1985). *The politics of education: Culture, power and liberation.* South Hadley, MA: Bergin & Garvey Publishers.

40. McLaren, P. (1999). A pedagogy of possibility: Reflecting upon Paulo Freire's politics of education. *Educational Researcher, 28,* 49–54, 56.

41. Bazemore, G., & Boba, R. (2007). 'Doing good' to 'make good': Community theory for practice in a restorative justice civic engagement reentry model. *Journal of Offender Rehabilitation, 46,* 25–56.

42. Farrall, S. (2005). On the existential aspects of desistance from crime. *Symbolic Interaction, 28,* 367–386.

43. Lynch, J. P. (2006). Prisoner reentry: Beyond program evaluations. *Criminology and Public Policy, 5,* 401–412.

Chapter Three: A Fragile Justice: Reconstruction's Organizational Origins, 1988–1992

1. Goldsby, W. (1988, May). *Notes from AFSC MOVE Memorial.* Archives of Reconstruction, Inc., Philadelphia, PA.

2. American Friends Service Committee (1990). *AFSC Progress Report.* Archives of AFSC, Philadelphia, PA.

3. Fattah, D. (1987, November). The house of Umoja as a case study for social change. *Annals of the American Academy of Political and Social Science, 494,* 37–41.

4. Fattah, D. (1969). Social disorder among Black youth. *School of Business Administration,* Temple University, Philadelphia.

5. Ford, L. (1990). Reconstruction: Progress Report, March 1989–March 1990. Archives of Reconstruction, Inc., Philadelphia, PA.

6. American Friends Service Committee. (2011). Mission statement and values. Retrieved from http://afsc.org/mission-and-values.

7. Lee, B. A., Price-Spratlen, T., & Kanan, J. W. (2003). Determinants of homelessness in metropolitan areas. *Journal of Urban Affairs, 25,* 335–355.

8. Levinson, D. (Ed.). 2004. *The Encyclopedia of Homelessness.* Thousand Oaks, CA: Sage.

9. Clark, R., & Giles, D. M. (1989, May 24). Inmate tensions incite food fight at Homesburg. *The Philadelphia Inquirer.* Retrieved from http://articles philly.com/1989-05-/24/news/26114737_1_prison-officials-prison-personnel-in mate

10. Asante, M. K. (1980). *Afrocentricity: The theory of social change.* Buffalo: Amulefi. p2–4,38.

11. James, S. V. (1962). The impact of the American Revolution on Quakers' ideas about their sect. *William and Mary Quarterly, 19,* 360–382.

12. Lorde, A. (1984). *Sister outsider.* Freedom, CA: Crossing Press. p63–64.

13. Johnson, R., & Bernard, T. J. (Eds.). (2004). *Life without parole: Living in prison today.* (3rd ed.). Los Angeles: Roxbury. p3,4.

14. Hassine, V. (Inmate AM4737). (2004). *Life Without Parole: Living in Prison Today* (3rd ed). Los Angeles: Roxbury.

Chapter Four: "There's No Progress Without a Woman In It" Women's Experiences in Reconstruction, Inc.

1. Du Bois, W. E. B. (1962). *Black reconstruction in America, 1860–1880*. New York: Atheneum/MacMillan. (Original work published 1935)

2. Thompson, A. C. (2008). *Releasing prisoners, redeeming communities: Reentry, race and politics*. New York: New York University Press. p45.

3. Szanton, S., & Gill, J. M. (2010). Facilitating resilience using a society-to-cells framework: A theory of nursing essentials applied to research and practice. *Advances in Nursing Science, 33*, 329–343.

4. Collins, P. H. (1991). *Black feminist thought: Knowledge, consciousness, and the politics of empowerment*. New York: Routledge.

5. Sasson, T., & Nelson, M. K. (1996). Danger, community, and the meaning of crime watch: An analysis of the discourses of African American and White participants. *Journal of Contemporary Ethnography, 25*, 171–200.

6. Watt, D. (2004). Traditional religious practices amongst African Caribbean mothers and community othermothers. *Black Theology, 2*, 195–212.

7. Collins, P. H. (1990). *Black feminist thought: Knowledge, consciousness, and empowerment*. Boston: Unwin Hyman. p147.

8. Kuykendall, E. H. (1983). Toward and ethic of nurturance. In J. Trebilcot (Ed.) *Mothering: Essays in Feminist Theory*. Totowan, NJ: Roman and Allanheld.

9. Collins, P. H. (1991). *Black feminist thought: Knowledge, consciousness, and the politics of empowerment*. New York: Routledge. p122,123.

10. Clutterbuck, D., & Kernaghan, S. (1994). *The power of empowerment*. London: Kogan Page. p94.

11. Drevdahl, D. (1995). Coming to voice: The power of emancipatory community interventions. *Advances in Nursing Science, 18*, 13–24.

12. Collins, P. H. (1991). *Black feminist thought: Knowledge, consciousness, and the politics of empowerment*. New York: Routledge.

13. Hirschman, A. O. (1970). *Exit, voice, and loyalty: Responses to decline in firms, organizations, and states*. Boston: Harvard University Press.

14. Lorde, A. (1984). *Sister outsider*. Freedom, CA: Crossing Press. p41.

15. Brockner, J., Ackerman G., Greenberg,J., Gelfand, M. J., Francesco, A. M., Chen, Z. X.,…Shapiro, D. (2001). Culture and procedural justice: The influence of power distance on reactions to voice. *Journal of Experimental Social Psychology, 37*, 300–315.

16. Collins, P. H. (1991). *Black feminist thought: Knowledge, consciousness, and the politics of empowerment*. New York: Routledge.

17. Haymes, S. N. (1995). *Race, culture, and the city: A pedagogy for Black urban struggle*. Albany: State University of New York Press.

18. Baker, H. A. (1991). *Workings of the spirit: The poetics of Afro-American women's writings*. Chicago: University of Chicago Press. p133.

19. Brockner, J., Ackerman G., Greenberg,J., Gelfand, M. J., Francesco, A. M., Chen, Z. X.,…Shapiro, D. (2001). Culture and procedural justice: The influence of power distance on reactions to voice." *Journal of Experimental Social Psychology, 37*, 300–315.

20. Christian, J. (2005). Riding the bus: Barriers to prison visitation and family management strategies. *Journal of Contemporary Criminal Justice, 21*, 31–48.

21. Drevdahl, D. (1995). Coming to voice: The power of emancipatory community interventions. *Advances in Nursing Science, 18*, 13–24.

22. Harris, M. K. (1987). Moving into the new millennium: Toward a feminist vision of justice. *Prison Journal, 67*, 27–38.

23. Collins, P. H. (1991). *Black feminist thought: Knowledge, consciousness, and the politics of empowerment.* New York: Routledge. p112.

24. Fanon, F. (1952). *Black skin, White masks.* New York: Grove.

25. Freire, P. (1970). *Pedagogy of the oppressed.* New York: Continuum.

26. Collins, P. H. (1991). *Black feminist thought: Knowledge, consciousness, and the politics of empowerment.* New York: Routledge. p112.

27. Ibid. p112.

28. Bazemore, G. & Maruna, S. (2009). Restorative justice in the reentry context: Building new theory and expanding the evidence base. *Victims and Offenders, 4*, 375–384.

29. Bellah, R. N., Madsen, R., Sullivan, W., Swidler, A., & Tipton, S.M. (1985). *Habits of the heart: Individualism and commitment in American life.* Berkeley: University of California Press.

30. Fry, L. W. (2003). Toward a theory of spiritual leadership. *Leadership Quarterly 14*, 693–727.

31. Fry, L. W., & Cohen, M. P. (2009). Spiritual leadership as a paradigm for organizational transformation and recovery from extended work hours cultures. *Journal of Business Ethics, 84*, 265–278.

32. Moon, G. W. (2002). Spiritual direction: Meaning, purpose, and implications for mental health professionals. *Journal of Psychology and Theology, 30*, 264–275.

33. Zalanga, S. (2004). Teaching and learning social theory to advance social transformation: Some insights, implications, and practical suggestions from Paulo Freire. *The Discourse of Sociological Practice, 6*, 7–26.

34. Boy Scouts of America (2011). Mission Statement. Retrieved from http://www.scouting.org /scoutsource/Media/mission.aspx

35. Dantley, M. E. (2003). Critical spirituality: Enhancing transformative leadership through critical theory and African American prophetic spirituality. *International Journal of Leadership in Education, 6*, 3.

36. Alston, J. A. (2005). Tempered radicals and servant leaders: Black females persevering in the superintendency. *Educational Administration Quarterly, 41*, 675–688.

37. Besecke, K. (2001). Speaking of meaning in modernity: Reflexive spirituality as a cultural resource. *Sociology of Religion, 62*, 365–381.

38. Collins, P. H. (1991). *Black feminist thought: Knowledge, consciousness, and the politics of empowerment.* New York: Routledge.

39. Dash, M. I. N., Jackson, J. & Rasor, S. C. (1997). *Hidden wholeness: An African American spirituality for individuals and communities.* Cleveland: United Church Press.

40. Dillard, C. B. (2006). *On spiritual strivings: Transforming an African American woman's academic life.* Albany: State University of New York Press.

41. Fry, L. W. (2003). Toward a theory of spiritual leadership. *Leadership Quarterly 14*, 693–727.

42. Lorde, A. (1984). *Sister outsider.* Freedom, CA: Crossing Press. p111.

43. Ibid. p111.

44. Andrews, D. P. (2002). *Practical theology for Black churches: Bridging Black theology and African American folk religion.* Louisville, KY: Westminster John Knox Press.

45. Besecke, K. (2001). Speaking of meaning in modernity: Reflexive spirituality as a cultural resource. *Sociology of Religion, 62*, 365–381.

46. Dash, M. I. N., Jackson, J. & Rasor, S. C. (1997). *Hidden wholeness: An African American spirituality for individuals and communities.* Cleveland: United Church Press.

47. Moon, G. W. (2002). Spiritual direction: Meaning, purpose, and implications for mental health professionals. *Journal of Psychology and Theology, 30,* 269.

48. Collins, P. H. (1991). *Black feminist thought: Knowledge, consciousness, and the politics of empowerment.* New York: Routledge. p158.

49. Baker, H. A. (1991). *Workings of the spirit: The poetics of Afro-American women's writings.* Chicago: University of Chicago Press.

50. Brown, K. M. (2004). Leadership for social justice and equity: Weaving a transformative framework and pedagogy. *Educational Administration Quarterly, 40,* 77–108.

51. Dillard, C., Tyson, C. A., & Abdur-Rashid, D. (2000). My soul is a witness: Affirming pedagogies of the spirit. *International Journal of Qualitative Studies in Education, 13,* 447–462.

52. Jonsson, J. H. (2010). Beyond empowerment: Changing local communities. *International Social Work, 53,* 393–401.

53. Collins, P. H. (1991). *Black feminist thought: Knowledge, consciousness, and the politics of empowerment.* New York: Routledge. p158.

54. Angelou, M. (1995). *Phenomenal woman: Four poems celebrating women.* New York: Random House. p5–6.

55. American Friends Service Committee. (1994, October 10). *The death of Barbara Moffett.* AFSC News Release.

56. Ibid.

57. Ibid.

58. Baker, H. A. (1991). *Workings of the spirit: The poetics of Afro-American women's writings.* Chicago: University of Chicago Press.

59. Dillard, C. B. (2006). *On spiritual strivings: Transforming an African American woman's academic life.* Albany: State University of New York Press.

60. Collins, P. H. (1991). *Black feminist thought: Knowledge, consciousness, and the politics of empowerment.* New York: Routledge.

61. Smith, B. (Ed.) (1983). *Home girls: A Black feminist anthology.* New York: Kitchen Table Women of Color Press.

62. Knight, N. (1980). Mao ZeDong's 'on contradiction' and 'on practice': Pre-liberation texts. *China Quarterly, 84,* 641–668.

63. Liu, J. (1971). Mao's 'On Contradiction.' *Studies in East European Thought, 11,* 71–89.

64. Tse-Tung, M. (2001) [1967]. *Selected works of Mao Tse-tung.* Honolulu: University Press of the Pacific. (Original work published 1967)

65. Tse-Tung, M. (1990). *On dialectical materialism.* New York: M.E. Sharpe. (Original work published 1937).

66. Churchill, W (1910, July 20). *Address to Parliament, in 2 Winston S. Churchill: His complete speeches, 1897–1963.* New York, London: Chelsea House Publishers.

67. Bloom, S. L. & Sreedhar, S. Y. (2008). The sanctuary model of trauma-informed organizational change. *Reclaiming Children and Youth*, *17*, 48–53.

68. Szanton, S., & Gill, J. M. (2010). From cells to society: A theory of resilience in nursing. *Advances in Nursing Science*, *33*, 329–343.

69. Walsh, F. (2003). Crisis, trauma, and challenges: A relational resilience approach for healing, transformation, and growth. *Smith College Studies in Social Work*, *74*, 49–72.

70. Watts-Jones, D. (2002). Healing internalized racism: The role of a within-group sanctuary among people of African descent. *Family Process*, *41*, 591–601.

71. Danesh, H. B. (2008). Creating a culture of healing in multiethnic communities: An integrative approach to prevention and amelioration of violence-induced conditions. *Journal of Community Psychology*, *36*, 814–832.

72. Dillard, C. B. (2006). *On spiritual strivings: Transforming an African American woman's academic life.* Albany: State University of New York Press.

73. Yehya, N. A., & Dutta, M. J. (2010). Health, religion, and meaning: A culture-centered study of Druze women. *Qualitative Health Research*, *20*, 845–858.

74. Font, R., Dolan-Del Vecchio, K., & Almeida, R. V. (1998). Finding the words: Instruments for a therapy of liberation." *Journal of Feminist Family Therapy*, *10*, 85–97.

75. Freire, P. (1970). *Pedagogy of the oppressed.* New York: Continuum.

76. Freire, P. (1978). *Education for critical consciousness.* New York: Seabury.

77. Freire, P. (1985). *The politics of education: Culture, power and liberation.* South Hadley, MA: Bergin & Garvey Publishers.

78. Martin-Baro, I. (1994). *Writings for a liberation psychology.* Cambridge, MA: Harvard University Press.

79. Bloom, S. L. & Sreedhar, S. Y. (2008). The sanctuary model of trauma-informed organizational change. *Reclaiming Children and Youth*, *17*, 49.

80. Belenky, M. F., Clinchy, B. M., Goldberger, N. R., & Tarule, J. M. (1986). *Women's ways of knowing: The development of self, voice and mind.* New York: Basic Books.

81. Keller, E. F. (1983). *A feeling for the organism: The life and works of Barbara McClintock.* New York: W.H. Freeman.

82. Blau, P. M. (1977). *Inequality and heterogeneity: A primitive theory of social structure.* New York: Free Press.

83. Chaskin, R. J., Brown, P., Venkatesh, S. & Vidal, A. (2001). *Building community capacity.* New York: Aldine de Gruyter.

84. Nye, N., & Glickman, N. J. (2000). Working together: Building capacity for community development. *Housing Policy Debate*, *11*, 163–198.

85. Lorde, A. (1984). *Sister outsider.* Freedom, CA: Crossing Press.

86. Marwell, G., & Oliver, P. (1993). *The critical mass in collective action: A micro-social theory.* New York: Cambridge University Press. p181.

87. Eden, D. (1992). Leadership and expectations: Pygmalion effects and other self-fulfilling prophecies in organizations. *Leadership Quarterly*, *3*, 287.

Chapter Five: A Pedagogy of Progress: Nurturing Community, 1993–1998

1.   Freire, P. (1970). *Pedagogy of the oppressed.* New York: Continuum.

2. Zalanga, S. (2004). Teaching and learning social theory to advance social transformation: Some insights, implications, and practical suggestions from Paulo Freire. *The Discourse of Sociological Practice, 6*, 7–26.

3. Cho, S. (2010). Politics of critical pedagogy and new social movements. *Educational Philosophy and Theory, 42*, 310–325.

4. McLaren, P. (1999). A pedagogy of possibility: Reflecting upon Paulo Freire's politics of education. *Educational Researcher, 28*, 49–54, 56.

5. Taylor, P. V. (1993). *The texts of Paulo Freire*. Buckingham, England: Open University Press.

6. Goodman, R. M., Speers, M. A., McLeroy, K., Fawcett, S., Kegler, M., Parker, E.,...Wallerstein, N. (1998). Identifying and defining the dimensional of community capacity to provide a basis for measurement. *Health, Education and Behavior, 25*, 258–278.

7. Chaskin, R. J. (2008). Resilience, community, and resilient communities: Conditioning contexts and collective action. *Child Care in Practice, 14*, 65–74.

8. Chaskin, R. J., Brown, P., Venkatesh, S. & Vidal, A. (2001). *Building community capacity*. New York: Aldine de Gruyter.

9. Morris, A. D. (1984). *The origins of the civil rights movement: Black communities organizing for change*. New York: Free Press. p284.

10. Gilbert, M., & Orlans, V. (2010). *Integrative therapy: 100 key points and techniques*. New York: Routledge.

11. Price-Spratlen, T. (2008). Urban destination selection among African Americans during the 1950s Great Migration. *Social Science History, 32*, 437–469.

12. Board meeting minutes (1992, November 19). Archives of Reconstruction, Inc., Philadelphia, PA.

13. Akbar, N. (1976). *The community of the self*. Chicago: Nation of Islam Office of Human Development.

14. Asante, M. K. (1980). *Afrocentricity: The theory of social change*. Buffalo: Amulefi.

15. Gilroy, P. (1993). *The Black Atlantic: Modernity and double consciousness*. Cambridge, MA: Harvard University Press.

16. Some, M. P. (1993). *Ritual: Power, healing and community*. New York: Penguin.

17. Blassingame, J. W. (1973). *The slave community: Plantation life in the antebellum south*. New York: Oxford University Press.

18. Asante, M. K. (1980). *Afrocentricity: The theory of social change*. Buffalo: Amulefi.

19. Nobles, W. (1974). Africanity: Its role in Black families. *Black Scholar, 5*, 10–17.

20. Ronnau, J. P., & Marlow, C. R. (1993). Family preservation and poverty: Valuing diversity. *Families in Society, 74*, 538–544.

21. Landry, P. (1993, February 23). A Graterford inmate is stabbed to death watching ball game. *Philadelphia Inquirer*, pB03.

22. Funk, L. K. (1993, February 26). Lockdown at Graterford prison is lifted. *The Morning Call*. Retrieved from http://articles.mcall.com/1993-02-26/news/2900616_1_lockdown-cells-graterford-state-prison

23. Ibid.

24. Reconstruction, Inc. Board Meeting Minutes (1993, March 18). Archives of Reconstruction, Inc., Philadelphia, PA.

25. Reconstruction, Inc. Board Meeting Minutes (1993, May 20). Archives of Reconstruction, Inc., Philadelphia, PA.

26. Ibid.

27. Goodman, R. M., Speers, M. A., McLeroy, K., Fawcett, S., Kegler, M., Parker, E.,…Wallerstein, N. (1998). Identifying and defining the dimensional of community capacity to provide a basis for measurement. *Health, Education and Behavior, 25*, 258–278.

28. Mazama, M. (2002). Afrocentricity and African spirituality. *Journal of Black Studies, 33*, 221.

29. Some, M. P. (1993). *Ritual: Power, healing and community.* New York: Penguin.

30. Regnier, R. H. (1994). The sacred circle: A process pedagogy of healing. *Interchange, 25*, 129.

31. Cochrane, J. R. (2008). Fire from above, fire from below: Health, justice and the persistence of the sacred. *Theoria, 116*, 67–96.

32. Diaz-Soto, L., Cervantes-Soon, C. G., Villarreal, E., & Campos, E. E. (2009). The Xicana sacred space: A communal circle of compromise for educational researchers. *Harvard Educational Review, 79*, 755–775.

33. Gotthold, J. J. (2009). Peeling the onion: Understanding layers of treatment. *Annals of the New York Academy of Sciences, 1159*, 301–312.

34. Wellwood, J. (2000). *Journey of the heart: The path of conscious love.* New York: Harper.

35. Zigarmi, D., Blanchard, K., O'Connor, M., & Edeburn, C. (2004). *The leader within: Learning enough about yourself to lead others.* New York: Prentice-Hall.

36. hooks, b. (1990). *Yearning: Race, gender, and cultural politics.* Boston: South End Press. p42.

37. Bellah, R. N., Madsen, R., Sullivan, W., Swidler, A., & Tipton, S.M. (1985). *Habits of the heart: Individualism and commitment in American life.* Berkeley: University of California Press.

38. Dillard, C. B. (2006). *On spiritual strivings: Transforming an African American woman's academic life.* Albany: State University of New York Press.

39. Haymes, S. N. (1995). *Race, culture, and the city: A pedagogy for Black urban struggle.* Albany: State University of New York Press.

40. Shirlow, P., & Murtagh, B. (2004). Capacity-building, representation and intracommunity conflict. *Urban Studies, 41*, 57–70.

41. Browning, C. R., Feinberg, S. L., & Dietz, R. (2004). The paradox of social organization: Networks, collective efficacy, and violent crime in urban neighborhoods. *Social Forces, 83*, 503–534.

42. Gilbert, M., & Orlans, V. (2010). *Integrative therapy: 100 key points and techniques.* New York: Routledge.

43. Turner, R. J., & Marino, F. (1994). Social support and social structure: A descriptive epidemiology. *Journal of Health and Social Behavior, 35*, 193–212.

44. Shirlow, P., & Murtagh, B. (2004). Capacity-building, representation and intracommunity conflict. *Urban Studies, 41*, 59.

45. Perkins, D. D., Brown, B. B., & Taylor, R. B. (1996). The ecology of empowerment: Predicting participation in community organizations. *Journal of Social Issues, 52*, 85–110.

46. Smyth, J., Angus, L., Down, B., & McInerney, P. (2009). *Activist and socially critical school and community renewal.* Rotterdam, The Neatherlands: Sense Publishers.

47. Reconstruction, Inc. Board meeting minutes (1993, May 20). Archives of Reconstruction, Inc., Philadelphia, PA.

48. Murray, L. W. (1921). Aboriginal sites in and near 'Teaoga,' now Athens, Pennsylvania. *American Anthropologist*, *23*(2), 184.

49. Randel, W. P. (1939). The place names of Tioga County, Pennsylvania. *American Speech*, *14*, 181–190.

50. Ganter, G. (2007). Red jacket and the decolonization of Republican virtue. *American Indian Quarterly*, *31*(4), 570.

51. Pattillo-McCoy, M. (1999). *Black picket fences: Privilege and peril among the Black middle class.* Chicago: University of Chicago Press.

52. Wilson, M. (2007, July 19). ...And stay out: Hakim Ali's using his years inside to help ex-cons stay on the up and up. *Philadelphia City Paper.* Retrieved from http://archives.citypaper.net/articles/2007/07/19/and-stay-out

53. Friends For Change (2011). General Organization Information. Retrieved from http://www.fatherpaulwashington.com

54. Goldsby, W. (1994, August 4). Letter to Board. Archives of Reconstruction, Inc., Philadelphia, PA.

55. Board Meeting Minutes (1994, September). Archives of Reconstruction, Inc., Philadelphia, PA.

56. Suarez, R. (1999). *The old neighborhood: What we lost in the great suburban migration, 1966–1999.* New York: Free Press.

57. Board Meeting Minutes (1994, November 11). Archives of Reconstruction, Inc., Philadelphia, PA.

58. Scribe (2011). Mission Statement. Retrieved from http://scribe.org/about/community visions.

59. Chepesiuk, R. (1999). *The war on drugs: An international encyclopedia.* Santa Barbara, CA: ABC-CLIO. p317.

60. Associated Press. (1995, April 15). It was the 'day of judgment' for rogue cops in Philadelphia. *The Philadelphia Inquirer.* Retrieved from: http://www.googieonline.com/revolution/body/drugs/legal/philadelphia.html

61. Guither, P. (2006, June 19). *Len Bias—the death that ushered in two decades of destruction.* Retrieved from http://www.drugwarrant.com/articles/len-bias-two-decades-of-destruction.

62. U. S. Sentencing Commission. (1995, February). Special Report to the Congress: Cocaine and Federal Sentencing Policy. Retrieved from http://www.ussc.gov/Legislative_and_ Public_Affairs/Congressional_Testimony_and_Reports/Drug_Topics/199502_RtC_Cocaine_S entencing_Policy/index.htm

63. White, S. A. (1999, June 4). Controlling police corruption. Poverty and prejudice: Paradoxes of U. S. drug policies. *EDGE: Ethics of Development in a Global Environment.* Retrieved from http://www.stanford.edu/class/e297c/poverty_prejudice/paradox/hwhite.html

64. De Vita, C. J. & Fleming, C. (2001). *Building capacity in nonprofit organizations.* Washington, DC: Urban Institute.

65. Powley, E. H., & Cameron, K. S. (2006). Organizational healing: Lived virtuousness amidst organizational crisis. *Journal of Management, Spirituality and Religion*, *3*, 13–33.

66. Hallett, T. (2003). Symbolic power and organizational culture. *Sociological Theory*, *21*, 128–149.

67. Ouchi, W. G., & Wilkins, A. L. (1985). Organizational culture. *Annual Review of Sociology*, *11*, 457–483.

68. Block, K. (2010). Cultivating inner and outer plantations: Property, industry, and slavery in early Quaker migration to the new world. *Early American Studies, 8,* 515–548.

69. Cantor, G. (1997). *Old roads of the Midwest.* Ann Arbor: University of Michigan Press.

70. Travis, J. (2000). *But they all come back: Rethinking prisoner reentry. Sentencing & Corrections: Issues for the 21st Century.* Papers from the Executive Sessions on Sentencing and Corrections (No. 7). U.S. Department of Justice, Office of Justice Programs. Washington, DC: National Institute of Justice.

71. Workman, K. (2009). Back to Churchill—an old vision for prisoner reintegration. *Policy Quarterly, 5,* 24–31.

72. Lofland, J. (1979). White-hot mobilization: Strategies of a millenarian movement. In M. Zald and J. McCarthy (Eds.), *Dynamics of Social Movements.* (pp. 156–166). Cambridge, MA: Winthrop. p165.

73. Etzioni, A. (1975). *A comparative analysis of complex organizations.* New York: Free Press.

74. McCarthy, J., & Zald, M. (1973). *The trend of social movements in America: Professionalization and resource mobilization.* Morristown, NJ: General Learning Press.

75. Olney, C. A. (2005). Using evaluation to adapt health information outreach to the complex environments of community-based organizations. *Journal of the Medical Library Association, 93,* pS59.

76. Kim, H., Shim, Y., Choi, D., Kim, S., & Cho, W. (2006). Community manager: A dynamic collaboration solution on heterogeneous environment. In *ACE/IEEE International Conference on Pervasive Services.* (pp. 39–46). Los Alamitos, CA: IEEE Press.

77. Tirado, M. D. (1970). The key to Chicano political power. *Chicano Journal of the Social Sciences and the Arts, 1,* 53–78.

78. Price-Spratlen, T. (2000). Safety among strangers: The Million Man March. In D. Constantine-Simms (Ed.), *The greatest taboo: Homosexuality in Black communities.* (pp. 44–66). Los Angeles: Alyson Books.

79. West, M. O. (1999). Like a river: The Million Man March and the Black nationalist tradition in the United States. *Journal of Historical Sociology, 12,* 81–100.

80. Goldsby, W. (1995, December 24). Personal Journal. In author's possession.

81. Ibid. (1996, January 31).

82. Lofland, J. (1979). White-hot mobilization: Strategies of a millenarian movement. In M. Zald and J. McCarthy (Eds.), *Dynamics of Social Movements.* (pp. 156–166). Cambridge, MA: Winthrop.

83. Olney, C. A. (2005). Using evaluation to adapt health information outreach to the complex environments of community-based organizations. *Journal of the Medical Library Association, 93,* S57–59.

84. Reconstruction, Inc. Board Meeting Minutes (1997, March 26). Archives of Reconstruction, Inc., Philadelphia, PA.

85. Asante, M. K. (1980). *Afrocentricity: The theory of social change.* Buffalo, NY: Amulefi Publishing Co.

86. Krogh, M., & Pillifant, A. (2004). Kemetic orthodoxy: Ancient Egyptian religion on the internet. *Sociology of Religion, 65,* 167–175.

Chapter Six: "And A Little Child Shall Lead Them"

1. Kiecolt, K. J. (2000). Self-concept change in social movements. In S. Stryker, T. J. Owens, & R. W .White (Eds.), *Self, Identity and Social Movements.* (pp. 111–131). Minneapolis: University of Minnesota Press.

2. Osterman, P. (2006). Overcoming oligarchy: Culture and agency in social movement organizations. *Administrative Science Quarterly, 51,* 622–649.

3. Ginwright, S. A. (2010). Peace out to revolution! Activism among African American youth: An argument for radical healing. *Young, 18,* 83.

4. Anderson, E. (2011). *The cosmopolitan canopy: Race and civility in everyday life.* New York: W.W. Norton & Co. p156.

5. Reconstruction, Inc. Board Meeting Minutes (1994, August 4). Archives of Reconstruction, Inc., Philadelphia, PA.

6. Graham, J. W. (1991). Servant leadership in organizations: Inspirational and moral. *Leadership Quarterly, 2,* 105–119.

7. Greenleaf, R. K. (1970). *The servant as leader.* Indianapolis, IN: Greenleaf Center.

8. Graham, J. W. (1991). Servant leadership in organizations: Inspirational and moral. *Leadership Quarterly, 2,* 111.

9. Kouzes, J. M., & Posner, B. Z. (1987). *The leadership challenge: How to get extraordinary things done in organizations.* San Francisco: Jossey-Bass.

10. Cottman, B. (2002, January 13). Board Meeting Minutes. Archives of Reconstruction, Inc., Philadelphia, PA.

11. Goldsby, W. (2001). Archival document. Archives of Reconstruction, Inc., Philadelphia, PA.

12. University of Pennsylvania Neighborhood Youth Network (2011). Mission Statement. Retrieved from http://www.stwing.upenn.edu/~rrodrigu/PYN/ youth.html

13. Ginwright, S. A. (2007). Black youth activism and the role of critical social capital in Black community organizations. *American Behavioral Scientist, 51,* 403–418.

14. Freire, P. (1970). *Pedagogy of the oppressed.* New York: Continuum. p15.

15. Geo-Clan (2011). *Mission Statement.* Retrieved from http://geoclan.com/blog

16. LEAD (2006). *Program summary.* Archives of Reconstruction, Inc., Philadelphia, PA.

17. Ginwright, S. A. (2010). Peace out to revolution! Activism among African American youth: an argument for radical healing. *Young, 18,* 77.

18. Ibid. p77–96.

19. Reconstruction 2006 Mid-year report (n.d.). Archives of Reconstruction, Inc., Philadelphia, PA.

20. Jordan, J. (1980). Poem for South African women. In *Passion: New Poems 1977–1980.* Boston: Beacon Press. Retrieved from: www.JuneJordan.com

21. Reconstruction, Inc. (2011). Mission Statement. Retrieved from http://www. reconstructioninc.org/drupal

22. Cass, J., & Curry, C. (2007, October). *America's cradle to prison pipeline.* A report of the Children's Defense Fund. Retrieved from http://www.childrensdefense.org/child-research-data-publications/data/cradle -prison-pipeline-report-2007-full-lowres.pdf

23. Western, B. (2006). *Punishment and inequality in America.* New York: Russell Sage Foundation.

24. The Sentencing Project. (2007). Women in the criminal justice system: Briefing sheets. Washington, DC: *The Sentencing Project.* Retrieved from http://www.sentencingproject.org/doc/publications/womenincj_total.pdf

25. Ibid.

26. Stack, C. (1974). *All our kin: Strategies for survival in a Black community.* New York: Harper & Row.

27. Aron, W. S. (1974). Student activism of the 1960s revisited: A multivariate analysis research note. *Social Forces, 52,* 408–414.

28. Gottlieb, D., & Heinsohn, A. L. (1973). Sociology and youth. *Sociological Quarterly, 14,* 249–270.

29. Ginwright, S. A. (2010). Peace out to revolution! Activism among African American youth: An argument for radical healing. *Young, 18,* 77–96.

30. Ager, R. D., Parquet, R., & Kreutzinger, S. (2008). The youth video project: An innovative program for substance abuse prevention. *Journal of Social Work Practice in the Addictions, 8,* 303–331.

31. Bradley, B. S., Deighton, J. & Selby, J. (2004). The 'voices' project: Capacity-building in community development for youth at risk. *Journal of Health Psychology, 9,* 197–212.

32. Checkoway, B, Allison, T., & Montoya, C. (2005). Youth participation in public policy at the municipal level. *Children and Youth Services Review, 27,* 1149–1162.

33. Cheadle, A., Wagner, E., Anderman, C., Walls, M., McBride, C., Bell, M. A.,…Pettigrew, E. (1998). Measuring community mobilization in the Seattle minority youth health project. *Evaluation Review, 22,* 699–716.

34. Sobeck, J., Agius, E., & Mayers, V. N. (2007). Supporting and sustaining grassroots youth organizations: The case of new Detroit. *Voluntas: International Journal of Voluntary and Nonprofit Organizations, 18,* 1–17.

35. Liss, S. (2005). *No place for children: Voices from juvenile detention.* Austin: University of Texas Press.

Chapter Seven: Building the Bridge Between Them, 1998–2007

1. Osterman, P. (2006). Overcoming oligarchy: Culture and agency in social movement organizations. *Administrative Science Quarterly, 51,* 622–649.

2. Edwards, B., & Marullo, S. (1995). Organizational mortality in a declining social movement. *American Sociological Review, 60,* 908–927.

3. Chaskin, R. J., Brown, P., Venkatesh, S. & Vidal, A. (2001). *Building community capacity.* New York: Aldine de Gruyter.

4. Goodman, R. M., Speers, M. A., McLeroy, K., Fawcett, S., Kegler, M., Parker, E.,…Wallerstein, N. (1998). Identifying and defining the dimensional of community capacity to provide a basis for measurement. *Health, Education and Behavior, 25,* 258–278.

5. Honadle, B. W. (1981). A capacity-building framework: A search for concept and purpose. *Public Administration Review, 41,* 575–580.

6. Steels, B. (2007). Applying a communitarian model of restorative justice and therapeutic jurisprudence: A social research project in Roebourne, WA. *International Journal of Rural Crime, 1,* 44–61.

7. ben-Jochannan, Y. A. A. (1988). *Africa: Mother of western civilization*. Baltimore, MD: Black Classic Press.

8. Nearing, S. (2006). *Civilization and beyond*. Gloucestershire, England: Echo Library. (Original work published 1975)

9. Antrop-Gonzalez, R. (2006). Toward the 'school as sanctuary' concept in multicultural urban education: Implications for small high school reform. *Curriculum Inquiry, 36*, 273–301.

10. Buskey, J. H. (1990). Historical context and contemporary setting of the learning sanctuary. *New Directions for Adult and Continuing Education, 46*, 15–25.

11. Taylor, P. V. (1993). *The texts of Paulo Freire*. Buckingham, England: Open University Press. p52.

12. De Vita, C. J. & Fleming, C. (2001). *Building capacity in nonprofit organizations*. Washington, DC: Urban Institute.

13. Powley, E. H., & Cameron, K. S. (2006). Organizational healing: Lived virtuousness amidst organizational crisis. *Journal of Management, Spirituality and Religion, 3*, 13–33.

14. Hallett, T. (2003). Symbolic power and organizational culture. *Sociological Theory, 21*, 128–149.

15. Ouchi, W. G., & Wilkins, A. L. (1985). Organizational culture. *Annual Review of Sociology, 11*, 457–483.

16. Freire, P. (1972). *Cultural action for freedom*. New York: Penguin. p24.

17. Alexander, M. (2010). *The new Jim Crow*. New York: Free Press.

18. Thompson, A. C. (2008). *Releasing prisoners, redeeming communities: Reentry, race and politics*. New York: New York University Press.

19. New African Voices Alliance [Bahiya Cabral Asante, Nkosi Ali Asante, Shina Ahad and William Goldsby]. (1997). Introduction. In Shafik Asante, *When spider webs unite: Challenging articles & essays on community, diversity and inclusion*. Toronto: Inclusion Press. p7–8.

20. Goodman, R. M., Speers, M. A., McLeroy, K., Fawcett, S., Kegler, M., Parker, E.,…Wallerstein, N. (1998). Identifying and defining the dimensional of community capacity to provide a basis for measurement. *Health, Education and Behavior, 25*, 258–278.

21. Chaskin, R. J., Brown, P., Venkatesh, S. & Vidal, A. (2001). *Building community capacity*. New York: Aldine de Gruyter.

22. Ibid.

23. Goodman, R. M., Speers, M. A., McLeroy, K., Fawcett, S., Kegler, M., Parker, E.,…Wallerstein, N. (1998). Identifying and defining the dimensional of community capacity to provide a basis for measurement. *Health, Education and Behavior, 25*, 258–278.

24. Asante, S. (1997). *When spider webs unite: Challenging articles & essays on community, diversity and inclusion*. Toronto: Inclusion Press. p13.

25. Stoecker, R. (1997). The CDC model of urban redevelopment: A critique and an alternative. *Journal of Urban Affairs, 19*, 1–22.

26. Cummings, S. L. (2001.) Community economic development as progressive politics: Toward a grassroots movement for economic justice. *Stanford Law Review, 54*, 399–493.

27. Goodpaster, G. S. (1969). An introduction to the community development corporation. *Journal of Urban Law, 46*, 603–666.

28. Kelling, G. L., & Coles, C. M. (1996). *Fixing broken windows: Restoring order and reducing crime in our communities*. New York: Free Press.

29. Price-Spratlen, T., & Santoro, W. A. (2011). Neighborhood disorder and individual community capacity: How incivilities inform three domains of psychosocial assessment. *Sociological Spectrum, 31*, 579–605.

30. Skogan, W. G. (1990). *Disorder and decline: Crime and the spiral of decay in American neighborhoods.* Berkeley: University of California Press.

31. McGovern, S. J. (2006). Philadelphia's neighborhood transformation initiative: A case study of mayoral leadership, bold planning, and conflict. *Housing Policy Debate, 17*, p529.

32. Royster, D. D. (2001, January 21). Letter to Editor. *Philadelphia Inquirer*, A05.

33. Massey, D. S., & Denton, N. A. (1993). *American Apartheid: Segregation and the making of the underclass.* Cambridge, MA: Harvard University Press.

34. McGovern, S. J. (2006). Philadelphia's neighborhood transformation initiative: A case study of mayoral leadership, bold planning, and conflict. *Housing Policy Debate, 17*, 529–570.

35. University of Pennsylvania Neighborhood Information System. (2010). Retrieved from http://cml.upenn.edu/nis/cBase

36. Moxley, D. P., Alvarez, A. R., Johnson, A. K., & Gutierrez, L. M. (2005). Appreciating the glocal in community practice: Camp Hill, Gaviotas and intentional community. *Journal of Community Practice, 13*, 1–7. p3.

37. Brooks, J. S., & Normore, A. H. (2010). Educational leadership and globalization: Literacy for a glocal perspective. *Educational Policy, 24*, 52–82.

38. Pearson, C. (2007). The quest for a glocal public theology. *International Journal of Public Theology, 1*, 151–172.

39. Massey, D. S., & Denton, N. A. (1993). *American Apartheid: Segregation and the making of the underclass.* Cambridge, MA: Harvard University Press.

40. Reconstruction, Inc. Draft Annual Report (2005–06). Archives of Reconstruction, Inc., Philadelphia, PA. p5.

41. Fight for Lifers (2011). Mission statement. Retrieved from www.reconstructioninc.org/drupal/node/49

42. Reconstruction Inc. Draft Annual Report (2005–06). Archives of Reconstruction, Inc., Philadelphia, PA. p6.

43. Knight, G. H. (1999, Summer). My perspective on the impact of the Bergoll decision. *The Magnifying Glass.*

44. Fight For Lifers (1999, Summer). An exhibit of 132 t-shirts with the names painted on them of the 132 women currently serving life without [the possibility of] parole were hung…and will remain on display until the end of October [1999]. *The Magnifying Glass.*

45. Fight For Lifers. (2002, Fall). *The Magnifying Glass.*

46. Camp, S. D., Klein-Safran, J., Kwan, O. K., Daggett, D. M., & Joseph, V. (2006). An exploration into participation in a faith-based prison program." *Criminology and Public Policy, 5*, 529–550.

47. Markway, J., & Worsham, D. (2009). The potency of faith in successful offender reentry. *Corrections Today, 71*, 98–99.

48. Roman, C. G., Wolff, A., Correa, V., & Buck, J. (2007). Assessing intermediate outcomes of a faith-based residential prisoner reentry program. *Research on Social Work Practice, 17*, 199–215.

49. Bell, L. A. (2007). Theoretical foundations for social justice education. In M. Adams, L. A. Bell, & P. Griffin (Eds). *Teaching for diversity and social justice* (pp. 1–14). New York: Routledge/Taylor & Francis Group.

50. Wahking, H. (1992). Spiritual growth through grace and forgiveness. *Journal of Psychology and Christianity, 11,* 198–206.

51. Abu-Jamal, M (2005, May 21). A half-life. *Taped speech, Fight for Lifers Conference, Temple University.* Archives of Reconstruction, Inc. Philadelphia, PA.

52. Murder Victim Families for Reconciliation. (2011). Organizational Background and Mission Statement. Retrieved from http://www.mvfr.org

53. Reconstruction, Inc. Draft Annual Report (2005–2006). Archives of Reconstruction, Inc., Philadelphia, PA.

54. Ibid.

55. Foner, J. (1996). Surviving the 'mental health' system with co-counseling. *Psychotherapy Patient, 9,* 107–123.

56. Nickerson, D. (1995). *An introduction to co-counseling.* Seattle: Rational Island.

57. Reconstruction, Inc. Draft Annual Report (2005—2006). Archives of Reconstruction, Inc., Philadelphia, PA.

58. Reconstruction, Inc. Mid-Fiscal Year Report (2006, December). Archives of Reconstruction, Inc., Philadelphia, PA.

59. Wilson, M. (2007, July 19). ....And stay out: Hakim Ali's using his years inside to help ex-cons stay on the up and up. *Philadelphia City Paper.* Retrieved from http://archives.citypaper.net/articles/2007/07/19/and-stay-out

60. Ibid.

61. Ibid.

Chapter Eight: More Than a Moment's Notice: Reconstruction's Recent Best Practices

1. Marable, M. (2001, September). Structural racism and American democracy: Historical and theoretical perspectives. Paper presented at United Nations Racism and Public Policy Conference, Durban, South Africa. Retrieved from http://www.unrisd.org/80256B3C005BCCF9/(httpAuxPages)/4DAC9FF0A00C10F680256B6D0057879C/$file/dmarable.pdf

2. Yen, Hope (2007, October 12). 2,002 die in custody in three years. *Associated Press.*

3. Cottman, B. (2008, January). *The suffering of the poor is the life blood of Capitalism.* Archives of Reconstruction, Inc., Philadelphia, PA.

4. Moore, P. A. (2008, January 17). How to destroy the public schools when the rich pay no taxes. *CounterPunch.* Retrieved from http://www.counter punch.org/2008/01/17/when-the-rich-pay-no-taxes

5. Goodman, R. M., Speers, M. A., McLeroy, K., Fawcett, S., Kegler, M., Parker, E.,...Wallerstein, N. (1998). Identifying and defining the dimensional of community capacity to provide a basis for measurement. *Health, Education and Behavior, 25,* 258–278.

6. Chaskin, R. J. (2008). Resilience, community, and resilient communities: Conditioning contexts and collective action. *Child Care in Practice, 14,* 65–74.

7. Chaskin, R. J., Brown, P., Venkatesh, S. & Vidal, A. (2001). *Building community capacity*. New York: Aldine de Gruyter.

8. Kretzmann, J. P., & McKnight, J. L. (1993). *Building communities from the inside out: A path toward finding and mobilizing a community's assets*. Chicago: ACTA Publications.

9. Verity, F. (2007). *Community capacity-building—a review of the literature*. South Australian Health Department, Health Promotion Branch, Adelaide.

10. Fox, K. J. (2010). Second chances: A comparison of civic engagement in offender reentry. *Criminal Justice Review, 35*, 335–353.

11. Henderson, M. L., & Hanley, D. (2006). Planning for quality: A strategy for reentry initiatives. *Western Criminology Review, 7*, 62–78.

12. Nixon, V., Clough, P. T., Staples, D., & Peterkin, Y. J. (2008). Life capacity beyond reentry: A critical examination of racism and prisoner reentry reform in the U.S. *Race/Ethnicity: Multidisciplinary Global Perspectives, 2*, 21–43.

13. Osher, F., Steadman, H. J., & Barr, H. (2003). A best practice approach to community reentry from jails for inmates with co-occurring disorders: The APIC Model. *Crime & Delinquency, 49*, 79–96.

14. Petersilia, J. (2004). What works in prisoner reentry? Reviewing and questioning the evidence. *Federal Probation, 68*, 4–8.

15. Taxman, F. S., Young, D., Byrne, J. M., Holsinger, A., & Anspach, D. (2002). *From prison safety to public safety: Innovations in offender reentry*. A Formative Evaluation of the Reentry Partnership Initiative (RPI), Bureau of Government Research.

16. Wilkinson, R. A. (Ed.). (2004). *The Association of State Correctional Administrators Reentry Best Practices: Director's Perspectives*. Middletown, CT: ASCA Publications. Retrieved from http://www.asca.net/system/assets/attachments/2075/Reentry_Best_Practices_Publication1.pdf?1296149357

17. Fox, K. J. (2010). Second chances: A comparison of civic engagement in offender reentry. *Criminal Justice Review, 35*, 335–353.

18. Mohr, L. B. (1969). Determinants of innovation in organizations. *Political Science Review, 63*, 111–126. p112.

19. Reconstruction, Inc. (2009) *Community capacity-building curriculum implementation*. Retrieved from www.reconstructioninc.org/drupal/capaccity-building-curriculum

20. Aday, R. H. (2003). *Aging prisoners: Crisis in American corrections*. Westport: Praeger.

21. Aday, R. H. (2006). Aging prisoners' concerns toward dying in prison. *OMEGA—Journal of Death and Dying, 52*, 199–216.

22. Bishop, A. J., & Merten, M. J. (2011). Lifestyle behaviors and the likelihood of comorbid health among older male offenders. *Journal of Correctional Healthcare, 17*, 24–25.

23. Williams, B., & Abraldes, R. (2007). Growing older: Challenges of prison and reentry for the aging population. In R. B. Greifinger (Ed.), *Public Health Behind Bars: From Prison to Communities*. New York: Springer.

24. Reconstruction, Inc. (2009). Partial transcript from a Rap Program Meeting. Archives of Reconstruction, Inc., Philadelphia, PA.

25. Font, R., Dolan-Del Vecchio, K., & Almeida, R. V. (1998). Finding the words: Instruments for a therapy of liberation." *Journal of Feminist Family Therapy, 10*, 85–97.

26. Hanna, F. J., Talley, W. B., & Guindon, M. H. (2000). The power of perception: Toward a model of cultural oppression and liberation. *Journal of Counseling and Development, 78*, 430–441.

27. Ivey, A. E. (1995). Psychotherapy as liberation. In J. G. Ponterotto, J. M. Casas, L. Suzuki, & C. M. Alexander (Eds.), *Handbook of Multicultural Counseling and Therapy.* (pp. 53–72). Beverly Hills, CA: Sage.

28. Continuing Opportunity for Family Education Enrichment. (2010). Organization background and mission. Retrieved from http://coffeecri—sis.org

29. Chaskin, R. J., Brown, P., Venkatesh, S. & Vidal, A. (2001). *Building community capacity.* New York: Aldine de Gruyter.

30. Goodman, R. M., Speers, M. A., McLeroy, K., Fawcett, S., Kegler, M., Parker, E.,…Wallerstein, N. (1998). Identifying and defining the dimensional of community capacity to provide a basis for measurement. *Health, Education and Behavior, 25*, 258–278.

31. Verity, F. (2007). Community capacity-building—a review of the literature. South Australian Health Department, Health Promotion Branch, Adelaide.

32. Katz, D., & Kahn, R. L. (1978). *The social psychology of organizations.* New York: Wiley.

33. Lester, D. L., & Parnell, J. A. (2008). Firm size and environmental scanning pursuits across organizational life cycle stages. *Journal of Small Business and Enterprise Development, 15*, 540–554.

34. Goodman, R. M., Speers, M. A., McLeroy, K., Fawcett, S., Kegler, M., Parker, E.,…Wallerstein, N. (1998). Identifying and defining the dimensional of community capacity to provide a basis for measurement. *Health, Education and Behavior, 25*, 258–278.

35. Mintzberg, H. (1984). Power and organizational life cycles. *Academy of Management Review, 9*, 207–224.

36. Nadler, D. A., & Tushman, M. (1999). The organization of the future: Strategic imperatives and core competencies for the 21st Century." *Organizational Dynamics, 28*, 45–60.

37. Reconstruction, Inc. (n.d.). *Internal memo.* Archives of Reconstruction, Inc., Philadelphia, P.A.

38. Pew Charitable Trust, Philadelphia Research Initiative. (2010). *A City Transformed: The Racial and Ethnic Changes in Philadelphia Over the Last 20 Years.* Retrieved from http://www.pewtrusts.org/uploadedFiles/wwwpewtrusts.org/Reports/Philadelphia_Resear ch _Initiative/Philadelphia-Population-Ethnic-Changes.pdf

39. Reconstruction, Inc. (2011, April). *Internal memo.* Archives of Reconstruction, Inc., Philadelphia, PA.

40. Ibid.

41. Reconstruction, Inc. (2011). *Organizational memo.* Archives of Reconstruction, Inc., Philadelphia, PA.

42. Sudbury, J. (2004). Globalized punishment, localized resistance: Prisons, Neoliberalism, and empire. *Souls, 6*, 55–65. p63.

43. Chaskin, R. J., Brown, P., Venkatesh, S. & Vidal, A. (2001). *Building community capacity.* New York: Aldine de Gruyter.

44. Youth Art and Self—Empowerment Project (YASP). Organization Information. Retrieved from http://www.yasproject.com

45. Exit-Us. Mission Statement. Retrieved from www.exitus.weebly.com

46. Garvin, D. A. (1993). Building a learning organization. *Harvard Business Review, 71*, 78–91.

47. Hallett, T. (2003). Symbolic power and organizational culture. *Sociological Theory, 21*, 128–149.

48. Lucas, C., & Kline, T. (2008). Understanding the influence of organizational culture and group dynamics on organizational change and learning. *Learning Organization, 15*, 277–287.

49. Powley, E. H., & Piderit, S. K. (2008). Tending wounds: Elements of the organizational healing process. *Journal of Applied Behavioral Science, 44*, 134–149.

50. Hild, C. M. (2006). Places and states of mind for healing. *ReVision, 29*, 12–19. p13.

51. Belk, R., Wallendorf, M., & Sherry, J. F. (1989). The sacred and the profane in consumer behavior: Theodicy on the odyssey. *Journal of Consumer Research, 16*, 1–38.

52. Siemiatycki, M. (2005). Contesting sacred urban space: The case of the Eruv. *Journal of International Migration and Integration, 6*, 255–270.

53. Wagner-Pacifici, R. (1994). *Discourse and destruction.* Chicago: University of Chicago Press.

54. Murray, L. W. (1921). Aboriginal sites in and near 'Teaoga,' now Athens, Pennsylvania. *American Anthropologist, 23*(2), 184–214.

55. Randel, W. P. (1939). The place names of Tioga County, Pennsylvania. *American Speech, 14*, 181–190.

56. Taney, Roger B. (1857). Dred Scott v. Sanford. The United States Supreme Court Decision. 60 U.S. 393. Retrieved from http://supreme.justia.com/ us/60/393/ case.html

57. Marks, D. F. (2002). Freedom, responsibility and power: Contrasting approaches to health psychology. *Journal of Health Psychology, 7*, 5–19.

58. Shiner, L. E. (1972). Sacred space, profane space, human space. *Journal of the American Academy of Religion, 40*, 425–436.

59. Tioga United. (2011). Mission Statement. Retrieved from http://www.volunteermatch/org/ search/org59994.jsp

60. Hild, C. M. (2006). Places and states of mind for healing. *ReVision, 29*, 12–19. p12–13.

61. Philadelphia City Planning Commission (2010). *Strategies for neighborhood revitalization.* Philadelphia, PA: Retrieved from http://www.philaplan ning.org/cpdiv/Tioga2010.pdf

62. Belk, R., Wallendorf, M., & Sherry, J. F. (1989). The sacred and the profane in consumer behavior: Theodicy on the odyssey. *Journal of Consumer Research, 16*, 1–38.

63. Hild, C. M. (2006). Places and states of mind for healing. *ReVision, 29*, 12–19.

64. Shiner, L. E. (1972). Sacred space, profane space, human space. *Journal of the American Academy of Religion, 40*, 425–436.

65. Blumenthal, D. R. (2002). Liturgies of anger. CrossCurrents, *52,* p198.

Chapter Nine: Transformative Collaborations
Toward a People's Democracy

1. Teeters, N. K., & Shearer, J. D. (1957). *The prison at Philadelphia, Cherry Hill.* New York: Columbia University Press. p84.

2. Abramsky, S. (2002). *Hard time blues: How politics built a prison nation.* New York: St. Martin's Press.

3. Alexander, M. (2010). *The new Jim Crow.* New York: Free Press.

4. Clear, T. (2007). *Imprisoning communities: How mass incarceration makes disadvantaged neighborhoods worse.* Oxford: Oxford University Press.

5. Pager, D. (2007). *Marked: Race, crime, and finding work in an era of mass incarceration.* Chicago: University of Chicago Press.

6. Thompson, A. C. (2008). *Releasing prisoners, redeeming communities: Reentry, race and politics.* New York: New York University Press.

7. Wacquant, L. (2001). Deadly symbiosis: When ghetto and prison meet and merge. *Punishment and Society, 3,* 95–133.

8. Wakefield, S., & Uggen, C. (2010). Incarceration and stratification. *Annual Review of Sociology, 36,* 387–406. p387.

9. The Pew Charitable Trusts, Pew Center on the States. (2009, March). *One in 31: The long reach of American corrections.* Retrieved from http://www.evidencebasedassociates.com/reports/pew_1in31_report.pdf)

10. Alexander, M. (2010). *The new Jim Crow.* New York: Free Press.

11. Petersilia, J. (2003). *When prisoners come home: Parole and prisoner reentry.* New York: Oxford.

12. Thompson, A. C. (2008). *Releasing prisoners, redeeming communities: Reentry, race and politics.* New York: New York University Press.

13. Travis, J. (2005). *But they all come back: Facing the challenges of prisoner reentry.* Washington, DC: Urban Institute Press.

14. Wacquant, L. (2001). Deadly symbiosis: When ghetto and prison meet and merge. *Punishment and Society, 3,* 95–133.

15. Kazemian, L. (2007). Desistance from crime: Theoretical, empirical, methodological, and policy considerations. *Journal of Contemporary Criminal Justice, 23,* 5–27. p.6–7

16. Clear, T. (2007). *Imprisoning communities: How mass incarceration makes disadvantaged neighborhoods worse.* Oxford: Oxford University Press.

17. Frost, N. A., & Clear, T. R. (2009). Understanding mass incarceration as a grand social experiment. *Studies in Law, Politics and Society, 47,* 159–191. p186–187.

18. Krisberg, B., & Marchionna, S. (2010, April 16). *A framework for evidence-based practices in local criminal justice systems: A work in progress* [3rd ed.]. The National Council on Crime and Delinquency. Retrieved from http://www.cepp. com/documents/EBDM%Framework.pdf

19. Ibid.

20. Freire, P. (1985). *The politics of education: Culture, power and liberation.* South Hadley, MA: Bergin & Garvey. p84–85.

21. Maddock, S., & Morgan, G. (1998). Barriers to transformation: Beyond bureaucracy and the market conditions for collaboration and social care. *International Journal of Public Sector Management, 11,* 234–251.

22. Mezirow, J. (1978). Perspective transformation. *Adult Education Quarterly, 28,* 100–110.

23. Sorokin, P. (1957). *Social & cultural dynamics: A study of change in major systems of art, truth, ethics, law and social relationships.* Boston: Extending Horizon.

24. Himmelman, A. T. (1996). On the theory and practice of transformational collaboration: Collaboration as a bridge from social service to social justice. In C. Huxman (ed). *Creating Collaborative Advantage.* (pp. 19–43). Thousand Oaks, CA: Sage. p28.

25. Lorde, A. (1984). *Sister outsider.* Freedom, CA: Crossing Press.

26. Danesh, H. B. (2008). Creating a culture of healing in multiethnic communities: An integrative approach to prevention and amelioration of violence-induced conditions. *Journal of Community Psychology, 36,* 814–832.

27. Walsh, F. (2003). Crisis, trauma, and challenges: A relational resilience approach for healing, transformation, and growth. *Smith College Studies in Social Work, 74,* 49–72.

28. Bloom, S. L. & Sreedhar, S. Y. (2008). The sanctuary model of trauma-informed organizational change. *Reclaiming Children and Youth, 17*, 48–53.

29. Cho, S. (2010). Politics of critical pedagogy and new social movements. *Educational Philosophy and Theory, 42*, 310–325.

30. Faust, D. (2007). A probation story. In J. Fuller & C. Townsend (Eds.), *National Association of Probation Executives Executive Exchange* (pp. 2–4). Retrieved from http://www.napehome.org

31. Evangelista, J., Corrigan, J. & Geoghegan, W. (2007). Utilizing a performance measurement system to enhance decision-making in a community corrections agency. In J. Fuller & C. Townsend (Eds.), *National Association of Probation Executives executive exchange* (pp. 5–9). Retrieved from http://www.napehome.org. p8.

32. Stern, K. (2011). Shackles and sunlight. *Fellowship, 77*, 12–17. p15.

33. Milk Not Jails. (2011). Mission Statement and goals. Retrieved from http://milknotjails.wordpress.com

34. King, R. S., Mauer, M., & Huling, T. (2003). *Big prisons, small towns: Prison economics in rural America*. The Sentencing Project. Retrieved from www.sentencingproject.org

35. Hooks, G., Mosher, C., Genter, S., Rotolo, T., & Lobao, L. (2004). The prison industry: Carceral expansion and employment in U.S. Counties, 1969–1994. *Social Science Quarterly, 85*, p37.

36. Ibid. p51.

37. Lambe, W. (2008, December). Small towns, big ideas: Case studies in small town community economic development. University of North Carolina at Chapel Hill. Retrieved from http://www.ucruralcenter.org

38. Bond, B. & Gittell, J. H. (2010). Cross-agency coordination of offender reentry: Testing outcomes of collaboration policies. *Journal of Criminal Justice, 38*, 118–129. p119.

39. Bazemore, G., & Boba, R. (2007). 'Doing good' to 'make good': Community theory for practice in a restorative justice civic engagement reentry model. *Journal of Offender Rehabilitation, 46*, 25–56.

40. Bazemore, G. & Maruna, S. (2009). Restorative justice in the reentry context: Building new theory and expanding the evidence base." *Victims and Offenders, 4*, 375–384.

41. Fletcher, L. E., & Weinstein, H. M. (2002). Violence and social repair: Rethinking the contribution of justice to reconciliation." *Human Rights Quarterly, 24*, 573–639.

42. Shields, C. M. (2004). Dialogic leadership for social justice: Overcoming pathologies of silence. *Educational Administration Quarterly, 40*, 109–132.

43. Pattillo, M. E. (1998). Sweet mothers and gangbangers: Managing crime in a Black middle class neighborhood. *Social Forces, 76*, 747–774.

44. Clear, T. (2007). *Imprisoning communities: How mass incarceration makes disadvantaged neighborhoods worse*. Oxford: Oxford University Press.

45. Ibid. p191.

46. Zhang, S. X., Roberts, R. E. L., & Callahan, V. J. (2006). Preventing parolees from returning to prison through community-based reintegration. *Crime & Delinquency, 52*, 551–571.

47. Burnett, R. & Maruna, S. (2006). The kindness of prisoners: Strengths-based resettlement in theory and in action. *Criminology & Criminal Justice, 6*, 83–106. p90.

48. Danesh, H. B. (2008). Creating a culture of healing in multiethnic communities: An integrative approach to prevention and amelioration of violence-induced conditions. *Journal of Community Psychology, 36*, 814–832.

49. Perry, A. R., Robinson, M. A., Alexander, R., & Moore, S. E. (2011). Post-prison community reentry and African American males: Implications for family therapy and health. *Handbook of African American Health, 6*, 197–214.

50. Regnier, R. H. (1994). The sacred circle: A process pedagogy of healing. *Interchange, 25*, 129–144.

51. Walker, L. (2010). Huikahi restorative circles: Group process for self-directed reentry planning and family healing. *European Journal of Probation, 2*, 76–95.

52. Green, G. P., & Haines, A. (2011). *Asset building and community development* (3rd ed). Newbury, CA: Sage.

53. Goodman, R. M., Speers, M. A., McLeroy, K., Fawcett, S., Kegler, M., Parker, E.,…Wallerstein, N. (1998). Identifying and defining the dimensional of community capacity to provide a basis for measurement. *Health, Education and Behavior, 25*, 258–278.

54. Kretzmann, J. P., & McKnight, J. L. (1993). *Building communities from the inside out: A path toward finding and mobilizing a community's assets.* Chicago: ACTA Publications.

55. Wenning, M. (2009). The return of rage. *Parrhesia, 8*, 89–99. p94–95.

56. Blumenthal, D. R. (2002). Liturgies of anger. CrossCurrents, *52*, 178–199. p198.

57. Fry, L. W. (2003). Toward a theory of spiritual leadership. *Leadership Quarterly 14*, 693–727.

58. Christian, J. (2005). Riding the bus: Barriers to prison visitation and family management strategies. *Journal of Contemporary Criminal Justice, 21*, 31–48.

59. Giordano, P. C., Cemkovich, S. A., & Rudolph, J. L. (2002). Gender, crime, and desistance: Toward a theory of cognitive transformation. *American Journal of Sociology, 107*, 990–1064.

60. Glueck, S., & Glueck, E. (1974). *Of delinquency and crime.* Springfield, IL: Thomas.

61. Kazemian, L. (2007). Desistance from crime: Theoretical, empirical, methodological, and policy considerations. *Journal of Contemporary Criminal Justice, 23*, 5–27.

62. Laub, J. H., & Sampson, R. J. (2003). *Shared beginnings, divergent lives: Delinquent boys to age 70.* Cambridge: Harvard University Press

63. Massoglia, M., & Uggen, C. (2010). Settling down and aging out: Toward an interactionist theory of desistance and the transition to adulthood. *American Journal of Sociology, 116*, 543–582.

64. Nixon, V., Clough, P. T., Staples, D., & Peterkin, Y. J. (2008). Life capacity beyond reentry: A critical examination of racism and prisoner reentry reform in the U.S. *Race/Ethnicity: Multidisciplinary Global Perspectives, 2*, 21–43.

65. Rose, D.R., & Clear, T. R. (2001, December). Incarceration, reentry and social capital: Social networks in the balance. Commissioned Paper for *From Prison to Home: The Effect of Incarceration and Reentry on Children, Families, and Communities, U. S. Department of Health and Human Services, The Urban Institute.* Retrieved from http://aspe.hhs.gov/hsp/prison2home02/rose.pdf

66. Coffee Consulting. (2009). *Evaluation of the prisoner re-entry initiative, final report.* U.S. Department of Labor. Bethesda, MD

67. Fasenfest, D. (2010). The glocal crisis and the politics of change. *Critical Sociology, 36*, 363–368. p364.

68. Ibid. p363–368.

69. Wakefield, S., Yeudall, F., Taron, C., Reynolds, J., & Skinner, A. (2007). Growing urban health: Community gardening in South-East Toronto. *Health Promotion International, 22*, 92–101.

70. Fasenfest, D. (2010). The glocal crisis and the politics of change. *Critical Sociology, 36*, 363–368. p364.

71. Ibid. p365.

72. Alexander, M. (2010). *The new Jim Crow.* New York: Free Press. p243, 245.

73. Ibid. p217, 222.

74. Rhine, E. E., & Thompson, A. C. (2011). The reentry movement in corrections: resiliency, fragility and prospects. *Criminal Law Bulletin, 47*, 177–209.

75. Sudbury, J. (2004). Globalized punishment, localized resistance: Prisons, Neoliberalism, and empire. *Souls, 6*, 55–65.

76. Sudbury, J. (2008). Rethinking global justice: Black women resist the transnational prison-industrial complex. *Souls, 10*, 344–360.

77. Thompson, A. C. (2008). *Releasing prisoners, redeeming communities: Reentry, race and politics.* New York: New York University Press.

78. Alexander, M. (2010). *The new Jim Crow.* New York: Free Press. p223.

79. Lorde, A. (1984). *Sister outsider.* Freedom, CA: Crossing Press.

80. Rhine, E. E., & Thompson, A. C. (2011). The reentry movement in corrections: resiliency, fragility and prospects. *Criminal Law Bulletin, 47*, p203.

81. Alexander, M. (2010). *The new Jim Crow.* New York: Free Press.

82. Harris, M. K. (1987). Moving into the new millennium: Toward a feminist vision of justice. *Prison Journal, 67*, 27–38.

83. Thompson, A. C. (2008). *Releasing prisoners, redeeming communities: Reentry, race and politics.* New York: New York University Press.

84. Kautzer, C., & Mendieta, E. (2004). Law and resistance in the prisons of empire: An interview with Angela Y. Davis. *Peace Review, 16*, 339–347.

85. Du Bois, W. E. B. (1969). *The souls of Black folk.* New York: Signet Books. (Original work published 1903).

86. Foner, E. (2002). *Black reconstruction: America's unfinished revolution.* New York: Harper Perennial Modern Classics.

87. Carson, C., & Shepard, K. (Eds). (2001). A call to conscience: The landmark speeches of Dr. Martin Luther King, Jr. New York: Grand Central Publishing.

88. Du Bois, W. E. B. (1969). *The souls of Black folk.* New York: Signet Books. (Original work published 1903) p110.

89. Stern, K. (2011). Shackles and sunlight. *Fellowship, 77*, 12–17.

Epilogue

1. Loury, G. C., & Western, B. (2010). The challenge of mass incarceration in America. *Daedalus, Journal of the American Academy of Arts & Sciences, 139*(3), 5–7.

2. Pew Center on the States. Public Safety Performance Project. (2008). *One in 100: Behind bars in America.* Washington, DC: The Pew Charitable Trusts.

3. Pew Center on the States. Public Safety Performance Project. (2010). *Prison count 2010: State population declines for the first time in 38 years.* Washington, DC: The Pew Charitable Trusts.

4. Austin, J., & Fabelo, T. (2004). *The diminishing returns of increased incarceration: A blueprint to improve public safety and reduce costs.* Washington, D.C.: JFA Institute. Retrieved from http://www.ajaassociates.com/BlueprintFinal.pdf

5. Useem, B., & Piehl, A. M. (2008). *Prison state: The challenge of mass incarceration.* New York: Cambridge University Press.

6. Travis, J. (2005). *But they all come back: Facing the challenges of prisoner reentry.* Washington, DC: Urban Institute Press.

7. Bush, G. W. (2004, January 20). 2004 *State of the Union Address.* Retrieved from http://www.americanrhetoric/com/speeches/stateoftheunion2004.htm

8. Rhine, E. E., & Thompson, A. C. (2011). The reentry movement in corrections: resiliency, fragility and prospects. *Criminal Law Bulletin, 47*, 177–209.

9. Justice Center, The Council of State Governments. State Leaders' National Forum on Reentry and Recidivism. Forum Agenda and Content. Retrieved from http://www.national reentry resourcecenter.org/forum-on-reentry-and-recidivism

10. Aos, S., Miller, M., & Drake, E. (2006, January). *Evidence-based adult correctional programs: What works and what does not.* Olympia: Washington State Institute for Public Policy. Retrieved from http://www.wsipp.wa.gov/rptfiles/06-01-1201.pdf

11. National Institute of Corrections. (2010, April 16). *A framework for evidence-based practices in local criminal justice systems: A work in progress* [3rd ed.] Retrieved from http://www.cepp.com/documents/EBDM%Framework.pdf

12. John Jay College of Criminal Justice. (2009, March 12). *"What works" for successful prisoner reentry? Hearings before the Subcommittee on Commerce, Justice, Science, and Related Agencies, of the House Appropriations Committee* (testimony of Jeremy Travis). Retrieved from http://www.jjay.cuny.edu/Travis_Congressional_Testimony.pdf

13. Barker, V. (2009). *The politics of imprisonment: How the democratic process shapes the way America punishes offenders.* New York: Oxford University Press.

14. Berman, D. A. (2008, December 8). Reorienting progressive perspectives for twenty-first century punishment realities. *Harvard Law and Policy Review Online.* Retrieved from http://www.hlpronline.com/Berman_HLPR_ 120808.pdf

15. Brown, M. (2009). *The culture of punishment: Prison, society, and spectacle.* New York: New York University Press.

16. Clear, T. (2007). *Imprisoning communities: How mass incarceration makes disadvantaged neighborhoods worse.* Oxford: Oxford University Press.

17. Loury, G. C., & Western, B. (2010). The challenge of mass incarceration in America. *Daedalus, Journal of the American Academy of Arts & Sciences, 139*(3), 5–7.

18. Frost, N. A. (2006). *The punitive state: Crime, punishment, and imprisonment across the United States.* New York: LFB Scholarly Publishing LLC.

19. Gottschalk, M. (2006). *The prison and the gallows: The politics of mass incarceration in America.* New York: Cambridge University Press.

20. Gottschalk, M. (2011). The past, present, and future of mass incarceration in the United States. *Criminology and Public Policy 10*(3), 483–504.

21. Perkinson, R. (2010). *Texas tough: The rise of America's prison empire.* New York, NY: Metropolitan Books.

22. Useem, B., & Piehl, A. M. (2008). *Prison state: The challenge of mass incarceration.* New York: Cambridge University Press.

23. Western, B. (2006). *Punishment and inequality in America.* New York: Russell Sage Foundation.

24. Weisberg, R., & Petersilia, J. (2010). The dangers of pyrrhic victories against mass incarceration. *Daedalus, 139*(3), 124–133.

25. Simon, J. (2012). Mass Incarceration: From Social Policy to Social Problem. In J. Petersilia & K. Reitz (Eds.), *Sentencing and Correctional Reform.* (pp.23–52). New York: Oxford University Press.

26. Western, B., & Pettit, B. (2010). Incarceration and Social Inequality. *Daedalus, 139*(3), 5–19.

27. Alexander, M. (2010). *The new Jim Crow.* New York: Free Press.

28. Peterson, R.D., & Krivo, L. J. (2010). *Divergent social worlds: Neighborhood crime and the racial-spatial divide.* New York, NY: Russell Sage Foundation.

29. Thompson, A. C. (2008). *Releasing prisoners, redeeming communities: Reentry, race and politics.* New York: New York University Press.

References

Abramsky, S. (2002). *Hard time blues: How politics built a prison nation*. New York: St. Martin's Press.

Aday, R. H. (2003). *Aging prisoners: Crisis in American corrections*. Westport, CT: Praeger.

Aday, R. H. (2006). Aging prisoners' concerns toward dying in prison. *OMEGA—Journal of Death and Dying, 52*, 199–216.

Abu-Jamal, M (2005, May 21). A halflife. *Taped speech, Fight for Lifers Conference, Temple University*. Archives of Reconstruction, Inc. Philadelphia, PA.

Ager, R. D., Parquet, R., & Kreutzinger, S. (2008). The youth video project: An innovative program for substance abuse prevention. *Journal of Social Work Practice in the Addictions, 8*, 303–331.

Akbar, N. (1976). *The community of the self*. Chicago: Nation of Islam Office of Human Development.

Alexander, M. (2010). *The new Jim Crow*. New York: Free Press.

Alston, J. A. (2005). Tempered radicals and servant leaders: Black females persevering in the superintendency. *Educational Administration Quarterly, 41*, 675–688.

American Friends Service Committee. (1994, October 10). *The death of Barbara Moffett*. AFSC News Release.

American Friends Service Committee. (2011). Mission statement and values. Retrieved from http://afsc.org/mission-and-values.

Anderson, E. (2011). *The cosmopolitan canopy: Race and civility in everyday life*. New York: W.W. Norton.

Andrews, D. P. (2002). *Practical theology for Black churches: Bridging Black theology and African American folk religion*. Louisville, KY: Westminster John Knox Press.

Angelou, M. (1995). *Phenomenal woman: Four poems celebrating women*. New York: Random House.

Antrop-Gonzalez, R. (2006). Toward the 'school as sanctuary' concept in multicultural urban education: Implications for small high school reform. *Curriculum Inquiry, 36*, 273–301.

Aron, W. S. (1974). Student activism of the 1960s revisited: A multivariate analysis research note. *Social Forces, 52*, 408–414.

Asante, M. K. (1980). *Afrocentricity: The theory of social change*. Buffalo, NY: Amulefi.

Asante, S. (1997). *When spider webs unite: Challenging articles & essays on community, diversity and inclusion*. Toronto: Inclusion Press.

Aos, S., Miller, M., & Drake, E. (2006, January). *Evidence-based adult correctional programs: What works and what does not*. Olympia: Washington State Institute for Public Policy. Retrieved from http://www.wsipp.wa.gov/rptfiles/06-01-1201.pdf

Associated Press. (1995, April 15). It was the 'day of judgment' for rogue cops in Philadelphia. *The Philadelphia Inquirer*. Retrieved from http://www.boogieonline.com/revolution/body/drugs/legal/philadelphia.html

Austin, J., & Fabelo, T. (2004). *The diminishing returns of increased incarceration: A blueprint to improve public safety and reduce costs*. Washington, D.C.: JFA Institute. Retrieved from http://www.jfa-associates.com/BlueprintFinal.pdf

Baker, H. A. (1991). *Workings of the spirit: The poetics of Afro-American women's writings*. Chicago: University of Chicago Press.

Barker, V. (2009). *The politics of imprisonment: How the democratic process shapes the way America punishes offenders.* New York: Oxford University Press.

Bazemore, G., & Boba, R. (2007). 'Doing good' to 'make good': Community theory for practice in a restorative justice civic engagement reentry model. *Journal of Offender Rehabilitation, 46,* 25–56.

Bazemore, G. & Maruna, S. (2009). Restorative justice in the reentry context: Building new theory and expanding the evidence base." *Victims and Offenders, 4,* 375–384.

Beam, J. (1986). Brother-to-brother: Words from the heart. In J. Beam (Ed.) *In the Life: A Black Gay Anthology* (pp230–242). Boston: Alyson Publications.

Belenky, M. F., Clinchy, B. M., Goldberger, N. R., & Tarule, J. M. (1986). *Women's ways of knowing: The development of self, voice and mind.* New York: Basic Books.

Belk, R., Wallendorf, M., & Sherry, J. F. (1989). The sacred and the profane in consumer behavior: Theodicy on the odyssey. *Journal of Consumer Research, 16,* 1–38.

Bell, L. A. (2007). Theoretical foundations for social justice education. In M. Adams, L. A. Bell, & P. Griffin (Eds.) *Teaching for diversity and social justice* (pp. 1–14). New York: Routledge/Taylor & Francis Group.

Bellah, R. N., Madsen, R., Sullivan, W., Swidler, A., & Tipton, S.M. (1985). *Habits of the heart: Individualism and commitment in American life.* Berkeley: University of California Press.

ben-Jochannan, Y. A. A. (1988). *Africa: Mother of Western civilization.* Baltimore, MD: Black Classic Press.

Berman, D. A. (2008, December 8). Reorienting progressive perspectives for twenty-first century punishment realities. *Harvard Law and Policy Review Online.* Retrieved from http://www.hlpronline.com/Berman_HLPR_120808.pdf

Besecke, K. (2001). Speaking of meaning in modernity: Reflexive spirituality as a cultural resource. *Sociology of Religion, 62,* 365–381.

Bishop, A. J., & Merten, M. J. (2011). Lifestyle behaviors and the likelihood of comorbid health among older male offenders. *Journal of Correctional Healthcare, 17,* 24–25.

Blassingame, J. W. (1973). *The slave community: Plantation life in the antebellum south.* New York: Oxford University Press.

Blau, P. M. (1977). *Inequality and heterogeneity: A primitive theory of social structure.* New York: Free Press.

Block, K. (2010). Cultivating inner and outer plantations: Property, industry, and slavery in early Quaker migration to the new world. *Early American Studies, 8,* 515–548.

Bloom, S. L. & Sreedhar, S. Y. (2008). The sanctuary model of trauma-informed organizational change. *Reclaiming Children and Youth, 17,* 48–53.

Blumenthal, D. R. (2002). Liturgies of anger. CrossCurrents, *52,* 178–199.

Bond, B. & Gittell, J. H. (2010). Cross-agency coordination of offender reentry: Testing outcomes of collaboration policies. *Journal of Criminal Justice, 38,* 118–129.

Boy Scouts of America (2011). Mission Statement. Retrieved from http://www.scouting.org/scoutsource/Media/mission.aspx)

Bradbury, J. (1986). *Travels in the interior of America in the years 1809, 1810, and 1811.* Lincoln: University of Nebraska Press. (Original work published 1819)

Bradley, B. S., Deighton, J. & Selby, J. (2004). The 'voices' project: Capacity-building in community development for youth at risk. *Journal of Health Psychology, 9,* 197–212.

Brockner, J., Ackerman G., Greenberg,J., Gelfand, M. J., Francesco, A. M., Chen, Z. X.,...Shapiro, D. (2001). Culture and procedural justice: The influence of power distance on reactions to voice. *Journal of Experimental Social Psychology, 37*, 300–315.

Brooks, J. S., & Normore, A. H. (2010). Educational leadership and globalization: Literacy for a glocal perspective. *Educational Policy, 24*, 52–82.

Brown, K. M. (2004). Leadership for social justice and equity: Weaving a transformative framework and pedagogy. *Educational Administration Quarterly, 40*, 77–108.

Brown, M. (2009). *The culture of punishment: Prison, society, and spectacle.* New York: New York University Press.

Browning, C. R., Feinberg, S. L., & Dietz, R. (2004). The paradox of social organization: Networks, collective efficacy, and violent crime in urban neighborhoods. *Social Forces, 83*, 503–534.

Burnett, R. & Maruna, S. (2006). The kindness of prisoners: Strengths-based resettlement in theory and in action. *Criminology & Criminal Justice, 6*, 83–106.

Bush, G. W. (2004, January 20). *2004 State of the Union Address.* Retrieved from http://www.americanrhetoric.com/speeches/stateoftheunion2004.htm

Buskey, J. H. (1990). Historical context and contemporary setting of the learning sanctuary. *New Directions for Adult and Continuing Education, 46*, 15–25.

Camp, S. D., Klein-Safran, J., Kwan, O. K., Daggett, D. M., & Joseph, V. (2006). An exploration into participation in a faith-based prison program. *Criminology and Public Policy, 5*, 529–550.

Cantor, G. (1997). *Old roads of the Midwest.* Ann Arbor: University of Michigan Press.

Carson, C., & Shepard, K. (Eds.) (2001). *A call to conscience: The landmark speeches of Dr. Martin Luther King, Jr.* New York: Grand Central Publishing.

Cass, J., & Curry, C. (2007, October). *America's cradle to prison pipeline.* A report of the Children's Defense Fund. Retrieved from http://www.childrensdefense.org/child-research-data-publications/data/cradle-prison-pipeline-report-2007-full-lowres.pdf

Chaskin, R. J. (2008). Resilience, community, and resilient communities: Conditioning contexts and collective action. *Child Care in Practice, 14*, 65–74.

Chaskin, R. J., Brown, P., Venkatesh, S. & Vidal, A. (2001). *Building community capacity.* New York: Aldine de Gruyter.

Cheadle, A., Wagner, E., Anderman, C., Walls, M., McBride, C., Bell, M. A.,... Pettigrew, E. (1998). Measuring community mobilization in the Seattle minority youth health project. *Evaluation Review, 22*, 699–716.

Checkoway, B, Allison, T., & Montoya, C. (2005). Youth participation in public policy at the municipal level. *Children and Youth Services Review, 27*, 1149–1162.

Chepesiuk, R. (2001). *The war on drugs: An international encyclopedia.* Santa Barbara, CA: ABC—CLIO.

Cho, S. (2010). Politics of critical pedagogy and new social movements. *Educational Philosophy and Theory, 42*, 310–325.

Christian, J. (2005). Riding the bus: Barriers to prison visitation and family management strategies. *Journal of Contemporary Criminal Justice, 21*, 31–48.

Churchill, W (1910, July 20). *Address to Parliament, in 2 Winston S. Churchill: His complete speeches, 1897–1963.* London, New York: Chelsea House Publishers.

Clark, R., & Giles, D. M. (1989, May 24). Inmate tensions incite food fight at Homesburg. *The Philadelphia Inquirer.* Retrieved from http://articles.philly.com/1989-05 /24/news/26114737 _1_prison-officials-prison -personnel-inmate

Clear, T. (2007). *Imprisoning communities: How mass incarceration makes disadvantaged neighborhoods worse.* Oxford: Oxford University Press.

Clutterbuck, D., & Kernaghan, S. (1994). *The power of empowerment.* London: Kogan Page.

Cochrane, J. R. (2008). Fire from above, fire from below: Health, justice and the persistence of the sacred. *Theoria, 116,* 67–96.

Coffee Consulting. (2009, January 13). *Evaluation of the prisoner re-entry initiative, final report.* U.S. Department of Labor, Employment and Training Administration Retrieved from http:www.doleta.gov.rexo/pdf/pri_final_report_ 011309.pdf

Collins, P. H. (1990). *Black feminist thought: Knowledge, consciousness, and empowerment.* Boston: Unwin Hyman.

Collins, P. H. (1991). *Black feminist thought: Knowledge, consciousness, and the politics of empowerment.* New York: Routledge.

Combahee River Collective. 1981. A Black feminist statement. In C. Moraga & G. Anzaldua (Eds.), *This Bridge Called My Back: Writings by Radical Women of Color* (pp 210–219). London: Persephone Press.

Cumbrie, S. A. (2001). The integration of mind-body-soul and the practice of humanistic nursing. *Holistic Nursing Practice, 15,* 56–62.

Cummings, S. L. (2001.) Community economic development as progressive politics: Toward a grassroots movement for economic justice. *Stanford Law Review, 54,* 399–493.

Danesh, H. B. (2008). Creating a culture of healing in multiethnic communities: An integrative approach to prevention and amelioration of violence-induced conditions. *Journal of Community Psychology, 36,* 814–832.

Dantley, M. E. (2003). Critical spirituality: Enhancing transformative leadership through critical theory and African American prophetic spirituality. *International Journal of Leadership in Education, 6,* 3–17.

Dash, M. I. N., Jackson, J. & Rasor, S. C. (1997). *Hidden wholeness: An African American spirituality for individuals and communities.* Cleveland, OH: United Church Press.

De Leon, G. (2000). *The therapeutic community: Theory, model, and method.* New York: Springer.

De Vita, C. J. & Fleming, C. (2001). *Building capacity in nonprofit organizations.* Washington, DC: Urban Institute.

Diaz-Soto, L., Cervantes-Soon, C. G., Villarreal, E., & Campos, E. E. (2009). The Xicana sacred space: A communal circle of compromise for educational researchers. *Harvard Educational Review, 79,* 755–775.

Dillard, C. B. (2006). *On spiritual strivings: Transforming an African American woman's academic life.* Albany: State University of New York Press.

Dillard, C., Tyson, C. A., & Abdur-Rashid, D. (2000). My soul is a witness: Affirming pedagogies of the spirit. *International Journal of Qualitative Studies in Education, 13,* 447–462.

Drake, S. C., & Cayton, H. R. (1962). *Black metropolis: A study of Negro life in a northern city* (2nd ed.). New York: Harper Torchbooks.

Drevdahl, D.(1995). Coming to voice: The power of emancipatory community interventions. *Advances in Nursing Science, 18,* 13–24.

Du Bois, W. E. B. (1962). *Black reconstruction in America, 1860–1880.* New York: Atheneum/ Macmillan. (Original work published 1935)

Du Bois, W. E. B. (1969). *The souls of Black folk.* New York: Signet Books. (Original work published 1903)

Eden, D. (1992). Leadership and expectations: Pygmalion effects and other self-fulfilling prophecies in organizations. *Leadership Quarterly, 3,* 271–305.

Edwards, B., & Marullo, S. (1995). Organizational mortality in a declining social movement. *American Sociological Review, 60,* 908–927.

Etzioni, A. (1975). *A comparative analysis of complex organizations.* New York: Free Press.

Evangelista, J., Corrigan, J. & Geoghegan, W. (2007). Utilizing a performance measurement system to enhance decision-making in a community corrections agency. In J. Fuller & C. Townsend (Eds.), *National Association of Probation Executives Executive Exchange* (pp. 5–9). Retrieved from http://www.napeho me.org

Fanon, F. (1952). *Black skin, White masks.* New York: Grove.

Farrall, S. (2005). On the existential aspects of desistance from crime. *Symbolic Interaction, 28,* 367–386.

Fasenfest, D. (2010). The glocal crisis and the politics of change. *Critical Sociology, 36,* 363–368.

Fattah, D. (1969). Social disorder among Black youth. *School of Business Administration, Temple University.*

Fattah, D. (1987). The house of Umoja as a case study for social change. *Annals of the American Academy of Political and Social Science, 494,* 37–41.

Faust, D. (2007). A probation story. In J. Fuller & C. Townsend (Eds.), *National Association of Probation Executives Executive Exchange* (pp. 2–4). Retrieved from http://www.napehome.org

Fellowship of Intentional Communities. (1959). *The intentional communities: 1959 yearbook of the Fellowship of Intentional Communities.* Yellow Springs, OH: Fellowship of Intentional Communities.

Fight for Lifers (1999, Summer). An exhibit of 132 T-shirts with the names painted on them of the 132 women currently serving life without [the possibility of] parole were hung...and will remain on display until the end of October [1999]. *The Magnifying Glass.*

Fletcher, L. E., & Weinstein, H. M. (2002). Violence and social repair: Rethinking the contribution of justice to reconciliation. *Human Rights Quarterly, 24,* 573–639.

Fletcher, R. C., & Sherk, J. (2009). *Mentoring former prisoners: A guide for reentry programs.* Philadelphia, PA: Public/Private Ventures.

Foner, E. (2002). *Black reconstruction: America's unfinished revolution.* New York: Harper Perennial Modern Classics.

Foner, J. (1996). Surviving the 'mental health' system with co-counseling. *Psychotherapy Patient, 9,* 107–123.

Font, R., Dolan-Del Vecchio, K., & Almeida, R. V. (1998). Finding the words: Instruments for a therapy of liberation. *Journal of Feminist Family Therapy, 10,* 85–97.

Ford, L. (1990). Reconstruction: Progress Report, March 1989–March 1990. Archives of Reconstruction, Inc. Philadelphia, PA.

Foster-Fishman, P. G., Berkowitz, S. L., Lounsbury, D. W., Jacobson, S., & Allen, N. A. (2001). Building collaborative capacity in community coalitions: A review and integrative framework. *American Journal of Community Psychology, 29,* 241–261.

Fox, K. J. (2010). Second chances: A comparison of civic engagement in offender reentry. *Criminal Justice Review, 35,* 335–353.

Freire, P. (1970). *Pedagogy of the oppressed.* New York: Continuum.

Freire, P. (1972). *Cultural action for freedom*. New York: Penguin.

Freire, P. (1978). *Education for critical consciousness*. New York: Seabury.

Freire, P. (1985). *The politics of education: Culture, power and liberation*. South Hadley, MA: Bergin & Garvey.

Frost, N. A. (2006). *The punitive state: Crime, punishment, and imprisonment across the United States*. New York: LFB Scholarly Publishing.

Frost, N. A., & Clear, T. R. (2009). Understanding mass incarceration as a grand social experiment. *Studies in Law, Politics and Society, 47*, 159–191.

Fry, L. W. (2003). Toward a theory of spiritual leadership. *Leadership Quarterly 14*, 693–727.

Fry, L. W., & Cohen, M. P. (2009). Spiritual leadership as a paradigm for organizational transformation and recovery from extended work hours cultures. *Journal of Business Ethics, 84*, 265–278.

Funk, L. K. (1993, February 26). Lockdown at Graterford prison is lifted. *The Morning Call*. Retrieved from http://articles.mcall.com/1993-02-26/news/2900616_1_lockdown-cells-graterford-state-prison

Ganter, G. (2007). Red jacket and the decolonization of Republican virtue. *American Indian Quarterly, 31*(4), 559–581.

Garvin, D. A. (1993). Building a learning organization. *Harvard Business Review, 71*, 78–91.

Gilbert, M., & Orlans, V. (2010). *Integrative therapy: 100 key points and techniques*. New York: Routledge.

Gilroy, P. (1993). *The Black Atlantic: Modernity and double consciousness*. Cambridge, MA: Harvard University Press.

Ginwright, S. A. (2007). Black youth activism and the role of critical social capital in Black community organizations. *American Behavioral Scientist, 51*, 403–418.

Ginwright, S. A. (2010). Peace out to revolution! Activism among African American youth: An argument for radical healing. *Young, 18*, 77–96.

Ginwright, S. A., & James, T. (2002). From assets to agents of change: Social justice, organizing, and youth development. *New Directions for Youth Development, 96*, 27–46.

Giordano, P. C., Cemkovich, S. A., & Rudolph, J. L. (2002). Gender, crime, and desistance: Toward a theory of cognitive transformation. *American Journal of Sociology, 107*, 990–1064.

Glueck, S., & Glueck, E. (1974). *Of delinquency and crime*. Springfield, IL: Thomas.

Goh, S. C. (1998). Toward a learning organization: The strategic building blocks. *SAM Advanced Management Journal, 63*, 15–22.

Goodman, R. M., Speers, M. A., McLeroy, K., Fawcett, S., Kegler, M., Parker, E.,…Wallerstein, N. (1998). Identifying and defining the dimensional of community capacity to provide a basis for measurement. *Health, Education and Behavior, 25*, 258–278.

Goodpaster, G. S. (1969). An introduction to the community development corporation. *Journal of Urban Law, 46*, 603–666.

Gotthold, J. J. (2009). Peeling the onion: Understanding layers of treatment. *Annals of the New York Academy of Sciences, 1159*, 301–312.

Gottlieb, D., & Heinsohn, A. L. (1973). Sociology and youth. *Sociological Quarterly, 14*, 249–270.

Gottschalk, M. (2006). *The prison and the gallows: The politics of mass incarceration in America*. New York: Cambridge University Press.

Gottschalk, M. (2011). The past, present, and future of mass incarceration in the United States. *Criminology and Public Policy 10*(3), 483–504.

Graham, J. W. (1991). Servant leadership in organizations: Inspirational and moral. *Leadership Quarterly, 2,* 105–119.

Green, G. P., & Haines, A. (2011). *Asset building and community development* (3rd ed.). Newbury, CA: Sage.

Greenleaf, R. K. (1970). *The servant as leader.* Indianapolis, IN: Greenleaf Center.

Grier, W. H., & Cobbs, P. M. (1992). *Black rage.* New York: Basic Books. (Original work published in 1968)

Griffin, J. W. (2002). *A letter to my father.* Bloomington, IN: Xlibris Corporation.

Guither, P. (2006, June 19). Len Bias—the death that ushered in two decades of destruction. Retrieved from http://www.drugwarrant.com/articles/len-bias-two-decades-of-destruction.

Hallett, T. (2003). Symbolic power and organizational culture. *Sociological Theory, 21,* 128–149.

Hamma, R. M. (1999). *Landscapes of the soul: A spirituality of place.* Notre Dame, IN: Ave Maria Press.

Hancock, M. (1994). Collaboration for youth development: Youth action programming. *National Civic Review, 83,* 139–145.

Hanna, F. J., Talley, W. B., & Guindon, M. H. (2000). The power of perception: Toward a model of cultural oppression and liberation. *Journal of Counseling and Development, 78,* 430–441.

Harris, M. K. (1987). Moving into the new millennium: Toward a feminist vision of justice. *Prison Journal, 67,* 27–38.

Hassine, V. (Inmate AM4737). (2004). *Life Without Parole: Living in Prison Today* (3rd ed.). Los Angeles: Roxbury.

Haymes, S. N. (1995). *Race, culture, and the city: A pedagogy for Black urban struggle.* Albany: State University of New York Press.

Henderson, M. L., & Hanley, D. (2006). Planning for quality: A strategy for reentry initiatives. *Western Criminology Review, 7,* 62–78.

Hild, C. M. (2006). Places and states of mind for healing. *ReVision, 29,* 12–19.

Himmelman, A. T. (1996). On the theory and practice of transformational collaboration: Collaboration as a bridge from social service to social justice. In C. Huxman (Ed.). *Creating Collaborative Advantage.* (pp. 19-43). Thousand Oaks, CA: Sage.

Hirschman, A. O. (1970). *Exit, voice, and loyalty: Responses to decline in firms, organizations, and states.* Boston: Harvard University Press.

Honadle, B. W. (1981). A capacity-building framework: A search for concept and purpose. *Public Administration Review, 41,* 575–580.

hooks, b. (1990). *Yearning: Race, gender, and cultural politics.* Boston: South End Press.

hooks, b. (1993). *Sisters of the yam: Black Women and self-recovery.* Boston: South End Press.

hooks, b. (1996). *Killing rage: Ending racism.* New York: Henry Holt & Co.

Hooks, G., Mosher, C., Genter, S., Rotolo, T., & Lobao, L. (2004). The prison industry: Carceral expansion and employment in U.S. Counties, 1969–1994. *Social Science Quarterly, 85,* 37–57.

Hooks, G., Mosher, C., Genter, S., Rotolo, T., & Lobao, L. (2010). Revisiting the impact of prison building on job growth: Education, incarceration, and county-level employment, 1976–2004. *Social Science Quarterly, 91,* 228–244.

Hunn, L. M. (2004). Africentric philosophy: A remedy for Eurocentric dominance. *New Directions for Adult and Continuing Education, 102,* 65–74.

Ivey, A. E. (1995). Psychotherapy as liberation. In J. G. Ponterotto, J. M. Casas, L. Suzuki, & C. M. Alexander (Eds.), *Handbook of Multicultural Counseling and Therapy.* (pp. 53–72). Beverly Hills, CA: Sage.

James, S. V. (1962). The impact of the American revolution on Quakers' ideas about their sect. *William and Mary Quarterly, 19,* 360–382.

John Jay College of Criminal Justice. (2009, March 12). *"What Works" for Successful Prisoner Reentry? Hearings before the Subcommittee on Commerce, Justice, Science, and Related Agencies, of the House Appropriations Committee* (testimony of Jeremy Travis). Retrieved from http://www.jjay.cuny.edu/Travis_Congressional_Testimony.pdf

Johnson, R., & Bernard, T. J. (Eds.). (2004). *Life without parole: Living in prison today.* (3rd ed.). Los Angeles: Roxbury.

Jonsson, J. H. (2010). Beyond empowerment: Changing local communities. *International Social Work, 53,* 393–401.

Jordan, J. (1980). Poem for South African women. In *Passion: New poems 1977–1980.* Boston: Beacon Press. Retrieved from: www.JuneJordan.com

Justice Center, The Council of State Governments. *State Leaders' National Forum on Reentry and Recidivism.* Forum Agenda and Content. Retrieved from http://www.nationalreentryresourcecenter.org/forum-on-reentry-and-recidivism

Katz, D., & Kahn, R. L. (1978). *The social psychology of organizations.* New York: Wiley.

Kautzer, C., & Mendieta, E. (2004). Law and resistance in the prisons of empire: An interview with Angela Y. Davis. *Peace Review, 16,* 339–347.

Kazemian, L. (2007). Desistance from crime: Theoretical, empirical, methodological, and policy considerations. *Journal of Contemporary Criminal Justice, 23,* 5–27.

Keller, E. F. (1983). *A feeling for the organism: The life and works of Barbara McClintock.* New York: W.H. Freeman.

Kelling, G. L., & Coles, C. M. (1996). *Fixing broken windows: Restoring order and reducing crime in our communities.* New York: Free Press.

Kennedy, D. M. (2002). A tale of one city: Reflections on the Boston gun project. In G. S. Katzmann (Ed.), *Securing Our Children's Future: New Approaches to Juvenile Justice and Youth Violence* (pp. 229–261). Washington, DC: Brookings Institution Press.

Kiecolt, K. J. (2000). Self-concept change in social movements. In S. Stryker, T. J. Owens, & R. W .White (Eds.), *Self, Identity and Social Movements.* (pp. 111–131). Minneapolis: University of Minnesota Press.

Kim, H., Shim, Y., Choi, D., Kim, S., & Cho, W. (2006). Community manager: A dynamic collaboration solution on heterogeneous environment. In *ACE/IEEE International Conference on Pervasive Services.* (pp. 39–46). Los Alamitos, CA: IEEE Press.

King, R. S., Mauer, M., & Huling, T. (2003, February). Big prisons, small towns: Prison economics in rural America. *The Sentencing Project.*

Klekar, R. F., & Ting, D. I. (2004). Using a collaborative approach with criminal justice clients: A promising narrative in rehabilitation. *Journal of Systemic Therapies, 23,* 64–77.

Knight, G. H. (1999, Summer). My perspective on the impact of the Bergoll decision. *The Magnifying Glass.*

Knight, N. (1980). Mao ZeDong's 'On contradiction' and 'On practice': Pre-liberation texts. *China Quarterly, 84,* 641–668.

Kouzes, J. M., & Posner, B. Z. (1987). *The leadership challenge: How to get extraordinary things done in organizations.* San Francisco: Jossey-Bass.

Kretzmann, J. P., & McKnight, J. L. (1993). *Building communities from the inside out: A path toward finding and mobilizing a community's assets.* Chicago: ACTA Publications.

Krisberg, B., & Marchionna, S. (2006, April). Attitudes of U.S. voters toward prisoner rehabilitation and reentry policies. *National Council on Crime and Delinquency.* Retrieved from http://www.need-crc.org/need/pubs/2006april_ focus_zogby.pdf

Krogh, M., & Pillifant, A. (2004). Kemetic orthodoxy: Ancient Egyptian religion on the internet. *Sociology of Religion, 65,* 167–175.

Kuykendall, E. H. (1983). Toward and ethic of nurturance. In J. Trebilcot (Ed.) *Mothering: Essays in Feminist Theory.* (pp.263–274). Totowan, NJ: Roman and Allanheld.

Lambe, W. (2008, December). Small towns, big ideas: Case studies in small town community economic development. *University of North Carolina at Chapel Hill.* Retrieved from http://www.ucruralcenter.org

Landry, P. (1993, February 23). A Graterford inmate is stabbed to death watching ball game. *Philadelphia Inquirer,* p. B03.

Laub, J. H., & Sampson, R. J. (2003). *Shared beginnings, divergent lives: Delinquent boys to age 70.* Cambridge: Harvard University Press.

Lee, B. A., Price-Spratlen, T., & Kanan, J. W. (2003). Determinants of homelessness in metropolitan areas. *Journal of Urban Affairs, 25,* 335–355.

Lester, D. L., & Parnell, J. A. (2008). Firm size and environmental scanning pursuits across organizational life cycle stages. *Journal of Small Business and Enterprise Development, 15,* 540–554.

Levinson, D. (Ed.). 2004. *The Encyclopedia of homelessness.* Thousand Oaks, CA: Sage.

Liss, S. (2005). *No place for children: Voices from juvenile detention.* Austin: University of Texas Press.

Liu, J. (1971). Mao's 'on contradiction.' *Studies in East European Thought, 11,* 71–89.

Lofland, J. (1979). White-hot mobilization: Strategies of a millenarian movement. In M. Zald and J. McCarthy (Eds.), *Dynamics of Social Movements.* (pp. 156–166). Cambridge, MA: Winthrop.

Lorde, A. (1980). *The cancer journals.* San Francisco: Aunt Lute Books.

Lorde, A. (1984). *Sister outsider.* Freedom, CA: Crossing Press.

Loury, G. C., & Western, B. (Eds.). (Summer, 2010). Mass incarceration [Special topic]. *Daedalus, Journal of the American Academy of Arts & Sciences, 139*(3).

Loury, G. C., & Western, B. (2010). The challenge of mass incarceration in America. *Daedalus, Journal of the American Academy of Arts & Sciences, 139*(3), 5–7.

Lucas, C., & Kline, T. (2008). Understanding the influence of organizational culture and group dynamics on organizational change and learning. *Learning Organization, 15,* 277–287.

Lynch, J. P. (2006). Prisoner reentry: Beyond program evaluations. *Criminology and Public Policy, 5,* 401–412.

Maddock, S., & Morgan, G. (1998). Barriers to transformation: Beyond bureaucracy and the market conditions for collaboration and social care. *International Journal of Public Sector Management, 11,* 234–251.

Mao, T. (2001) [1967]. *Selected works of Mao Tse-tung.* Honolulu: University Press of the Pacific. (Original work published 1967)

Mao, T. (1990). *On dialectical materialism.* New York: M.E. Sharpe. (Original work published 1937)

Marable, M. (2001, September 3). Structural racism and American democracy: Historical and theoretical perspectives. Paper presented at *United Nations Racism and Public Policy Conference,* Durban, South Africa. Retrieved from http://www.unrisd.org/80256B3C005BCCF9/ (httpAuxPages)/4DAC9FF0A00C10F680256B6D0057879C/$file/dmarable.pdf

Marks, D. F. (2002). Freedom, responsibility and power: Contrasting approaches to health psychology. *Journal of Health Psychology, 7,* 5–19.

Markway, J., & Worsham, D. (2009). The potency of faith in successful offender reentry. *Corrections Today, 71,* 98–99.

Martin-Baro, I. (1994). *Writings for a liberation psychology.* Cambridge, MA: Harvard University Press.

Maruna, S. (2001). *Making good: How ex-convicts reform and rebuild their lives.* Washington, DC: American Psychological Association.

Maruna, S., LeBel, T. P., Mitchell, N., & Naples, M. (2004). Pygmalion in the reintegration process: Desistance from crime through the looking glass. *Psychology, Crime & Law, 10,* 271–281.

Marwell, G., & Oliver, P. (1993). *The critical mass in collective action: A micro-social theory.* New York: Cambridge University Press.

Massey, D. S., & Denton, N. A. (1993). *American apartheid: Segregation and the making of the underclass.* Cambridge, MA: Harvard University Press.

Massoglia, M., & Uggen, C. (2010). Settling down and aging out: Toward an interactionist theory of desistance and the transition to adulthood. *American Journal of Sociology, 116,* 543–582.

Mazama, M. (2002). Afrocentricity and African spirituality. *Journal of Black Studies, 33,* 218–234.

McCarthy, J., & Zald, M. (1973). *The trend of social movements in America: Professionalization and resource mobilization.* Morristown, NJ: General Learning Press.

McCoy, C. (2010, May 9). 25 years later: Lessons of the MOVE tragedy. *The Philadelphia Inquirer,* pp.B1,B5.

McGovern, S. J. (2006). Philadelphia's neighborhood transformation initiative: A case study of mayoral leadership, bold planning, and conflict. *Housing Policy Debate, 17,* 529–570.

McLaren, P. (1999). A pedagogy of possibility: Reflecting upon Paulo Freire's politics of education. *Educational Researcher, 28,* 49–54, 56.

Mezirow, J. (1978). Perspective transformation. *Adult Education Quarterly, 28,* 100–110.

Mills, A., & Codd, H. (2008). Prisoner's families and offender management: Mobilizing social capital. *Probation Journal, 55,* 9–24.

Mintzberg, H. (1984). Power and organizational life cycles. *Academy of Management Review, 9,* 207–224.

Mohr, L. B. (1969). Determinants of innovation in organizations. *Political Science Review, 63,* 111–126.

Moon, G. W. (2002). Spiritual direction: Meaning, purpose, and implications for mental health professionals. *Journal of Psychology and Theology, 30,* 264–275.

Moore, P. A. (2008, January 17). How to destroy the public schools when the rich pay no taxes. *CounterPunch.* Retrieved from http://www.counterpunch.org/ 2008/01/17/when-the-rich-pay-no-taxes

Morris, A. D. (1984). *The origins of the civil rights movement: Black communities organizing for change.* New York: Free Press.

Moxley, D. P., Alvarez, A. R., Johnson, A. K., & Gutierrez, L. M. (2005). Appreciating the glocal in community practice: Camp Hill, Gaviotas and intentional community. *Journal of Community Practice, 13,* 1–7.

Murray, L. W. (1921). Aboriginal sites in and near 'Teaoga,' now Athens, Pennsylvania. *American Anthropologist, 23*(2), 184–214.

Nadler, D. A., & Tushman, M. (1999). The organization of the future: Strategic imperatives and core competencies for the 21st century. *Organizational Dynamics, 28*, 45–60.

National Institute of Corrections. (2010, April 16). *A framework for evidence-based practices in local criminal justice systems: A work in progress* (3rd ed.) Retrieved from http://www.cepp.com/documents/EBDM%Framework.pdf

Nearing, S. (2006). *Civilization and beyond.* Fairford, England: Echo Library. (Original work published 1975)

New African Voices Alliance [Bahiya Cabral Asante, Nkosi Ali Asante, Shina Ahad and William Goldsby]. (1997). Introduction. In Shafik Asante, *When Spider Webs Unite: Challenging Articles & Essays on Community, Diversity and Inclusion.* (pp. 5–8). Toronto: Inclusion Press.

Nickerson, D. (1995). *An introduction to co-counseling.* Seattle: Rational Island.

Nixon, V., Clough, P. T., Staples, D., & Peterkin, Y. J. (2008). Life capacity beyond reentry: A critical examination of racism and prisoner reentry reform in the U.S. *Race/Ethnicity: Multidisciplinary Global Perspectives, 2*, 21–43.

Nobles, W. (1974). Africanity: Its role in Black families. *Black Scholar, 5*, 10–17.

Nye, N., & Glickman, N. J. (2000). Working together: Building capacity for community development. *Housing Policy Debate, 11*, 163–198.

O'Connor, J. (1987). *The meaning of crisis.* New York: Basil Blackwell.

Olney, C. A. (2005). Using evaluation to adapt health information outreach to the complex environments of community-based organizations. *Journal of the Medical Library Association, 93*, S57–S67.

Osher, F., Steadman, H. J., & Barr, H. (2003). A best practice approach to community reentry from jails for inmates with co-occurring disorders: The APIC Model. *Crime & Delinquency, 49*, 79–96.

Osterman, P. (2006). Overcoming oligarchy: Culture and agency in social movement organizations. *Administrative Science Quarterly, 51*, 622–649.

Ouchi, W. G., & Wilkins, A. L. (1985). Organizational culture. *Annual Review of Sociology, 11*, 457–483.

Pager, D. (2007). *Marked: Race, crime, and finding work in an era of mass incarceration.* Chicago: University of Chicago Press.

Pattillo, M. E. (1998). Sweet mothers and gangbangers: Managing crime in a Black middle class neighborhood. *Social Forces, 76*, 747–774.

Pattillo-McCoy, M. (1999). *Black picket fences: Privilege and peril among the Black middle class.* Chicago: University of Chicago Press.

Pearson, C. M., & Clair, J. A. (1998). Reframing crisis management. *Academy of Management Review, 23*, 59–76.

Pearson, C. (2007). The quest for a glocal public theology. *International Journal of Public Theology, 1*, 151–172.

Perkins, D. D., Brown, B. B., & Taylor, R. B. (1996). The ecology of empowerment: Predicting participation in community organizations. *Journal of Social Issues, 52*, 85–110.

Perkinson, R. (2010). *Texas tough: The rise of America's prison empire.* NY: Metropolitan Books.

Perry, A. R., Robinson, M. A., Alexander, R., & Moore, S. E. (2011). Post-prison community reentry and African American males: Implications for family therapy and health. *Handbook of African American Health*, *6*, 197–214.

Petersilia, J. (2003). *When prisoners come home: Parole and prisoner reentry.* New York: Oxford University Press.

Petersilia, J. (2004). What works in prisoner reentry? Reviewing and questioning the evidence. *Federal Probation*, *68*, 4–8.

Peterson, R.D., & Krivo, L. J. (2010). *Divergent social worlds: Neighborhood crime and the racial-spatial divide.* New York, NY: Russell Sage Foundation.

Pew Center on the States. Public Safety Performance Project. (2008). *One in 100: Behind bars in America.* Washington, DC: The Pew Charitable Trusts.

Pew Center on the States. Public Safety Performance Project. (2010). *Prison count 2010: State population declines for the first time in 38 years.* Washington, DC: The Pew Charitable Trusts.

Pew Charitable Trusts, Pew Center on the States. (2009, March). *One in 31: The long reach of American corrections.* Retrieved from http://www.evidencebasedassociates.com/reports/pew_1in 31_report.pdf

Pew Charitable Trust, Philadelphia Research Initiative. (2010). *A city transformed: The racial and ethnic changes in Philadelphia over the last 20 years.* Retrieved from http://www.pewtrusts.org/ uploaded Files/wwwpewtrustorg/Reports/Philadelphia_Research_Initiative/Philadelphia-Population-Ethnic-Changes.pdf

Philadelphia City Planning Commission (2010). *Strategies for neighborhood revitalization.* Philadelphia, PA: Retrieved from http://www.philaplan ning.org/cpdiv/Tioga2010.pdf

Powley, E. H., & Cameron, K. S. (2006). Organizational healing: Lived virtuousness amidst organizational crisis. *Journal of Management, Spirituality and Religion*, *3*, 13–33.

Powley, E. H., & Piderit, S. K. (2008). Tending wounds: Elements of the organizational healing process. *Journal of Applied Behavioral Science*, *44*, 134–149.

Prasad, A., & Prasad, P. (1993). Reconceptualizing alienation in management inquiry: Critical organizational scholarship and workplace. *Journal of Management Inquiry*, *2*, 169–183.

Price-Spratlen, T. (2000). Safety among strangers: The Million Man March. In D. Constantine-Simms (Ed.), *The Greatest Taboo: Homosexuality in Black Communities.* (pp. 44–66). Los Angeles: Alyson Books.

Price-Spratlen, T. (2008). Urban destination selection among African Americans during the 1950s Great Migration. *Social Science History*, *32*, 437–469.

Price-Spratlen, T., & Santoro, W. A. (2011). Neighborhood disorder and individual community capacity: How incivilities inform three domains of psychosocial assessment. *Sociological Spectrum*, *31*, 579–605.

Randel, W. P. (1939). The place names of Tioga County, Pennsylvania. *American Speech*, *14*, 181–190.

Regnier, R. H. (1994). The sacred circle: A process pedagogy of healing. *Interchange*, *25*, 129–144.

Rhine, E. E., & Thompson, A. C. (2011). The reentry movement in corrections: resiliency, fragility and prospects. *Criminal Law Bulletin*, *47*, 177–209.

Riggs, M. (1989). *Tongues untied* (Documentary Film). United States: Strand Releasing.

Roman, C. G., Wolff, A., Correa, V., & Buck, J. (2007). Assessing intermediate outcomes of a faith-based residential prisoner reentry program. *Research on Social Work Practice*, *17*, 199–215.

Ronnau, J. P., & Marlow, C. R. (1993). Family preservation and poverty: Valuing diversity. *Families in Society, 74*, 538–544.

Rose, D.R., & Clear, T. R. (2001, December). Incarceration, reentry and social capital: Social networks in the balance. Commissioned paper for *From Prison to Home: The Effect of Incarceration and Reentry on Children, Families, and Communities, U.S. Department of Health and Human Services, The Urban Institute*. Retrieved from http://aspe.hhs.gov/hsp/prison2home02/rose.pdf

Royster, D. D. (2001, January 21). An open letter to Mayor Street: What now for abandoned buildings? [Letter to the editor]. *Philadelphia Inquirer*, pA05.

Sasson, T., & Nelson, M. K. (1996). Danger, community, and the meaning of crime watch: An analysis of the discourses of African American and White participants. *Journal of Contemporary Ethnography, 25*, 171–200.

Shields, C. M. (2004). Dialogic leadership for social justice: Overcoming pathologies of silence. *Educational Administration Quarterly, 40*, 109–132.

Shiner, L. E. (1972). Sacred space, profane space, human space. *Journal of the American Academy of Religion, 40*, 425–436.

Shirlow, P., & Murtagh, B. (2004). Capacity-building, representation and intracommunity conflict. *Urban Studies, 41*, 57–70.

Siemiatycki, M. (2005). Contesting sacred urban space: The case of the Eruv. *Journal of International Migration and Integration, 6*, 255–270.

Simon, J. (2012). Mass Incarceration: From Social Policy to Social Problem. In J. Petersilia & K. Reitz (Eds.), *Sentencing and Correctional Reform* (pp.23–52). New York: Oxford University Press.

Skogan, W. G. (1990). *Disorder and decline: Crime and the spiral of decay in American neighborhoods*. Berkeley: University of California Press.

Smith, B. (Ed.) (1983). *Home girls: A Black feminist anthology*. New York: Kitchen Table Women of Color Press.

Smyth, J., Angus, L., Down, B., & McInerney, P. (2009). *Activist and socially critical school and community renewal*. Rotterdam: Sense Publishers.

Snow, D. A., & Phillips, C. L. (1980). The Lofland-Stark Conversion Model: A critical reassessment. *Social Problems, 27*, 430–447.

Sobeck, J., Agius, E., & Mayers, V. N. (2007). Supporting and sustaining grassroots youth organizations: The case of new Detroit. *Voluntas: International Journal of Voluntary and Nonprofit Organizations, 18*, 1–17.

Some, M. P. (1993). *Ritual: Power, healing and community*. New York: Penguin.

Sorokin, P. (1957). *Social & cultural dynamics: A study of change in major systems of art, truth, ethics, law and social relationships*. Boston: Extending Horizon.

Stack, C. (1974). *All our kin: Strategies for survival in a Black community*. New York: Harper & Row.

Staples, J. S. (2000). Violence in schools: Rage against a broken world. *Annals of the Association of American Political and Social Science, 567*, 30–41.

Steels, B. (2007). Applying a communitarian model of restorative justice and therapeutic jurisprudence: A social research project in Roebourne, WA. *International Journal of Rural Crime, 1*, 44–61.

Stern, K. (2011). Shackles and sunlight. *Fellowship, 77*, 12–17.

Stoecker, R. (1997). The CDC model of urban redevelopment: A critique and an alternative. *Journal of Urban Affairs, 19*, 1–22.

Suarez, R. (1999). *The old neighborhood: What we lost in the great suburban migration, 1966–1999*. New York: Free Press.

Sudbury, J. (2004). Globalized punishment, localized resistance: Prisons, neoliberalism, and empire. *Souls, 6*, 55–65.

Sudbury, J. (2008). Rethinking global justice: Black women resist the transnational prison-industrial complex. *Souls, 10*, 344–360.

Szanton, S., & Gill, J. M. (2010). Facilitating resilience using a society-to-cells framework: A theory of nursing essentials applied to research and practice. *Advances in Nursing Science, 33*, 329–343.

Taney, Roger B. (1857). *Dred Scott v. Sanford*. The United States Supreme Court Decision. 60 U.S. 393. Retrieved from http://supreme.justia.com/us/60/393/ case.html

Taxman, F., Young, D., & Byrne, J. (2004). With eyes wide open: Formalizing community and social control intervention in offender reintegration programs. In S. Maruna and R. Immarigeon (Eds.), *After Crime and Punishment: Pathways to Offender Reintegration* (pp. 233–260). Portland, OR: Willand.

Taxman, F. S., Young, D., Byrne, J. M., Holsinger, A., & Anspach, D. (2002). From prison safety to public safety: Innovations in offender reentry. A formative evaluation of the Reentry Partnership Initiative (RPI), Bureau of Government Research.

Taylor, P. V. (1993). *The texts of Paulo Freire*. Buckingham, England: Open University Press.

Teeters, N. K., & Shearer, J. D. (1957). *The prison at Philadelphia, Cherry Hill*. New York: Columbia University Press.

The Sentencing Project. *Women in the criminal justice system: Briefing sheets*. (2007). Retrieved from http://www.sentencingproject.org/doc/publications/ womenincj_total.pdf

Thompson, A. C. (2008). *Releasing prisoners, redeeming communities: Reentry, race and politics*. New York: New York University Press.

Tirado, M. D. (1970). The key to Chicano political power. *Chicano Journal of the Social Sciences and the Arts, 1*, 53–78.

Trauffer, H. C. V., Bekker, C., Bocarnea, M., & Winston, B. E. (2010). Towards an understanding of discernment: A conceptual paper. *Leadership & Organization Development Journal, 31*, 176–184.

Travis, J. (2000). *But they all come back: Rethinking prisoner reentry. sentencing & corrections: Issues for the 21st century*. Papers from the Executive Sessions on Sentencing and Corrections (No. 7). U.S. Department of Justice, Office of Justice Programs. Washington, DC: National Institute of Justice.

Travis, J. (2005). *But they all come back: Facing the challenges of prisoner reentry*. Washington, DC: Urban Institute Press.

Turner, B. A. (1976). The organizational and intergenerational development of disasters. *Administrative Science Quarterly, 21*, 378–397.

Turner, R. J., & Marino, F. (1994). Social support and social structure: A descriptive epidemiology. *Journal of Health and Social Behavior, 35*, 193–212.

Uggen, C., Manza, J., & Thompson, M. (2006). Citizenship, democracy, and the civic reintegration of criminal offenders. *Annals of the American Academy of Political and Social Science, 605*, 281–310.

University of California, Berkley. National Abandoned Infants Assistance Resource Center. (2006). *Spirituality: A powerful force in women's recovery.* Retrieved from: http://aia.berkeley.edu/media/pdf/spirituality_issue_brief.pdf.

University of Pennsylvania Neighborhood Information System. 2010. http://cml.upenn.edu/nis/

U.S. Department of Justice, Office of Justice Programs, Bureau of Justice Statistics. (2009, December). *Prisoners in 2008.* (NCJ Publication No. 228417). [Rev 2010, June]. Retrieved from http://bjs.ojp.usdoj.gov/content/ pub/pdf/p08.pdf

U.S. Sentencing Commission. (1995, February). Special Report to the Congress: Cocaine and Federal Sentencing Policy. Retrieved from http://www.ussc.gov/Legislative_and_Public_Affairs/ Congressional_Testimony_and_Reports/DrugTopics/199502_RtC_Cocaine_Sentencing_ Policy/index.htm

Useem, B., & Piehl, A. M. (2008). *Prison state: The challenge of mass incarceration.* New York: Cambridge University Press.

Verity, F. (2007). *Community capacity-building-a review of the literature.* South Australian Health Department, Health Promotion Branch, Adelaide.

Visher, C. A., & Travis, J. (2003). Transitions from prison to community: Understanding individual pathways. *Annual Review of Sociology, 29,* 89–113.

Wacquant, L. (2001). Deadly symbiosis: When ghetto and prison meet and merge. *Punishment and Society, 3,* 95–133.

Wagner-Pacifici, R. (1994). *Discourse and destruction.* Chicago: University of Chicago Press.

Wahking, H. (1992). Spiritual growth through grace and forgiveness. *Journal of Psychology and Christianity, 11,* 198–206.

Wakefield, S., & Uggen, C. (2010). Incarceration and stratification. *Annual Review of Sociology, 36,* 387–406.

Wakefield, S., Yeudall, F., Taron, C., Reynolds, J., & Skinner, A. (2007). Growing urban health: Community gardening in South-East Toronto. *Health Promotion International, 22,* 92–101.

Walker, L. (2010). Huikahi restorative circles: Group process for self-directed reentry planning and family healing. *European Journal of Probation, 2,* 76–95.

Walsh, F. (2003). Crisis, trauma, and challenges: A relational resilience approach for healing, transformation, and growth. *Smith College Studies in Social Work, 74,* 49–72.

Watt, D. (2004). Traditional religious practices amongst African Caribbean mothers and community othermothers. *Black Theology, 2,* 195–212.

Watts-Jones, D. (2002). Healing internalized racism: The role of a within-group sanctuary among people of African descent. *Family Process, 41,* 591–601.

Wellwood, J. (2000). *Journey of the heart: The path of conscious love.* New York: Harper.

Wenning, M. (2009). The return of rage. *Parrhesia, 8,* 89–99.

West, M. O. (1999). Like a river: The Million Man March and the Black Nationalist tradition in the United States. *Journal of Historical Sociology, 12,* 81–100.

Western, B. (2006). *Punishment and inequality in America.* New York: Russell Sage Foundation.

Western, B., & Pettit, B. (2010). Incarceration and social inequality. *Daedalus, The Journal of the American Academy of Arts and Sciences, 139*(3), 5–19.

Western, B., & Wildeman, C. (2009). The Black family and mass incarceration. *Annals of the American Academy of Political and Social Science, 621,* 221–242.

Weisberg, R., & Petersilia, J. (2010). The dangers of pyrrhic victories against mass incarceration. *Daedalus, The Journal of the American Academy of Arts and Sciences, 139*(3), 124–133.

White, S. A. (1999, June 4). Controlling police corruption. Poverty and prejudice: Paradoxes of U. S. drug policies. *EDGE: Ethics of Development in a Global Environment.* Retrieved from http://www.stanford.edu/class/e297c/poverty_ prejudice/paradox/hwhite.html

Wilkinson, R. A. (Ed.). (2004). *The Association of State Correctional Administrators Reentry Best Practices: Director's Perspectives.* Middletown, CT: ASCA Publications. Retrieved from http://www.asca.net/system/assets/attachments/2075/Reentry_Best_Practices_Publicatio n-1.pdf?1296149357

Williams, B., & Abraldes, R. (2007). Growing older: Challenges of prison and reentry for the aging population. In R. B. Greifinger (Ed.), *Public Health Behind Bars: From Prison to Communities.* (pp. 56–72). New York: Springer.

Williams, E. J. (2011). *The big house in a small town: Prisons, communities, and economics in rural America.* New York: Praeger.

Williams, S. T. (2007). *Blue rage, Black redemption: A memoir.* New York: Touchstone.

Wilson, M. (2007, July 19). ...And stay out: Hakim Ali's using his years inside to help ex-cons stay on the up and up. *Philadelphia City Paper.* Retrieved from http://archives.Citypaper .net/articles/2007/07/19/and-stay-out

Wilson, W. J. (1996). *When work disappears: The world of the new urban poor.* New York: Knopf.

Workman, K. (2009). Back to Churchill—an old vision for prisoner reintegration. *Policy Quarterly, 5*, 24–31.

Yehya, N. A., & Dutta, M. J. (2010). Health, religion, and meaning: A culture-centered study of Druze women. *Qualitative Health Research, 20*, 845–858.

Yen, Hope (2007, October 12). 2,002 die in custody in three years. *Associated Press.*

Zalanga, S. (2004). Teaching and learning social theory to advance social transformation: Some insights, implications, and practical suggestions from Paulo Freire. *The Discourse of Sociological Practice, 6*, 7–26.

Zhang, S. X., Roberts, R. E. L., & Callahan, V. J. (2006). Preventing parolees from returning to prison through community-based reintegration. *Crime & Delinquency, 52*, 551–571.

Zigarmi, D., Blanchard, K., O'Connor, M., & Edeburn, C. (2004). *The leader within: Learning enough about yourself to lead others.* New York: Prentice-Hall.

Index

ROCHELLE BROCK &
RICHARD GREGGORY JOHNSON III,
Executive Editors

Black Studies and Critical Thinking is an interdisciplinary series which examines the intellectual traditions of and cultural contributions made by people of African descent throughout the world. Whether it is in literature, art, music, science, or academics, these contributions are vast and far-reaching. As we work to stretch the boundaries of knowledge and understanding of issues critical to the Black experience, this series offers a unique opportunity to study the social, economic, and political forces that have shaped the historic experience of Black America, and that continue to determine our future. Black Studies and Critical Thinking is positioned at the forefront of research on the Black experience, and is the source for dynamic, innovative, and creative exploration of the most vital issues facing African Americans. The series invites contributions from all disciplines but is specially suited for cultural studies, anthropology, history, sociology, literature, art, and music.

Subjects of interest include (but are not limited to):

- EDUCATION
- SOCIOLOGY
- HISTORY
- MEDIA/COMMUNICATION
- RELIGION/THEOLOGY
- WOMEN'S STUDIES

- POLICY STUDIES
- ADVERTISING
- AFRICAN AMERICAN STUDIES
- POLITICAL SCIENCE
- LGBT STUDIES

For additional information about this series or for the submission of manuscripts, please contact Dr. Brock (Indiana University Northwest) at brock2@iun.edu or Dr. Johnson (University of San Francisco) at rgjohnsoniii@usfca.edu.

To order other books in this series, please contact our Customer Service Department:

(800) 770-LANG (within the U.S.)
(212) 647-7706 (outside the U.S.)
(212) 647-7707 FAX

Or browse online by series at www.peterlang.com.